# ENCYCLOPEDIA OF
# ORGANIZED CRIME
## IN THE UNITED STATES

# ENCYCLOPEDIA OF ORGANIZED CRIME IN THE UNITED STATES

## From Capone's Chicago to the New Urban Underworld

### Robert J. Kelly

**GREENWOOD PRESS**
Westport, Connecticut • London

**Library of Congress Cataloging–in–Publication Data**

Kelly, Robert J.
    Encyclopedia of organized crime in the United States : from
Capone's Chicago to the new urban underworld / Robert J. Kelly.
      p.  cm.
    Includes bibliographical references and index.
    ISBN 0–313–30653–2 (alk. paper)
    1. Organized crime—United States Encyclopedias.   I. Title.
HV6446.K43   2000
364.1'06'0973—dc21        99–33801

British Library Cataloguing in Publication Data is available.

Library of Congress Catalog Card Number: 99–33801
ISBN: 0–313–30653–2

First published in 2000

Greenwood Press, 88 Post Road West, Westport, CT 06881
An imprint of Greenwood Publishing Group, Inc.
www.greenwood.com

Printed in the United States of America

♾™

The paper used in this book complies with the
Permanent Paper Standard issued by the National
Information Standards Organization (Z39.48–1984).

10 9 8 7 6 5 4 3 2

For Rose Giarrusso,
with love and affection

# CONTENTS

# INTRODUCTION

This encyclopedia is about a special kind of crime. It is not about muggers, burglars, adolescent car thieves, or the miscellaneous violence that infests our cities. It is about crime that is organized, businesslike, "professional"—crime that is so thoroughly a part of our lives, ingrained in our institutions, and integrated into our economy and politics that we often fail to notice it or recognize its forms and face it when it appears.

Numerous government officials, law enforcement specialists, and social scientists have described organized crime as part of the American way of life. While many organized criminals themselves have national and ethnic roots in other cultures and societies, the fundamental criminal methods and ways of thought are not alien. Rather than being an alien conspiracy originating outside the United States, organized crime is indeed American—woven into the fabric of our society so thoroughly that we do not easily recognize it as special or different, immensely wealthy, or powerful. A remarkable thing about it is not that we have put up with it for so long but that we have become so used to it that we no longer regard it as something that has to be tolerated.

Organized crime has always been a subject of fascination in popular culture and a major criminal justice concern for more than a half century. Books and films about it are abundant, and many such as *The Godfather* novel and films have a worldwide popularity. The names of famous (or infamous) gangsters with their colorful aliases and street names are almost as well known to the public as they are to law enforcement officials. Most important, organized crime has survived changing ideas of what is illegal: As bootlegging gave way to drug trafficking and as prostitution expands into video pornography on the Internet, organized crime continues to resist suppression and eradication.

Although it takes many forms and exists in many different cultures and societies, it has certain basic features and components. First, it is organized, and whether it is like a corporation in its structure of authority and power with

"Godfathers" analogous to chief executive officers or an informal network of criminal activity conducted from time to time by a gang of local hoodlums, it has an existence and permanence that go beyond individual membership. Because it is organized, it differs from street crime, which is more episodic and does not typically involve the degree of planning or the interconnected linkages of legal and illegal activities that are characteristic of most organized criminals. Second, organized crime is protected, depending on corruption and bribery of police and regulatory criminal justice agencies. Third, organized criminal activity encompasses a wide range of illegal activities whose main objective is to provide goods and services to a demanding public that has an appetite for illicit goods—drugs, for example—and services including various types of gambling, loansharking, and sexual activities that are legally forbidden. Based on these descriptions, organized crime can be broadly defined as a persisting form of criminal activity tied to a client-public that demands goods and services defined as illegal. Further, it is a structure or network of individuals who produce, supply, protect, or distribute those goods and services and use the profits earned to expand their activities into other illegitimate or legitimate activities and do so by intimidating victims and criminal rivals who compete for customers by means of violence and corrupting police and public officials with the aim of getting their protection.

Although organized crime thrives in cities and is popularly associated with immigrants, its social and economic roots reach back into the early history of the United States. That heritage is represented by the famous outlaw gangs of the western frontier—lawless bands led by the Daltons, the James brothers, Jesse and Frank, and Billy the Kid. Many of these gangs developed out of groups of gunmen regulators who enforced order in large areas ruled by powerful wealthy families of ranchers and cattle barons. As early as the 1890s, there had been allegations that Italian immigrants were bringing with them a secret criminal organization called the Mafia. After World War I in 1919, the immigration renewed fear of an alien criminal conspiracy. However, Irish and Jewish gangsters had a grip on public notoriety. In the late 1930s and 1940s Thomas Dewey, Samuel Seabury, William O'Dwyer, District Attorney of Brooklyn, and the federal Treasury officers in Chicago exposed gangs of racketeers, extortionists, and murderers. In 1951 the Kefauver Committee of the U.S. Senate concluded in a sensational report to the nation that there was a nationwide organization of the Mafia in the United States. Since that time, the debate over the involvement of Italian Americans in organized crime has centered on the existence of a Mafia, also known as La Cosa Nostra, in the United States.

It has been fiction, and not fact, that made organized crime and Italian domination of it a household idea in America and elsewhere. The *Godfather* films of the early and mid-1970s made the character of Don Vito Corleone and his family symbolically representative of the power, influence, and wealth of organized crime. But, as will be seen, organized crime in the United States wears many faces, and this is a truth that is often ignored or forgotten.

After several failures to successfully prosecute John Gotti, the boss of the Gambino crime family, the government finally managed to obtain a conviction in 1992. The prosecution of the "Teflon Don" was hailed as a major blow against the underworld, and the press talked enthusiastically about the "twilight of the Godfathers." A half century earlier, Herbert Asbury, an investigative journalist and crime historian, breathed a sigh of relief in his book *The Gangs of New York* because he believed that the gangster, the street hoodlum, had receded into the American past. Asbury had in mind the demise of violent street gangs like the armies of young toughs that battled in the slums of New York City. But even then, Asbury was guilty of wishful thinking because as he wrote their obituaries in the middle of the Prohibition era, many individuals from these great brawling street gangs were forming into a national crime syndicate of immense power and durability. Requiems for American gangsters are nothing new, and they are usually premature. As events would demonstrate, the American gangster was not an endangered species.

Asbury's forlorn hopes and those of more contemporary observers looking at the turmoil in the ranks of organized crime as proof of its decline only point up the hazards of attempting to predict its future. This is especially true of La Cosa Nostra. The misplaced optimism of law enforcement predictions of the Mafia's demise, despite its long reign, is at least understandable. It is well to remember that the war waged against La Cosa Nostra began in earnest with the efforts of Attorney General Robert Kennedy in the 1960s and has continued for three decades with many successes: Major crime bosses have been toppled; crime families have been destroyed by turncoats and informers; Mafia strongholds in New York, Chicago, Philadelphia, Boston, Cleveland, New Orleans, and Kansas City find themselves still under constant surveillance and siege. It was, therefore, an easy—if not bold—prediction that the Mafia, battered by aggressive investigations and weakened by an incompetent and fearful leadership, would fade out of existence as had Irish and Jewish criminal groups before it.

Along with the famous Pizza Connection trials that imprisoned the Mafia's National Commission (its leadership) and the virus of betrayal that the testimony of Salvatore Gravano represented, which shattered the vaunted code of silence, the death knell for the "men of respect and honor" has been continually sounded, accompanied by intense speculation about other crime groups replacing the Italians. An industry of prediction arose identifying emerging groups that might become the kings of the underworld.

What is the future of organized crime in the United States? This question seems simple and clear enough, but it belies the complexities of contemporary criminal activity here and abroad. Organized crime is no longer a parochial activity of neighborhood rackets and local gangsters; it is increasingly international in scope and technically more sophisticated. One of the reasons perhaps that La Cosa Nostra survived as long as it has is that it made the changes needed to survive. As a criminal organization it responded to opportunities for crime and to techniques of crime prevention developed by a law enforcement establishment determined to destroy it. But it is questionable about how rapidly the Italian Mafia in the United States is likely to decline and whether it will ever follow the sociological and economic pathways of Irish and Jewish criminal organizations by virtually disappearing altogether. That the Mafia is hardly the power it once was during the three decades of the post–World War II period seems beyond dispute. It has lost substantial control of many of the labor unions, including the Teamsters, that were important sources of power and influence. La Cosa Nostra racketeers scarcely have the clout and control they once enjoyed over the waterfront through the International Longshoremen's Association. Moreover, the federal government continues the process of weeding the Mafia out of legitimate businesses and industries, from fish wholesaling to waste collection and construction.

In some cities La Cosa Nostra no longer has a dominant presence. Cleveland is a good example of federal law enforcement determination and success in neutralizing an influential crime family. However, while the federal law enforcement agencies can be justifiably gratified with their crime control efforts, they must acknowledge that in no city other than Cleveland have they completely eliminated a Mafia crime family. By their reckoning, that leaves 23 regions where there are still active La Cosa Nostra criminal conspiracies that, at the very least, involve profitable illegal gambling activities and loansharking operations.

With the highly publicized arrests and convictions of top La Cosa Nostra bosses, it might be expected that interest among potential candidates seeking membership would decline. Contrary to expectation, membership totals in New York's Mafia families are not diminishing. For instance, at the time of the McClelland Senate hearings in the late 1950s and early 1960s, the Genovese crime family in the New York area showed 114 members. When the FBI released information on the composition of the same family in 1988, there were nearly 200 inducted members. Similarly, for the other New York crime families—the Bonanno, Luchese, Gambino, and Colombo groups—hundreds of known members were listed on government charts. These numbers are interesting when we allow for the fact of 25 years of developing sophistication in anticrime technology.

For some observers the criminal subculture that provides recruits and "soldiers" for the La Cosa Nostra has been weakened by a number of factors in spite of membership stability. First is the growth of the federal law enforcement agencies with concurrent jurisdiction and a strong incentive to make corruption cases. Mafia/police alliances and long-term corrupt relationships have been inhibited as a result. Second, federal prosecutors have become much more sophisticated in their use of RICO (Racketeer Influenced and Corrupt Organizations Act) and CCE (Continuing Criminal Enterprise) statutes. Entire Mafia "crews" are being convicted, not just individuals, and the sentences delivered are long and tough. In 1985, each of the leaders of the five La Cosa

Nostra crime families in New York received prison terms of at least 100 years; most of them and their principal deputies are in prison for life without parole. Third, the price of loyalty, the legendary rule of "omerta" (silence), has thus become very high for many members. Those who might otherwise serve 3 years rather than inform often change their minds when 15-year RICO terms become common. John Gotti, head of the Gambino crime family, is serving a life sentence without parole because Salvatore Gravano, his underboss (who admitted participation in 19 murders) chose to testify against him and turn an expected life sentence into a mere five years. The federal government now reports over a hundred mafiosi in its Witness Security Program, compared to just a handful a decade ago.

A factor contributing to the gradual erosion of Mafia power is incompetence. With generational cultural assimilation and economic mobility promoted by legitimate opportunities now widely available for Italian American youth with promise, education, and drive, the Mafia is no longer an attractive employer; it is obliged to recruit almost exclusively among uneducated, tough felons and requires, in most cases, that they, the recruits, commit serious crimes to be admitted into the organization.

La Cosa Nostra is considered to be the epitome of traditional organized crime in the United States. But it is by no means the only organized criminal association that law enforcement is concerned with. New ethnic gangs—Chinese, Russian, African, Latin American, and Jamaican—as well as American outlaw motorcycle gangs have come into prominence.

Tomorrow's gangsters will not be just mafiosi but Chinese, Mexican, Russian, Caribbean, and African. More than today, organized crime will be a broader threat from a host of different nationalities and regions. It is also likely that no one group will be as powerful and dominating as La Cosa Nostra. However, because of new racial, ethnic, and cultural diversity, law enforcement will face new crime challenges.

In addition, there is always the possibility that new, emerging criminal groups will join forces. Imagine La Cosa Nostra crime family members purchasing heroin and cocaine from Chinese, Nigerian, and Colombian suppliers and distributing it in partnership with Puerto Rican and Dominican street gangs. Russian mobsters have been accomplices of Mafia members in fuel-tax scams, and Sicilian mafiosi have operated gambling establishments in the United States with Albanians and Cubans. Asian organized crime may be destined to become an amalgam of Chinese, Vietnamese, and Korean groups.

Of even greater concern is that these new criminal associations are creating and maintaining international and transcontinental links with criminal groups in Europe, Asia, and Latin America. For example, the Russian mafia has migrated to Germany, Poland, Hungary, Austria, the United States, and Canada. Similarly, the Chinese Triads in Hong Kong operate a worldwide counterfeit credit card conspiracy and participate in drug trafficking all over the globe.

The tasks facing law enforcement not only in the United States but worldwide were delineated by President Bill Clinton in two addresses to the General Assembly of the United Nations in 1995 and 1996. The president indicated and reiterated that law enforcement alone cannot be counted on to contain the growth of organized crime. According to the President, international cooperation among nations in terms of cooperation in joint anticrime task forces, regulations concerning money-laundering and information sharing among criminal justice agencies is essential. The United States is a choice locale for criminal groups of all sorts because it is an incredibly rich market for both legal and illegal products— especially narcotics. For this reason, narcotics are the most important product criminal groups seek to handle and the reason why federal officials in the United States and throughout the world have assigned drug enforcement a top priority.

Is law enforcement the key factor in the war on drugs? As will be seen, the conditions that promote organized crime, including drug trafficking, cannot be remedied only by law enforcement efforts. The tragedy of crime and narcotics lies in the conditions of the inner-city communities that are filled with hopeless people whose despair leads to impulsive behavior designed to offer gratification, behavior that leads to desperate actions, crime, and violence. The ghettos and neglected and impoverished communities at large continue to be the breeding grounds for organized crime that they have always been.

There is a tendency to think of nontraditional new ethnic organized crime as a distinctly modern phenomenon. This is why La Cosa Nostra is such a useful prism through which to see the development and evolution of organized crime in America as it enters the twenty-first century. The new organized crime is in many ways an old, familiar story.

The *Encyclopedia of Organized Crime in the United States* offers a reference source on the developmental history of organized crime in America. It presents descriptions and analyses on issues, personalities, and trends throughout the twentieth century in America.

The *Encyclopedia* also examines the conditions that produced criminal activists and organizations. Organized crime flourishes in the United States because there exists a strong and persistent demand for illegal goods and services which presents an opportunity to make enormous profits. While the persistence of organized crime on a large scale in the United States may be registered in organizational terms that go beyond the personalities of particular gangsters and racketeers, the *Encyclopedia* concentrates on the individual criminal whose personality, lifestyle, and relationships with other criminals, law enforcement, and the public shapes the nature of his criminal enterprises.

It is probably impossible to produce a work of this kind without errors of omission. Comprehensiveness, of course, does not require completeness; nor is completeness even possible in an encyclopedia covering a dynamic and growing field. Although the length of the entries is not unrelated to their importance, other factors, such as the degree of current or recent interest in it, the consequences of individual careers or activities or aspects of organized criminal behavior, and official law enforcement responses to this type of crime, have also figured in determining length. Also, in striving for the highest level of accessibility appropriate to topics or personal activities and careers, each entry had to be fully intelligible, no matter how complex, to the reader. I trust that all of the entries have something of value for any interested reader, even though some give more specialized and technical information than others. The entries include "suggested readings" and are cross-referenced to other entries under "see also." A number of entries are accompanied by photographs or by tables and figures because of their significance and importance. A main entry that is mentioned in another entry is followed by an asterisk (*) to indicate that separate treatment of that subject matter is included in the text. The book begins with a list of acronyms—to aid the reader in identifying organizations referred to in the entries—and a timeline of important events.

# ACRONYMS

| | |
|---|---|
| AFL-CIO | American Federation of Labor and Congress of Industrial Organizations |
| AOC | Asian organized crime |
| BATF | Bureau of Alcohol, Tobacco and Firearms |
| BCCI | Bank of Credit and Commerce International |
| CCBA | Chinese Consolidated Benevolent Association |
| CCE | Continuing Criminal Enterprise |
| CD | certificate of deposit |
| CFCs | chlorofluorocarbons |
| CIA | Central Intelligence Agency |
| CMIR | Currency, Monetary Instrument Report |
| CNP | Colombian National Police |
| CTR | Currency Transaction Report |
| DAS | Department of Administrative Security |
| DEA | Drug Enforcement Administration |
| DOJ | Department of Justice |
| FARC | Revolutionary Armed Forces of Colombia |
| FBI | Federal Bureau of Investigation |
| FDIC | Federal Deposit Insurance Corporation |
| Fin CEN | Financial Crime Enforcement Network |
| FOBs | Fresh off the Boats |
| GAO | General Accounting Office |
| HEREIU | Hotel Employees and Restaurant Employees International Union |
| IACRL | Italian-American Civil Rights League |

| | |
|---|---|
| IBT | International Brotherhood of Teamsters |
| ILA | International Longshoremen's Association |
| INS | Immigration and Naturalization Service |
| IRS | Internal Revenue Service |
| JBM | Junior Black Mafia |
| JLP | Jamaica Labor Party |
| LCN | La Cosa Nostra |
| LIUNA | Laborers' International Union of North America |
| NYSOCTF | New York State Organized Crime Task Force |
| OC | organized crime |
| OCRS | Organized Crime and Racketeering Section |
| PCC | Pennsylvania Crime Commission |
| PCOC | President's Commission on Organized Crime |
| PNP | People's National Party |
| POBOB | Pissed Off Bastards of Bloomington |
| RICO | Racketeer Influenced and Corrupt Organizations |
| SEC | Securities and Exchange Commission |
| TFR | Task Force Report |
| TYJK | Toa Yuai Jigyo Kumiani |
| UAW | United Auto Workers |
| UBG | United Bamboo Gang |
| UCR | Uniform Crime Reports |
| UFCW | United Food and Commercial Workers International Union |
| USW | United Seafood Workers |
| WASP | White Anglo-Saxon Protestant |
| WITSEC | Witness Security Program |

# TIMELINE

| | |
|---|---|
| 1860–1880 | Although organized crime thrives in cities and is popularly associated with immigrant groups, its social and economic roots are deeply embedded in American history. The famous outlaw gangs of the western frontiers—the lawless bands led by the James brothers, the Youngers, and the Daltons—represent a cultural heritage of organized criminal activity. And as the nation grew during the period of industrialization and urbanization, the "robber barons," ancestors of some of America's foremost families, transformed, often through extralegal tactics, the wealth of the frontier into financial empires. As they amassed their fortunes, the use of gangs of enforcers, violence, bribery, corruption, and other activities currently associated with organized crime proved economically expedient and therefore morally tolerable. When the opportunities provided by the western frontier disappeared, those Americans striving for success and security, along with millions of European immigrants, turned toward the cities. The growth of the American city and the influx of immigrants created the modern era—and dilemma—of organized crime. |

In this tumultuous period of the Civil War, immigration, urbanization, frontier development, and enormous economic growth in the form of industrial expansion, the large cities witnessed the formation of large street gangs who worked for local politicians during electoral campaigns and were offered some protection from police in criminal activities mainly directed at exploiting immigrants and slum dwellers. The gangs forged partnerships with local political machines and shared profits earned in the extensive vice industries. Many infamous criminals over the subsequent decades developed their skills and contacts in these gangs. Men like "Lucky" Luciano, Meyer Lansky, and Frank Costello who became top syndicate leaders later on began their careers in the gangs.

| 1878 | The Italian government launches an anti-Mafia campaign. Many mafiosi leave Sicily for North African ports, where there are colonies of Italians, or immigrate (often illegally) to the United States. Most of those who come to America settle in the major urban areas in New York, Boston, Chicago, New Orleans, Kansas City, and St. Louis (all places that will later be home for La Cosa Nostra crime families). |
|------|------|
| 1882 | Enactment of the Chinese Exclusion Act creates anti-Asian sentiments and isolates Chinese into "Chinatowns," ethnic enclaves cut off from the mainstream of white society. Chinese immigrants form Tongs for protection against discrimination. |
| 1891 | William Hennessey, New Orleans chief of police, is murdered when he intervenes in a dispute between rival Mafia factions. Seventeen Italians are arrested, and a mob storms the jail and lynches 11 of them. For the first time in the United States, there is public discussion of a secret criminal organization from Italy that operates in New Orleans. |
| 1899 | The Tongs in New York City go to war. The causes are conflicting gambling interests in Chinatown. In 1913, the street war between the Hip Sing and On Leong Tongs is ended with the signing of a peace treaty that the Chinese government and the New York City police arranged. |
| 1903 | Evidence of La Mano Nera (The Black Hand) surfaces in Brooklyn, New York. The Black Hand becomes a fearsome symbol of Italian extortionists and terrorists who commit crimes against other Italians. |
| 1915 | Al Capone joins the Five Points gang in New York. |
| 1920 | The Eighteenth Amendment to the U.S. Constitution, which outlaws the manufacture, sale, distribution, and transportation of alcoholic beverages, goes into effect and begins the Prohibition Era. Criminal gangs that had functioned in two fields—violent crime (including robbery, murder, burglary, and extortion) and crimes associated with electoral politics (vote fixing, intimidation of citizens at voting polls, ballot box stuffing, etc.)—now find new criminal opportunities in a vast subterranean world of speakeasies and bootlegging. Casper Holstein, the man who invented the modern "numbers game," puts together a gambling syndicate in Harlem. Holstein's group is among the first formally organized groups of African American criminals operating in the United States. In Chicago, Johnny Torrio, anxious to take over the Colosimo mob and exploit Prohibition, has "Big Jim" shot and killed in his own restaurant. Torrio gives Capone, his top lieutenant and suspected leader in the Colosimo execution, 25 percent of the existing prostitution rackets profits and 50 percent of the bootleg profits. |

1925            A gang war rocks the streets of Chicago in the aftermath of
                Charles Dion O'Banion's murder. O'Banion led a coalition of
                bootleggers and gamblers opposed to the Capone organization's
                encroachments on their territories and customers.

1926            As the Chicago gang war rages, "Hymie" Weiss and Vincent
                Drucci orchestrate an armed attacked in broad daylight against
                Capone headquarters at the Hawthorne Inn, in Cicero—a suburb
                of Chicago. A 1,000 rounds are fired by machine guns, but Ca-
                pone survives unscathed. An innocent bystander is killed. Less
                than a month later, Hymie Weiss is machine-gunned to death in
                an ambush set up in an apartment house across the street from his
                headquarters.

1927            "War of Sicilian Succession": Within the Unione Siciliano a strug-
                gle breaks out between Capone's choice for president, Tony Lom-
                bardo, and Joseph Aiello, an associate of the Genna brothers, who
                are major Chicago bootleggers and influential mafiosi. The con-
                flict spills over into New York, Buffalo, and St. Louis. Capone's
                gunmen force Aiello out after Aiello hires assassins to kill Ca-
                pone.

1928            Arnold "The Brain" Rothstein, a major racketeer and creative
                criminal innovator, is shot and killed on November 6. On Decem-
                ber 5, the National Crime Syndicate is formed at the Statler Hotel
                in Cleveland, Ohio, when 23 mafiosi from Chicago, New York,
                Detroit, St. Louis, Tampa, Philadelphia, Buffalo, and Newark
                gather to discuss mutual problems and interests. Many of those
                attending, Joseph Profaci, Charles "Lucky" Luciano, Vincent
                Mangano, and Joseph Magliocco, eventually head Mafia crime
                families.

1929            St. Valentine's Day Massacre: The Chicago gang war that started
                in 1925 comes to a bloody conclusion on February 14 in a garage
                on the north side of Chicago. Four men—dressed as police offi-
                cers—brutally murder seven members of Bugs Moran's gang.
                Shaken by events, Moran goes into hiding. When interrogated by
                police, he allegedly said of the grisly murders that shocked the
                entire nation, "Only Capone kills like that."
                   Between May 13 and 16, a major underworld conclave is con-
                vened in Atlantic City, New Jersey. About 30 gang leaders from
                around the country attend. The country is divided into spheres of
                influence and gang territories. Disputes and conflicts among gangs
                are to be taken to a nine-member national "commission" for res-
                olution and conciliation.

1930–1931       The Castellammarese War: In March the two major factions in
                the New York Mafia take sides in a struggle for domination
                of the rackets. The Maranzano group, consisting of mobsters
                from the Castellammarese del Golfo region of Sicily, go to war

against a group headed by Joseph ("Joe the Boss") Masseria. Masseria's gang is allied with many non-Italians such as Meyer Lansky and "Bugsy" Siegel. As the war goes against Masseria, five of his top men, including Luciano and Genovese, execute him and make peace. Maranzano, however, fearing the betrayal of Masseria's executioners, plans their murder. Instead, he is murdered on September 10, 1931. In the aftermath of the Castellammarese War, the five Cosa Nostra crime families in New York emerge.

On September 15, Luciano resurrects the "Commission" as an authoritative body in the Mafia and gets agreement that there shall be no "Boss of Bosses." New York is divided among 5 crime families, with 24 others around the country, 9 of which sit on the "Commission" to arbitrate disputes. Thus, the Mafia was "Americanized."

| | |
|---|---|
| 1931 | Al Capone is convicted of tax evasion and sentenced to 11 years in prison, never to return to mob leadership. |
| 1933 | Prohibition is repealed. Organized criminals turn to other illicit enterprises to compensate for the loss of a major source of income. |
| 1935 | Dutch Schultz is murdered in Newark, New Jersey, by his rivals in New York City who fear his plans to take over their rackets and murder special prosecutor Thomas Dewey. |
| 1936 | "Lucky Luciano," the most powerful gangster in New York and perhaps the United States, is sentenced to 30 to 50 years in prison on prostitution charges. |
| 1937 | Colonel Fulgencio Batista invites Meyer Lansky of New York to organize and operate the major Cuban hotel gambling casinos. "Bugsy" Siegel goes to California to organize the filmmaking trade unions and the gambling enterprises. |
| 1938 | A Mafia narcotics syndicate is set up in Kansas City and St. Louis. |
| 1940–1941 | Abe "Kid Twist" Reles, an assassin and member of "Murder, Inc.," provides evidence against syndicate members and their political allies in Brooklyn and Manhattan. On November 12, 1941, Reles suspiciously "falls" to his death from a six-story window in a heavily guarded Coney Island hotel. |
| 1942 | The U.S. Naval Intelligence Office in New York seeks the help of waterfront gangsters against Nazi sabotage activities. "Lucky" Luciano agrees to fight wartime espionage on the New York docks and orders the International Longshoremen's Association to cooperate with the navy. |
| 1944 | Louis "Lepke" Buchalter is electrocuted in Sing Sing Prison, New York. He is the only mob boss ever to go to the electric chair. |

1946            The Hobbs Act becomes law. It makes interference with interstate
                commerce for criminal purposes a federal crime. Until 1970, with
                the enactment of RICO, the Hobbs Act is the most frequently used
                prosecutorial weapon against organized crime.
                    On January 3, 1946, "Lucky" Luciano is released from prison
                for his patriotic efforts during the war and deported to Italy by
                the then-Governor Thomas Dewey, who had prosecuted and ob-
                tained a conviction against him.

1947            "Bugsy" Siegel is murdered by his mob associates for problems
                with hotel/casino operations in Las Vegas.

1950–1951       The Kefauver Committee convenes hearings on crime in inter-
                state commerce. In an unprecedented move, the Committee tel-
                evises its hearings around the country. The Committee spends
                12 months investigating organized crime. Many law enforce-
                ment officials, public officials, and journalists testify. Interest-
                ingly, all of the criminal offenders subpoenaed to testify deny
                membership in the Mafia. Several powerful mob figures in-
                cluding Joseph Adonis and Frank Costello are exposed before
                a fascinated public. The hearings put "taking the Fifth Amend-
                ment" (invoking the constitutional right to refuse to answer
                because of self-incrimination) into the American vocabulary.
                The hearings alert the public to the dangers of organized crime
                in the United States and mark a change of policy by the FBI
                that for years denied the existence of a mafia operating in the
                United States.

1957            On October 25, Albert ("The Mad Hatter") Anastasia, head of a
                Cosa Nostra crime family and the individual who directed the
                notorious "Murder, Inc." assassination team, is murdered in a bar-
                bershop in the Sheraton Hotel in New York City.
                    On November 19 in Apalachin, New York, a meeting of some
                60 organized crime bosses in the United States is uncovered by
                state police. According to one of those invited, the meeting was
                arranged to discuss the execution of Albert Anastasia, the removal
                of Frank Costello as boss of the Luciano crime family, and the
                arrangement for drug trafficking in the United States by members
                of the Sicilian and Corsican mafias.

1960            Jamaican "Posses" make their appearance in the marijuana dis-
                tribution systems in many major American cities. Mostly Ras-
                tafarians, they locate in urban areas with sizable Jamaican
                populations.
                    The "Gallo-Profaci War" erupts in Brooklyn, New York. After
                much bloodletting a fragile truce is arranged, but mob bosses con-
                tinue to suspect each other of conspiracies. La Cosa Nostra is
                momentarily in turmoil.

1963    To a shocked nation, Joseph Valachi reveals the existence of La Cosa Nostra before the U.S. Senate Subcommittee on Investigations. Valachi, a "made member" of the Genovese crime family, describes the structure of LCN in New York City and the internal organization of the crime families across the nation. For the first time the public learns from the televised hearings of a national "Crime Commission" that makes decisions about interfamily disputes and the succession of crime family bosses.

1964    The "Banana War": A plot hatched by Joseph Bonanno, head of a Cosa Nostra crime family bearing his name, to seize control of mob interests by assassinating Thomas Luchese and Carlo Gambino, New York Crime family bosses, fails and sparks gang warfare. Bonanno is apparently "kidnapped" by his cousin Giuseppe Magaddino, head of the Buffalo LCN, on orders of the Commission until he agrees to retire and end the war. Bonanno accepts the national Commission's proposal only if his son is permitted to head his family. The Commission agrees, and he is released, leaving him in effective control until his retirement for health reasons in 1968.

In the "French Connection" case, New York City police and federal authorities intercept and confiscate the largest shipment of heroin (116 pounds) ever to reach the United States. Along with local drug dealers, three Frenchmen from the Marseilles underworld and Corsican mafia are caught and convicted. The mastermind of the drug plot escapes the police net and returns to France.

1965    Nigerian heroin smuggling into the United States is uncovered. The importing methods are dangerous and often fatal to the "mules" (the couriers). Small bags of heroin are swallowed and settle in the stomach cavity or are deposited in other body orifices. If a bag should rupture, the carrier is likely to die.

Jeff Fort organizes several Chicago street gangs into a coalition that forms the base for his crime syndicate, the El Rukns—a major African American extortion ring in Chicago.

1966    "Little Apalachin" meeting: Top Mafia bosses meet at the LaStella restaurant in Queens, New York. Included at the meeting are Santos Trafficante of Tampa, Florida; Carlos Marcello of New Orleans, Louisiana; and Carlos Gambino, Joseph Colombo, Mike Miranda, and Tommy Eboli of New York City.

1967    Leroy "Nicky" Barnes, an African American gangster impressed by the tightly structured efficiency of La Cosa Nostra, becomes the ghetto kingpin of heroin distribution in the New York area. While serving a prison sentence, Barnes and Joseph ("Crazy Joe") Gallo of the Colombo crime family become friendly, and a drug connection develops, with the Mafia providing Barnes's organization with supplies of heroin.

The U.S. Department of Justice establishes the first "Strike Force" in Buffalo, New York, to investigate and bring convictions against the Magaddino crime family. The Strike Force is composed of agents from several federal agencies and local police. The Buffalo Strike Force becomes a model for Task Force operations to control and contain organized crime throughout the country.

The Task Force on Organized Crime of the President's Commission on Law Enforcement and Administration of Justice reported to President Lyndon Johnson its principal findings that organized crime was a "society" and at its core were 24 groups in the United States totaling 5,000 members of Italian origins and ancestry. The landmark report went on to detail the structure of each organized crime group, or "family," and presented a series of recommendations to control them.

1970        RICO becomes law. The crime of racketeering is established as part of the Organized Crime Control Act. The Racketeer Influenced and Corrupt Organizations (RICO) section of that act, Title IX, 18 United States Code S1961, becomes the most potent weapon against organized crime in years to come. RICO makes it unlawful to acquire, operate, or receive income from an enterprise through a pattern of racketeering activity. *Racketeering* is defined broadly. Also included in the act are provisions for a Witness Security and Protection Program, to provide for the safety of government witnesses, and expansion of the use of electronic surveillance.

1971        Colombian drug traffickers establish cartels, including smuggling routes and street sales distribution systems in the United States. The Medellin and Cali cartels of Colombia will become the major suppliers of cocaine to the United States.

Joseph Colombo, crime family boss, is shot in the head by an African American gunman at the Italian-American Unity Day rally in Columbus Circle, New York City. His assailant is killed immediately by unidentified gunmen in the crowd. Law enforcement officials speculate that the attack (which eventually leads to Colombo's death) was approved by Carlo Gambino and other mob bosses displeased with Colombo's public antics, which antagonized the federal government. Others believed that Colombo's rival, Joe Gallo, engineered the assassination attempt.

1972        Joseph ("Crazy Joe") Gallo is assassinated in Umberto's Clam House in "Little Italy," New York City. Again law enforcement is puzzled by the motive: Was it to avenge Colombo, or was Gallo just another Gambino victim in a strategy to gain control of all the New York crime families?

In July, three months after Gallo's murder, Gaetano (Tommy

Ryan) Eboli, interim boss of the Genovese crime family, is murdered in Brooklyn.

In October, the Brooklyn district attorney issues subpoenas for almost 700 people, most of them known criminals, in connection with a joint police/FBI investigation of Paul Vario, a capo in the Luchese crime family, who operates a junkyard in Brooklyn. It is alleged that the property serves as a meeting place and operational center for vice activities and assorted crimes. Under police surveillance, it is established that Vario's trailer was visited by members of all the crime families and numerous corrupt public officials.

In December, the Knapp Commission finds that a "majority" of police in New York City are involved in some sort of crime or wrongdoing. The influence of organized crime on law enforcement is underscored in the Commission's findings and recommendations for reform.

1975       On July 30, James Hoffa, former head of the powerful Teamsters Union, disappears. There is little doubt that he was murdered by the very gangsters he made rich through easy access to Teamster labor union pension funds.

Sam ("Momo") Giancana, onetime head of the Chicago mafia (a.k.a. the "Chicago Outfit"), is murdered in the basement of his home. Giancana was scheduled to appear before a Senate committee investigating CIA connections, Mafia involvements in Castro assassination plots, and President John F. Kennedy's murder in 1963.

1976       The Task Force on Organized Crime issues a report with recommendations for state and local criminal justice agencies.

Carlo Gambino dies of natural causes. His death marks a milestone in the history of organized crime in the United States. Considered the most powerful Mafia capo, his death produces a succession crisis in the crime family among the warring factions.

1977       The Casino Control Act legalizing casino gambling in Atlantic City is approved by New Jersey voters. Skeptics predict that Atlantic City will be dominated by La Cosa Nostra.

1980–1981  The "Funzi" Tieri prosecution: After the assassination of Thomas Eboli, the head of the Genovese crime family, Francisco Tieri supervised large-scale gambling, extortion, and loansharking operations in several states. In 1980, based on testimony from Jimmy "The Weasel" Fratianno, Tieri becomes the first LCN boss tried and convicted under RICO. Another significant feature of the Tieri case is that it is one of several prosecutions designed to prove in court that La Cosa Nostra exists as a continuing illegal enterprise, that Tieri was the boss of one of its families, and that he committed various organized crimes in that capacity.

On March 21, Angelo Bruno, boss of the Philadelphia Cosa Nostra crime family and member of the Mafia's Commission, is shot and killed. His death is followed by turmoil and violent competition for control of the Philadelphia/Atlantic City crime network.

1982    As federal prosecutors begin to use RICO as a legal tool, trials involving mob bosses become more frequent. Cleveland Mafia leader James Licavoli is convicted as head of the Denver-based Cosa Nostra crime family.

1984    Nicholas Civella and the leadership of the Kansas City, Missouri, Cosa Nostra crime family are indicted under RICO for murder, conspiracy, and skimming from Las Vegas casinos.

Anthony "Tony Ducks" Corallo, head of the Luchese Cosa Nostra crime family in New York City, is indicted with others for conspiracies to operate illegal garbage collection associations in Nassau and Suffolk counties on Long Island, New York.

Frank Balistieri, boss of the Milwaukee Cosa Nostra crime family, is convicted of extortion under the Hobbs Act.

1985    Family bosses in Cleveland, Chicago, Milwaukee, and Kansas City are convicted and receive lengthy sentences for conspiring to skim vast sums of cash from Las Vegas casinos that they controlled through the use of Teamster pension funds.

The hierarchy of the Patriarca family, which operated out of Providence, Rhode Island, and Boston, Massachusetts, is convicted on multiple RICO counts ranging from loansharking to murder.

An all-out federal assault is launched against the Philadelphia Cosa Nostra family, which would lead to life in prison for its violent boss Nicky ("Little Nicky") Scarfo.

In New Orleans, Louisiana, La Cosa Nostra never recovers its strength and influence from the conviction of its boss Carlos Marcello.

In New York, U.S. Attorney Rudolph Giuliani (later to be elected mayor of New York City) announces the "Commission case," charging that the national Commission of La Cosa Nostra itself is a criminal enterprise. All five local bosses are indicted, among them Colombo crime family acting boss Gerald (Gerry Lang) Langella (Langella is acting boss because Carmine ["The Snake"] Persico, the Colombo LCN boss, was already imprisoned on other charges); Anthony ("Tony Ducks") Corallo, the Luchese Cosa Nostra boss; Philip ("Rusty") Rastelli, the Bonanno Cosa Nostra boss; the Genovese Cosa Nostra boss, Anthony ("Fat Tony") Salerno; and Paul Castellano, the Gambino Cosa Nostra boss, who is assassinated in December before he could be convicted.

John Gotti, the capo who will be convicted of Castellano's murder in 1992, emerges as head of the Gambino Mafia network.

At the international level, Tommaso Buscetta, a powerful Sicilian capo mafioso, is extradited to Italy from Brazil. He informs and provides evidence on hundreds of mafiosi, many of whom are involved in the heroin smuggling operation in the United States called the "Pizza Connection."

**1986**
The President's Commission on Organized Crime issues its report in which it spells out a clear connection between labor racketeering and corruption. It also refers to the banking industry's failure to comply adequately with the Bank Secrecy Act as a cause of money laundering. Its report on narcotics observes that drug trafficking is the most widespread and lucrative organized crime activity in the United States.

Leaders of the Colombo Cosa Nostra crime family are convicted on RICO charges. And for the first time, the government seeks civil RICO remedies to recover illicit profits.

**1987**
Jeff Fort, leader of the El Rukns (a powerful African American criminal group in Chicago), and some of his associates are convicted of plotting terrorist activities linked with Libyan President Muammar Gadhafi. This is the first time that American organized crime groups appear to be involved in terrorism.

The "Pizza Connection" case concludes with the conviction of 35 members of the New York and Sicilian Cosa Nostra.

**1989**
Michael Markowitz is shot to death on May 2. He was arrested in connection with the Russian bootleg gasoline and fuel oil scams, and allegedly killed on orders of La Cosa Nostra to prevent his cooperation with law enforcement.

**1991**
Raymond Patriarca, boss of the New England Cosa Nostra crime family, and four associates plead guilty to charges of operating a racketeering enterprise—namely, their mafia networks in Rhode Island, Massachusetts, Connecticut, New Hampshire, and Maine.

**1992**
The Drug Enforcement Administration arrests 165 persons for drug trafficking and money laundering. They are members of, or affiliated with, the Cali cocaine cartel in Colombia and the Sicilian Cosa Nostra.

John Gotti, the boss of the Gambino Cosa Nostra crime family, is sentenced to life in prison without the possibility of parole. The testimony of Gotti's underboss, Salvatore ("Sammy the Bull") Gravano, is instrumental in convicting Gotti. The trial and conviction symbolize a major change in the Mafia's culture of omerta (secrecy). No longer is the code of silence sacred among members of La Cosa Nostra.

Sicilian investigative magistrates Giovanni Falcone and Paolo Borsellino are killed within months of each other by Coreleonsi mafiosi. The result is public outrage and the beginnings of an anti-

Mafia campaign that cripples the government and hastens the downfall and indictment of Giulio Andreotti, former prime minister of the country.

1993        Pablo Escobar, leader of the Medellín cocaine cartel in Colombia, is killed in a shootout with Colombian police and paramilitary forces.

Guo Liang Chi ("Ah Kay"), head of the Fuk Ching Tong in the United States, is arrested in Hong Kong for alien smuggling. The Fuk Ching is considered the most powerful Asian criminal organization operating in the United States.

The trial of Salvatore ("Toto") Riina, capo di tutti capi (boss of all bosses) in Sicily, begins in Palermo. Riina is accused of masterminding more than 100 murders and the growth of the Sicilian mafia in the heroin and cocaine markets.

1994        Jacob Dobrer, a Russian emigre and a "vory" (a crime boss), admits that he operated a fuel tax scheme and evaded nearly $50 million in taxes. His Russian organized crime group worked with the Gambino crime family, paying a "mob tax" of millions in order to do business.

Japan's Yakuza (crime syndicates) branch out into China using legitimate fronts such as karaoke bars, hotels, and restaurants to disguise their criminal activities, as they had done in Australia, the Philippines, and the United States.

1995        Clifford Wong Chi-fai, president of the Tung On Tong, is sentenced to life in prison for murder. Chi-fai formed an alliance with the Sun Yee On Triad to provide security for illegal gambling activities. The conviction is a breakthrough because it is the first time a Chinese community-based association is convicted under the RICO statute.

1996        Salvatore Gravano is released from the Witness Security Program after providing testimony in dozens of cases involving Cosa Nostra members and associates. A murder contract for $500,000 has been placed on his life by La Cosa Nostra.

"Pacho" Herrera-Buitrago, a charter member of the Cali cartel, a kingpin in the cocaine trade, surrenders to Colombian authorities.

1997        Vincent "The Chin" Gigante is tried and convicted of murder and racketeering enterprises as head of the Genovese crime family after seven years of court battles over whether he was mentally capable of understanding the charges against him.

Members of the Bloods and the Crips, California-based African American street gangs that originated in the ghettos of Los Angeles, are being imitated in East Coast cities such as New York, Philadelphia, Atlanta, Miami, Baltimore, and Boston by ghetto youths in African American communities.

1998–1999     Evidence from international crime analysis centers on increased
              linkages among criminal organizations themselves (e.g., Colom-
              bian cocaine cartels and heroin trafficking Mafia families in Italy)
              and between them and terrorist organizations, which serve to make
              criminal organizations more violent and terrorist organizations,
              such as Colombia's FARC (The Armed Revolutionary Forces of
              Colombia) and M-19 (Movimiento 19 de April), more criminal.

              Also, there are other disturbing international trends that impact
              on the United States. Money laundering has emerged as the num-
              ber one crime worldwide. In the United States at the end of the
              twentieth century, the impact on the recovery of money laundering
              in drug profits alone is estimated to be more than $75 billion
              annually. Laundered drug money returned to the United States can
              buy anything, entire industries, commercial enterprises, real estate,
              even a voice in politics and government.

# A

**ABREGO, JUAN GARCIA.** ("Dollface," "The Doll") (b. 1944, Matamoros, Mexico—incarcerated, U.S. prison). Mexican drug cartel leader.

Abrego was born into a family, some of whose members were well-known smugglers such as the legendary "godfather" of crime in Matamoros, Juan Guerra, a major figure in Mexico's drug trade. Abrego emerged as the head of the Gulf cartel, which controlled drug trafficking along the Gulf of Mexico and throughout northeastern Mexico. A heavyset, curly haired drug czar called "Dollface" or "The Doll" by his subordinates, he took the methods and techniques of the Cali cocaine cartel* and put together a drug organization that was compartmentalized into "cells" to ensure security. Abrego pioneered the Mexican role in cocaine trafficking and over a decade built an empire estimated to be worth $10 billion. He accepted cocaine in payment for transporting the Colombian cartels' loads and did so by guaranteeing delivery anywhere in the United States for 50 percent of a load with all risks assumed by his trafficking cartel.

Dollface paid millions of dollars in bribes and put together a group of gunmen and thugs that included law enforcement officers who provided security for his operations. Dozens of people, on both sides of the Mexican–U.S. border, were murdered.

By 1990, Abrego was indicted in the United States, and by 1996, he was arrested in Monterrey, the capital of the Mexican state Neuvo León, which borders Texas, and quickly flown to the United States, where a $2 million reward had been offered for his capture.

About 60 members of Abrego's group are serving time in American prisons, and it has weakened the Gulf cartel's competitive edge with rival drug cartels in Juarez and Tijuana. At the time of his arrest and extradition, Juan Abrego's power had been declining: Cali cut off his drug supplies because of his high-profile notoriety and because the government officials he had bribed and cor-

Anthony Joseph Accardo. Reproduced from
the Collections of the Library of Congress.

rupted were out of office. Abrego became a sacrificial lamb, it seems, because
Mexico needed to show some substantial progress in cracking down on drug
traffickers. Like his counterparts in the American Cosa Nostra, the primary wit-
ness/informant against Abrego was a Mexican American FBI agent who, by
pretending to be corrupt, successfully infiltrated the Gulf cartel. *See also* LA-
TINO ORGANIZED CRIME; MEXICAN ORGANIZED CRIME IN THE
UNITED STATES; PISTONE, JOSEPH

**SUGGESTED READING:** Peter A. Lupsha, "Transnational Narco-Corruption and Narco
Investment: A Focus on Mexico," *Transnational Organized Crime* (Spring 1995): 84–
101.

**ACCARDO, ANTHONY JOSEPH.** ("Joe Batters," "Big Tuna") (b. 1906, Chicago, IL—d. May 29, 1992, Chicago, IL). Head of the Chicago Outfit,* the
Chicago crime syndicate.

   Accardo began his criminal career as an enforcer in the Capone crime syndicate, where he earned the nickname "Joe Batters" because of his skill with a
baseball bat in collecting debts and in urging reluctant customers of vice to use
Alphonse Capone's* services. Despite humble origins in an impoverished Italian
section of Chicago, Accardo demonstrated intelligence in using violence and

verbal persuasion—a skill not overlooked by Capone, who was always on the lookout for bright gangsters.

His criminal career goes back to 1922 for petty offenses. Accardo was long suspected in at least two major murders—that of Joseph Aiello, a Mafia leader in Chicago who caused problems for Al Capone's consolidation of syndicate activities, and as a participant in the infamous St. Valentine's Day Massacre* in 1929 where seven of Capone's rivals in the George "Bugs" Moran* gang were brutally killed. With all this and the notoriety of being the head of the Chicago Outfit for decades, Accardo spent only one day in jail.

Accardo climbed his way to the top of organized crime in Chicago in 1929 when Capone served a brief jail term in Philadelphia on a gun possession charge. At that point, Accardo was appointed head of the enforcement wing of the Outfit. He handled problems with skill and resoluteness, often resorting to the baseball bat in order to leave tangible, horrifying evidence of what cheating or competing with the Outfit meant. One mob associate became well known for the brutality and suffering he experienced when he crossed Accardo. William "Action" Jackson, who as a mob collector of gambling monies forgot who he was collecting for, was found hanging from a meat hook in a Chicago suburban basement. He had been beaten mercilessly around his genitals and carved with a razor, and his eyes had been burned out with a blowtorch. He died more from the shock of the beating than his wounds.

Accardo followed Capone's organizational philosophy of allowing non-Italians into the organization. After he became head of the Chicago mob in 1943, Accardo kept Jake Guzik* in place as the financial brains of the organization and the "connection guy" whose prime function was to maintain and spread mob profit centers and corrupt public officials. Accardo was a great believer, as were his mentors, Al Capone and Frank "The Enforcer" Nitti,* in mob alliances with politicians. During Accardo's reign as boss, nearly 100 judges and other court personnel in Cook County (Chicago) had been convicted of bribery to fix criminal cases. Longtime mayor Richard Daley, who was alleged to have connections with the Outfit, disbanded a Chicago Police Department investigative unit. The stated reason was cost cutting in the city's government; the real reason, however, was very likely to have been a move to reduce surveillance on the mob.

Accardo shared power as boss. Paul "The Waiter" Ricca* and, later, Joseph John Aiuppa* played important roles running the mob. In 1958, Accardo "retired" from active involvement, spending most of his time in Palm Springs, California, but he was instrumental in selecting Sam Giancana* as mob boss. The other nickname, "Big Tuna," was given him after he caught a 400-pound tuna during a Florida fishing trip. In 1984, in an appearance before a Senate investigative committee, Joe Batters denied any role in the Chicago syndicate. *See also* CAPONE, ALPHONSE; CHICAGO OUTFIT; GIANCANA, SAM; ST. VALENTINE'S DAY MASSACRE

SUGGESTED READING: William F. Roemer, Jr., *Accardo: The Genuine Godfather*. 1995.

**ADONIS, JOSEPH.** (b. Giuseppe Doto, Nov. 22, 1902, Mantemarano, Italy— d. 1972, Milan, Italy). New York syndicate* racketeer and political fixer.*

Joe Adonis sided with "Joe the Boss" Masseria* during the Castellammarese War,* which was fought on the streets of American cities in 1930 among Sicilian mafiosi. Masseria lost the war and his life; Adonis was reputedly one of his boss's assassins.

He entered the United States illegally and took the name "Adonis" to reflect his handsome appearance. Like many of his youthful associates—Charles "Lucky" Luciano,* Vito Genovese,* Albert Anastasia*—Adonis soared up the criminal ladder of success during Prohibition (*see* PROHIBITION AND ORGANIZED CRIME*). His partnerships with powerful bootleggers* and mafiosi enabled him to create legitimate businesses. Throughout his career, he cultivated political figures, many of whom patronized his restaurant "Joe's Italian Kitchen," located around the criminal court buildings in downtown Brooklyn. Posing as a restauranteur, he functioned as an intermediary between the syndicate and public officials. His power as a racketeer extended beyond the New York Cosa Nostra rackets. In New Jersey, Adonis operated a large-scale gambling operation and an auto conveying company under contract with the Ford Corporation. His "Duke's Restaurant" in Cliffside, New Jersey, was known for its food and as a meeting place for gangsters and corrupt police.

In 1956, facing contempt and perjury charges based on his appearance before the Kefauver Committee,* he agreed to deportation. Adonis lived well in Milan, Italy, until his death in 1972. *See also* CASTELLAMMARESE WAR; COSTELLO, FRANK; LUCIANO, CHARLES "LUCKY"

SUGGESTED READING: Humbert S. Nelli, *The Business of Crime*. 1976.

**AFRICAN AMERICAN ORGANIZED CRIME.** Leroy "Nicky" Barnes,* "Mr. Untouchable," was a heroin kingpin during the 1970s in the Harlem ghetto. He understood that cooperation between crime groups was preferable to violence, because violence drew the police. But drugs in the 1980s and 1990s changed the world Barnes lived in. The African American godfathers today live in ghettos bristling with weapons and filled with teenagers willing to use them.

African Americans were not visible in nineteenth-century organized crime enterprises. Indeed, they entered the twentieth century with no history of a leadership role or an active affiliation in any organized criminal gang. In the first two decades of the twentieth century—when Caribbean and native-born African Americans migrated in large numbers into large northeastern and midwestern cities—illegal gambling,* illegal alcohol-drinking establishments, and other illegal vice activities evolved in these newly settled African American communities. Many of these businesses were owned and operated by African Americans. While there continues to be lively debate about the degree to which African American criminal organizations are independently run and the extent of their threat in the years ahead, historically, African American involvement in organized crime has been greatest in the traditional vices such as gambling, drugs, and prostitution and, to a lesser degree, loansharking,* theft, and fencing.*

Descriptions of African American organized gangs include a broad grouping that includes criminals made up of African Americans, Jamaicans, West Indians, Nigerians, Haitians, and others. Two principal types of organized crime networks among African Americans are identified as based on social and cultural bonds. First, a *domestic kinship network* is generally headed by a dominant male and includes close relatives. The second is an *associational network*, which is based on friendships developed in street gangs, prison, or neighborhood peer groups. Research shows that African American organized crime groups prey almost exclusively on each other and that this occurs mostly in their own areas, particularly within the inner cities.

The recent exodus of businesses and jobs out of cities to overseas locales, combined with the transformation of the American occupational system to a service-oriented economy, has led to an increase in the number of subpoverty wage-level jobs for the lower-strata workforce. The abandonment of the cities by both affluent whites and African Americans has left behind an underclass that is increasingly minority and poor in composition. Municipal tax bases have eroded in large cities, making it difficult for city officials to meet the needs of their citizens. Governmental policy changes and cutbacks in social programs in the 1980s have also widened the income gap between the poor and the affluent, quickening the instability of the inner-city African American family, already fragile and traumatized by neglect and racism. The effects on children have been devastating: By the early 1990s half of all African American children lived in female-headed households, and a similar proportion lived in poverty. These enervating factors impinge on African American family life in ways that make crime attractive as an alternative to the squalor and misery of the impoverished ghettos. Although some African Americans have moved successfully into the mainstream in recent decades, the inner-city poor are worse off today than at any time since the Great Depression.

African Americans in New York City controlled numbers* banks during the 1920s and 1930s. Kinship networks were the common organizational bonds, but they were not always headed by males. One popular African American female policy banker, Stephanie St. Clair,* known as "Madame Queen of Policy," testified in 1930 before the Seabury Committee (*see* SEABURY INVESTIGATIONS*) that she operated a policy bank from 1923 to 1928 and that the police took her money and kept arresting her runners. Outraged by the unscrupulous behavior and male chauvinism of the police department, she placed several paid advertisements in local Harlem newspapers and made serious charges of graft and corruption against them. Almost immediately she was arrested on what she termed a "framed charge" and was sent to jail for eight months.

The economic fixation of the African American community with numbers may be explained by viewing numbers gambling groups as a substitute for the legitimate financial institutions that were conspicuously absent in impoverished communities. The fact that career criminals did not control the African American gambling enterprises and organizations suggests that numbers were a communal response to the absence of legitimate organizations that could provide jobs, ready capital, and financial resources to a hard-pressed community.

Numbers players typically placed a small amount of money with a runner (an agent who takes the bets from players) whom they trusted, hoping to receive a generous return if they "hit" a winning number. Apart from their chief purpose of generating money, numbers gambling banks created jobs and were a source of ready capital in the African American community. In addition, a usury industry sprang up to serve the clientele of the numbers game. This species of an illegal appended enterprise may have broadened its scope beyond the gambling needs of the minority community and taken on a life of its own. The extent to which numbers became an integral part of the economy in African American communities is suggested by J. Saunders Redding, who characterized the pervasiveness of numbers gambling as "the fever that has struck all classes and conditions of men."

Before Dutch Schultz's* gang, a white criminal organization, seized much of the Harlem policy racket and consolidated its control, numbers were not a criminal monopoly or cartel operation. It consisted of many independent bankers (mostly African Americans) who conducted the game, each for themselves, each providing the requisite operating capital and each taking the profits. Early Harlem policy rackets were led by gambling "kings" and "queens" who were unsettled by the intrusions of white gangs that freely employed violence and cunning. The influence on corrupted political officials was the major tool employed by white competitors in the confrontation between community-based African American operators and alien white gangs. Schultz reportedly murdered 40 people in his takeover of the policy kingdom.

The rise of African American organized crime groups in the post–World War II era seems to have coincided with the rise of African American political consciousness and the awakening of political and social militancy. Major African American traffickers in drugs surfaced at approximately the same time, in the early and mid-1960s, when the pressures for jobs, educational reform, fair housing, and a greater share of political power intensified. Apparently, a combination of factors coalesced, some with unanticipated consequences, that produced legitimate and illegitimate opportunities for African Americans. In the wake of sweeping reforms, African Americans gained greater control over their communities, and as their political strength grew, criminal elements were able to take advantage of the correlative declines of white power and the increase of

African American influence within the ghetto crime scene. They were more able than at any other time to wrest the ghetto's lucrative rackets from white syndicates. African Americans became less dependent on La Cosa Nostra's* political and police clout and could bargain independently with white gangsters, who were no longer able to operate as freely in the ghettos.

The civil rights movement set in motion African American social and economic mobility and no doubt diminished the power of white crime groups that had dominated these communities until then. As the ghettos developed their newfound strength and discovered that they had political punch, the political agent, the operator, the political machine functionary, not unfamiliar in white communities, who had connections in the "administration" or city hall, appeared on the scene. As the ghettos became more politically assertive and economically more viable, a host of new actors arose—among them the "minority middlemen," the power brokers, those who were equally comfortable in the official world of government and business and in the shadows of opportunism and crime, where favors are arranged, deals are made, and money, when properly placed, can shield and immunize its possessors from the criminal justice system.

The African American underworld is not a homogeneous, monolithic structure of power and influence wielded only by America's blacks. Since the late 1960s in New York City, New Jersey, Baltimore, Washington, D.C., cities in Florida and California, and Toronto, Canada, the Rastafarians have engaged principally in marijuana and cocaine smuggling on a comparatively large scale. The Rastafarian movement originated in Jamaica in the early 1930s. It centered on the belief that the coronation of Prince Ras Tafari Makonnen as Emperor Haile Selassie I of Ethiopia was the prophesied black king and that the time of deliverance for blacks would be near. Ganja (marijuana) is used as a religious sacrament among the members. A close-knit group centered in a religious ideology with political overtones that deify Ethiopia's former emperor, Haile Selassie, the "Rastas" have achieved something of a détente with white organized crime families and other African American criminal groups. The Rastas have gained territorial control over the criminal economy (temporarily, at least) in the West Indian and Jamaican communities in the United States. Whether they are hierarchically organized with descending positions from boss downward to the street worker is not known. It is probable that, as with other ghetto-bound criminal groups, a flexible system of patron and client relations exists.

Crack is to ghetto gangsters as alcohol was to the white gangsters during the Prohibition (see PROHIBITION AND ORGANIZED CRIME*) era. Prohibition made the alcohol gangsters rich; similarly, crack is the lucrative illegal product of today's drug dealers. Crack is more available to small-time ghetto gangsters than heroin, mainly because the initial investment is within the reach of small-time traffickers. A puzzling thing about crack cocaine is that it did not begin rotting American's urban landscape sooner. References to the recipe that used heat and baking soda to turn cocaine into hydrochloride, or powder, and into the smokable form of freebase called "crack" appeared throughout the 1970s in underground literature, media interviews, and even congressional testimony. What turned crack into a craze was mass marketing. Cocaine powder required an investment of at least $75 for a gram but a "hit" of crack as little as $5. Enormous profits may be made by converting cocaine into crack.

At the same time, for African Americans and Hispanic ghetto dwellers, one of their most important problems, one that confronted white ethnic immigrants decades earlier, was how to escape poverty through socially approved means when these means were virtually closed. When legitimate means are not available, this problem is resolved to some extent by indulging in criminal activities.

Every large, urban African American ghetto has criminal organizations operating in its midst. Some of these gangs are large and some small. These criminal enterprises are usually led by local African Americans called "homeys."

Large powerful drug syndicates, like those of Frank Lucas and Leroy "Nicky" Barnes, spread beyond the ghetto in the late 1960s and 1970s. The level of sophistication and scope of trafficking in these organizations show that it was planned carefully. For example, Frank Lucas and his brothers (Vernon Lee, Lee Van, Larry, and Ezell) employed relatives as a hedge against security breaches in their international narcotics smuggling operations. Their group was known as the "Country Boys." Lucas did not restrict his trafficking to wholesaling but sought to control a network from Indochina to street-level sales in America's ghettos. All the trademarks of a sophisticated organization that resemble La Cosa Nostra operations were apparent in the Lucas group: Personnel were selected because they were trustworthy and reliable blood relatives, not because of some sentimental friendship or childhood attachment; a division of labor was constructed whereby participants knew only what was necessary for them to function; and state-of-the-art technologies in transportation, processing, and packaging were vigorously exploited in the drug business.

In many urban ghettos, crack cocaine is the currency of the informal economy. The gangs that developed around it reflect the dynamics of the trafficking systems that have emerged. In these respects, modern minority criminal groups— African American organized crime, in particular—have little structural resemblance to La Cosa Nostra crime families. Still, these groups are no less dangerous, nor are they likely to be short-lived or only drug dependent since the gangs may thrive beyond the demand for crack and transform themselves to meet the illegal market conditions of other commodities in demand. Crack enables minority groups to generate essential criminal assets (the use of violence and the availability and distribution of illegal commodities). Once established, these groups can explore other criminal opportunities, as did the white criminal groups that emerged to serve the demand of illicit alcohol. *See also* BARNES, LEROY "NICKY"; CRIPS AND BLOODS; EL RUKNS; FORT, JEFF

**SUGGESTED READING:** Rufus Schatzberg and Robert J. Kelly, *African-American Organized Crime: A Social History.* 1997.

**AGRON, EVSEI.** (b. St. Petersburg, Russia—d. May 4, 1985, Brooklyn, NY). Russian crime boss, New York.

A self-proclaimed "Russian godfather," Agron came to the United States in 1975 and within a few years built a criminal enterprise in the Brighton Beach section of New York City known as "Little Odessa." In Soviet Russia, Argon had been an assassin and black market operator who had spent years in prison. His reputation for violence preceded him, and when Argon arrived in Brighton Beach, he was feared.

Within a short period of time, Argon managed to acquire some businesses and involved himself in a profitable but highly dangerous fuel tax scam where through a complex maze of companies taxes on gasoline could be evaded. Profits were enormous. The swindle involved members of the New York La Cosa Nostra* and Agron's chief aide, Morat Balagula. Compared to his boss Agron, Balagula could not have been more different: Where Agron was a street ruffian who found himself in fights in Little Odessa neighborhoods, Balagula, an educated man, took care of the complex financial aspects of Agron's criminal schemes. The relationship must have deteriorated as Balagula continued to earn millions in the gasoline scam with his Cosa Nostra partners, whereas Agron did little but exploit his subordinate.

In January 1984, Agron was shot in the neck as he exited a garage in the Brooklyn apartment building where he lived. He survived that attack but was killed in May 1985 while his bodyguard looked on. Balagula moved in on Agron's businesses and positions in the Russian underworld soon after his boss's death.

Balagula did not enjoy his rise to power very long. In 1986 he was convicted in Philadelphia on credit card theft. He fled the country rather than face prison but was later found and extradited to the United States in 1989, where he is now in federal prison. *See also* IVANKOV, VYACHESLAV; RUSSIAN ORGANIZED CRIME

**SUGGESTED READING:** Phil Williams, *Russian Organized Crime.* 1997.


**AIUPPA, JOSEPH JOHN.** ("Joey Doves") (b. 1907, Sicily—   ). Chicago Outfit* leader in 1980s and 1990s.

Sam Giancana's* fall as the street boss of the Chicago Outfit in the mid-1960s meant that the retired leaders—Paul "The Waiter" Ricca* and Anthony Joseph Accardo*—had to return and pick up the reins of power. Joey Aiuppa also came back after Ricca's death and assumed control. He acquired his nickname—"Joey Doves"—early in his criminal career when he was arrested and convicted of illegally possessing and transporting birds, morning doves, from Kansas City to Chicago. Otherwise, his demeanor could be menacing, a man who was all business, never cracking a smile or making a joke.

Aiuppa was entrusted with restoring the Outfit's rackets and profits after Giancana's mishandling of government probes. Because of his reputation as an intelligent, diplomatically imaginative corrupter of police and politicians, and with his willingness to use force to discipline wayward gangsters, it is believed that Aiuppa arranged the assassination of Giancana in 1975 when "Momo" was scheduled to testify before Congress about the mob's role in Operation Mongoose*—a mob/CIA plot to assassinate Cuba's dictator, Fidel Castro. "Joey Doves" learned to corrupt law enforcement and politicians during his apprenticeship under Alphonse Capone*—a master at the properly placed bribe. He also appreciated the value of information and cultivated individuals with access to grand jury proceedings and law enforcement operations directed at the underworld and made good use of this knowledge in evading arrests throughout a long career. Never one to leave a stone unturned, John Roselli's* murder in 1976 was attributed to Aiuppa, who suspected that Giancana's close friend and associate with ties to Cuba and the Florida gambling rackets run by Santos Trafficante, Jr.* might be likely to talk to the government. FBI theories suggest more down-to-earth motives having nothing to do with international intrigues. According to the FBI, Giancana and Roselli failed to share the proceeds from gambling ship operations that were arranged in Mexico with the Outfit's money, and this deeply angered Accardo and Aiuppa.

For whatever reasons, Aiuppa supposedly got rid of Giancana and Roselli only to face a new horror with the antics of Tony "The Ant" Spilotro.* In 1986, Aiuppa, already an elderly man, was convicted of a conspiracy to skim monies from Las Vegas, Nevada,* casinos. Spilotro had been the Outfit's representative in Las Vegas whose job it was to ensure that the skimming of gambling profits proceeded smoothly. It did not. The Ant's high profile and reckless criminal activity got him into trouble with Joey Doves. Aiuppa and his associates blamed Spilotro; two badly beaten bodies, identified as Tony Spilotro and his brother Michael, were discovered in a shallow grave in an Indiana cornfield not far from a farm owned by Joey Doves.

**SUGGESTED READING:** Nicholas Pileggi, *Casino.* 1995.


**ALEX, GUS.** ("Gussie") (b. 1916—d. ?). Chicago Outfit boss in the 1970s and 1980s.

The career of Gus Alex illustrates two important realities about organized crime: First, his criminal activities dispel the myth that Italians are the exclusive force in organized crime; they do not discriminate against other ethnics just because of their ethnic identities—Alex was of Greek ethnic background. Second, Alex operated extortion and vice rackets as part of the Chicago Outfit,* demonstrating that without the corruption of segments of the political system, organized crime could not survive intact. As with Murray ("The Camel") Joseph Humphreys "The Waiter" and Jake Guzik,* Alex enjoyed the trust of Alphonse Capone,* Anthony Accardo,* Paul Ricca,* Frank "The Enforcer" Nitti,* and Sam Giancana*—important leaders of the Chicago Outfit—because of his skills in vice racketeering and his sly cultivations of police and politicians.

In the 1950s and 1960s, Alex appeared many times before the McClelland Committee* and took the Fifth Amendment, declining, respectively, to answer any questions.

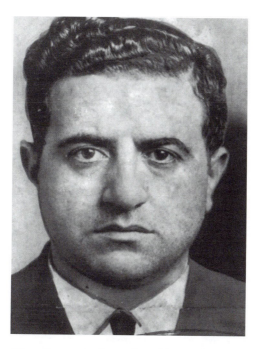

Albert Anastasia. Reproduced from the Collections of the Library of Congress.

Apart from his chief interests in Chicago rackets, Alex is alleged to have
handled skimming operations in Las Vegas casinos and functioned as a top
courier of underworld cash deposited in secret banks in Switzerland. In 1992,
an associate of Gus Alex's, Leonard Patrick,* rather than face more jail time
agreed to become a government witness and wore a wire. As a result of Patrick's
testimony and electronic surveillance information, in 1995 Alex and his crew's
main enforcer were found guilty of extortion. At the age of 76, Gus Alex was
sentenced to 15 years.

**AMERICAN MAFIA.** *See* LA COSA NOSTRA

**ANASTASIA, ALBERT.** ("Lord High Executioner," "The Mad Hatter") (b. Umberto Anastasio, Sept. 26, 1902, Tropea, Italy—d. Oct. 25, 1957, New York
City). Crime family boss, Murder, Inc.*
    On October 25, 1957, while getting a haircut and shave in the barbershop of
the Park Sheraton Hotel in midtown Manhattan, Albert Anastasia, head of one
of the most important crime families in the United States, the Mangano* crime
family, was assassinated. As with most mob killings, the Anastasia murder remains unsolved, but it is reliably rumored that Joseph Profaci,* another godfather, was given the contract and passed it on to the Gallo brothers, Larry and

Joseph Gallo.* The man behind this sensational rubout, which was carried out in the morning in a crowded section of Manhattan, was Vito Genovese,* whose motive in killing Anastasia was to weaken further his rival Frank Costello* for control of the Luciano crime family.* Anastasia and Costello were close friends; in the early days of the Castellammarese War,* Anastasia was a top triggerman for Luciano; he allegedly was part of the four-man death squad that murdered "Joe the Boss" Masseria* in a Coney Island restaurant in 1931, which ended the factional fighting among Sicilians and created the modern Cosa Nostra.

Anastasia was born "Anastasio" in Italy. Between 1917 and 1920 he jumped ship in the United States and became a dockhand. By 1921, he was arrested for murder, and it is believed that he changed his name to avoid embarrassing his family. His brother Anthony Anastasio* ("Tough Tony") would later become the unofficial ruler of the Brooklyn waterfront as head of Local 1814 of the International Longshoreman's Association. Throughout his life, Anastasia did not hesitate to murder when he was threatened by other gangsters or witnesses in cases against him. Given his willingness to murder, it is not surprising that with Louis Buchalter* he would operate Murder, Inc., a selected hit squad of experienced assassins serving the needs of the National Crime Syndicate. Some estimates suggest that in its ten years the enforcement arm of the syndicate may have murdered 400 to 500 people. Unlike "Lepke" Buchalter and other members of Murder, Inc., Anastasia was never prosecuted for any of its crimes.

During World War II, Anastasia served in the U.S. Army stateside. Prior to that, and after his military service, he was imprisoned for short periods on gun possession and tax evasion. The waterfront connection with his brother has a significance that goes beyond the exploitation of the ILA's union. As the war engulfed the United States, fear of waterfront sabotage of the Lend-Lease Program (war aid to Great Britain) encouraged the U.S. Navy to seek the help of Mafia bosses with influence among dockworkers. The idea was to enlist the assistance of longshoremen in an antiespionage campaign the Nazis might launch against American shipping and port facilities along the Eastern seaboard. Joseph "Socks" Lanza* on the New York piers was approached, but he deferred to Meyer Lansky* and Frank Costello, who, in turn, sought the help of Charles "Lucky" Luciano,* who at the time was imprisoned in New York State. Anastasia, according to one theory, persuaded his brother "Tough Tony" to destroy the French luxury liner S.S. *Normandie*, which was being converted into a troop ship. The idea was to show just how vulnerable to saboteurs the New York waterfront could be; Luciano's cooperation would then be eagerly sought and a pardon from prison more likely if it would facilitate his aid in helping the war effort. Indeed, after the *Normandie* incident, Luciano was moved to a more convenient location, closer to his associates. At war's end, Lucky was pardoned.

Albert Anastasia's violent temperament knew no bounds. In 1951, Philip Mangano was murdered and his brother, Vincent Mangano,* head of the crime family in which Anastasia was a capo, was permanently missing. Mangano never accepted the closeness of Anastasia with Luciano, Costello, and Joe Adonis.*

Anastasia claimed self-defense and was accepted by the other bosses as the new don of the Mangano crime family. Over the years, Anastasia's family often provided the muscle Costello needed to foil the ambitions of Vito Genovese,* who wanted the crown of the Luciano family, with Lucky permanently deported to Italy.

But Anastasia was a loose cannon by any standard. Even a killer like Genovese had the presence of mind not to harm innocent civilians if it could be avoided. Not so for the "The Mad Hatter." In 1952, Anastasia ordered the execution of Arnold Schuster, a young salesman who was a prime witness in the arrest of career bank thief Willie Sutton. Anastasia violated a cardinal principle of the organized underworld: We only kill each other; outsiders, including police, prosecutors, journalists, and the general public, were not to be killed.

Apart from other violations of the Cosa Nostra code (like selling memberships), Anastasia's execution was necessary if Genovese intended to take over the Luciano crime family because Costello's protection was dependent on Anastasia's loyalty and friendship. Thus, by killing Anastasia, Costello would be too weak to confront Genovese. Anastasia's murder in October 1957 was a carefully planned mob hit that required the neutralization of Albert's bodyguards, detailed knowledge of his day-to-day habits, and the complicity of the heads of the other crime families who had to believe that Anastasia had become a dangerous liability for the other crime families. The murder went smoothly, and the Cosa Nostra was dramatically changed, if not permanently weakened. *See also* ANASTASIO, ANTHONY; BUCHALTER, LOUIS; MURDER, INC.

**SUGGESTED READING:** Burton Turkus and Sid Feder, *Murder, Inc.* 1951, 1992.

**ANASTASIO, ANTHONY.** ("Tough Tony") (b. 1906, Tropea, Italy—d. 1963, New York). Major waterfront racketeer.

As vice president of the International Longshoremen's Association and head of Local 1814, "Tough Tony" Anastasio ruled the Brooklyn waterfront for three decades. Because he had the power of his brother Albert's crime family behind him, few would dare to challenge his authority in the ILA. It is believed that during World War II Tony Anastasio arranged for the sabotage of the French luxury liner the S.S. *Normandie*, moored at a New York pier, in order to demonstrate to federal authorities that the docks could not be considered safe from Nazi sabotage unless the Mafia received concessions including the eventual pardon of Charles "Lucky" Luciano,* who was serving a 50-year sentence on prostitution charges. Concessions were made, and the Mafia helped the U.S. Navy secure the safety of the waterfront.

Anastasio's power was directly related to his brother's power. Anastasio kept the original spelling of his name, which his brother, Albert Anastasia,* changed because of the notoriety associated with his criminal career. Throughout the 1950s the mob grip on the waterfront was tight. Shipping companies had no choice but to make informal arrangements for cargo loading and unloading with the mob; dockworkers who protested against unfair and dangerous work conditions, including the "shape-up" where men were hired only if they "kicked back" part of their wages, were found floating in the harbor. The stevedores survived by "dummying up": See nothing, hear nothing, say nothing. For years these conditions existed; public outrage in the late 1950s forced the government to create a waterfront commission in 1953 (Bi-state Waterfront Commission), which monitored union practices in hiring and setting work conditions.

When Albert Anastasia was assassinated in 1957, Tony Anastasio lost power and was reduced to a figurehead. Carlo Gambino,* the new boss, appointed his son-in-law, Anthony Scotto,* to the leadership of Local 1814. Shortly before his death of natural causes in 1963, Tough Tony began to talk to the Department of Justice. How much he revealed about mob operations on the waterfront is not known. *See also* ANASTASIA, ALBERT; COSTELLO, FRANK

**SUGGESTED READING:** John H. Davis, *Mafia Dynasty.* 1993.

**ANGIULO, GENNARO.** ("Jerry") (b. 1919, Boston, MA—   ). Boston Mafia racketeer and gambler.

Jerry Angiulo and his brothers constituted a mini-Mafia gang all by themselves. Born in the North End of Boston, Angiulo was the second-oldest son of an Italian immigrant who ran a "mom-and-pop" grocery store that also functioned as gambling center when Giovannina Angiulo had to support seven children after her husband's early death.

Angiulo had the distinction of graduating from Boston English High School in 1936, which raised his hopes of becoming a criminal lawyer, but the realities of the depression and the lure of quick bootlegging and gambling money pulled Angiulo in another direction: into a life of crime when a golden opportunity arose in the early 1950s. The Kefauver Committee* was planning to conduct hearings in Boston, and the local Mafia boss, Joseph Lombardo, decided it would be well to close down gambling in order to take the wind out of Kefauver's sails. Angiulo was not a La Cosa Nostra* member at the time and sought permission from Lombardo to operate the numbers* gambling with the understanding that he would have no Mafia protection. Lombardo agreed.

When Lombardo was succeeded by a new boss, Philip Bruccola, the arrangement broke down when too much law enforcement heat forced Bruccola to flee to Sicily. Angiulo was then subjected to heavy extortion payments from several mobsters that threatened his gambling business. Finally, he approached Raymond L. S. Patriarca,* in Providence, Rhode Island, who had emerged as the Cosa Nostra boss of all New England. Guaranteed a sizable percentage of Angiulo's profits, Patriarca offered his protection, which meant that several phone calls were made to Boston gangsters indicating that Angiulo and Patriarca were partners—and that was that. To further ensure his stature with the mob, Angiulo was "made" in the Patriarca crime family and became the boss of Boston, representing Patriarca and La Cosa Nostra* interests.

For many Mafia soldiers, Angiulo was a "back door" man, no matter what rank he had in the organization. When Patriarca died in 1984, the underboss of the crime family, Henry Tameleo, was in prison; as the number-three man in the organization, Angiulo claimed a right to become boss. He did not get it. Many members of the organization resented the way Angiulo got into the mob: Moneymaking was important, to be sure, but it was not enough for many who had to run the supreme risk of "making your bones"* (committing a murder) to be inducted as soldiers.*

Because Angiulo had corrupted so many Boston police officers (45 were implicated in his racketeering enterprises), he was under investigation by the federal government. Heavy surveillance and electronic intercepts culminated in a federal racketeering prosecution that would have meant almost 200 years in prison. That fact, no doubt, figured into the decision to abandon Angiulo and reduce him in rank to a mere soldier. In 1986, he was convicted on racketeering charges and sentenced to 45 years' imprisonment.

**SUGGESTED READING:** Gerard O'Neill and Dick Lehr, *The Underboss: The Rise and Fall of a Mafia Family.* 1989.

**ANNENBERG, MOSES.** ("Moe") (b. 1878, East Prussia—d. 1942, Palm Springs, CA). Gambling czar and newspaper racketeer.

Moe Annenberg had made his name as a brutally effective circulation manager for the William Randolph Hearst papers in Chicago in the first decades of the twentieth century. He later moved to Milwaukee, Wisconsin, in 1907 and then to San Francisco, California, in roughly the same capacity as a newspaperman. In 1920, the great newspaper mogul, Hearst, brought him to New York City to work as circulation boss of the entire Hearst chain.

Annenberg was a tall, rangy man who could be quite friendly and jovial but also very violent. He was a German Jewish immigrant, born in a village in East Prussia near the Russian border. Brought to Chicago as a boy in 1885, he grew up on the tumultuous South Side. His father was a peddler and a grocer. Moe and his brother Max went to work selling newspapers and were caught up in the vicious circulation struggles that pitted Hearst's *American* and *Examiner* newspapers against the conservative *Tribune.* All the contending parties hired gangs of sluggers and ex-boxers who used guns and blackjacks to persuade newsstands to feature one paper and ignore competitors. Delivery trucks were attacked, bundles of newspapers destroyed, newsstands firebombed, and in the end, people killed.

Under Hearst, Annenberg was one of the highest-paid circulation men in the entire country. He rose from the slums and poverty of the South Side of Chicago to accumulate one of the largest individual incomes in the country. Realizing the money to be made in gambling—legal and illegal—in 1922 he had seized control of the *Daily Racing Form,* the bookies' Bible, and began to build an empire of his own. By 1926 his various private businesses became so profitable that he quit the Hearst Company. By this time Annenberg found the Nation-Wide News Service in association with the biggest gambler on the East Coast, Frank Erickson, who was a close associate of Charles "Lucky" Luciano,* Meyer Lansky,* and Frank Costello.*

In 1929, Alphonse Capone* brought Annenberg into the underworld's Atlantic City, New Jersey,* Conference, which laid much of the foundation for a National Crime Syndicate built upon vices such as gambling. Annenberg worked out the details of a syndicate racing wire—a telegraphic information service featuring racetrack results around the country.

Annenberg had a respectable facade: By the 1930s he owned the prestigious *Philadelphia Inquirer*, but he also did business with gangsters as an equal. The racing wire and information service made him rich. The service acquired its information from telegraph and telephone wires hooked up in nearly 30 major racetracks, and from these tracks, they moved the information to 225 cities in 30 states where poolrooms and horse parlors operated illegal gambling* enterprises. It was an intricate and profitable criminal enterprise. Annenberg lived in palatial homes in four states and occupied luxurious hotel suites in New York and Philadelphia; he invested in hotels, office buildings, garages, movie theaters, bowling alleys, liquor stores, and laundries, among other legitimate businesses—all in an effort to achieve the status of "respectability" and public acceptance as a man of prestige and influence.

But Moe was destined to experience some of what Al Capone endured: a confrontation with the IRS over tax evasion. In 1939, Moe and his son Walter were indicted. All together the government claimed he owed $9.5 million in unpaid taxes. He saved his son by pleading guilty, for which he received a three-year prison term and a tax lien of $9.5 million in settlement. Walter would go on legitimately, and during the Nixon administration, he would become ambassador to the Court of Saint James (England) and emerge as a major philanthropist after his government service. Moe would have been proud. *See also* ILLEGAL GAMBLING

**SUGGESTED READING:** Joseph Gies, *The Colonel of Chicago: A Biography of Robert McCormick.* 1979.


**APALACHIN MEETING.** On November 14, 1957, an underworld conference was uncovered quite by accident in a rural upstate New York community by state troopers. It provided the most compelling proof until then of a nationwide Mafia conspiracy. In and around the home of Joseph Barbara, a local businessman, but also a mafioso, police arrested 58 gangsters of Italian background from all over the country. Among them were La Cosa Nostra* crime family bosses such as Vito Genovese* (New York City), Nicholas Civella* (Kansas City), Carlo Gambino* (New York City), Stefano Magaddino* (Buffalo, New York), and Santos Trafficante* (Tampa, Florida). Of the 58, 50 had arrest records, 35 had criminal convictions, and 23 had served prison terms. Among those who managed to flee and avoid detention were James Lanza, boss of the San Francisco crime family, Thomas Luchese, head of the Luchese crime family* in New York City, Sam Giancana* of Chicago, and Joe Zerilli* of Detroit.

Since 1931, the Mafia Commission* had met every five years in secret with no such problems. The most recent meeting in 1956, also at Barbara's home in Apalachin, occurred without incident. At the conclave, Joe Zerilli of Detroit and Angelo Bruno* of Philadelphia were added to the National Commission, bringing it to nine members.

Since 1956, a number of crises had enveloped the Cosa Nostra: There were squabbles over admission of new members; over the violence of Vito Genovese against Frank Costello* in his quest for control of the Luciano crime family* and his assassination of Albert Anastasia* just 20 days before the Apalachin meeting convened; over the purging of Mafia members deemed unreliable; and over the need to formulate a Cosa Nostra policy on narcotics concerning the relationship of American Cosa Nostra groups to heroin trafficking groups of the Sicilian mafia. Earlier in 1957, as Joseph Bonanno revealed in his book *Man of Honor*, meetings had taken place in Palermo, Sicily, involving Charles "Lucky" Luciano* and Frank Coppola with members of the Sicilian mafia. Bonanno does not say much beyond the suggestion that the Sicilians were urged to form a "Commission" to handle disputes. The real purpose of the meeting in Palermo, according to Ralph Salerno, was to formalize heroin trafficking procedures in the United States.

The Apalachin meeting hurt the Cosa Nostra because it provided the public with evidence of a national criminal conspiracy and forced FBI director J. Edgar Hoover* to acknowledge the existence of a secret crime syndicate and take action against it. *See also* ANASTASIA, ALBERT; COMMISSION; GENOVESE, VITO; LA COSA NOSTRA

**SUGGESTED READINGS:** Joseph Bonanno, *A Man of Honor*. 1983; Ralph Salerno and John S. Tompkins, *The Crime Confederation*. 1969.

**ASIAN ORGANIZED CRIME.** Asian organized crime (AOC) groups have emerged as one of the most violent criminal enterprises operating in big-city Chinatowns across America. With their origins going back centuries, Chinese Triads,* criminally influenced Tongs,* the Japanese Yakuza* (a.k.a. Boryokudan), and the Vietnamese and Korean criminal organizations are criminally diverse. They are involved in murder, extortion, kidnaping, gambling, fraud, counterfeiting, prostitution, weapons trafficking, drug trafficking, money laundering, alien smuggling, and armed home invasions. More disturbing, law enforcement reports show a trend toward more brutal and more deadly home invasions and an increase in execution-style murders. AOC presents a major challenge for law enforcement. Language and cultural barriers are significant. In addition, because AOC operations are so criminally diverse and have spread to nearly every corner of the world, an extraordinary cooperative effort between foreign law enforcement and the United States, as well as among U.S. agencies, is required to cripple these organizations.

A complex and fluid relationship exists between Triads, Tongs, street gangs, and American Chinese organized crime groups. Some of these groups evolved from street gangs into sophisticated organizations that rival the traditional mob in their violence, economic impact, and expansion of illegal operations. Particularly in the drug trade, various groups cooperate at different levels to get the product to its final destination. Frequently, higher-level Asian groups provide support to the lower-level street gangs. In exchange, the street gangs act as enforcers for the higher-level group, including performing contract murders and protecting illegal operations.

Asian organized criminal groups originated as secret societies in their homelands to resist oppressive political regimes. After the political threat subsided, these societies began using their power and organization to capitalize on criminal opportunities.

Asian immigrants have been coming to this country since the mid-1800s. Like the Italians with Little Italy, and the Greeks with Greektown, they settled into ethnic enclaves known as Chinatowns. In the late 1960s, the United States experienced a dramatic influx of Asian immigration. Among the new arrivals were members of these criminal organizations. Like many immigrants new to the United States, Asians were subject to discrimination and, out of necessity, organized for self-protection and self-preservation. These Asian criminal groups found opportunities to exploit the organizational power represented by the new immigrants. Although these groups have spread internationally, they maintain allegiance to their parent organizations back in Asia.

Experts have noted some similarities in the evolution of AOC and that of homegrown American organized criminal groups. The organizational structure of most AOC groups is hierarchical, with subgroups emerging based upon ethnicity or geography. A charismatic leader emerges and is able to instill and maintain loyalty to the organization. Historically, loyalty to the family and the organization is highly valued. Lower-level and younger members are used to insulate leaders. Each group relies heavily on corrupt public officials and institutions to operate without interference, and they use front organizations to conceal their illegal activity. Finally, using fear of retribution and violence, both groups initially preyed upon immigrants from their respective ethnic backgrounds.

The major difference between AOC and the traditional mob is in the rate of assimilation into the American mainstream. While the mob will venture into all areas of American life in search of new enterprises, Asian immigrants are more provincial and less likely to venture into other communities for legitimate and illegitimate business or social opportunities. Just as this disposition inhibits economic mobility for noncriminal immigrants, it has slowed the expansion of AOC outside the Asian community.

AOC groups have developed alliances with other major crime syndicates including traditional organized crime, as well as the Russian mafia and Colombian drug cartels.* The alliance appears to be one of reciprocation. Chinese groups are a source of heroin for the mob, and it in turn provides loansharking* capital and weapons to Chinese street gangs.* They perform contract killings on each other's behalf and cooperate in illegal gambling* operations. As early as 1973, the FBI monitored and documented a meeting between the acting boss of the Bonanno crime family* of New York and leaders of the Japanese Boryokudan (Yakuza) to introduce them to the lucrative pornography business in Hawaii. More recently, there has been increasing evidence of direct contact between the Boryokudan and traditional organized crime groups across the United States. Future topics of mutual interest between these two organizations will likely include money laundering opportunities.

Korean, Laotian, Thai, Cambodian, and Filipino crime groups are also active in the United States but currently present less of a threat owing to a smaller membership base and less formal organization. However, they are known to be as violent and criminally motivated as other prominent Asian crime groups. In Chicago, they are primarily involved in gambling, extortion, money laundering, prostitution, drug trafficking, and loansharking. Korean organized crime groups generally control drugs and prostitution within their own community. Thai and Laotian criminal groups involve themselves in trafficking and heroin, whereas Filipino groups move large amounts of cocaine and methamphetamines—a psychoactive drug that is again spreading into the American population. *See also* CHINESE STREET GANGS; CHINESE TRIADS; TONGS; VIETNAMESE ORGANIZED CRIME; YAKUZA

**SUGGESTED READING:** Ko-lin Chin, *Chinatown Gangs: Extortion, Enterprise, and Ethnicity.* 1996.

**ATLANTIC CITY, NEW JERSEY.** Casino gambling.*
Atlantic City became the second major tourist destination to establish casino gambling. The first casinos in Atlantic City were opened in 1978, and unlike Las Vegas, Nevada,* extensive controls were implemented on gambling and the casino licensing process. At the ceremony signing of the Casino Control bill, the governor exclaimed, "Organized crime is not welcome in Atlantic City! . . . Keep the hell out of our state!"

Ironically, the genesis of organized crime in Atlantic City has, like Las Vegas, similar beginnings. In the 1920s, Atlantic City was a popular summer resort for celebrities, politicians, and gangsters. Indeed, in 1929, an underworld conference convened at the President Hotel hosted by Enoch "Nucky" Johnson, the boss of the city. Alphonse Capone,* Jake Guzik,* "Moe" Dalitz,* Abner Zwillman,* Frank Costello,* Charles "Lucky" Luciano,* Meyer Lansky,* and many others attended and reached important agreements on bookmaking, gambling, bootlegging, and violence that would form the basis and agenda for organized crime throughout the century.

In the present day, casino gambling in Atlantic City has been a successful source of revenue by any measure. Its strong regulatory structure has resulted in surprisingly few substantiated allegations of organized crime involvement in its casinos. However, there appear to be criminal penetrations in the ancillary services and workforces that service the casinos/hotels.

There is some evidence that the service vending agencies and businesses have been tainted by organized crime. A New Jersey state government report in 1971 indicated that Local 54 of the Hotel and Restaurant Employees International Union was under "substantial influence" of organized crime. Local 54 was controlled by Frank Gerace, an associate of Nicky Scarfo,* head of the Bruno crime family in Philadelphia.

**SUGGESTED READING:** Craig A. Zendazian, *Who Pays? Casino Gambling, Hidden Interests and Organized Crime.* 1993.

**BANANA WAR.** *See* BONANNO, JOSEPH

**BANK OF CREDIT AND COMMERCE INTERNATIONAL.** In July 1991, bank regulators in many countries seized the assets of the London-based BCCI to recover some $10 billion lost by hundreds of thousands of creditors. Referred to in the press as the "bank of crooks and criminals international," BCCI was founded and financed by Pakistanis and Arabs. Agha Hasan Abedi, the founder of the bank, was responsible for most of its illegal activities.

BCCI functioned as a full-service bank to terrorists and drug traffickers despite its associations and affiliations with influential political leaders in the United States such as former President Jimmy Carter, Washington lawyer and political insider Clark Clifford, and Utah Senator Orrin Hatch, who sought to protect the bank in the early phases of the criminal investigation.

The notorious terrorist leader Abu Nidal maintained a $60 million account at the London branch of BCCI, and the bank laundered money for the Medellín cocaine cartel and Golden Triangle drug lord Khun Sa. The Golden Triangle refers to the opium-growing highlands in southeast Asia including Thailand, Laos, and Myanmar. In 1988, the U.S. government accused BCCI of laundering $14 million for the Medellín cartel. The scheme worked as follows: Cash from the traffickers was electronically placed in certificates of deposit (CDs) in BCCI banks in Europe, Central America, South America, and the Caribbean. Using the CDs as collateral, BCCI officials created a loan at other branches and permitted the narcotics traffickers of the cartel to withdraw the funds. The bank repaid the loan with the funds from the CDs.

In 1990, BCCI pleaded guilty to laundering drug money and paid a $15 million fine, and two of its employees received long prison sentences. In 1991 as the investigation deepened, it was clear that money laundering* was integral to bank operations; it also carried on a "Ponzi" scheme where early investors took out loans that they did not repay and other depositors took the losses of poorly secured loans. *See also* BANK SECRECY ACT; COLOMBIAN DRUG CARTELS; MONEY LAUNDERING; POLITICAL CORRUPTION; SINDONA, MICHELE

**SUGGESTED READING:** Jonathan Ready, *The Outlaw Bank.* 1993.

**BANK SECRECY ACT.** The Bank Secrecy Act became law in 1970 and was designed specifically to block criminal opportunities in "laundering" illicit cash through legitimate channels. The act spelled out three requirements for banks and individuals.

First, banks are obliged to file a Currency Transaction Report (CTR) for deposits, withdrawals, or exchanges of funds more than $10,000. Second, a Currency and Monetary Instrument Report (CMIR) must be filed with the U.S. Customs Service if more than $10,000 in cash leaves or enters the United States. Third, citizens having bank accounts in foreign countries must declare them on their federal tax returns. Violations of these provisions can result in criminal penalties up to $500,000. Through the IRS, U.S. Customs Service, Federal Reserve Bank, SEC (Securities and Exchange Commission), and FDIC (Federal Deposit Insurance Corporation), the U.S. Treasury Department is responsible for enforcement of these provisions.

Until 1985, the government failed to do an effective job. However, the prosecution of Bank of Boston officials involving the J. Gennaro Angiulo* network of the Raymond L. S. Patriarca* crime family represented a significant change in compliance enforcement; by 1990 the IRS Criminal Investigation Division had processed more than 1,000 convictions in only three years for crimes relating to money laundering.* Because of the growing volume of financial transactions since 1990—for example, in 1992, 9 million CTRs were filed, reporting more than $417 billion in currency transactions—the Financial Crime Enforcement Network (Fin CEN) was established to support law enforcement agencies in identifying money laundering activities.

In 1994, the Bank Secrecy Act was amended, making it illegal to engage in multiple cash transactions just under $10,000 if it is a willful effort to avoid the CTR requirement. The government is confident that the Bank Secrecy Act is an effective tool against organized crime. The President's Commission Report (1986) urged that similar laws on the state level be enacted. By 1998, half the states implemented similar banking requirements and criminal reviews of currency transaction violations.

**SUGGESTED READING:** Marilyn B. Petersen, *A Guide to the Financial Analysis of Personal and Corporate Bank Records.* 1998.

**BARNES, LEROY "NICKY."** ("Mr. Untouchable") (b. March, 1933, New York City—    ). Major African American organized crime* figure and drug trafficker.

According to the New York City Police Department and the Drug Enforcement Administration's Joint Task Force, "Nicky" Barnes was one of the biggest heroin dealers in the United States during the 1970s. In his home base, Harlem, a black ghetto, he was regarded as powerful as any Mafia don* in the New York La Cosa Nostra* crime families. Furthermore, though frequently arrested in his youth, since 1973 he had not been convicted of any charges brought against him—hence, his nickname, "Mr. Untouchable."

To street people, Barnes was a charismatic figure, but to law enforcement, he represented a shift in the power bases of organized criminals in the minority communities that had until the mid-1970s been dominated by La Cosa Nostra. However, Barnes was not totally free of Mafia connections, and far from taking over, from becoming a "black godfather," Barnes was used by the Mafia, playing a typical role of ghetto gangster, that of a visible street ace in the rackets but little more than a narcotics distributor whose success was primarily due to his alliance with Joseph Gallo,* an influential member of the Joseph Profaci*/ Colombo crime family* in New York. Barnes is said to have met Gallo during a 1965 stay in Greenhaven Prison and had a connection with Carmine "The Cigar" Galante,* a capo* and major drug trafficker in the Bonanno crime family* who before his assassination in 1979 was considered a candidate for the title "boss of bosses."

Barnes conducted his criminal affairs in a mafialike manner: He consulted a "Council of 12" that he formed in Harlem, which consisted of African American drug dealers who met from time to time to set up and maintain drug distribution territories. Police intelligence reports suggested that Barnes shrewdly put together "buffers," layers of dealers, street retailers, buyers, transporters, and enforcers between him and the actual drugs, creating an arrest-proof narcotics operation.

Like Alphonse Capone* and John Gotti,* Nicky Barnes lived flamboyantly, driving fancy cars, wearing expensive clothing, and displaying his presumptive benevolence for the community by handing out turkeys to needy families on Thanksgiving and Christmas, which was done with a flair for publicity that would do credit to modern politicians and show business stars.

His early life is largely a mystery. What is certain is that he could not avoid the drug dealing that went on, and still does, in the streets of the Harlem ghetto. An early arrest as a street junkie sent Barnes off to rehabilitation in Lexington, Kentucky, where he kicked the habit. He never went back to drug or alcohol abuse after that.

Police reports indicate that in the 1950s when Barnes was in his twenties he began dealing and piecing together his network, enlisting in the process other known major drug violators. Initially these efforts to create a drug consortium as a basis for a "Black Mafia" were rejected by his street competitors, so Barnes went it alone.

In 1965 he was arrested and sent to Greenhaven Correctional Facility on a 25-years-to-life sentence on narcotics violations. While in prison he became friendly with "Crazy Joe" Gallo and acquired information and contacts that would lead to his release two years later when Barnes's mob lawyer was able to successfully challenge the testimony that jailed him. He then proceeded to create his drug empire with the help of his Mafia friends. It is alleged that Gallo wanted to become a major force in the New York underworld but that he lacked troops; he suggested that Barnes help him recruit African Americans. Gallo had serious problems with the heads of the Profaci/Colombo crime family bosses and perhaps decided to break with tradition and form alliances with non-Italians in order to gain easy access to minority communities and build up his own "crime family."

In any case, Barnes was able to secure large quantities of pure heroin from Italian suppliers. He then set up drug mills to process the heroin for street distribution and erected an elaborate delivery system, buying and selling in Pennsylvania, Arizona, Illinois, and Canada.

Gradually he began to take over the street operations in drugs from Cosa Nostra groups that had controlled Harlem until "Mr. Untouchable" arrived. But rather than lead to frictions and violent conflicts, Barnes was able to displace Cosa Nostra drug dealers by sharing profits with his erstwhile competitors—as long as money was made in areas where Cosa Nostra gangsters could not venture, they were content to allow Barnes to operate as one of their partners.

From 1968 until 1978, Barnes lived a lavish life, earning large sums of money in heroin dealing and beating the government on tax evasion charges. Barnes seemed immune to prosecution. And while he was increasingly influential in the huge Harlem drug scene, he began investing in legitimate businesses—in gasoline stations, travel agencies, real estate, and other retail businesses.

In 1978 a narcotics strike force brought Nicky Barnes to justice. He was sentenced to life and a fine of $125,000 for narcotics violations. After serving some hard time and irritated by rumors that his former associates were taking advantage of his wife and personal fortune, Barnes agreed to cooperate with authorities to win freedom in the Witness Security Program.* He was able to help in the conviction of nearly 12 of his former associates. On other matters concerning the international drug trafficking mechanisms he was believed to have created, nothing materialized, mainly because mafiosi, not Barnes, controlled the flow of drugs from southern Europe and Sicily to the United States. Indeed, after Barnes's departure, the drug rackets continued to flourish and even grow in the minority ghettos. *See also* JUNIOR BLACK MAFIA; MATTHEWS, FRANK

**SUGGESTED READING:** Rufus Schatzberg and Robert J. Kelly, *African-American Organized Crime: A Social History.* 1997.

**BATTLE, JOSÉ MIGUEL.** ("El Padrino" [The Godfather], "El Gordo" [The Fat Man] (b. 1929, Havana, Cuba—    ). Cuban American crime boss.

Since his arrival more than three decades ago in the United States, José Battle had become one of the most powerful gangsters in south Florida, New Jersey, and New York. He had been a vice cop in Havana when the Castro revolution swept President Fulgencia Batista out of the country.

Battle's entry into organized crime began in the 1950s when as a police officer in Havana he became acquainted with crime czar Meyer Lansky* and the Mafia boss of Tampa, Florida, Santos Trafficante Jr.,* both of whom operated gambling casinos in plush hotels. These Mafia connections were later parlayed into a "criminal license" to open Cuban-controlled gambling operations in Miami, where many Cuban exiles and anti-Castro partisans lived. By 1967 he moved to Union City, New Jersey, another Cuban exile settlement, and opened a bar that served as a numbers* drop for a gambling operation that extended to west New York and smaller towns in Hudson County. Along the way, Battle allied himself with Joseph (Joe Bayonne) Zicarelli, a capo* in the Bonanno crime family,* and James Napoli, a capo in the northern New Jersey branch of the Genovese crime family.*

Like many other Cuban American racketeers, Battle was a veteran of the failed Bay of Pigs invasion of 1961 where Cuban exiles trained by the CIA had attempted to overthrow Fidel Castro's government.

Within a decade, Battle's organization, known as "the Corporation," developed into a criminal empire stretching across New York City, New Jersey, and Florida, controlling illegal numbers outlets with a force of nearly 2,500 members.

El Padrino (the Godfather), as Battle is known, managed to achieve considerable power without attracting much media attention. It was the President's Commission on Organized Crime, which held a hearing on illegal gambling in 1985, that finally revealed Battle's operation. The profile of the crime commission showed not only his control over illegal lotteries but the penetration of legitimate businesses in the Latino community. Legitimate finance and mortgage companies, travel agencies, and real estate companies influenced or owned by the Corporation or its individual operatives enabled Battle to launder monies and funds illegally obtained in gambling and drug enterprises.

In fact, cocaine smuggling is a major activity of Latino organized crime* groups, and it generates millions of illegal dollars that need to be "washed" (made to appear legitimate) by putting them through legitimate business accounts, which a man like Battle has access to in Latino retail businesses and other service-type establishments where the flow of cash transactions is high.

Cuban organized crime in the United States was strengthened with the Marielito exodus from Cuba when President Jimmy Carter permitted tens of thousands of refugees from Mariel, Cuba, to be settled in south Florida. Many were mental patients, others genuine victims of the Castro regime, and still others career criminals who moved into the Latino underworld in American cities. Many Marielitos became "mules" (drug couriers), shuttling marijuana and cocaine from Miami to other parts of the country. Along with embittered Bay of Pigs veterans trained in weapons who could function as syndicate enforcers, the influx of Marielitos helped Battle further enlarge his empire. The hardened criminals and CIA-trained hit* men ruthlessly intimidated criminal competitors and ordinary citizens in Latino communities up and down the East Coast.

In the 1980s, Battle's Corporation attempted to seize the lottery operations of "Spanish" Raymond Marquez, the legendary Puerto Rican numbers* boss, who created outlets throughout neighborhoods in New York City. Firebombing and arson were the techniques of persuasion, but these backfired when Battle's associates were charged and convicted. No one talked, however, and he fled to Florida. From then on, El Padrino created buffers who insulated him from crimes he ordered to be carried out. He began to organize his crime syndicate like a crime family, with specific duties assigned to individual henchmen. Corrupters, for example, were designated to bribe politicians in various locales to ignore Battle's criminal enterprises.

In the 1990s, the Corporation has diversified its operations; Bolita, the Spanish numbers game, is but one of several illicit businesses that make up the Battle gang portfolio: video poker machines can be found in bars, bodegas (grocery stores), and other businesses in Latino communities in south Florida. With expansion of his criminal enterprises, Battle has become something of a recluse, staying behind the high-security walls and fences of his estate in Dade County, Florida, or in Lima, Peru. It is alleged that his wealth is invested in several legitimate businesses, or it is funneled into money laundering schemes. The Corporation goes on, continually expanding into territories that were once under the control of Mafia crime families. According to law enforcement officials, the Corporation is now so large and powerful that it need not pay tribute to the Cosa Nostra. *See also* LATINO ORGANIZED CRIME

**SUGGESTED READING:** President's Commission on Organized Crime, *Organized Crime and Gambling Hearings III*. 1985.

**"BEING PROPOSED."** Recruitment and Mafia Induction ceremony.

A candidate for membership in a La Cosa Nostra* crime family is recruited because he is considered valuable to the organization. A candidate must be one who recognizes the authority of the family and the LCN as greater, or at least more important to him, than that of society. He will have proven himself in several ways: as a useful minor functionary in the local area and in several actual bouts with society and the law. This requirement that prospective members must prove themselves by committing crimes has made penetration of the LCN by law enforcement agents almost impossible.

In recent years, several law enforcement agents have managed to become "associates" (a nonmember who works with or for members). FBI agent Joseph Pistone* managed to penetrate groups within the Bonanno* and Colombo crime families* but never took the final step of "making your bones"* (committing murder).

A person who is to be inducted ought to have an arrest record. Being arrested occasionally is not taken as an indication of rash or foolhardy behavior but simply a statistical probability. For the criminal organization, an arrest on suspicion or an actual crime is a good test of how an individual acts under stress—

whether they are frightened, impulsive, stupid, or manage to keep their heads and behave rationally and coolly. Can one be frightened into cooperation by the police or can one keep one's mouth shut? That is the test of reliability.

It is always helpful if the future member has been convicted and served time in jail or prison. The experience is a severe test for a young man, and he will be observed carefully. Full-fledged membership will come when his proficiency is rewarded in tangible form. But formal membership is not just dependent on the quality of the candidate. Like other organizations, Cosa Nostra may open and close its "books" from time to time so that there may be a long waiting list. The most important entry requirements, the ability for violence and moneymaking, are likely to facilitate membership.

The blood and fire ritual of initiation is no longer uniformly practiced by all LCN groups. One requirement applies nationally: Everyone must be Italian, at least on their father's side. In the traditional initiation ceremony, the future member joins a group of members including the boss,* underboss,* consigliere,* capos,* and his sponsor. Rules are explained concerning how the individual should conduct himself. He is sworn to secrecy and pledges his loyalty to the family, promising to commit murder if called upon. The oath is made with blood drawn and mixed with the sponsor's, and a picture of a Catholic saint is burned. A circle is formed (called a "tie-in") and then ceremoniously broken, at which point the new member is invited to join hands and re-form it, symbolizing acceptance. One thereafter is introduced to other mafia members as a "friend of ours." *See also* GRAVANO, "SAMMY THE BULL"; MAFIA; "MAKING YOUR BONES"; PISTONE, JOSEPH; VALACHI, JOSEPH

**SUGGESTED READINGS:** Peter Maas, *Underboss: Sammy the Bull Gravano's Story of Life in the Mafia.* 1997; Peter Maas, *The Valachi Papers.* 1968.


**BINAGGIO, CHARLES.** (b. 1909, TX—d. April 6, 1950, Kansas City, MO). Political boss* and La Cosa Nostra* figure.

On April 6, 1950, headlines reported the gangland assassinations of Charles Binaggio and Charles Gargotta in Kansas City. Binaggio was the underworld gambling lord of Kansas City as well as one of the most powerful political bosses in Missouri. Gargotta was a feared gunman who worked for Binaggio. The real significance of the murders was that they occurred in the Democratic Party headquarters. The tie between politics and crime in Missouri was a factor that spurred the formation of the Kefauver Committee,* which was the first major congressional examination of organized crime after World War II.

Other underworld murders have been more sensational—"Joe the Boss" Masseria,* Dutch Schultz,* Charles Dion O'Banion,* Paul Castellano,* Angelo Bruno,* and Bugsy Siegel,* to mention a few—but Binaggio's death in the First District Democratic Club was in many ways more significant because he was the successor to Tom Pendergast, the presidential king maker, who helped

Harry Truman move from rural obscurity in the U.S. Senate to the White House. Indeed, Binaggio was a mafia member and the only one to have accumulated more political clout than Frank Costello* in New York. Binaggio was a gangster/political boss on the verge of national prominence.

Before Kansas City and politics, Binaggio moved around in Texas and Colorado, accumulating arrests for vagrancy and carrying a concealed weapon. In 1932, he arrived in Kansas City and joined North Side boss Johnny Lazia, who was a protégé of Tom Pendergast's. Lazia was involved in gambling and bootlegging but also seriously involved in electoral politics, through which he obtained protection for his vice rackets. Fearing that his tax problems would turn him into an informant, the mob murdered him in 1934 as Binaggio moved into his slot in the rackets and political machine.

Within six years, Binaggio was in a position to challenge the Pendergast political juggernaut that controlled politics in Missouri. To consolidate his political power in the state and region, Binaggio sought financial support from the Cosa Nostra crime families around the country. They responded with nearly a quarter of a million dollars, but Binaggio could not deliver on his promises, especially when information of his deals with the mob leaked to the press. To avoid further embarrassment, the St. Louis Police Department blocked mob efforts to open up the city. Also, the mob suspected that Binaggio pocketed much of the money they put up and failed to make deals with the governor that would help the mob.

Binaggio was killed in a manner that signaled the reason for his murder: two bullet holes arranged in two straight rows, forming two deuces, or "Little Joe"— the mob's signal for a welsher.

**SUGGESTED READING:** Alfred Steinberg, *The Bosses.* 1972.


**BIOFF, WILLIE MORRIS.** ("William Nelson") (b. 1900, Russia—d. Nov. 4, 1955, Phoenix, AZ). Hollywood gangster and movie racketeer.

On November 4, 1955, Willie Bioff was blown to bits in a car explosion in front of his home in Phoenix, Arizona. The murder was mob retaliation for his cooperation with authorities in 1941 against members of the Chicago Outfit*— the old Alphonse Capone* crime organization. He testified against the top leaders of the syndicate including Frank "The Enforcer" Nitti,* Paul "The Waiter" Ricca,* John Roselli,* Phil D'Andrea, and Charlie ("Cherry Nose") Gioe for their role in union racketeering and extortion in the motion picture industry.

Before Hollywood, Bioff was a shakedown artist in Chicago, extorting money from kosher butchers. He arrived in America at age five, grew up on the southwest side of Chicago, and made it through the third grade. As a young man, he joined the labor movement and did muscle work for the political ward bosses and the Teamsters Union.*

His connections with the Capone organization while he was organizing the kosher butchers put him in contact with George E. Browne, business agent for

Local 2 of the Stagehands union, which included movie projectionists, electricians, carpenters, and other theater workers. The union was already gangster ridden when Bioff came on the scene, but limited in its criminal ambitions. Bioff was the bridge to the National Crime Syndicate that would organize the country, especially Hollywood. Browne was recruited by the Capone outfit, with Bioff as its agent. In 1934, criminals around the country—such as Louis Buchalter,* Charles "Lucky" Luciano,* and Frank Costello* of New York, Abner Zwillman* of New Jersey, Big Al Polizzi of Cleveland, and Jack Dragna of Los Angeles—made arrangements to ensure that Browne would become president of the Stagehands national union, the International Alliance of Theatrical Stage Employees.

Browne appointed Bioff to a union position, and the two, in partnership with important mob figures, began to extort from Hollywood film studios such as RKO and Twentieth Century–Fox under the threat of closing down theaters throughout the country.

When Bioff arrived in Hollywood in 1935, he found other hoodlums already on hand, moving around the studios and talent agencies. John Roselli,* "Bugsy" Siegel,* and Mickey Cohen* would soon arrive. Roselli did labor conciliation work (strikebreaking) for the film producers, and Siegel had clout in the union, representing movie extras. Frank Costello was close to Harry Cohn of Columbia Studios and George Wood of the powerful William Morris Agency.

Bioff did not have to "corrupt" Hollywood as such—it was an environment filled with former garment industry moguls from the East Coast who had developed relationships with gangsters many years before Hollywood was invented. Indeed, the film studio bosses used the gangsters to discipline the unions and the workforce. Bioff revitalized Local 37 of the Stagehands union and demanded $2 million from the studios to avert a strike.

Between 1936 and 1940, Bioff extracted $1.1 million in fees to ensure labor peace. With Bioff and Browne, the studios were no longer subjected to strikes and wage demands. But the Bioff-Browne leadership of the Stagehands cost the consumer: Wages and tickets were jacked up in theaters across the country.

The sweet racket came tumbling down in 1941 when a group of dissident union members in Local 37 asked Carey McWilliams, a radical labor attorney from Los Angeles, to help them break the grip of the mob on the union. McWilliams uncovered enough damning evidence of corruption to force investigations. As a result, Bioff was sentenced to ten years; after three years in prison, he decided to testify against the Chicago bosses who were behind the entire racketeering enterprise. Nitti committed suicide, and the other gangsters did three years and were paroled in a scandal that rocked the Truman administration—perhaps a favor from the Pendergast machine to the Chicago mob.

Once out of jail, Bioff changed his name and relocated to Phoenix, Arizona, befriending upcoming politician Senator Barry Goldwater in the process. Bioff's mistake was that he surfaced only a few years after putting powerful hoodlums behind bars. They never forgot it. His body was literally torn to pieces by a bomb explosion. It was revenge and a lesson for others who might be tempted to talk.

**SUGGESTED READING:** Malcolm Johnson, "In Hollywood," in *Mafia, USA*, ed. Nicholas Gage. 1972.

**BLACK GANGSTER DISCIPLE NATION.** *See* AFRICAN AMERICAN ORGANIZED CRIME

**THE BLACK HAND (LA MANO NERA).** Italian extortion racket.

The term "The Black Hand" refers to an early twentieth-century criminal activity that terrorized Italian immigrants in the teeming ethnic slums of American cities. Gangs of extortionists sometimes numbering only a few preyed upon their immigrant countrymen with threats, bombings, kidnapings, and other types of intimidation accompanied by a letter stamped with the fearsome symbol of a black handprint and a menacing dagger. Black Hand notes stressed the dire consequences of refusing demands for money.

Black Hand extortion notes usually were sent to immigrant businessmen, professionals within the ethnic community, prominent people (such as the opera singer Enrico Caruso), and even gangsters. Johnny Torrio* and Alphonse Capone* launched their criminal careers in Chicago when "Big Jim" Colosimo, Torrio's cousin, was being shaken down by local Black Handers who demanded a percentage of his prostitution racket profits.

The problem was made more difficult by the fact that so few law enforcement officers were Italian speaking or of Italian background in police departments in cities such as New York, Chicago, Philadelphia, and New Orleans. In New York City in 1904, for example, of nearly 20,000 police officers, only 11 understood Italian, which was the language spoken by almost 25 percent of the city's 2 million inhabitants. (Similar situations today confront law enforcement in communities where Asian—Chinese, Vietnamese, Laotian—and Russian criminals prey upon their communities; few police speak the languages, and few members of these communities have been recruited into the police.)

In 1905, the situation became so desperate that the New York City Police Department formed a special squad of Italian-speaking police officers to confront the Black Hand extortion problem in the Italian communities. Led by Italian-born Sergeant Joseph Petrosino,* the "Italian Branch" attempted to develop intelligence on Black Handers operating in the ghettos and tried to allay the fears and suspicions of Italian immigrants who were being victimized by extortion schemes. Petrosino succeeded in his education campaigns, doing much to eliminate the natural distrust of the Italian immigrants toward the police. In their home country, police traditionally exploited the peasants; and suspicions of the police were heightened by the fact that most police officers in America could barely communicate with the newcomers.

The Black Handers who held the community in the grip of fear were typically primitive country thieves from Sicily and southern Italy, transplanted to American cities. The problem was intensified by an Italian government policy of encouraging the emigration of convicts and those under special surveillance. Hence, it was easy for Italian criminals to obtain a passport and a clean police report.

The most infamous Black Hand extortionist was Ignazio Saietta, known as "Lupo the Wolf." He came from Sicily in 1899 and gained an awesome reputation as a murderer and extortionist with at least 60 murder victims to his credit.

By 1908, there were almost 500 Black Hand offenses reported to the police, and it was estimated by Petrosino's squad that for every one reported at least 250 victims remained silent for fear of reprisals. Black Hand rings operating in Chicago were even more widespread. Despite the fear in the community, Petrosino's efforts were effective: In 1908 there were 44 bombings in New York with 70 arrests; and of the 400 extortion complaints, 215 people were arrested, with numerous mafiosi being deported on the Italian squad's evidence.

Early in 1909 Petrosino went to Palermo, Sicily, to gather information. He was murdered in the streets because the mafiosi saw him as a serious threat.

In the 1920s with Prohibition (*See* PROHIBITION AND ORGANIZED CRIME*) under way and a source of income easily available in the bootlegging industry, the Black Hand virtually disappeared. Not only were illegal alcohol industries attracting potential extortionists, but the federal government was enforcing the mail fraud statutes effectively, and the cultural assimilation of Italians made the former immigrants more "Americanized" and less fearful of petty immigrant hoodlums. *See also* CAPONE, ALPHONSE; LA COSA NOSTRA; MAFIA; TORRIO, JOHNNY; WHITE HAND SOCIETY; ZIPS

**SUGGESTED READINGS:** Arrigo Petacco, *Joe Petrosino*. 1974; Thomas Pittson and Francesco Cordasco, *Black Hand: A Chapter in Ethnic Crime*. 1977.

**BLACK MAFIA.** *See* BARNES, NICKY

**BLOODS.** *See* CRIPS AND BLOODS

**BOIARDO, "RICHIE THE BOOT."** (b. Ruggerio Boiardo, 1891, Palermo, Sicily—d. 1984, Livingston, NJ). Luchese crime family* boss in New Jersey.

Boiardo was born in Italy and arrived in the United States as a young child. From Chicago he drifted to Newark, New Jersey, and during Prohibition (*see* PROHIBITION AND ORGANIZED CRIME*), he accumulated wealth and achieved power through political influence.

In the 1930s and 1940s, Richie the Boot was a one-man mafia murder machine. Boiardo was a leading light in the Luchese crime family's New Jersey faction, who disposed of murder victims for Luchese and other friendly crime families on his huge estate in Livingston, New Jersey. For bodies that were supposed to disappear—as opposed to those left in plain view as an object lesson—Boiardo burned them in a large crematorium hidden in a corner of his 100-acre estate. The rest of the estate featured a 30-room mansion with life-size statues of Boiardo and members of his family. Boiardo also used the crematorium as an execution chamber for certain victims he wanted to kill personally, usually by beating them to death with the assistance of his son Anthony, an apprentice in the murder trade. For amusement, the elder Boiardo, Richie the Boot, occasionally liked to dispose of live victims by tying them to an iron grill in his oven and slowly roasting them to death. When not busy killing in this grotesque manner, he liked to putter around his vegetable garden, which contained still another sign of his psychosis, a large sign reading "Godfather's Garden," apparently meant to deter raccoons.

Apart from Boiardo's chamber of horrors, he had the distinction of being the oldest mafioso ever brought to trial: At 89 years of age, he went to trial in New Jersey, facing racketeering, extortion, and murder conspiracy charges but was eventually released because of health considerations.

In the 1930s, Boiardo joined Abner Zwillman* in bootlegging, gambling, and other rackets associated with labor unions and hijacking along the New Jersey waterfront. Later, in testimony before the McClelland Committee,* Joseph Valachi* identified Boiardo as a powerful figure in La Cosa Nostra.* He, of course, denied that he was heavily involved in illegal gambling and loansharking* activities. He died in November 1984 at the age of 93 and was still considered a person with influence in extortion rackets in Essex County, New Jersey.

**SUGGESTED READING:** Ernest Volkman, *Gangsters*. 1998.


**BONANNO, JOSEPH.** ("Don Peppino," "Joe Bananas") (b. Jan. 18, 1905, Castellammarese del Golfo, Sicily—   ). Mafia* crime family boss and a founder of La Cosa Nostra.*

Joseph Bonanno emerged from the "Joe the Boss" Masseria–Salvatore Maranzano* conflict, known as the Castellammarese War,* as a don heading one of the original Cosa Nostra crime families that bears his name. Bonanno came to New York from Sicily in 1924. Taking up residence in an Italian ethnic community in Brooklyn, New York, he became involved in extortion activities and bootlegging.

By the 1930s, Bonanno was a man of wealth, deriving income from several legitimate businesses. He was also a participant in the war among mafiosi, and when it ended, he was named by Charles "Lucky" Luciano* as the head of a "crime family" that actually was a remnant of the Maranzano faction during the Castellammarese War. Crime family wealth multiplied, and Bonanno was soon a millionaire with many business interests both legitimate and illegitimate. These opportunities included dairy and cheese processing plants, clothing firms, a funeral parlor, a soft drink corporation, and a laundry service.

Although he was arrested several times, Bonanno did not serve a prison term until 1983, when he proudly published his autobiography. The book became a

Joseph Bonanno. Reproduced from the Collections
of the Library of Congress.

best-seller, but it horrified his criminal colleagues and puzzled law enforcement
officials because it revealed so many aspects of the Cosa Nostra that until then
they could only surmise. Indeed, Bonanno's gall in publishing details about
various criminal personalities put him in prison when he refused to give under
oath more details in court about the Mafia and its ruling "Commission."* Rudolph Giuliani, at that time a U.S. attorney in New York, used the published
material to open the "Commission Case" against the rulers of Cosa Nostra.

Bonanno's ambitions knew no bounds. By the 1960s he had invaded the
Southwest of the United States, settling in Tucson and making it the base of his
operations in Arizona and California. He also had a keen interest in Las Vegas,
Nevada,* with its gambling enterprises and potential for generating and amass-
ing still more wealth. The infiltration of Las Vegas meant conflict with the
powerful Chicago Mafia, and after several skirmishes with Chicago Outfit*
gangsters, an arrangement was reached providing Bonanno with many modest
opportunities to invest in and exploit casino revenues.

Preoccupation with enterprises in the West led to grumbling and growing
opposition within the family whose soldiers* and principal criminal activities
were located in the New York area. Benign neglect sowed the seeds of internal

revolt and encroachments by other families over Bonanno gambling interests and vice territories. In addition to these tensions, Carmine "The Cigar" Galante, a Bonanno underboss* and drug trafficker, went to prison on narcotics charges. Clearly, Bonanno chose to ignore the rulings of the National Commission of Cosa Nostra, which discouraged drug trafficking by American Cosa Nostra members at the 1957 Apalachin meeting.*

Perhaps he feared retaliation, so when his close colleague and friend Joseph Profaci* died in 1962, Bonanno decided to act. Profaci's successor Joseph Magliocco and Bonanno were related; the Profaci and Bonanno families were bonded together even more closely by the marriage of Bonanno's son Salvatore to Profaci's niece Rosalie. Relations with Mafia bosses Stefano Magaddino* of Buffalo (a cousin from Sicily), Nick Civella of Kansas City, Carlos Marcello* of Louisiana, and Santos Trafficante, Jr.* of Tampa, Florida, were good enough to encourage Bonanno to challenge other bosses who held seats on the Commission. A plot was set in motion to eliminate Carlo Gambino* and Gaetano Luchese* of New York and Frank DeSimmone of Los Angeles, but it was betrayed by Joseph Colombo, Jr.,* a soldier in the Profaci crime family who had been entrusted with carrying out the murders. Believing the conspiracy could not succeed, Colombo revealed the details to the intended victims.

Magliocco, who participated in the murder conspiracy, and Bonanno were both ordered to appear before the Mafia Commission to explain their actions. Magliocco admitted his complicity, but because of a mortal illness, he was permitted to retire and was replaced as boss by Joseph Colombo. And when Bonanno flatly refused to appear, the Commission stripped him of his authority as boss of his family and appointed a family defector, Gasper DiGregorio,* to be acting boss. The decision set off the "Banana War." Fighting broke out between Bonanno loyalists, led by Joseph's son Salvatore, and dissidents, led by the DiGregorio faction. In October 1964, Joe Bonanno was presumably kidnapped at gunpoint in Midtown Manhattan. He was missing for 19 months while the war dragged on without resolution. Magaddino held Bonanno prisoner during this time, hoping to persuade him to quit the Mafia as the Commission demanded. But Bonanno refused and warned others that the Commission had no right to dethrone a boss. Finally, a compromise was reached. Federal officials, on the other hand, believed that the kidnapping was a hoax staged by Bonanno to avoid a grand jury investigation that targeted him.

Bonanno was released and allowed to return to his Tucson, Arizona, home. His son would not succeed him. In January 1966, Bonanno reported to a federal court and was released after posting $150,000 bond, which an incredulous prosecutor strongly opposed. In May of that year the Banana War raged on when an ambush staged by DiGregorio against Salvatore Bonanno in Brooklyn led to gunfire in the streets of Brooklyn. Another settlement was arranged in order to stop the bloodshed and get back to business. This plan worked, and Bonanno retired—but not for long: In 1979, he was indicted and convicted of obstruction of justice; and in 1983 he stunned the underworld with the publication of his book *A Man of Honor*, which proved to be his undoing. Aging and ailing, he refused to answer questions about the Mafia Commission discussed in his book and was again jailed.

Bonanno's life symbolized an era of organized crime. He was the last of the original bosses of the 1931 American Mafia and insisted even at the end of his career that he was a man of his "cultural tradition"—not a career criminal. *See also* CASTELLAMMARESE WAR; COMMISSION; GAMBINO, CARLO; GENOVESE, VITO; LA COSA NOSTRA

SUGGESTED READINGS: Joseph Bonanno, with S. Lalli, *A Man of Honor: The Auto-biography of Joseph Bonanno.* 1983; Gay Talese, *Honor Thy Father.* 1971.

**BONANNO CRIME FAMILY.** In 1968, Joseph Bonanno,* the founding god-father of the Bonanno crime family,* was forced into a semiretirement in Arizona as a result of a heart attack and events that had led to his kidnapping by a cousin, La Cosa Nostra* Mafia chief Stephano Magaddino* of Buffalo, and an internal war, the "Banana War," within his own crime family.

Bonanno went to Arizona, and it marked the end of an era. A succession of bosses followed including several former capos,* among them Philip Rastelli* in the early 1980s. Bonanno hoped that his son Salvatore "Bill" Bonanno could assume the reins of power, but that was not to be. Before the relatively un-eventful leadership of Rastelli and Natale Evola, the National Commission* of La Cosa Nostra had to confront the ever dangerous and violent Carmine "The Cigar" Galante,* whose drug trafficking in Canada and the United States kept him imprisoned for many years. When he was released, he made it clear that he expected to become not only boss of the Bonanno family but boss of bosses of the American Mafia,* no matter how much blood would have to be spilled. This nightmare ended in 1979 when Galante was murdered after threatened mob bosses let out a contract on "The Cigar."

According to law enforcement intelligence surveys, the Bonanno family is involved in all forms of vice activity including hard-core pornography. And their penetrations of the legitimate marketplace have enabled Bonanno crime family members to reap profits from pizza shops throughout New York, New Jersey, Delaware, Pennsylvania, and Connecticut. In the 1990s, after close FBI sur-veillance and based on the famous undercover penetration by Joseph Pistone* (a.k.a. "Donnie Brasco"), it is estimated that the crime family has approximately 125 members and nearly 300 associates. *See also* BONANNO, JOSEPH; PIS-TONE, JOSEPH

SUGGESTED READING: Bill Bonanno, *Bound By Honor: A Mafioso's Story.* 1999; Joseph Pistone with Richard Woodley, *Donnie Brasco: My Undercover Life in the Mafia.* 1987.

**BOOTLEGGER.** A person who made, sold, smuggled, and transported alcoholic beverages during the period of Prohibition (1920–1933) in the United States when the manufacture, sale, and distribution of alcoholic products for personal consumption was illegal. Most of the criminal syndicates that have operated in America for the remainder of the century were put together during the Prohibition Era. Engaging in bootlegging was a very lucrative enterprise that yielded huge profits in a country that culturally opposed alcohol abstinence. *See also* O'BANION, CHARLES DION; PROHIBITION AND ORGANIZED CRIME; TORRIO, JOHNNY

**BORYOKUDAN.** *See* YAKUZA

**BOSS (DON).** The boss (don) of a crime family is the supreme leader of the gang or criminal network. Historically, the Italian term "don" applied to the leaders of Mafia* crime families but now is generically applied to any gang leader. "Godfather" (*compare*) is another term that describes bosses of organized criminal enterprises.

The primary functions of the boss are to maintain order and to maximize profits in the various criminal and noncriminal enterprises of the family. Subject to the possibility of being overruled by the Commission,* the authority of the boss within the crime family is absolute. He is the final arbiter in all matters relating to his territories, soldiers,* capos,* and enterprises under his authority. Some La Cosa Nostra* bosses are members of the Commission. Each boss of the estimated 24 crime groups throughout the United States who is not a Commission member has a designated boss-representative (*avvocato*) on the Commission.

Members of a crime family are likely to believe that they elect their own boss, but until recently, this has been rare. The crime family, according to precedent and tradition, submits the name of the man of its choice to the Commission, which makes the final decision. However, that role of the Commission seems to have been abandoned; or it is a function that the Commission of La Cosa Nostra may no longer choose to enforce. In December 1985, when Paul Castellano,* head of the Gambino crime family,* was assassinated in Midtown Manhattan, the capos of the family met and chose John Gotti* by acclamation to be the new boss. All the Commission could do then was to affirm the decision of the crime family leaders.

Each boss knows each of the others personally. Accordingly, each crime family is linked with every other in some form or other—through marriage and blood establishing kinship relations among bosses and leaders or through joint cooperative enterprises that create alliances and agreements. Respect and fear are elements in the relationships among bosses that constitute mechanisms of stability and peaceful coexistence. A boss is also the person who can initiate arrangements and agreements with nonmember organized criminals operating in their territories and communities. Charles "Lucky" Luciano* was famous for putting together criminal confederations that included Italians, Irish, Jews, and even African Americans. In recent years the FBI has focused its attention on the Cosa Nostra crime family bosses as a way of containing and destroying the

criminal enterprises of the families. *See also* CAPO; CONSIGLIERE; SOL-
DIERS; UNDERBOSS

**SUGGESTED READING:** Donald R. Cressey, *Theft of a Nation: The Structure and
Operations of Organized Crime in America.* 1969.

**BROOKLIER, DOMINIC.** ("Jimmy Regace") (b. Dominic Brucceleri, 1914—
d. 1984, Tucson, AZ, Federal Prison). Los Angeles La Cosa Nostra* boss.

Brooklier was originally part of Mickey Cohen's* California gambling operations until he joined Jack Dragna,* a mafioso in Los Angeles. To smooth his
transition from Cohen to Dragna, Brooklier attempted to assassinate Cohen as
he left a restaurant, but the murder plot failed, and real problems prevailed
between Cohen's group and Californian mafiosi.

Under Brooklier, the Los Angeles crime family was small and depended on
members of the Chicago Outfit* such as John Roselli* for support and "Bugsy"
Siegel* of New York, who were themselves engaged in movie industry racketeering. Brooklier and his men concentrated on small-time pornography, extortion, and burglaries.

Brooklier developed a stormy relationship with Jimmy "The Weasel" Fra-
tianno,* whom he had to rely on but rightly suspected of informing to the FBI.
When Nick Licata, a capo* in the Los Angeles Cosa Nostra, died in 1974,
Brooklier was named to replace him. But by 1978, Brooklier was incarcerated,
and Fratianno was named acting boss. When Brooklier returned, he ousted
Jimmy the Weasel, who was by this time providing the FBI with information.
When a murder contract was placed on his life, Fratianno implicated Brooklier
in the February 1977 murder of San Diego gangster Frank ("The Bomp") Bom-
pensiero. However, Brooklier was acquitted of conspiracy in that murder and
sought help from the Chicago and Cleveland Mafia members in getting rid of
Fratianno. Fratianno had by this time entered the federal Witness Security Program.*

Brooklier was convicted in 1978 with other members of his crime family on
racketeering and extortion of bookmakers and pornographers. He did not survive
the five-year sentence and died in prison in 1984.

**SUGGESTED READING:** Ovid Demaris, *The Last Mafioso.* 1981.

**BRUNO, ANGELO.** ("Ange," "The Docile Don") (b. Angelo Bruno Annaloro,
1910, Villalba, Sicily—d. Mar. 21, 1980, Philadelphia, PA). Leader of Philadelphia Cosa Nostra* family.

Raised in South Philadelphia, where his parents operated a small grocery
store, Bruno was arrested in 1935 for operating an illegal still above his father's
business and again in 1940 for possession of illegal gambling receipts. Apart
from still another gambling arrest in 1953, he remained out of jail until 1970,
when he was remanded (until 1973) for refusing to answer questions put to him
by the New Jersey Commission of Investigation. In 1956, because of his success

in the Philadelphia rackets, Bruno was made underboss, second in command, of the crime family. By 1959, he was named boss, a rank he would hold for the next 21 years, during which time his criminal influence would extend into New Jersey, Delaware, Maryland, and New York.

Known as the "Docile Don" because of his reputation for seeking nonviolent, negotiated solutions to problems, Bruno survived government anticrime campaigns in the 1960s and 1970s relatively unscathed. A combination of cunning and shrewdness enabled him to avoid arrest.

Bruno did not fit the image of the flashy, Capone-style gangster: he lived modestly with his wife and two children and seemed more like a small-time businessman than a powerful mobster. Like other prominent underworld figures, he disapproved of narcotics but could do little to stop drug dealing among his associates. He cleverly disguised his illegitimate businesses by forming partnerships and investing indirectly into legitimate businesses through friends and relatives. In fact, he reported and paid income taxes on earnings from a vending machine business that he owned legitimately. This business also provided him with the expertise and knowledge to penetrate the lucrative casinos in Atlantic City, New Jersey.*

His success in legitimate enterprises and the decision to permit other crime families opportunities in and around Atlantic City produced tensions within his organization. Bruno's talent in legitimate business may have been his undoing. He was increasingly cut off from the street crime upon which many of his subordinates depended, and their discontent mounted: A struggle for control of the family instigated by his top associates would eventually lead to his assassination.

The Bruno crime family was not an illicit enterprise as such. Rather, it was a power structure, membership in which provided distinct advantages in carrying on illegal activities. The organization fashioned by Bruno created partnerships in various illicit enterprises, thereby spreading and minimizing risks and making it possible to exploit capital resources and expertise. In gambling and loan-sharking* operations, for example, associates of Mafia members took a percentage of the profits earned from clients they recruited. Since their income was linked to their personal initiative, there was little need for much vigilance—everyone had an incentive to do well. And because these criminal enterprises were decentralized, the threat of criminal conspiracy prosecutions was minimized. The system maximized independence, required low levels of administration, and insulated the family leadership from overt complicity in criminal activities.

Among those who participated in family enterprises, a central principle was that the businesses of members or their associates were protected from raids by other members or by outsiders. This was a distinct advantage of membership or affiliation.

The Bruno crime family was part of a national system of crime organizations. This meant that its members could call upon contacts in other cities in their legal and illegal businesses. Members, their associates, and their customers constituted a complex system of mutual obligations and exchange of favors. Members and associates of the Bruno family carried on their legal and illegal businesses within the informal framework of rules and obligations. The quasi-governmental functions of the family constituted the most important way that associations with the family had an impact on the business activities of those within its influence.

Like many important organized crime figures, Bruno was still active as he approached his seventieth birthday. His chief criminal skills lay in his ability to blur the distinctions between underworld activities and legitimate business interests. The key to his longevity as an underworld leader was his capacity to ensure earnings for his associates and to minimize the violence characteristic of criminal enterprises. Few organized crime figures before him evaded notoriety and imprisonment as he had. Nonetheless, dissatisfaction existed in the crime family.

Bruno was killed in 1980 by a shotgun blast to his head as he sat in his car in front of his South Philadelphia home. After his death, the crime family was torn apart by warfare among its competing factions. By 1988, two family bosses who had conspired to kill Bruno were themselves killed, along with nine other Mafia members and their associates. A third boss, Nicky Scarfo,* a protégé of Bruno's, was imprisoned for life. The strength and durability of the crime family that Bruno had carefully nurtured were severely and irreversibly damaged. *See also* SCARFO, NICKY

**SUGGESTED READINGS:** Mark H. Haller, *Life Under Bruno: The Economics of an Organized Crime Family.* 1991; Pennsylvania Crime Commission, *Organized Crime in Pennsylvania.* 1990.


**BUCHALTER, LOUIS.** ("Lepke") (b. Feb. 12, 1897, New York City—d. Mar. 4, 1944, Sing Sing Prison, New York). Syndicate boss and industrial racketeer.

"Lepke" (a Yiddish term of affection meaning "Little Louis") grew up in a respectable but destitute middle-class Jewish family. His brothers went into pharmacy and dentistry, and Louis Buchalter went into the mob. After several arrests and time served in prison for burglaries in 1922, he joined Jacob "Gurrah" Shapiro*—another apprentice of Arnold "The Brain" Rothstein*—and began working for gangsters such as "Little Augie" Orgen,* who sold strong-arm violence to either unions or employers, whoever paid more, during the tumultuous era of labor organization activities.

Lepke's personal appearance belied his viciousness. His slender build and conservative clothing projected an image of a dignified businessman rather than a violent racketeer. The garment industry was the setting for Buchalter's activities and betrayal and murder of his boss Orgen. Lepke and Shapiro then took control of several garment union locals. His criminal innovations were notable in this area of industrial racketeering: Instead of sluggers and gunmen terrorizing

Louis "Lepke" Buchalter. Reproduced from the Collections of the
Library of Congress.

union members during strikes, Lepke also infiltrated his hoodlums directly into
the locals, thus avoiding relentless street battles for union control. From control
of tailors and cloth cutters, Lepke moved into the unions of bakery drivers,
poultry workers, cleaning and dyeing, handbags, shoes, millinery, leather, and
eventually restaurant workers. The "protection" costs to businesses in these industries amounted to more than $10 million a year during the Great Depression.

Closely associated with Charles "Lucky" Luciano,* Frank Costello,* Meyer
Lansky,* Dutch Schultz,* and Joseph Adonis,* Lepke became part of the new
crime syndicate that developed during Prohibition (*see* PROHIBITION AND
ORGANIZED CRIME*). In the early 1930s, syndicate bosses realized they
needed a special enforcement arm to maintain discipline in their growing criminal industries, and they needed to instill fear among potential informers and
intimidate witnesses and others from testifying about their rackets. Murder, Inc.*
was formed, controlled by Lepke, Gurrah Shapiro, and Albert Anastasia.* Over
a period of several years, hundreds of murders (hits*) were carried out by the
gruesome team of mob assassins.

Until 1937, Buchalter earned millions and lived well. Then prosecutor
Thomas E. Dewey* launched an investigation against him. Lepke went into
hiding when the Federal Narcotics Bureau developed a case against him and

Shapiro. A manhunt for Lepke (who was hidden by Anastasia in various New York hideouts) failed, so pressure was put on all mob operations to surrender him. Between 1937 and 1939, when Lepke finally gave himself up to J. Edgar Hoover*—an arrest arranged by Broadway gossip columnist Walter Winchell*— some 60 to 80 potential witnesses in cases against him had been murdered or intimidated or just disappeared.

In 1941, he and two others, Mendy Weiss and Louis Capone, were convicted on evidence of murder furnished by one of his contract killers, "Kid Twist" Reles,* from the Murder, Inc. crew. In 1944, Lepke was electrocuted—the only major organized crime figure to be executed by the state.

**SUGGESTED READING:** Alan Block, *East Side–West Side: Organizing Crime in New York, 1930–1950.* 1998.


**BUSCETTA, TOMMASO.** ("Don Massino") (b. 1927, Palermo, Sicily—Federal Witness Protection Program). Sicilian Mafia* boss, drug trafficker, and defector/1980s.

Don Massino Buscetta's credentials as a ranking mafia leader were established by thick police dossiers dating back two, even three, decades in Italy, Brazil, Mexico, Canada, and the United States. He had traveled everywhere, read books, and was articulate in three languages. Where Joseph Valachi,* Jimmy "The Weasel" Fratianno,* and "Sammy the Bull" Gravano* had seen La Cosa Nostra* from the ground up, Don Masino had known it from the top down since World War II.

How valuable was Buscetta as an informant? And why did he choose to betray his mafia oath of silence? In a gang conflict known as the "Great Mafia War" (1981–1983) involving most of the Sicilian Mafia networks in Sicily, Italy, Europe, and America, Buscetta lost a brother, two sons, three nephews, and a son-in-law. Revenge? No doubt about it. His testimony in the important Pizza Connection* case in New York City helped convict 35 members of the New York and Sicilian Cosa Nostra. Likewise, his testimony in 1986 at the Palermo "maxitrials" led to the convictions of 435 members of the Sicilian Mafia. In 1996, Buscetta was the primary witness against Giulio Andreotti, several times prime minister of Italy, for his protection of the Mafia.

The Mafia of the 1970s and 1980s Buscetta described in his testimony in the United States and in Italy was global, unitary and governed from the top down by a Cupola (a commission of powerful dons constituting the supreme governing body) with absolute powers over life, death, money, and policy. The line of command rose geometrically in a pyramid whose base covered practically every village in Sicily. (Its extension to every corner of the Italian mainland would come later when Giovanni Falcone and Paulo Borsellino, investigative magistrates murdered by the Mafia in 1992, uncovered its extensive intercontinental reach.) At the Mafia base were the capifamiglia (family bosses). Every three contiguous crime families answered to a capomandamento (a representative boss), who served on provincial commissions dominated in turn by the Central Commission, or Cupola, in Palermo, Sicily.

This chain of command was amply verified by other pentiti (Mafia defectors), but Buscetta's version is considered definitive. His other motives for revealing what he knew were that, as he said, the Mafia had changed and degenerated because of drugs. The ideals—respect, honor, courage, tradition—had been sacrificed to greed. Now, women, children, and distant relatives were killed. Buscetta laid out two tremendous accounts on which the Mafia was guilty: its capture of the worldwide heroin market and its secret heroin network in the United States, which he admitted he had helped to build.

**SUGGESTED READING:** Tim Shawcross and Martin Young, *Men of Honour: The Confessions of Tommaso Buscetta.* 1987.

**BUTTON MAN.** *See* SOLDIERS

# C

**CALI COCAINE CARTEL.** Over 20 years ago, Colombian drug trafficker Carlos Lehder-Rivas* convinced some Medellín, Colombia, area traffickers to pool their drug shipments, thus cutting their individual chances of financial ruin if a single shipment was seized. The method brought the traffickers profits beyond their dreams and led to the foundation of the Medellín cartel.

A similar federation of traffickers was formed in the city of Cali, some 200 miles south of Medellín. The Cali mafia grew from a small criminal gang founded in the early 1970s by Gilberto Rodriguez-Orejuela* and José Santacruz-Londono.* The gang originally confined themselves to counterfeiting and kidnapping, but gradually expanded into the smuggling of cocaine base from Peru and Bolivia to Colombia for conversion into cocaine. The group evolved into a loose association of five major independent drug trafficking organizations now called the Cali mafia.

The Cali mafia leaders directed a vast global network of cocaine production, transportation, wholesale distribution, and money laundering operations. They shared certain resources when their interests coincided. The member organizations were the Rodriguez-Orejuela brothers; José Santacruz-Londono (deceased); Helmer Herrera-Buitrago*; the Urdinola-Grajales brothers; and the Grajales-Lemos and Grajales-Posso organization.

Cali drug traffickers export hundreds of tons of cocaine into the United States annually and launder billions of dollars in drug proceeds. Their drug money initially meant economic boom for that city of 2 million residents, and the Cali mafia operated with virtual impunity for over 15 years. Their tactics of intimidation and corruption caused bribed officials to overlook illegal activities. One Cali businessman was quoted anonymously in the *Los Angeles Times* (1985), to say Cali had become "a sewer of corruption and violence. The narco-traffickers have taken over. They control businesses, politics, everything."

When the Colombian government took an antidrug stance in the mid- to late

1980s, the Medellín drug mafia reacted with a wave of narcoterrorism. Hundreds of Colombian police officers, judges, government officials, journalists, and ordinary private citizens were murdered by drug mafia *sicarios* (assassins). This savage violence allegedly included the murder of Justice Minister Rodrigo Lara-Bonilla (April 1984); the kidnapping and murder of Colombian Attorney General Carlos Mauro Hoyos Jimenez (January 1988); the assassination of presidential candidate Luis Carlos Galan (August 1989); the bombing of Avianca flight 203, which killed 110 people (November 1989); and the bombing of the Department of Administrative Security (DAS) Headquarters, which killed 50 people and wounded 200 (December 1989).

During 1995, the Colombian National Police (CNP) reported that 25,525 Colombians were murdered. Today Colombia has an annual homicide rate of 70 murders per 100,000 inhabitants, compared to the U.S. rate of 9. These gruesome numbers reveal the magnitude of Colombia's current crime problem.

Unlike their Medellín predecessors, who used intimidation and terror to bolster their power, the Cali mafia prefer to appear as legitimate businessmen. They employ bribes and pressure as ways of doing business, although they are not adverse to killing competitors or double-crossers. For example, when Drug Enforcement Administration (DEA) Operation Green Ice in 1992 resulted in the arrest of 165 traffickers worldwide and $54 million in cash and property being seized, Cali bosses retaliated against suspected informants by having them immersed in barrels of acid. However, Cali traffickers typically do not inflict acts of violent terrorism on the general population, as did their Medellín counterparts.

Since June 1995, the seven top leaders of the Cali mafia have either been arrested or have surrendered to Colombian authorities. The year 1995 will be remembered as a historic period in international and domestic drug law enforcement. With the arrest of six of the seven top leaders of the Cali mafia, significant enforcement gains against the world's most notorious drug traffickers were realized. During the first half of fiscal year 1995, DEA arrests increased by almost 18 percent over the same time period in fiscal year 1994.

The arrest of six of the seven top Cali drug lords represented a real blow to the most sophisticated organized crime syndicate in history. Having operated with virtual impunity in Colombia for the past 15 years, the Cali mafia's reach and influence extended into many nations, including the United States. Numerous homicides in the United States, including the murder of the editor of *El Diario* in 1992 and an innocent businessman in Baltimore in 1991, were the calling card of the Cali mafia.

The Cali mafia's annual profits were estimated at between $4 and $8 billion a year, and the organization operated like a well-run multinational business. They were able to run their global enterprise through a sophisticated system of telephones, faxes, pagers, and computers and employed an intelligence network that rivaled those of the most developed nations. The Cali drug lords controlled the Cali airport, the taxi system, and the phone company. They knew who came and went in Cali, who talked to the police, and who was cooperating with U.S. law enforcement agencies.

Despite the massive and unprecedented levels of influence the Cali mafia wielded, the CNP, in cooperation with the DEA and other U.S. agencies, tracked down the mafia leaders and brought them to justice. Within just a few months, the Cali mafia leadership was captured or surrendered to Colombian authorities.

But police work alone could not have brought the mafia down. The turning point in the struggle against the Cali mafia occurred simultaneously with the U.S. government's decision not to fully certify the Government of Colombia during the annual certification process in March. When the president withheld full approval of the Colombian government's performance on narcotics control for the first time since the certification process has been in force, and with months of congressional scrutiny of Colombia's slow progress on arresting major drug mafia leaders, Colombian government leaders began to act decisively against the Cali group.

In June 1995, after a four-year investigation, the DEA and the U.S. Customs Service indicted 62 individuals on drug conspiracy charges. In what is called the "Cornerstone" case, Cali mafia operatives in the United States, including attorneys in Miami, were charged with conducting business for the Rodriguez-Orejuela brothers, Santa Cruz-Londono, and Helmer Herrera-Buitrago.

In many instances, the Cali mafia conducted financial operations within the United States, depending on front companies and other money laundering techniques to disguise the source of their profits. In phase two of a complex money laundering investigation called "Operation Green Ice," the DEA worked with other federal, state, and local agencies to target the illegal uses of *casas de cambio* (money exchanges) along the southwest border, shut down businesses laundering drug proceeds for the Cali mafia, and created businesses posing as money laundering organizations through which the mafia laundered their funds.

The Cali mafia's influence, however, has not been limited to white-collar businesses. Within the United States, Cali mafia surrogates (members of homegrown violent drug gangs) have turned many communities into virtual war zones. Violent drug traffickers who operated in cities and towns from Michigan to Texas to California joined the Cali mafia leaders as targets of the DEA in 1995.

In a major case, the DEA worked with other federal, state, and local law enforcement agencies to dismantle the Larry Hoover organization (the Black Gangster Disciple Nation) in Chicago. When Hoover continued to run a drug trafficking and money laundering operation from the Vienna Correctional Center, he was removed from that prison, and 40 of his senior Black Gangster Disciple Nation officials were arrested. *See also* COLOMBIAN DRUG CARTELS; ESCOBAR, PABLO EMILIO GAVOROA; HERRERA-BUITRAGO, HELMER; MONEY LAUNDERING; OCHOA, JORGE LUIS VASQUEZ

**SUGGESTED READING:** Robert Nieves, *Colombian Cocaine Cartels*. 1997.


**CAMORRA.** Created by prisoners in Italian jails as a protective society, the Camorra (meaning "fight" or "quarrel" in Spanish), a Neapolitan crime organization, emerged in the early nineteenth century and became the mainland version of the Sicilian Mafia in Italy. Even more than the Mafia, the Camorra organized itself into well-structured gangs that engaged in vice activities and extortion. Each gang (a paranze) was supervised by a caporegime (a boss); several gangs would make up the 12 families that constituted the organization.

The Camorra exerted tight political and economic control in Naples and Campania, the southern Italian province in which opposition to the Spanish Bourbon kings was intense. The political turmoil in Naples clearly played a role in the creation of this secret society that came to dominate the politics and economics of Naples for nearly a century.

Within the families, capos held ultimate power; they were responsible for assigning each member to a specific job including robbery, extortion, murder, and so on. The capo also decided on the extortion "tax" each businessman or worker would pay. All criminal revenues were handed over to the family boss, who then divided the monies for distribution to corrupted officials and members. New recruits, called "picciotti" (beginners), were placed on probation and tested by criminal acts that would reveal their intelligence, courage, loyalty, and cunning, similar to Mafia recruitment tactics.

In America during the late nineteenth century, the Camorra had parity with the Mafia in New Orleans and New York, where many Sicilian and Neapolitan immigrants settled. In large measure, the Camorra controlled Brooklyn in New York City through World War I, when immigration temporarily stopped; but in New Orleans the Mafia overpowered the Camorristi in bloody battles for control in certain waterfront areas. Under Don Pelligrino Morano, the Brooklyn Camorra held the upper hand over the Mafia, which was then, by 1914, controlled by the Morello mafia family. During a meeting ostensibly designed to work out problems, Morano and a five-man execution squad assassinated Morello in broad daylight. Morano was arrogant enough to think that no witness would dare to come forward and accuse him. He was mistaken. Not everyone felt duty bound to keep their lips sealed. A witness talked, and Morano was convicted and sentenced to life in prison. Ironically, instead of eliminating the Mafia, the Camorrista plot strengthened the Mafia's position in America. By the 1920s, the surviving Camorristi, including Vito Genovese,* were absorbed into various mafia factions.

While the Camorra could not sustain itself as a separate criminal entity in the United States because the great immigrant enclaves smothered individual ethnic identity, in Naples and Campania, it is still a viable and dangerous entity. *See also* LA COSA NOSTRA; MAFIA

**SUGGESTED READING:** James Walston, "See Naples and Die: Organized Crime in Campania," in *Organized Crime: A Global Perspective*, ed. Robert J. Kelly. 1986.

**CAPO.** A capo or "caporegime," is a captain or second-echelon leader in a La Cosa Nostra* crime family. Reporting to the boss (don)* or underboss (sottocapo),* a capo oversees the activities of subordinate crews* of soldiers* (members of the crime family). Interestingly, the term "capo di tutti capi" (boss of all bosses) is generally, and rarely, applied to a particularly powerful boss who commands respect and exercises authority over other bosses. Salvatore Maranzano* relished this title, and when the Castellammarese War* ended in victory, he declared himself "boss of all bosses" of Cosa Nostra. It proved to be an elusive and dangerous title: He was murdered within months of his ascension to the top position. The new mafia men, many of whom were thoroughly Americanized, would not hear of a despot/boss running things as if he were a Caesar.

Capos represent the management and administration of the working levels of the crime family when considered from a business standpoint. The capo is the chief of an operating unit. "Caporegime" and "capodecina"—terms synonymous with "capo"—represent historical structural facts: a capodecina would be a "leader of ten" men or soldiers; a caporegime is a "leader of a troop" of soldiers.

All capos in a crime family are of equal status, no matter how many men each supervises, but capos may vary in wealth, infamy, or influence among soldiers and even bosses. The number of capos within a crime family varies with the size of the family (in 1985, the largest crime family in the United States, the Gambino crime family,* had 28 capos and nearly 800 soldiers), and the number of capos would depend on the specialized businesses the family conducts.

Each capo usually has a couple of top soldiers who work closely with him supervising and managing the crew. Capos typically deal with the underboss and boss on important matters and offer a percentage of monies earned illicitly as "tribute" to their boss, who in turn provides protection and resources. *See also* BOSS (DON); COMMISSION; LA COSA NOSTRA; UNDERBOSS (SOTTOCAPO)

**SUGGESTED READING:** Donald R. Cressey, *Theft of the Nation: The Structure and Operations of Organized Crime in America.* 1969.


**CAPONE, ALPHONSE.** ("Big Al," "Snorky," "Scarface") (b. Jan. 17, 1899, Brooklyn, NY—d. Jan. 25, 1947, Palm Island, Miami, FL). Major crime leader in the United States.

Capone belongs to that handful of successful criminals who have enjoyed public admiration during their careers. Among that group, Al Capone as a master criminal stands second only to Jesse James. And just as Jesse James's popularity benefited from the Civil War tragedy, Capone's celebrity derives in large part from the war between the government and the people over Prohibition (*see* PROHIBITION AND ORGANIZED CRIME*).

It is hard to imagine now the fame and success Capone achieved. Estimates are that in 1927 when he was only 28 years old his organization took in some $105 million; he was able to demonstrate his power publicly by humiliating his handpicked mayor, Joseph Klenha, on the steps of the town hall in Cicero,

Alphonse "Scarface" Capone. Reproduced from the
Collections of the Library of Congress.

Illinois—a small, outlying suburb of Chicago—while a police officer looked
on. In 1930, journalism students at the Medill School in Chicago chose Capone
as one of the ten most outstanding persons in the world, along with Mahatma
Gandhi, Albert Einstein, and Henry Ford.

Countless films, melodramas, and books have been written about Capone. He
was among a handful of criminals who could use the media to entertain and
mislead the public. He also knew that he symbolized the public's discontent
with social and cultural policies (Prohibition) and economic trends (the 1929
Wall Street collapse) in the country.

Al Capone was born into a working-class family in Brooklyn, New York, in
1899. Typically, the family was large and close-knit except for the eldest son,
Vincenzo, who ran away from home at age 16 and went west to become a
Prohibition agent known as Richard (Two-Gun) Harte. Al was a bright pupil
but had little use for school. Minor squabbles with the law and working as a
bouncer in a saloon-whorehouse produced the scar on his left cheek. As a young
man, he learned the way of the streets in Brooklyn and joined a gang run by a
slightly older man, Johnny Torrio,* who would later play a fateful role in Capone's life in Chicago.

Torrio and his partner Frankie Yale* operated a brothel in Brooklyn and hired the burly young Capone as a bouncer. Within two years, Capone was facing murder charges, and Torrio had relocated in Chicago to join his uncle "Big Jim" Colosimo to fend off Black Hand extortionists who wanted a piece of Colosimo's profitable prostitution empire.

The Black Hand (La Mano Nera)* was not synonymous with Mafia or any other secret society. It was simply a crude method of extortion with a long Italian—chiefly Sicilian—tradition, transplanted to America during the mass immigrations of the 1880s. The majority of its practitioners in America were Italians with criminal records in their native land who had joined the migration to the United States to victimize their compatriots. The Black Hand threat was met head-on: Capone and Torrio dispatched the extortionists with skill and efficiency.

By the time Capone arrived in Chicago, Torrio was at odds with Colosimo over bootlegging. Torrio wanted Colosimo to move his organization into bootlegging because of its potential for huge financial opportunities; but Colosimo was not interested. Torrio's ambition could not be constrained by an order from a contented whoremaster forbidding any involvement in this profitable racket. Torrio realized that Big Jim would have to be eliminated. Together with Capone, Torrio arranged Big Jim's assassination. However, there are only suspicions not proof, that Capone participated in the actual murder. In any case, Big Al's position with Torrio was strengthened after Colosimo's murder. Capone proved himself willing and able—and resourceful—when serious problems arose.

Prohibition spawned a huge industry in which Capone used violence freely and ruthlessly to eliminate and intimidate rivals. And much of this was possible because, thanks to Prohibition, a casual disregard of everyday law became part of American life. Many Americans realized, perhaps for the first time, that the law of the land could be misguided, even downright wrong, and therefore might be ignored.

Capone made the most of the situation, riding to fame and fortune on its ironies and hypocrisies. Some feared him, some loved him, and given the hypocrisy of Prohibition, many despised him and rooted for him at the same time. Chicago's power structure drank his booze even as they condemned him as a "dago" thug, but his ability to nimbly circumvent a preposterous law earned him a reputation of grudging respect that eclipsed those of other mobsters. He was volatile, violent, and more visible than any other racketeer, but he had a political flair, a flamboyant urge to be seen in public.

Bootlegging dragged the gangsters to center stage. As Capone himself noted, manufacturing, importing, and serving alcohol brought him into contact with virtually every level of society, from the spacious penthouses along Lake Shore Drive to the crowded shacks on the South Side. The visibility proved, in the long run, to be a tremendous liability, exposing him to unrelenting law enforcement scrutiny. It was as if Prohibition had been a lure and a gigantic trap to ensnare the racketeers. For these reasons, many racketeers were relieved by

Repeal. Those who wished to remain in the business went legitimate; others returned to their core businesses in gambling and vice.

The Torrio-Capone gang moved quickly to take over criminal territories by crushing competitors. With gangsters who offered serious resistance, compromises were arranged.

Torrio mapped out Chicago along a grid that staked out gang territories, hoping that cooperation would deter the violence and bad publicity.

Assassination attempts among the gangs were not as random or arbitrary as they seemed; in fact, they were highly predictable. They were often preceded by threats and warnings, and they were all accomplished for specific reasons— usually revenge.

The skein is traceable to the Charles Dion O'Banion* murder and the struggle that followed between George "Bugs" Moran's* North Side gang and the Capone organization. Nearly every major gun battle contributed to the vendetta. These were not the only gangs in Chicago, but they were so large and influential and had formed so many alliances with smaller gangs and bootleggers* that the Capone-Moran rivalry defined the racketeering environment in Chicago and throughout much of the country. With every murder this pattern became clearer—killings would beget more killings. It is interesting to note that Capone, contrary to the behavior of many Italian (and other white ethnic) gangsters, organized black bootleggers, protected them from the police, and shared profits equitably with them. His willingness to work with blacks displayed his ability to build a broad-based economic coalition, which contributed to his political power.

Prohibition spawned not only the huge illegal alcohol industry but the violence and gangs. Capone consolidated his power not by plotting murders but by running the organization that he and Torrio cobbled together and attempted to keep functioning. The mayhem began when some gangs violated each other's territories, so Capone took care to stay behind the front lines of machine gun shootouts in the streets, bombings, and "one-way" rides, which was the fate of many gangsters in the streets of Chicago.

As the fighting among the gangs intensified, in 1924 Capone and Torrio arranged the murder of Dion O'Banion, head of the powerful North Side gang.

Years earlier in 1920, Torrio put together a bootleg syndicate, which included all the major gangs in Cook County and the Chicago suburbs. The idea was to create a business out of Prohibition; several gang leaders owned and operated breweries and distilleries, but by Torrio's gang treaty, they were to receive their supplies from Torrio as well as protection of deliveries, shipments, and trucks. The syndicate would furnish gunmen, when needed, and corrupt law enforcement, where needed, and intimidate saloon keepers and "speakeasies" (illegal bars) into buying beer and whiskey from the syndicate.

The Torrio organization expanded into towns surrounding Chicago including Cicero. In 1923, reform candidate William ("Decent") Dever was elected mayor. He swiftly moved against the syndicate, ordering police to raid alcohol and vice establishments. But the corruption was too deeply ingrained, and police action failed to make much of a difference. Still, Torrio and Capone feared that reform might catch on, so a deal was arranged with corrupt officials in Cicero who would tolerate vice for help in reelection campaigns.

In the election of 1924, Al and his brother Frank brazenly led a group of 200 gunmen into Cicero to ensure the victory of Republican candidates. In the melee with police, Frank Capone was killed, but Cicero became the headquarters of the syndicate—and remained so throughout Capone's career.

The election of a reform mayor in Chicago created instability when protection broke down and encouraged competitive moves by various gang bosses. Again, Chicago became a battleground, with rebellion in the ranks of Torrio's carefully crafted but fragile syndicate. On the South Side, Spike O'Donnell's gang began hijacking Torrio's beer trucks; on the West Side, Dion O'Banion feuded with the Genna brothers, who operated gin stills in "Little Italy." In November 1924, O'Banion was murdered in his florist shop by gunman associated with Torrio and Capone. O'Banion's gang struck back: In early 1925, Capone's car was raked by gunfire, and shortly after, Torrio was attacked in front of his home and seriously wounded. When he recovered, he left Chicago forever, leaving the tattered syndicate in Capone's hands. Al Capone was 26 years old.

As the war raged against the North Side gangs under Earl "Hymie" Weiss,* an O'Banion loyalist, Capone inherited an organization that was actually a hierarchy of four men in which he served as the senior partner of the others who participated in specific enterprises. Al was surrounded by his brother Ralph, Frank "The Enforcer" Nitti,* and Jake Guzik* ("Greasy Thumb"), who handled the books and payoffs. The group was multiethnic, with loose ties to the local mafia organization.

Gang wars were bad for the image of the bootlegger and bad for business. So in 1926, a truce was arranged among the warring gangs, principally between Vincent ("The Schemer") Drucci, Bugs Moran—the leaders of the North Side gang—and Capone's forces. When the shooting subsided, at least for the time, many in Chicago began to realize that they needed Big Al despite the mayhem and violence. No longer just a goon but the head of a powerful and lucrative business enterprise (albeit on illegal one), the "Big Fellow" embraced the role of "boss" and public figure whose outlandish costumes and gratuitous charity enthralled the nation. His rackets employed hundreds, if not thousands, of people caught up in the freeze and misery of the worst economic depression of the twentieth century. Indeed, the entire city of Chicago required the services of the Capone organization, one way or the other. The police needed his payoffs because they could not survive on their civil service salaries, nor could they be expected to keep order; newspapers needed the image of "Scarface" with his bodyguards, armored-plated limousine, colorful suits, and big-spending ways to sell papers; and the city's numerous speakeasies needed him to keep them supplied. Most of all, the political machine needed Capone's money and vote-generating ability to stay in office and keep the peace among the murderous gangs. Al Capone, the gangster, bootlegger, gunman, and corrupter, became, paradoxically, a force of public community stability, doing more perhaps in maintaining law and order than the police.

The public ambivalence toward Capone certainly had much to do with the phenomenon of Prohibition. By 1927, Prohibition was entering its tenth year and had turned hundreds of thousands of otherwise law-abiding citizens into lawbreakers. Because of Prohibition, a casual disregard of the law became part of the American way of life. Capone and others like him exploited this cultural sickness.

There were those who recognized Capone as a creature of bad law and un-informed social policy but feared him; others loved him—especially when he boisterously claimed, fully aware of the ironies and hypocrisies of Prohibition, that he was a businessman giving the public what it wants. Many, perhaps most, despised his coarseness and brutality but rooted for him nonetheless because he keenly felt the contradictions and conflicts Prohibition created and acted ac-cordingly.

Capone was both Robin Hood and Public Enemy Number One, the vil-lain/hero who fed hungry, out-of-work citizens from soup kitchens operated by retail food suppliers "encouraged" by Al to provide the bread and soup. Was he a big-city Jesse James? A bandit with a conscience, stealing from the well-to-do to help the poor? Or were all his stunts and generosity carefully calculated to rehabilitate his image and to ingratiate himself with the public who were his customers, clients, and victims? His maneuvers gave his reputation a temporary boost, but he missed the opportunity to go beyond the hoodlum label when the horrendous St. Valentine's Day Massacre* occurred. His political power, which was crucial to his racketeering enterprises, was based solely on corruption. As his trial for tax evasion and the detailed newspaper accounts would suggest, although he did an efficient job of redistributing some wealth, it was also true that Big Al stole as much from the poor as he did from the rich—possibly more through his control of unions and extortion activities of small businesses. Indeed, his natural victims were the small people, and the glittering wealth he displayed came largely out of the pockets of the working people who were tempted into his speakeasies, gambling dens, and brothels.

The year 1929 is a benchmark in Capone's life and in the nation's history. The racketeering coalition he had built reached across ethnic boundaries and derived illicit wealth from Jews, blacks, Italians, Irish, Polish, and WASP com-munities; he was not the only bootlegger in Chicago but clearly the most dom-inant. The same was true in vice and gambling; Capone's move into labor racketeering and the infiltration of legitimate businesses made it difficult to de-scribe him as just another thug or hoodlum. Bugs Moran was a hoodlum, Dion O'Banion and Spike O'Donnell were gangsters, and Guzik was a racketeer. Capone appeared to have transcended these labels: He was all of these at one time or another, but he was also something else—a feared political boss with wealth and powerful connections, legal and illegal. No one, least of all Capone, could say what he earned. He naturally avoided banks and saved nothing beyond stashes of cash he kept in his homes. He was a pipeline through which huge quantities of money passed; when he needed funds, he dipped into the stream and helped himself. Political circumstances favored him: The mayor needed him, the Police Department drooled greedily for bribes and got them; the public wanted his booze, gambling, and whores, even though it was becoming apparent that his presence was worrisome and disturbing.

St. Valentine's Day 1929 was cold and windy. The plot to assassinate Bugs Moran was engineered by "Machine Gun" Jack McGurn (Vincent Gebaldi), a Capone killer who had miraculously survived a murder plot in 1928 hatched by Moran and carried out by Pete and Frank Gusenberg, two reckless shooters with the North Side gang who trapped McGurn in a phone booth and cut it in half with machine fire. McGurn turned to his lethal tasks with an industry fed by a lust for revenge. He had murdered many times for Capone in the past, and this time he urged that the entire Moran gang be eliminated once and for all. Capone approved and set the stage for the most notorious mass murder in American history, a cold-blooded execution that would eventually do as much to end Big Al's career as the combined forces of the U.S. government. Capone would be in Florida vacationing and entertaining—an airtight alibi; the "hit"* itself would be seen as retaliation among rival gangs involved in unending street battles whose only victims were each other. Press complaints would be token and quickly forgotten in a decade where mob violence regularly rocked the streets; and by now, the police seemed indifferent and inured to gangland murder. None of this was to be, however.

McGurn sprung a shrewd trap for Moran that must have seemed inspired to Capone. An assassination squad of the finest talents in the underworld was assembled from out of town so they would not be recognized by any survivors. The novel twist was the use of police uniforms and a police car to get into the garage at 2122 North Clark Street. McGurn lured the gang into the garage by offering truckloads of Canadian distilled whiskey for a good price. The transactions on the first load went well; the second load was easier to arrange and provided the occasion for the murder contract.

Moran's lateness in arriving at the garage saved his life. He and two associates were on their way to the garage when they spotted the police car and decided to wait until it departed. The gang in the garage suspected nothing more than a shakedown by the cops. McGurn's "cops," Fred "Killer" Burke of St. Louis, John Scalise and Albert Anselmi of New York, and Joseph Lolardo, brother of the murdered leader of the Unione Siciliana, entered the garage, lined up the occupants (who were fooled by the police disguises), disarmed them, and shot them down with pistols, shotguns, and machine guns. McGurn's plan, which was designed to confuse the victims and witnesses alike, scared Moran away. Brilliant though it was, the murder plan had proven to be too clever. The murders were gruesome. Highball, a German Shepherd belonging to the garage mechanic, bayed and howled throughout the slaughter and continued lunging on his chain, blood-splattered, crying for his dead master.

As word spread, the shock of the enormity of the event was heightened by newspaper reports of the German Shepherd's insane baying, which vibrated throughout the garage and the neighborhood.

Because of the massacre and the national press coverage, Capone was unable to dissociate himself from the slaughter as he had with so many other ghastly gangland hits. The "Big Fellow's" glamor turned grisly as the details of the murders surfaced in the media. Soon after, President Herbert Hoover asked Treasury Secretary Andrew Mellon if he had gotten this fellow Capone yet. When told no, he said, "I want that man in jail."

To avoid further negative publicity and changing public attitudes toward the savagery of the bootleg wars, Capone spent a year in a Pennsylvania jail on a weapons carrying violation. But that was not sufficient to cool public anger. Washington began to apply heat: Something had to be done.

A tax evasion case against Capone was begun in 1929. By October 1931 he was convicted of income tax evasion and faced a sentence of 11 years. Within a year, appeals were exhausted, and in 1932, Capone entered the federal prison in Atlanta. He was transferred to the newly constructed Alcatraz facility in 1934, where it was discovered that he suffered from an advanced case of syphilis. With his good behavior and illness, he was released in 1939.

In the last six years of his life, Capone was an invalid and recluse living in a world of fantasies and delusions in his Florida island fortress. Apart from the disabling illness, Capone resembled the fallen Napoleon in his island prison: dissolute, often confused, without hope or purpose. In 1947, Capone died at his Florida villa following a stroke. He was 48 years old.

Other members of Capone's organization were convicted of tax evasion and assorted other crimes; Frank Nitti, Capone's top enforcer, committed suicide in 1944 rather than face charges of labor racketeering, which would mean another term in Leavenworth federal prison.

The complicated network of overlapping rackets formerly known as the Torrio organization, later as the Capone organization, is now called the Chicago Outfit.*

The Outfit has had a unique leadership of former Capone associates and continued well after Prohibition and Capone's death to influence and effect criminal activity in Chicago, in the Midwest, in the gambling casinos of Nevada, and in the California film industry. *See also* ACCARDO, ANTHONY JOSEPH; GIANCANA, SAM

**SUGGESTED READINGS:** Laurence Bergreen, *Capone: The Man and the Era.* 1994; John Kobler, *Capone: The Life and World of Al Capone.* 1971.

**CASINO GAMBLING.** *See* ATLANTIC CITY, NEW JERSEY

## CASSO, ANTHONY "GASPIPE." (b. May 21, 1940, New York City—Witness Security Program). Crime family boss/informer.

Consistent with modern trends in crime family leadership successions, Anthony "Gaspipe" Casso became boss because he was the most violent capo* (leader) in the Luchese crime family.* His "nickname" originates from his early career in safecracking and as a vicious enforcer along the Red Hook waterfront in Brooklyn. Early on he became an underboss in the family because of his association with Vic Amuso, the family boss.

Casso was known not only for his violent temper and his frightful reputation with a piece of gaspipe that he used to chastise loanshark debtors or informers but also for his lavish lifestyle. He sported a half-million-dollar diamond ring, lived in a million-dollar house in an upscale section of Brooklyn, wore very expensive clothes, and ran up restaurant tabs of thousands of dollars.

In 1991, Amuso was imprisoned, and Casso became acting boss while he was facing murder and racketeering charges. He became a fugitive when convicted and was at large for nearly three years before he was captured without a struggle in his hideaway home in Mount Olivet, New Jersey. Casso was hiding, but he was still active in the affairs of his crime family: While a fugitive, Casso was reported to have ordered the murder of 11 persons and plotted with Vincent "The Chin" Gigante,* head of the Genovese crime family,* against John Gotti,* head of the Gambino crime family," in retaliation for the unauthorized murder of Paul Castellano,* the former head of the Gambinos. Gotti violated La Cosa Nostra* rules when he ordered Castellano's murder without the National Commission* sanction.

By 1994 Casso had become a government witness rather than face life imprisonment. *See also* CORRALLO, "TONY DUCKS"; REINA, GAETANO "TOMMY"

SUGGESTED READING: Jerry Capeci and Gene Mustain, *Gotti: Rise and Fall.* 1996.

## CASTELLAMMARESE WAR. (1930–1931). By 1930 Prohibition was fully established as an underground institution tolerated by millions of citizens from all walks of life. Illegal alcohol was the tool the Mafia needed to break out of the bonds of "Little Italy" and conduct its businesses and provide its numerous services to a wider public. A struggle ensued for domination of Mafia criminal opportunities between two factions, one led by "Joe the Boss" Masseria* and the other by Salvatore Maranzano,* a mafioso whose supporters and retainers came from the Sicilian coastal town of Castellammare del Golfo.

Maranzano was seen as the upstart and antagonist in the conflict. He was tall, an ex-seminarian who studied for the priesthood and straitlaced in matters of sex. His supporters, many of whom were fairly recent immigrants, made up a *fratallanze* (a brotherhood). In contrast, there was Masseria, crude, squat, gluttonous, whose family consisted of more "Americanized" Italians (not all Sicilians) who also associated with non-Sicilians and had Irish and Jewish criminal partners in their ventures.

The war raged with murders and retaliations; many of the more infamous gangsters of later generations were pitted against each other in this struggle for power. Charles "Lucky" Luciano,* Frank Costello,* and Vito Genovese* were with Masseria; Maranzano had Joseph Profaci,* Joseph Bonanno,* Joseph Magliocco, and Stephano Magaddino.* When it became clear that the war was nothing but an old Sicilian feud transplanted to American cities, a secret underground developed in the two vendetta-prone mafia groups. The war became complicated by a third side led by Luciano, a top deputy of Masseria. Men from both sides became impatient with the warring mafia chiefs and decided who of the two bosses to eliminate in order to end the bloody and economically costly war.

On April 15, 1931, Masseria was coaxed out of his Manhattan stronghold to lunch at a restaurant, the Nuova Villa Tammaro, in the Coney Island section of Brooklyn. After lunch, Luciano retreated to the toilet, and four assassins murdered Masseria as he played solitaire. The murder was never solved. Luciano was never investigated.

Peace was made with Maranzano, but suspicions on both sides persisted. Maranzano had been arranging for Luciano's murder when in September 1931 he himself was killed in his office by the very men he plotted against.

The outcome of the Castellammarese War was a powerful structure of crime families that has continued to this day. *See also* LA COSA NOSTRA; PROHIBITION AND ORGANIZED CRIME

**SUGGESTED READING:** Virgil W. Peterson, *The Mob: 200 Years of Organized Crime in New York.* 1983.

**CASTELLANO, PAUL.** ("Big Paul," "The Pope") (b. 1915, Brooklyn, NY—d. Dec. 16, 1985, New York). Cosa Nostra crime family boss.

Paul Castellano was elevated to boss of the Gambino crime family* in 1976, soon after Carlo Gambino* died. In time, he consolidated his command of the largest, most powerful crime family in the United States with the help of his relatives and loyal associates. The new godfather owned or controlled many businesses in New York, New Jersey, Connecticut, Pennsylvania, and Florida. He was something of an expert on labor unions and contracts—a skill he acquired, no doubt, from his brother-in-law and cousin Carlo Gambino. Castellano dressed elegantly and favored fashionable restaurants. If asked, he said he was a butcher.

"Big Paul," as he was known among his mob associates, had varied interests that mingled the legal and illegal: waste cartage in Nassau County, New York, road construction in New Jersey, supermarkets, cement, trucking, linens, liquor, restaurants, nightclubs, video arcades, and then stock frauds, "bust-out" scams, extortion, bribery, and murder.

Paul Castellano was the first major La Cosa Nostra* boss to have been born in the United States. His parents emigrated from Sicily at the turn of the century, and by the time he was 19, Castellano was arrested for armed robbery. Though of short duration, the experience of prison must have been distasteful for the future godfather: it was not until 1957 that he became visible again to law enforcement at the Cosa Nostra conclave in Apalachia, New York.

Before Carlo Gambino died in 1976, he made Castellano, who was married to Gambino's sister, the head of the crime family, although the natural choice should have been Aniello Dellacroce,* Gambino's long-standing, highly respected underboss. Gambino treasured family ties and wanted relatives in key positions of the family power structure; but that decision polarized the family and set the stage for a major rebellion.

Going into the 1980s, the Gambino crime family was a large confederation of clans and factions with as many as 28 capos heading "crews"* all over the metropolitan New York area, New Jersey, Pennsylvania, and Connecticut. Its sheer size and many interests mitigated against its functioning as a unitary entity except if collectively challenged by outsiders. Naturally, no other group would dare to take on the Gambino family, given its collective firepower. The tensions that would eventually shake the family to its foundations, which failed to materialize when Gambino himself died, surfaced when the family's underboss, Aniello Dellacroce, died in early December 1985.

Castellano may have extended and realized the mission of his mentor, Carlo Gambino, by integrating the criminal empire into the legitimate side of society. Despite the use of the term "Pope," which some of the "button men" (criminal members) in the family used derisively to refer to the boss because of his aloofness from the rank and file, the godfather's wing of the family was more white collar than the rough and tough blue-collar Dellacroce faction. The family drifted apart into those crews preoccupied with gambling, hijacking, loansharking,* drugs, and mafia discipline and those siding with Castellano, who were more involved in labor racketeering, bid-rigging in construction, trucking, waste cartage, meat wholesaling, and the garment industries. While Dellacroce lived, there was a fitful peace because he demanded loyalty to the boss.

For Castellano, the idea was to change the image of the LCN from a frighteningly ruthless band of killers and thugs into briefcase-carrying entrepreneurs—not tame, but naughty, and violent only in extreme necessity. Business dealings with the LCN might be considered risque, and maybe even risky, but not scary and certainly not depraved. Castellano embraced this image as his grip on the reins of power was strengthened and firmed up. He regarded himself as a businessman who regrettably associated with unsavory people out of loyalty to the past and because, from time to time, they, the thugs, could be useful. The boss was more at ease with chicken king Frank Perdue than with John Gotti.*

The chief complaint of the Gotti types was that their muscle subsidized these modernizing trends by generating the capital through their rackets that could be safely invested into legitimate enterprises. And without credible threats of violence, many of the business projects that men like Castellano pursued would not have succeeded.

Consequently, over time, the street mafia reconstituted itself beyond the

Pope's orbit. Young lieutenants like John Gotti developed powerful bands of hoodlums with an attitude, street punks who wanted a "McMafia"—a fast gangster gig that yielded instant fortunes. That meant drugs and other dangerous enterprises. Gotti's crews and associates were loyal first to him rather than the godfather. These trends set in motion an erosion of power that eventually would end in the godfather's death.

From the standpoint of the "good mafia" side of the Gambino family, Gotti was a symbol of everything that was wrong with the LCN. His arrests and trials that recurred with depressing regularity demonstrated outrageous contempt for the tradition among gang bosses of keeping a low profile. Gotti projected the image of the "Dapper Don," the garish gangster who could not be repressed, and his attitudes toward the old-timers, the "Mustache Petes,"* sent shivers of fear through the LCN establishment. Here was a man who was vain, vulgar, a media star sought after and fawned upon. As Gotti wrested more power from Castellano, the street crews, abandoned by Big Paul (who in his new incarnation was Mr. Castellano, businessman), developed their own influence. And these were unrelated to the networks of relationships woven by Castellano. The conditions necessary for the godfather's removal were emergent. The first was the availability of power, which, having been vacated by Castellano, was there, lying in the streets. By 1984, it became obvious that power no longer resided in the godfather; a steady stream of meetings, sit-downs,* and decisions came increasingly from the Bergin Hunt and Fish Club and the Ravenite. Power had lost its moorings. In the mythology of the LCN, power was embraced fully by the boss; he dispensed it as he saw fit; it could not become available except at the price of an act that would be heretical and violent or one sanctioned by his peers.

Dellacroce's death rattle in early December 1985 was also the pronouncement on Castellano's fate. Rumors and criticisms that Big Paul had abdicated his duties as boss were fueled by other alarming developments about FBI surveillance and wiretaps and what they could reveal about other bosses and associates. The godfather's impending trial might also disclose incriminating evidence against other families. So that while they may not have actually sanctioned a hit,* the other family bosses could live with it. And the final straw was Castellano's unilateral decision to make his driver, Thomas Bilotti, his new underboss. This was simply unthinkable. It showed a reckless disregard for mob protocol; the inarticulate, pit bull Bilotti was not leadership material. All of these matters, some immediate, others developing over a period of time, congealed and came together like an irresistible current to carry the assassination plot forward; in short, the events uncoiled the mainspring of revolt.

Two weeks after Dellacroce's death from lung cancer, Castellano was shot dead in the crowded streets of Midtown Manhattan. His successor, the chief conspirator against him, was John Gotti. *See also* GAMBINO, CARLO; GOTTI, JOHN; LA COSA NOSTRA

**SUGGESTED READING:** Joseph O'Brien and Andris Kurins, *Boss of Bosses: The FBI and Paul Castellano.* 1991.

**CHAMBERS BROTHERS.** A Detroit crack cocaine network operation founded in 1983 by the four Chambers brothers evolved in just a few years to some 200 crack houses that employed up to 500 people, mostly teenagers recruited from their hometown, Marianna, Arkansas. In 1988, during a drug conspiracy case against 14 members of the Chambers brothers gang, law enforcement authorities suggested that the drug network "once supplied half the city's crack." Police allege that the Chambers's drug profits amounted to $1 million a week. A rigid set of rules often posted on crack house walls governed behavior. The gang leaders warned that crack and money were not to be carried simultaneously; speeding while driving was prohibited; and the use of lavish automobiles for business purposes was discouraged. Quality-control managers posed as crack buyers to keep an eye on the product.

Everyone in Marianna, Arkansas, knew that Larry, Willie, Billy Joe, and Otis Chambers were drug dealers in Detroit. Many young people were lured to Detroit by the prospect of easy money and the fast life in the city famous for automobiles. But not everyone returned in chauffeured limousines. At their trial in 1988 a witness described the vicious discipline the brothers employed to control their workers. After the Chambers brothers were locked up in Detroit, the city's drug trade was reduced to chaos. Much of the drug trade fell into the hands of street sellers and rip-off artists. *See also* EL RUKNS; YOUNG BOYS, INC.

**SUGGESTED READING:** Harold Abadinsky, *Organized Crime.* 1997.

**CHAN, EDDIE T. C.** (b. n.d., Hong Kong—   ). Tong boss and Chinatown racketeer.

A former Hong Kong police sergeant who fled because of extensive involvement in corruption, Chan arrived in New York City's Chinatown in the mid-1970s. Soon after his arrival, he opened restaurants and a funeral parlor. Even with his affiliation with Triad* societies in the former British colony, he was victimized in an extortion plot by the notorious Ghost Shadows street gang. Later, as a successful businessman, he was elected president of the On Leong Tong and made contacts with local and federal politicians.

Law enforcement authorities charged that Chan became closely affiliated with the Ghost Shadows and their extortion activities. He was also accused of being involved in fraudulent activities associated with the Continental King Leong Corporation, an investment company he established. A Triad member in Hong Kong identified him as the "Dragon Head" (crime boss) of New York's Chinatown underworld before hearings of the President's Commission on Organized

Crime in 1983, charges Chan denied. When he was subpoenaed by the Commission to testify, he fled the United States.

**SUGGESTED READING:** Ko-lin Chin, *Chinatown Gangs: Extortion, Enterprise, and Ethnicity.* 1996.

**CHICAGO OUTFIT.** Cosa Nostra crime organization.

Ever since Alphonse Capone* led the major crime organization in Chicago, the Outfit, as it is known throughout the nation's underworld and law enforcement community, it has remained a formidable racketeering combine that runs everything from diaper services to funeral parlors. Its efficiency is envied throughout the Mafia. Anthony Joseph Accardo,* also known as "Joe Batters," who had been a thug and chauffeur for Al Capone, with cunning and skill rose to the top of the organization, and has been over the years the chief architect of the intricate power plays that made the Outfit the dominant force in the rackets from the Great Lakes to the West Coast.

Discipline has been the Outfit's guiding management principle. The Chicago mob imposes a "street tax" on all illegal activities and on some legitimate ones as well. Bookies, hookers, drug dealers, and even owners of restaurants, bars, and parking lots pay from 10 percent to 50 percent of their gross revenues, depending upon the profitability of their operations and the amount of protection paid to the police to keep them running. The Outfit maintains especially tight discipline over its internal security.

Chicago insurance executive Allen Dorfman, a sophisticated money manager, pioneered the use of union welfare and pension funds to finance an underworld bank in the 1960s. First he funneled loans from the Teamsters Union's* Central States pension fund to several casino-hotels in Las Vegas, Nevada.* Then he showed Accardo and associates how to establish health care organizations in which participating doctors and dentists gave the Outfit kickbacks after overcharging union patients. Dorfman personally received kickbacks for processing the Teamster loans and insurance claims but knew too much about the Outfit's unusual finances. He was gunned down in broad daylight in a suburban Chicago parking lot in 1983 when Outfit bosses believed that he might talk to prosecutors.

Another case of discipline mixed with paranoia involves Outfit strongman Anthony "The Ant" Spilotro.* Spilotro was stationed in Las Vegas to watch casino skimming, making sure that the money flowed back to his bosses in Chicago and Kansas City. Known as "The Ant" because of his squat appearance and toughness, he failed to keep a low-business profile but operated out of a Las Vegas fast-food store called the Food Factory. From there he dabbled in real estate and set up burglary and fencing rings on the strip and ran a prostitution business servicing hotels around the famous strip. With these preoccupations, The Ant did not discipline the skimming operation, and the FBI penetrated it, leading to the conviction of two of the Outfit's godfathers, Joseph

John Aiuppa\* and Jackie Cerone. Imprisoned with them were several other gang leaders including the Kansas City mob's top money man, Carl DeLuna.

In June 1985, the Outfit meted out its punishment for Spilotro's delinquencies in Las Vegas: He and his brother Michael were found buried in an Indiana cornfield. They were the victims of the Outfit's rules: They neglected their jobs, so they suffered the fatal consequences.

The Outfit is an example of Chicago's evolving organized crime. Several of its features make it distinctive from the Mafia crime families around the country. Although it is rooted in La Cosa Nostra,\* ever since Al Capone's days membership has not been restricted to Italians—indeed, the Outfit was and remains an ethnic melting pot, with Jews, Irish, Poles, and even African Americans part of its operational core. Entry into the Outfit is not a highly ritualized event, as with certain New York Mafia families; a handshake is enough. More important, the leadership is not solely under the control of a single boss sitting on top of the crime pyramid. "Elder statesmen," retired bosses who have relaxed control of the active street operations and day-to-day activities of Outfit crews, still exercise power in the decision-making component of the organization. Anthony Accardo shared power with Paul "The Waiter" Ricca, Jackie Cerone, Sam Giancana,\* and Joey Aiuppa and would step back in when a crisis emerged. For those who think that the Outfit's importance is overshadowed by the New York Cosa Nostra, just remember that there are two national crime syndicates in the United States: Chicago and the rest.

**SUGGESTED READINGS:** Howard Abandinsky, *Organized Crime*, 5th ed. 1997; John Landesco, *Organized Crime in Chicago*. 1929; reprint 1968.


**CHINESE STREET GANGS.** With growth of the Chinese population in the United States after the enactment of the Immigration and Naturalization Act in 1965, eliminating national origins quotas, gangs began to appear in the Chinese communities of New York City, San Francisco, Los Angeles, Boston, and Chicago. These gangs were alleged to have been involved in illegal gambling,\* extortion, promoting of prostitution, burglary, and robbery. Gang shootouts often erupted in Chinese communities, resulting in the injury or death of innocent bystanders.

The gangs are also alleged to be closely associated with Chinese community organizations known as "Tongs."\* Owing to their pervasive and consistent involvement in illegal gambling, prostitution, opium trafficking, and violence, the Tongs are considered by American law enforcement authorities as criminal enterprises. These associations, however, are registered with the American government as nonprofit organizations and, in many respects, are legitimate groups.

Chinese Tongs and gangs are also believed to be increasingly tied to organized criminal groups in Taiwan and China. Since the early 1980s, the activities of Chinese gangs and Tongs have been the subject of great concern and scrutiny by officials in the United States and Canada. Public hearings were convened to discuss the emergence of the so-called nontraditional organized crime groups. Asian or Chinese gang task forces have been established in San Francisco, Los Angeles, Monterey Park (California), New York, Vancouver, and Toronto to cope with Asian crime groups. The Drug Enforcement Administration in New York City also has an Asian Heroin Group (also known as Group 41), which deals mainly with drug trafficking among the Chinese. Other cities such as Oakland, Chicago, Boston, Dallas, Houston, and Arlington, Virginia, have also devoted law enforcement resources to Chinese gangs. The Immigration and Naturalization Service has established special task forces in Washington, New York, Boston, Houston, San Francisco, and Los Angeles to deal exclusively with Chinese offenders. In order to more effectively attack the internationally active Chinese crime groups, federal agents in the United States have begun to work closely with law enforcement agencies abroad. Chinese crime groups are now considered by law enforcement authorities as the second most serious organized crime problem in America. It is speculated that Chinese criminal groups may surpass Italian organized crime groups in the near future.

Most Chinese gangs in New York City, especially the Tong-affiliated gangs, have more than one leader or faction and are active in more than one location. For example, the Flying Dragons has two or more Dai Dai Los (Big Big Brothers) who are very close to certain officers or members of the Hip Sing Tong. These Dai Dai Los control six factions of the gang, three in Manhattan and three in Queens, New York. Each faction has about 15 members and its own factional Dai Lo (Big Brother). More often than not, the factions are at odds with one another. Each street-level Dai Lo is in charge of several lower-level street criminals known as Ma Jais (Little Horses) or Lian Jais (Little Kids).

The Dai Dai Los take orders from one or more Tong officers or members, who are known as Ah Kung (Grandpa) or Sook Fu (Uncle) among the gang members (Figure 1). The Dai Dai Los then convey the orders to the Dai Los, who then relay them to the Yee Los or Sam Los, and the street-level leader eventually gives the orders to the Ma Jais. Most directives from the Tong relate to gambling debt collection or protection of Tong-supported gambling and prostitution houses.

The Ma Jais seem to have no idea of who their factional Dai Los are, not to mention the Dai Dai Los and the Ah Kungs or Sook Fus. They take orders only from their immediate leader, that is, the street-level Dai Lo. They are taught by the gang not to ask questions about the leadership structure. Likewise, the street-level Dai Los are familiar only with the immediate leaders—the Dai Los—and rarely talk to their Dai Dai Los or Ah Kungs directly. Thus, there is evidence that Tong-affiliated Chinese gangs are highly hierarchical. Young gang members may see those above their immediate leaders only once—at the initiation ceremony for induction.

In sum, the gangs and the Tongs are linked through certain Tong members and gang leaders. If a Tong needs help from its affiliated gang, the message will be conveyed to the Dai Dai Lo by the Ah Kung.

**Figure 1**
**Typical Organizational Structure of Tong-Affiliated and Non-Tong-Affiliated Gangs**

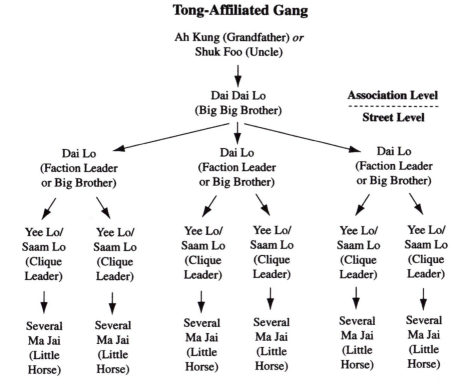

## Tong-Affiliated Gang

Ah Kung (Grandfather) *or*
Shuk Foo (Uncle)

Dai Dai Lo
(Big Big Brother)

**Association Level**
- - - - - - - - - - - - - - - - - -
**Street Level**

| Dai Lo (Faction Leader or Big Brother) | Dai Lo (Faction Leader or Big Brother) | Dai Lo (Faction Leader or Big Brother) |

Yee Lo/Saam Lo (Clique Leader)

Several Ma Jai (Little Horse)

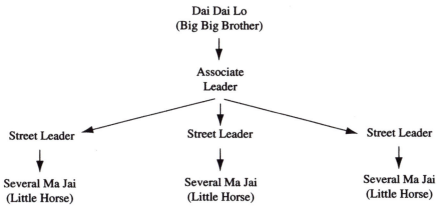

## Non-Tong-Affiliated Gang

Dai Dai Lo
(Big Big Brother)

Associate Leader

Street Leader

Several Ma Jai (Little Horse)

*Source:* Adapted from Ko-lin Chin, Robert J. Kelly, and Jeffrey Fagan, "Gangs and Social Order in Chinatown." Final Report, National Institute of Justice, U.S. Department of Justice, Washington, D.C. 1990.

Chinese street gangs first appeared in San Francisco in the late 1950s. The first juvenile gang was known as the "Bugs" and was formed by American-born Chinese. The Bugs were heavily involved in burglary and were easily identified by their mode of dress, which included high-heeled, "Beetle"-type boots.

In 1964, young immigrants organized the first foreign-born Chinese gang in San Francisco, which was known as the Wah Ching (Youth of China). The main goal of the gang was to protect members from American-born Chinese. After the immigration restrictions were eased a year later, the Wah Ching rapidly evolved into a powerful gang by recruiting its members from new immigrants. Later, the Hop Sing Tong hired Wah Ching members as lookouts for its gambling establishments. One of the Wah Ching leaders, unhappy with Hop Sing's control over the gang, left it in 1969 to form the Yau Lai (or Yo Le), which later became the Joe Fong Boys.

Besides working as lookouts for the gambling casinos, members of Wah Ching and Joe Fong Boys began to prey upon retail businesses in their community. Most store operators paid extortion money to the gangs regularly to avoid being disturbed. The stores of those businessmen who refused to pay the gang were often vandalized or destroyed.

As Wah Ching and Joe Fong Boys proceeded to become the most dominant gangs in San Francisco's Chinatown, street violence broke out. One of the most vicious incidents took place in September 1977, at the Golden Dragon Restaurant in San Francisco's Chinatown. In order to avenge a shootout, three Joe Fong Boys armed with guns entered the restaurant to attack the Wah Ching. The gunmen recklessly opened fire on the customers. Five people were killed and 11 seriously wounded.

When some of the Wah Ching members from San Francisco moved to Los Angeles in 1965, they established the Los Angeles Wah Ching by recruiting immigrant students who needed protection from Mexican gangs.

In the Los Angeles area, Chinese gangs are also active in Monterey Park, which is known as "Little Taipei." The Asian gangs are struggling for control of the lucrative criminal enterprises in Los Angeles and San Gabriel Valley, including gambling, illegal-alien smuggling, extortion, protection, and narcotic distribution rackets.

The number of Chinese gangs in New York City surpasses that in any other American city. New York is now considered the power base of Chinese organized crime in the United States. The first Chinese street gang, the Continentals, was formed in 1961 by native-born Chinese high school students for self-protection. It had as many as 100 members and fought not only Puerto Ricans and African Americans but also Italians and other whites. Unlike Chinese gangs that emerged later, the Continentals were not affiliated with any tongs.

During their emergence stage, Chinese gangs were, in essence, martial arts clubs headed by Kung Fu masters who were Tong members. Gang members were mainly involved in martial arts, driving away American-born young Chinese from Chinatown and protecting the community from rowdy visitors.

During the late 1960s and early 1970s, the gangs transformed themselves completely from self-help groups to community predators. They terrorized the community by demanding food and money from businesses and robbed illegal gambling establishments. When the youth gangs started to shake down merchants and gamblers who were Tong members, the Tongs finally decided to hire the gangs as their street soldiers to protect themselves from robbery and extortion and to solidify the Tong's power position within the community.

By the mid-1970s some gangs in Chinatown became inseparable from certain Tongs. Gang members lived in apartments rented to them by the Tongs and patronized restaurants owned by the Tongs. Gang membership became a full-time occupation for the youths, who detached themselves almost completely from school and family. Despite all the security provided by gang membership, members still had to protect themselves, not only from rival gangs but also from rival factions within the same gang as gang conflicts reached an all-time high. Although gang members were offered membership and jobs by the Tongs, they were too powerful to be fully controlled by the Tongs. As a result, the community continued to experience an increase in extortion and robbery.

The most violent year in the history of New York City's Chinatown was 1976. The violence reached an explosive stage when Man Bun Lee, a former president of the Chinese Consolidated Benevolent Association (CCBA) who publicly requested that law enforcement officials get tough with Chinese gangs, was stabbed five times by a hired assassin. Although Lee survived, the incident brought a clear message to the community: No one who antagonizes the gangs is safe. Intergang and intragang wars often erupted in the streets of Manhattan's Chinatown. Merchants were terrorized by gang members who were heavily involved in theft, robbery, and extortion. Merchants who refused to pay put their lives in jeopardy. Official statistics also showed that the complaint rates for violent crimes within the Fifth Precinct reached an all-time high in 1976.

In the 1980s, new gangs, such as the Fook Ching, White Tigers, Tung On, Green Dragons, and Golden Star, emerged in Chinatown and in the outer boroughs of Queens and Brooklyn, following the relocation patterns of Chinese businesses and residents.

The White Tigers became the dominant gang in the newly established Asian community in Flushing, Queens, in the early 1980s. Local police officers and community leaders indicate that most Chinese businesses in the area are often extorted or robbed by the gang. Besides Queens, the northern area of Manhattan's Chinatown is also the scene of White Tigers' activity.

The Tung On is a relatively new but rapidly growing Chinese gang. It was formed by former Ching Yee members and controls the new commercial areas on Division Street and East Broadway, the territory of the Tung On Association. In May 1985, the notoriety of the Tung On reached its peak when two factions of the gang were involved in a major shootout. Seven were wounded, including a four-year-old Chinese boy who was shot in the head as he walked along the street with his uncle.

The Born-to-Kill (or the Canal Boys) was formed by ex-members of the Ghost Shadows and Flying Dragons. Members of the gang were predominantly Vietnamese or Vietnamese Chinese. The gang occupies an area at the outskirts of Manhattan Chinatown, where many Vietnamese or Vietnamese Chinese retail shops are located. The Born-to-Kill, like the Green Dragons, has a violent reputation and is not affiliated with an adult group. In the early 1990s, the gang was involved in a series of violent confrontations with other Chinese gangs. For a while, the Born-to-Kill was the most feared Asian gang in New York City. However, the gang's second-in-command was killed by rival gang members in the summer of 1991, and mourners, while attending his funeral in Linden, New Jersey, were shot at by three gunmen. Later, the leader of the gang and several members were convicted of murder, extortion, and other racketeering activities. Currently, the gang is on the verge of dissolution.

Beyond the cities of San Francisco, Los Angeles, and New York, where Chinese gangs were first established, gangs are also reported to be active in Oakland, Dallas, Houston, Falls Church, Virginia, Arlington, Philadelphia, Chicago, and Boston. Media and law enforcement agencies in Southern California, Louisiana, Texas, Florida, Massachusetts, Virginia, Illinois, and Pennsylvania have also reported the existence of Vietnamese gangs in their jurisdictions. *See also* ASIAN ORGANIZED CRIME; CHINESE TRIADS; TONGS

**SUGGESTED READINGS:** Thomas J. English, *Born to Kill*. 1995; Peter Kwong, *The New Chinatown*. 1988.

**CHINESE TRIADS.** Chinese Triads are the oldest Asian crime organizations operating in the United States and probably the greatest threat. The word *Triad* is derived from the triangle, the three points representing heaven, earth, and man. Their operations were established in China in the late 1800s as resistance groups attempting to overthrow the Ching Dynasty, which ruled China from the seventeenth century until 1912. Between 1840 and 1912, the Triads began to shift from idealistic revolutionary groups to criminal enterprises. By the 1900s, they were fully immersed in corruption, with no allegiance to their earlier idealism. Many Triad members fled to Hong Kong and the United States after an unsuccessful insurrection against the Ching Dynasty from 1870 to 1920, and early decades of the twentieth century. They soon discovered that Hong Kong was a haven for criminal activity. Gambling, prostitution, and labor markets were among the new lucrative areas to tap. Upon the collapse of the Chinese Nationalist government in 1949, more members fled to Taiwan and Hong Kong, reinforcing an already formidable presence in Hong Kong. The Triads weathered a bloody inter-Triad power struggle in the mid-1950s and emerged stronger despite efforts by the Hong Kong government to control their growth and influence.

The internal structure of a majority of Triad groups tends to be nonhierarchical and informal, with each faction run by an autonomous area boss. The factions

**Figure 2**
**Chinese Triad**

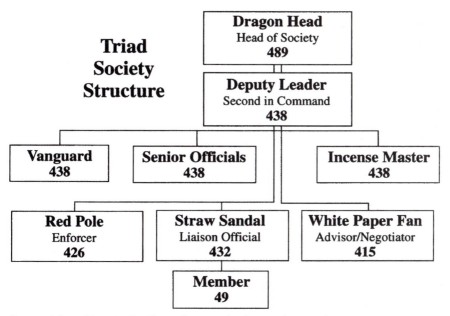

*Source:* Adapted from Ko-lin Chin, *Chinese Subculture and Criminality.* Westport, CT: Green-
    wood Press, 1990.

are independent of the parent organization for planning and executing particular
criminal activity. The groups are bound not by deep familial or organization ties
but by their criminal goal of accumulating wealth. The factions operating within
a Triad range from street gangs to highly sophisticated crime syndicates.

Existing for over 200 years in secrecy, Triads cultivated rituals and codes,
many of which are still practiced today. Officers are identified by number, always starting with a "4," referring to the Chinese tenet that the world is surrounded by four seas. Initiation ceremonies and oaths were designed to promote
unity and loyalty and strongly discourage betrayal. In one ceremony, a chicken
is beheaded to signify the consequences of betraying the group.

The Triads operate internationally and are linked throughout Hong Kong,
China, and Taiwan. The Royal Hong Kong Police estimate worldwide Triad
membership to be in the hundreds of thousands, with size and influence of the
Triads varying greatly.

Rank in a Triad (except for the lowest status) is designated by three digits
(see Figure 2). A "489," or Shan Chu (Dragon Head), is the leader or "Hill
Chief"; a "438," or Heung Chu (Incense Master), is the Triad member in charge
of ceremonies; a "432," or Cho Hai (Straw Sandal), serves as a messenger and

communications specialist; a "426," or Hung Kuan (Red Pole), is an enforcer; and a "49," or Kow Jai, is an ordinary member.

Some of the better known Triads include the following.

### United Bamboo Gang (UBG) Triad

The Chuk Luen Bong, which, when translated, means United Bamboo Gang, was formed in 1956 in a village near Taipei, Taiwan. The group grew from a street gang of exiles from Hong Kong and China, banding together to resist local gangs, into the largest Triad in Taiwan. They were able to form corrupt alliances with government officials who used gang members to perform assassinations. The organization soon expanded internationally.

UBG members and associates in the United States are involved in drug trafficking, money laundering, contract murder, extortion, bank fraud, illegal gambling,* prostitution, alien smuggling, and weapons trafficking. Each chapter of the UBG contributes to a common fund in the United States to support its leaders, members, and activities. These funds are often used to pay legal fees of indicated members and to support families of incarcerated members. The UBG also has an established network capable of providing members with guns, narcotics, and fraudulent passports and identification. Its ability to produce counterfeit identification and its sophisticated network allow members sought by law enforcement to be easily transported out of the country.

### 14K Group

Based in Hong Kong, the 14K was formed in the 1950s by former members of another Triad society called the Hung Fat Shan; it is perhaps the most well-known Triad society. The Hung Fat Shan Triads were headquartered at 14 Po Wah Road and consequently became known as the 14 Triads. After winning control of various rackets, they became the most powerful Triad in Hong Kong and changed their name to the "14K."

The 14Ks are involved in illegal gambling, extortion, prostitution, drug trafficking, murder, money laundering, illegal alien smuggling, and firearms smuggling. Law enforcement sources also report that 14K drug trafficking proceeds are laundered through East Coast casinos, and counterfeit U.S. currency is smuggled from Hong Kong through San Francisco.

Each chapter of the 14K operates autonomously and without the coordinated effort common with other Asian organizations. Past attempts at unity have failed. The lack of hierarchy and central organization and the diversity of criminal activities have led to turf battles among 14K chapters and make it difficult for law enforcement to focus its efforts. In addition, successful law enforcement efforts against one faction or leader have had little effect on the rest of the organization.

### Sun Yee On

Established in Hong Kong in 1919, the Sun Yee On is involved in alien smuggling, extortion, loansharking, illegal gambling, blackmail, and prostitution. Members of this group are natives of Chiu Chau and possess a strong group identity. The group is extremely cautious about admitting new members; however, it interacts with numerous U.S.-based Asian gangs and some criminally influenced Tongs. The Sun Yee On follow traditional Triad rituals, adhere to a strict command and control structure, and are extremely disciplined. It has been reported that the Sun Yee On Triad has significant control over the movie industry in Hong Kong, and competition with other Triads and non-Triad criminal groups for control has been bloody.

### Wo Hop To

Founded in 1908 in Hong Kong, the Wo Hop To has traditionally been heavily involved in gambling and drug trafficking. In the United States, it is involved in heroin trafficking, murder, gambling, extortion, and loansharking.* Peter Chong has been identified as the leader of the Wo Hop To and has been successful in recruiting new members on the West Coast. A power struggle between Wo Hop To and rival organizations led to the 1991 shooting death of the leader of the rival group. After an extensive nationwide investigation into Wo Hop To criminal activities in 1992, the FBI arrested ten individuals on charges of murder for hire, conspiracy to distribute heroin, and illegal weapons possession. Law enforcement experts report that the Wo Hop To will be a formidable organized crime group in the United States.

**SUGGESTED READING:** Ko-lin Chin, Robert J. Kelly, and Jeffrey Fagan, "Chinese Organized Crime in America" in *Handbook of Organized Crime in the United States*, ed. Robert J. Kelly, Ko-lin Chin, and Rufus Schatzberg. 1994.

**CIVELLA, NICHOLAS.** (b. 1912, Kansas City, MO—d. 1983, in federal custody). Kansas City Cosa Nostra* boss.

Not a well-known figure throughout the nation, Civella was nonetheless an important link between the Teamsters Union* and the criminal groups that exploited the huge pension funds of the International Brotherhood of Teamsters.* And although he was barred by the Nevada Gaming Commission from entering its casinos, Civella was active in the mob's skimming operations.

The son of Italian immigrants, his youth was filled with delinquency and crime. By 1957 his criminal stature enabled him to attend the Apalachin meeting* in upstate New York.

Kansas City during Civella's period as the crime boss was not much more that a satellite of the Chicago Outfit.* In 1980 Civella faced a prison term on bribery, and a year later, he was indicted on a Las Vegas skimming conspiracy. The most sensational criminal activity in which he participated had to do with the attempt to bribe Senator Howard W. Cannon of Nevada; Civella was implicated in the conspiracy with Teamster boss Roy L. Williams.

Throughout his life, he denied the existence of the Mafia or even that organized crime existed.

**SUGGESTED READING:** Nicholas Pileggi, *Casino*. 1995.

**COHEN, MICKEY.** (b. Michael Harris Cohen, July 29, 1914, Brooklyn, NY—d. 1976, Los Angeles, CA). Racketeer, gambler in California for Chicago syndicate.

Cohen dropped out of school in the sixth grade and worked in Los Angeles as a sparring partner to prepare boxers for upcoming fights. In his teens, he left home to become a boxer in Cleveland, Ohio, where he fell in with bootleggers* and gangsters. He embraced the gangster lifestyle rather than return to the drudgery of the small grocery store his mother operated. Eventually, he came to the attention of the Chicago Outfit,* which was impressed with his nerve and cunning; Cohen's involvements with Alphonse Capone* and other mob bosses inflated his reputation as a strongman with brains and opened up opportunities for him in gambling enterprises.

Cohen moved back to the West Coast and joined "Bugsy" Siegel* of the New York syndicate in loansharking,* gambling, and movie industry rackets. With Siegel's assassination in 1947, Cohen emerged as the undisputed boss representing Chicago underworld interests. He lived sumptuously in a large mansion fully equipped with sophisticated security devices.

Cohen identified with the Hollywood mystique, moved in fashionable circles, and lavishly entertained many of the movie industry's biggest stars. He was noted for his expensive clothes and fastidious taste in food and for his obsessive personal hygiene: He showered many times a day and washed his hands constantly. Apart from his chief preoccupations with vice and movie racketeering in which he played a role in manipulating the labor unions, he bought a haberdashery, invested in a supermarket chain, and dabbled in the promotion of prizefighters.

Having achieved notoriety with his open connections with movie stars, law enforcement officials, politicians, and hoodlums in a community that thrived on publicity and flamboyance, in 1947 Cohen agreed to raise money and material support for the Jewish struggle in Palestine. He met with Menachem Begin, at the time one of the leaders of the Irgun, a radical underground group believed to be a terrorist organization. Cohen's contacts with Teamsters and stevedores persuaded Begin and other Jewish activists that he could assemble war surplus and ordnance for shipment to the Irgun and the more moderate Haganah statehood movement. Nearly $1 million was collected for the Israeli cause at Hollywood benefits and functions that Cohen arranged. But according to Mafia informants, the entire scheme was nothing more than an elaborate and callous scam. Three months after the funds had been collected, Cohen claimed that the ship and supplies destined for Jews fighting in Palestine was mysteriously sunk. Cohen also claimed that the funds donated were used to buy weapons and bribe government officials.

In November 1950, Cohen testified before the Kefauver Committee* of the U.S. Senate investigating racketeering and illegal gambling activities in the United States. Asked to explain his many arrests in Cleveland, Chicago, and Los Angeles, as well as his scale of living, he denied he was a racketeer and said that his principal business was a tailor shop and that his affluence was attributable to his knowledge of sports and his sheer luck in betting. Even less convincingly, he claimed that he was the beneficiary of gifts in the amount of $300,000 from friends and Hollywood associates. Within two years of his appearance before the Senate committee, he was convicted of tax evasion and served two years at the McNeil Island federal prison in Washington.

While serving a 15-year sentence on tax evasion in the Atlanta Federal Penitentiary, Cohen was assaulted by an inmate in 1963 and was partially paralyzed from a head injury. He was released in 1972, moved to a modest abode in southern California, and faded from public view until 1974, when he attracted attention by meeting with the Hearsts about the sensational events surrounding the 1974 kidnapping of their daughter, Patricia, by the Symbionese Liberation Army. Cohen intimated that he could locate Patty Hearst and arrange for her safe return.

Cohen wrote a book in 1975 about his colorful life and made television appearances in which he described the underworld as full of misfits and freaks. His rejection of his former way of life may have been an effort to change his thuggish image and to vindicate himself. He urged the government to vigorously prosecute organized criminals and to root out corrupt government officials, without which, he said, racketeers could not flourish. He died of stomach cancer at the University of California Medical Center in 1976.

**SUGGESTED READING:** Mickey Cohen and John Peer Nugent, *Mickey Cohen: In My Own Words.* 1975.

**COLL, VINCENT "MAD DOG."** ("The Mad Mick") (b. 1909, Manhattan, NY—d. Feb. 9, 1932, New York). New York gangster and hit man.

On February 9, 1932, Vincent ("Mad Dog") Coll was in a drugstore not far from the home of Owney Madden,* a New York bootlegger* and underworld figure. Coll called Madden and threatened to kill him unless he was given money. The conversation dragged on, and the call was traced to a phone booth in a drugstore on Twenty-third Street near London Terrace, close to Madden's apartment house. A limousine with three men pulled up to the store. One of the men entered the store with a Thompson submachine gun and opened fire. Coll was riddled with bullets and killed instantly. A week earlier, four gunmen broke into a house in the north Bronx based on a tip that Coll would be playing cards there. Three people were killed and two wounded. Coll showed up a half hour after the shooting of his gang.

Vincent Coll began his criminal career as a hit man and enforcer for Dutch Schultz.* Straight out of "Hell's Kitchen," an Irish ghetto on the west side of Manhattan, Coll and his brother Peter worked as rum runners for Schultz until the spring of 1931, when they had a parting of the ways. Coll and his gang of Schultz dissidents began raiding the Dutchman's beer drops, and vicious warfare quickly broke out. In May of 1931, Schultz's gunmen killed 24-year-old

Peter Coll, Vincent's brother, on a Harlem street corner. In a rage, Coll killed four of Schultz's men. As the war raged, some 20 people were killed on both sides.

Because he lacked resources, Coll attempted to intimidate other gangsters by demanding money and help in his vendetta against Schultz. Kidnapping Owney Madden's partner and Jack Diamond's* men for ransom made Coll an outlaw—dangerous to both law-abiding citizens and mobsters. In July 1931 Coll picked up his "Mad Dog" nickname when in a shootout with some of Dutch Schultz's men in Spanish Harlem five children were hit by machine gun fire, and one died in the melee. An outraged public demanded he be caught dead or alive. Coll had to go. The mob had lined up against him. Miraculously he beat the child shooting charges with the help of his lawyer, Sam Leibowitz, but he had not escaped the wrath of the underworld. Still, even though he was an outcast, in September 1931, as the Castellammarese War* was nearing its end, the apparent victor, Salvatore Maranzano,* hired Coll to assassinate potential Mafia rivals Charles "Lucky" Luciano,* Frank Costello,* and Vito Genovese.* The plot failed because the victims anticipated the double-cross and had Maranzano executed instead. Coll managed to walk away, pocketing a $25,000 advance payment.

By the end of 1931, Luciano, Madden, Costello, Meyer Lansky,* and even Schultz decided that Coll was a serious liability. Despite his luck, he was finally trapped and murdered by his former partners and colleagues.

**SUGGESTED READING:** Luc Sante, *Low Life*. 1991.

**COLOMBIAN DRUG CARTELS.** In less than a decade the Medellín and Cali cocaine cartels* controlled more than half the world's cocaine supply, from coca plant farmers in Bolivia and Peru to giant jungle laboratories in Colombia, fleets of aircraft and boats, assassins on motorcycles wielding machine pistols with lethal accuracy, and a vast web of distributors stretching into every major American city.

By the middle of the 1980s the cartels were earning more than $2 billion per year, tax free. The impact of this illicit enterprise was simply staggering: The government of Colombia became deeply corrupted at all levels; assassinations of police, competitors, and cartel informers occurred almost daily; the rate of drug addiction in the country soared; and the effects in the United States, as "coke" and "crack" crept into the nation's ghettos and middle-class communities, were devastating, addicting the poor and young, spreading misery and chaos. By 1988, 6 million Americans would use cocaine regularly. Cocaine would become the first drug to be declared a threat to America's national security.

In the early 1970s, the Colombian drug traffickers, also known as the "narcomafia," supplied marijuana and cocaine for La Cosa Nostra* and Mexican and Cuban crime groups. But as the cocaine business expanded into a hugely profitable enterprise, a number of traffickers decided to create their own smuggling and distribution operations. As a result, the cartels were formed. The Drug Enforcement Administration defines the cartels as independent trafficking organizations that have pooled their resources. Of the Colombian cartels, the Medellín (named for the Colombian city that is its home base) and the Cali (from Cali, Colombia) at various times have been considered the largest and most powerful.

It has been speculated that these two cartels may control over 80 percent of the cocaine sent to the United States. Both the Medellín and Cali cartels are deeply entrenched in New York; New Jersey; Miami, Florida; Los Angeles, California; and Houston, Texas. They are well organized, building upon cultural traditions similar to the Sicilian Mafia of strong family ties, honorable social banditry, distrust of government, and the combination of criminal and entrepreneurial skills. It is estimated that the cartels employ thousands of people in Colombia and indirectly in the United States. These include those who deal directly with the illicit product—including farmers who grow cocoa, smugglers, small-time distributors, and street pushers—and those who tend the structure— accountants who keep records, chemists who process the drugs, lawyers who provide legal counsel, and cooperative politicians and law enforcement officials corrupted by the cartels who facilitate the overall operations of transport and distribution.

Many of the characteristics of other organized crime groups may be seen in the cartels. They control the prices of drugs; they eliminate competition; they avoid prosecution through the use of violence and corruption; and they use other criminal activities and legitimate businesses to hide and launder their profits (see Figures 3 and 4).

Those most directly involved in Cartel activities are limited to Colombians and are often blood relatives. A U.S. government study conducted by the Department of Justice described the cartels as having an onionlike layering of organizational power, with kingpins at the center, directing operations but insulated by layer upon layer of protective subordinates. On the fringes and margins of the trafficking mafia are public officials, business and community leaders, and journalists who are bought and paid for by the cartels.

It must be said that there are also many judges, politicians, police officials, and community leaders who resist the corruption and crippling of the society and relentlessly combat the cartels. But those who cannot be bought are subject to assassination, intimidation, and acts of violence against themselves and their families. The cartels' willingness to kill opponents and informants is widely recognized: They have even smuggled hit men into the United States to commit contract murders.

The cartels' involvement in multiple criminal enterprises is limited for the most part to activities associated with the drug business, but that has not meant that other criminal activities have been completely abandoned. Before cocaine

Figure 3
Colombian Drug Cartel

# TRAFFICKING ORGANIZATIONS

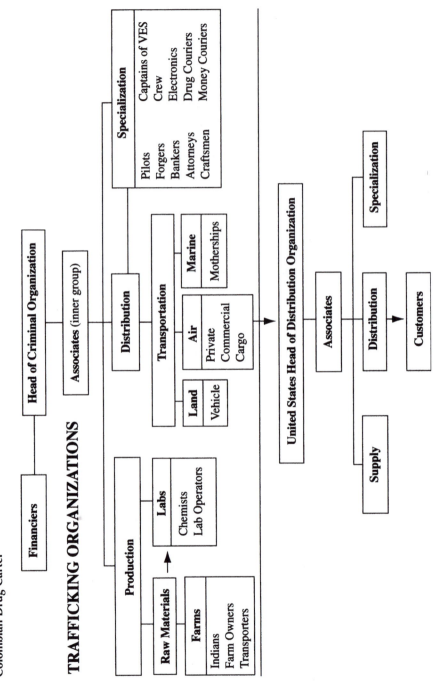

*Source:* U.S. Drug Enforcement Administration, "The Cocaine Threat to the United States." Arlington, VA. 1995.

**Figure 4**
**Typical Colombian Cocaine Organization**

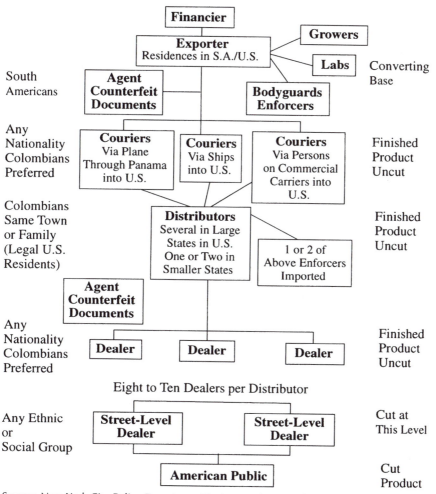

South Americans

Any Nationality Colombians Preferred

Colombians Same Town or Family (Legal U.S. Residents)

Any Nationality Colombians Preferred

Any Ethnic or Social Group

*Source:* New York City Police Department Testimony, Organized Crime Control Bureau, July 11, 1983. New York Police Department.

emerged as the major source of criminal income and as the principal criminal business, Colombian criminals were involved, and many remain active in, counterfeiting currencies, especially U.S. money, and forging travel documents including passports. Few, if any, groups, rival the Colombian drug cartels in financial resources, power, and control of drug trafficking.

With the decline of the Medellín and Cali cartels in the late 1980s and early 1990s, other groups in Bogotá and Barranquilla have emerged to fill the void and meet the insatiable demand of American markets. Unfortunately, Colombia's national economy is so intertwined with narcotics trafficking that short of major dismantling of the cartels—which seems unlikely, given the inflow of drug money into politics at the national level—the drug problem will persist. *See also* ESCOBAR, PABLO EMILIO GAVOROA; OCHOA, JORGE LUIS VASQUEZ

**SUGGESTED READING:** Patrick Clawson and Rensselaer Lee III, *The Andean Cocaine Industry.* 1996.

**COLOMBO, JOSEPH, JR.** ("Joey") (b. 1914, Brooklyn, NY—d. May 22, 1978, Brooklyn, NY). Head of the Colombo crime family* and Italian-American Civil Rights League.

Joseph Colombo became head of the Profaci crime family because two Mafia bosses, Carlo Gambino* and Gaetano Luchese,* placed him there at the top of one of the oldest and most powerful La Cosa Nostra* organizations in the United States. Becoming a boss was a reward for revealing a murder plot that targeted Luchese and Gambino that he, Colombo, had been asked to organize by another mob boss. Gambino and Luchese were supposed to be murdered by Colombo on behalf of Joseph Bonanno,* head of the Bonanno crime family.* Of course when the murder scheme was uncovered, all of the principals, Bonanno, Stephano Magaddino,* and Magliocco, denied it. This was 1964; Colombo was 40, the youngest Mafia boss in the country.

In many ways, Colombo and his bitter rival Joseph Gallo* were alike: Both appreciated the importance of image and tried to manipulate public opinion about the Mafia; both questioned the rule regarding secrecy; and both sought to maximize their power in the underworld through public relations in the upperworld by deflecting attention away from their criminal identities and careers. However, the public image proved to be too costly for both men. Anthony Colombo, Joe's father, who was a member of La Cosa Nostra,* had been assassinated in 1938 for some infraction of the rules. Joe himself became a member of the Profaci family after serving as a goon on the docks, running gambling and loansharking* operations in Brooklyn and Nassau County and participating in hijackings at Kennedy Airport. He without hesitating "made his bones"* (committed murder) when called upon to do so.

Colombo's rise to the top of the crime family depended upon his keen sense of the opposing bosses aligning themselves in anticipation of a major power struggle that could be as bloody as the Castellammarese War* of the 1930s. Colombo correctly chose the winning side and was rewarded with the leadership of the Profaci family under the patronage of the powerful Carlo Gambino.

The new boss reshuffled the family by introducing new strategies to mask its overt criminal activities. First, everyone in the organization had to have a legitimate job—including the boss. Colombo listed his occupation as a salesman for the Cantalupo Realty Company in Brooklyn. Others were "employed" as butchers, bakers, truck drivers, saloon keepers, and so on, anything that looked legitimate. Second, the most fateful move was to create the Italian-American Civil Rights League (IACRL) in 1970 to counter the negative stereotyping and discrimination Americans of Italian descent experienced in everyday life. At least that was the publicly announced purpose of the organization; the real motive was to intimidate the FBI, whose surveillance led to the arrest and prosecution of Colombo's son. The Civil Rights League members picketed FBI headquarters in Manhattan, demanding the end of law enforcement discrimination. The protests generated a good deal of media coverage, with Colombo appearing on television talk shows with other civil rights activists, hoping by his appearances to legitimate his campaign against the FBI. The first mass rally in Columbus Circle was a success; prominent citizens of Italian American background and political and social leaders lent their names and endorsed the League's objectives. Indeed, the Civil Rights League managed to persuade the producers of the highly successful *Godfather* film to delete any references to "Mafia" or "Cosa Nostra." Here was an absurd spectacle of a Mafia boss leading a campaign that denied the existence of the Mafia. But even this worked for a while: The attorney general, the chief law enforcement officer of the United States, and Nelson Rockefeller, governor of New York state, ordered their employees not to make references to Mafia or La Cosa Nostra* in official documents.

But with all of Colombo's success, or because of it, not everyone was pleased, especially his mentor, Carlo Gambino. Gambino was not the only mob boss dissatisfied with the League's activities—either because Colombo did not share the financial fruits of the League contributions, rallies, and subscription campaigns for its announced children programs or because the League drew unwanted attention to the underworld. Despite the successes of his 1970 rally and sponsored dinners and fund-raising events, what Colombo was doing greatly annoyed the FBI. By the middle of 1971, just before the League's second mass rally at Columbus Circle, the federal government had nearly 20 percent of the Colombo crime family under indictment on various charges. Other mob bosses wondered how and against whom law enforcement would move against next.

At the annual Unity Day rally scheduled by the League for June 28, 1971, it was estimated that only 10,000 people attended. Rumors had it that Carlo Gambino and other mob bosses frowned on the rally and wanted it discontinued, and prominent sponsors were quietly urged to ignore the rally. As the rally proceeded with reporters and others crowded around the podium, Jerome Johnson, a lone African American with camera equipment representing himself as a journalist, approached Colombo and shot him at point blank range in the head and neck. Johnson was immediately shot to death. Colombo survived but in a comatose state until his death seven years later in 1978.

The shooting prompted many theories; among the most widespread was the view that Joey Gallo authorized and organized the hit. Suspicion centered on Gallo because he led an internal insurrection against Profaci and was also disgruntled with Colombo's leadership of the crime family. Further, Gallo was known to have African American criminal associates. Another perspective on the shooting focused on the stealthy Carlo Gambino, who, it was believed, may have decided to let the Gallo forces deal with Colombo. In any event, whoever was behind the attempted murder of Joe Colombo, the plot succeeded in dooming the League and in precipitating the end of Colombo and Gallo—two potential threats to Gambino's power. Less than a year after Colombo's shooting, Joe Gallo was murdered in Little Italy—presumably in revenge for the Colombo shooting.

**SUGGESTED READINGS:** Peter Diapoulos and Steven Linakis, *The Sixth Family*. 1981; Nicholas Gage, ed., *Mafia, U.S.A.* 1972.

**COLOMBO CRIME FAMILY.** The Profaci-Colombo crime family would be a more accurate description of this mafia organization. Joseph Profaci* was a "founding godfather" appointed by Salvatore Maranzano* as a crime family boss at the end of the Castellammarese War* in 1931. He remained head of the family he created until his death from natural causes in 1962. His successor, Joseph Magliocco, was indecisive and incompetent but pressed on with an internal war against the Joseph Gallo* faction of the family and relied on Joseph Bonanno* because Magliocco believed that Gaetano Luchese* and Carlo Gambino* were behind the Gallo plot to take over the Profaci organization. Bonanno and Magliocco conspired to kill Gambino and Luchese and brought Joseph Colombo, Jr. into the plot. But Colombo warned Gambino, and the murder plan failed. Magliocco was forced out, Bonanno went into hiding, and Colombo became family boss of the Profaci crime family until he was shot in 1971.

Shortly after Colombo's shooting, the leadership of the Colombo crime family passed to Vincent Aloi and Thomas DiBella, who functioned as mere caretakers until a real boss emerged. Eventually the leadership passed to Carmine "The Snake" Persico.* Persico, however, was constantly running afoul of the law, passing 10 of his last 13 years prior to 1985 in various prisons. Jerry "Lang" Langella held the boss position for a while, until 1986, when Persico was sentenced to 100 years in prison. Victor Orena was named boss. A war has raged within the ranks between the Orena faction and a group of soldiers* loyal to Carmine Persico who designated his son, Alphonse "Allie Boy" Persico, as interim boss.

In the late 1990s, Colombo crime family members numbering around 120, with 200 to 300 associates, appear to be engaged in low-level rather than high-profile criminal activity. Government successes in prosecuting ordinary members and upper-echelon bosses at the top of the pyramid have meant fewer criminal opportunities and a stagnation of the crime family as an organization.

**SUGGESTED READING:** Ralph Salemo and John Tompkins, *The Crime Confederation*. 1969.

**COMMISSION.** (Mafia regulatory body).
Based on evidence from defectors such as Joseph Valachi,* Angelo Lonardo,

and "Sammy the Bull" Gravano,* and information obtained through electronic surveillance, La Cosa Nostra* in its formative period formed a ruling body called the "Commission." When Charles "Lucky" Luciano succeeded in eliminating Salvatore Maranzano,* one of the chief protagonists in the Castellammarese War* fought in 1930–31, a board of powerful bosses was created to replace the position of "boss of bosses."

The Commission consists of the dons or bosses of the most powerful crime families in the nation. Its membership varies between 9 and 12 members. It is not a representative body or elected judicial assembly, but most of its functions are judicial. Cosa Nostra families in Dallas, Kansas City, Pittsburgh, and so on, do not have members on the Commission. They will have a representative from a more powerful family from New York or Chicago looking after their interests. The group serves as a board of directors that resolves and arbitrates disputes between crime families. It may authorize the execution of Cosa Nostra members, approve the initiation of new members into the families, and promote joint criminal ventures among families.

Actually, according to Joseph Bonanno* in his autobiography *A Man of Honor*, and Angelo Lonardo, a boss of the Cleveland Cosa Nostra family who cooperated with law enforcement authorities in order to obtain leniency, there are two Commissions operating in the United States. There is the National Commission, with authority across the 20-odd families in the United States, and a regional body composed of the bosses of the 5 families in the New York area.

In 1986, the U.S. attorney in New York, Rudolph Giuliani, brought forward his "Commission Case" where a number of New York bosses were convicted of conducting the affairs of the "commission of La Cosa Nostra" in a pattern of racketeering that violated the RICO statutes. In January 1987, Anthony Salerno,* boss of the Genovese crime family,* "Tony Ducks" Corallo,* head of the Luchese crime family,* and Carmine "The Snake" Persico,* head of the Colombo crime family,* were sentenced to 100 years' imprisonment, as were several capos and underbosses who received long jail terms without the possibility of parole. *See also* BONANNO, JOSEPH; LA COSA NOSTRA; RICO

**SUGGESTED READING:** President's Commission on Organized Crime, *The Impact: Organized Crime Today.* 1986.

**CONGRESSIONAL INVESTIGATIONS OF ORGANIZED CRIME.** Among significant government efforts to enhance the public understanding of organized crime have been congressional inquiries dating back to 1950 when the Kefauver Committee* (U.S. Senate Special Committee to Investigate Organized Crime in Interstate Commerce) came into being. Seven years after Kefauver, in 1958, the McClelland Committee* (Senate Select Committee on Improper Activities in the Labor or Management Field) revealed the workings of La Cosa Nostra* in the United States and the links between it and the Teamsters Union. In the late 1960s and early 1980s crime commissions on organized crime* (1967 and 1983), authorized by presidential order, deepened the public's knowledge and understanding of criminal enterprises and their participants.

In 1988, the Nunn Committee (U.S. Senate Permanent Subcommittee on Investigations) held hearings on organized crime 25 years after Joseph Valachi's* testimony on La Cosa Nostra before the McClelland Committee. In a voluminous report of 1,300 pages, the Committee reviewed the progress and limitations in the government's struggle with the underworld. Earlier in 1980 this same Committee held public, televised hearings and issued a report on organized crime and violence; in 1984, the Committee profiled crime in the mid-Atlantic region of the United States and put out a report on waterfront corruption. Similarly, the Senate Committee on the Judiciary in 1983 held hearings and issued several reports on organized crime in America.

The investigative arm of the U.S. Congress, the U.S. General Accounting Office (GAO), undertook investigations at the request of various congressional committees in both houses on the Congress. In 1989, the GAO published two reports that, examined the effectiveness of Department of Justice organized crime strike forces, and in another investigation, the GAO described and assessed the influence and impact of Colombian, Jamaican, and Vietnamese criminal gangs operating in the United States.

These investigations and reports assisted the Congress in its efforts to expose the problem of organized crime. They also provided information to law enforcement, researchers, and the general public.

**SUGGESTED READINGS:** U.S. General Accounting Office, *Nontraditional Organized Crime* (1989); U.S. General Accounting Office, *Organized Crime: Issues Concerning Strike Forces* (1989); U.S. Senate, *Organized Crime: 25 Years After Valachi* (1990); President's Commission on Organized Crime, *Profile on Organized Crime: Mid Atlantic Region* (1984).

**CONSIGLIERE.** A counselor or a staff adviser to a boss (don)* and his underboss (sottocapo).* On the same level as the underboss, the person occupying this position is a staff officer rather than a line officer such as a capo* in the organization. Counselors are likely to be experienced career criminals, appointed by the boss. Counselors do not issue orders or command "soldiers"*; they are neutral advisers to all crime family* members, including the boss and underboss. The consigliere is also a mafia family historian whose advice is based on precedent and tradition, and it frequently reflects the wishes of the boss, of whom he is a close confidant. The consigliere therefore enjoys considerable influence and power. Although the consigliere has no subordinates, capos, or soldiers reporting and answering to him directly, he is given a piece of the action of many members, in return for his advice. Usually, a consigliere will have served as a capo with his own "crew"* (group) of soldiers who will set aside for him, as will a boss, profits from both illegal and legal enterprises. *See also* BOSS (DON); CAPO; CRIME FAMILY; SOLDIERS; UNDERBOSS (SOTTO CAPO)

**SUGGESTED READING:** Francis A. J. Ianni, *A Family Business: Kinship and Social Control in Organized Crime.* 1972.

**CONTRACT.** A misleading term that actually describes a murder assignment authorized by authority figures in criminal organizations against persons who have violated agreements or divulged vital secrets about individuals or the operations of the criminal firm to law enforcement authorities or criminal competitors.

A murder contract is, strictly speaking, a business decision in which some asset of the criminal enterprise, lethal violence, is utilized to resolve a problem.

The rules governing murder and the dynamics of the process are fascinating and at the same time appalling: Murder is committed for purely business reasons—not for revenge or passion, although the rule is routinely violated. Second, murders in the course of business must be approved by the executive heads of criminal organizations. The grounds for murder contracts or "hits"* are fairly simple and straight-forward. Anyone threatening the integrity of a criminal enterprise by revealing it to the police or criminal competitors is likely to be killed, and anyone violating the rules of the organization may be murdered.

Once a contract is let, those ordering the assassination are isolated from the actual killer(s). The murder contract may be passed to a second party, who assigns the "hit man" or killer. By passing the job off to those further removed, the corroboration necessary for a conviction is weakened.

The assassins are given the identity of the victim and background relevant to his or her murder. Sometimes a "fingerman" (identifier) is used to point out the victim. When the deed is done, the killers vanish. Often criminal organizations prefer "outside talent"—assassins from another region—because establishing their identity would be difficult and unlikely.

Frank "The Enforcer" Nitti* in an unusually unguarded moment of revelation for him remarked that local executioners might know the victim and begin thinking about grieving children, wives, and parents, whereas an outsider pulls the trigger on a perfect stranger and is only concerned with a swift, clean murder and quick disappearance. Sympathy for the victim is minimized. Murder, Inc.,* an underworld murder machine consisting of professional killers, is a good example of the logic of contract killing in action. Albert Anastasia,* a top mafioso and La Cosa Nostra* boss, supervised Murder, Inc., which worked for Louis Buchalter* and the Cosa Nostra bosses involved in racketeering and vice in the New York City metropolitan region. The members of the murder corporation took outside contracts in different parts of the country. It worked very well and was only uncovered when member "Kid Twist" Reles* was arrested on murder charges. To reduce his sentence, he revealed his membership in the organization and the details about its grisly business.

**SUGGESTED READING:** Sid Feder and Burton Turkus, *Murder, Inc.* 1951.

**COPPOLA, "TRIGGER MIKE."** (b. Michael Coppola, 1904—d. 1966, New York). Luciano crime family* capo.*

When Charles "Lucky" Luciano* was imprisoned on prostitution charges in 1936 and Vito Genovese* left the country to avoid a murder indictment, "Trigger Mike" Coppola assumed the stewardship of the crime family's rackets. For a brutal gunman like Coppola, this was a big step up the ladder of the criminal hierarchy. For a person who was little more than a goon, Coppola had authority over the artichoke supply and the numbers* operation in Harlem, which yielded $1 million a year.

Trigger Mike's real problems stemmed not from law enforcement but from the women in his life. His first wife, according to Ann Coppola, the second wife, overheard Coppola's plans to assassinate a New York Republican Party activist, Joseph Scottoriggio (who was subsequently murdered in 1946 because he opposed Vito Marcantonio—a Luchese political hack). Eventually Coppola silenced his first wife by killing her before she testified against him.

The second Mrs. Coppola was also harshly treated and beaten badly to keep her from talking about her husband's criminal activities. When Coppola was in prison, Ann absconded to Europe with $250,000 of the mob's money. In 1962 in Rome she wrote to Attorney General Robert F. Kennedy* about her husband's criminal activities and also sent an angry note to her husband and then killed herself with an overdose of sleeping pills.

Coppola left prison in 1963 and went into obscurity, abandoned by La Cosa Nostra* because he allowed his wives to learn the secrets of the organization and violate his oath.

**SUGGESTED READING:** James Mills, *The Underground Empire: Where Crime and Governments Meet.* 1986.

**CORALLO, "TONY DUCKS."** (b. Anthony Corallo, 1913, New York City—   ). Luchese crime family* boss/Commission* member.

Corallo acquired his street name "Tony Ducks" because of his wily ways of ducking convictions. But in 1986 he and other La Cosa Nostra* crime bosses were convicted of being members of the Mafia* Commission and sentenced to 100 years in prison—a jail term he could not "duck."

In the East Harlem, New York, community where he grew up, Corallo's youth was filled with criminal acts typical for an aspiring mafioso. As a member of the crime family that became known as the Luchese family, Corallo drifted into union activities and eventually gained control of Local 239 of the Teamsters in New York City. He was closely linked with Johnny Dio* in the 1950s, and with the support of Jimmy Hoffa* of the Teamsters, who seized control of five Teamster locals in New York and used the union as a basis for extortion and shakedowns of businesses in the transport industries.

Corallo did not limit his criminal activities to union racketeering. In 1962 Corallo received a two-year sentence for bribing a judge in a fraudulent bankruptcy case; in 1968 he was convicted for his part in a kickback scheme involving the Water Commission of New York City. Corallo attempted to secure a lucrative city reservoir cleaning contract for a payoff to a city official over-whelmed with gambling and stock investment debts. For this scheme Corallo received a three-year sentence. He then became boss of the Luchese crime family.

In the 1980s Corallo faced charges of bid-rigging in New York's waste dis-posal industry. The government's case that Corallo and his associates frustrated competition among garbage haulers and illegally set up territories for preferred businesses was based on an electronic bug placed in Tony Ducks's car. Finally, in 1986, the "Commission case" was successfully prosecuted against several heads of the New York Mafia families including Corallo, claiming that they participated in extorting monies from cement suppliers in the construction in-dustry and that each was a participant in the Cosa Nostra Commission. All were convicted to long prison terms.

**SUGGESTED READING:** Howard Blum, *Gangland: How the FBI Broke the Mob.* 1993.

**COSA NOSTRA.** *See* LA COSA NOSTRA

**COSTELLO, FRANK.** ("Prime Minister of the Underworld," "King of the Slots") (b. Francesco Castiglia, Jan. 26, 1891, Calabria, Italy—d. Feb. 1973, Sands Point, NY). Syndicate gambling boss and La Cosa Nostra* political fixer.*

Known late in his career as the "Prime Minister of the Underworld" because of his political connections and influence with judges and politicians, Frank Costello began his criminal life in gambling enterprises: "King of the Slots" was another title he bore early on in the Italian American underworld and the huge gambling syndicates located in New York.

Costello arrived in New York when he was 5 years old; his family settled into East Harlem, an Italian ghetto at the turn of the century. His criminal career began in his adolescence with petty offenses; then at 24 years old he served a year in jail for carrying a concealed gun. It was a lesson well learned: Costello would not return to prison for the next 37 years. As with many Italian criminals, he affected an Irish surname that could not hurt with a police department and political machine (Tammany Hall) dominated by the Irish.

By 1923, Costello was a successful bootlegger* and later claimed that he was a partner of Joseph Kennedy, father of John and Robert E. Kennedy*; together Costello and Kennedy shipped illegal liquor into the United States. With his wide-ranging interests in racketeering, gambling, and bootlegging and his lack of ethnic bigotry (he worked often with non-Italians such as Frank Erickson and Meyer Lansky*), Costello developed contacts and influence among police and politicians. In the late 1920s and early 1930s he bribed police commissioners in New York City and opened gambling casinos such as the plush Piping Rock in Saratoga, New York. Fiorello La Guardia,* the reform mayor of New York, waged a campaign against Costello's slot machines in New York and vowed to rid the city of the vice rackets. With his growing influence, Costello was not deterred by the mayor. He managed an invitation by Senator Huey Long to take his machines to Louisiana.

But reform movements sweeping the city led to the imprisonment of Charles "Lucky" Luciano* and the flight of Vito Genovese* to Italy. Genovese was facing a murder indictment. With the top men gone, Costello became acting boss of the Luciano crime family.* In that capacity, he maintained close relationships with Albert Anastasia,* head of the Vincent Mangano* Cosa Nostra family.

Costello's image, however, was not that of a dangerous mafia boss but, rather, of a philanthropist and political activist. In 1951, that carefully woven image of a public-minded citizen was dismantled at the Kefauver Committee* hearings. Millions of Americans witnessed Costello's anxiety and anger as he was questioned about his criminal ties. Refusing to be televised, the cameras focused quite dramatically on his nervous hands. In 1952, the government moved against him on tax evasion charges, which were overturned because they were based on illegal wiretaps. The information from the phone surveillance did do damage in that it revealed his connections with many politicians, gangsters, and law enforcement officials.

In May 1957, an attempt was made on his life by a Genovese gunman. Later in October, his longtime supporter in the Cosa Nostra, Albert Anastasia, was murdered. Costello realized that his leadership of the family was in jeopardy, and rather than fight, he retired.

It is believed that he arranged an act of revenge along with Luciano (who was living as a deportee in Italy), Lansky, and Carlo Gambino* to have Genovese framed in a drug scheme that led to Genovese's imprisonment in 1959, where he died ten years later.

More than any Cosa Nostra boss, Costello sought to create a secure bond between the underworld and the upperworld through corruption and bribery. In that sense, he was far more dangerous than many of the gun-toting gangsters that solved problems and sought power through brutal violence. *See also* ANASTASIA, ALBERT; GENOVESE, VITO; GIGANTE, VINCENT "THE CHIN"; LUCIANO, CHARLES "LUCKY"

**SUGGESTED READING:** George Wolfe, with J. DiMora, *Frank Costello: Prime Minister of the Underworld.* 1974.

**COUNSELOR.** *See* CONSIGLIERE

**CREW.** In La Cosa Nostra* in the United States, the term refers to a subunit of a crime family* headed by a capo,* a captain in the family. Each crew has some autonomy, relying on the talents and resources of fellow crew members to earn money for the family. In exchange for a "tax" or percentage of their earnings, paid to the boss of the family for the protection the family provides, the crew is protected from molestation by rivals and even the police. The reputation of a crew chief or capo is directly related to the money he earns and sends up to the boss.

Crews may vary in size, from a handful or a half-dozen men to sometimes 20 or 30 soldiers* operating numerous vice activities, drug trafficking, racketeering, and extortion.

**SUGGESTED READING:** Peter Maas, *Underboss: Sammy the Bull Gravano's Life in the Mafia.* 1997.


**CRIME COMMISSIONS ON ORGANIZED CRIME.** The effort to control and contain organized crime has produced several strategies: new police techniques (electronic surveillance, infiltration through undercover work of criminal groups, Witness Security Program*); new laws (RICO* and immunity statutes); and public crime commissions at the state, municipal, and national levels.

Three types of crime commissions exist in the United States: those that are government funded, bipartisan groups where investigators have police status but no arrest authority (e.g., the former Pennsylvania Crime Commission); commissions funded by the private sector with no law enforcement authority at all (e.g., the Chicago Crime Commission); and government-sponsored temporary groups authorized to investigate, with subpoena power, specific phenomena or incidents (e.g., Knapp Commission on Police Corruption in New York City; President's Commission on Organized Crime).

Citizen crime commissions have been useful in developing and disseminating information and in focusing public attention on organized crime. Commission hearings, reports, and publicity about community crime trends and specific incidents are ways of galvanizing community attitudes and reducing ignorance about such problems.

Over the past 35 years, there have been two investigations of organized crime authorized directly by a president. Each in its own way abetted efforts to control organized crime. The first, the 1967 Task Force Report on Organized Crime, focused almost entirely on La Cosa Nostra.* The second, the President's Commission on Organized Crime (PCOC), was appointed in July 1983 and submitted a report on the problems of organized criminality in April 1986. The President's Commission expanded the scope of the 1967 Task Force to include groups with varied ethnic identities and whose activities go beyond the traditional La Cosa Nostra parameters.

The 1967 Task Force did more to change the criminal justice system in the United States regarding organized crime than any other set of events or factors, not because it accurately described the phenomenon of organized crime (it did not) but because it elevated the issue to one of national concern, which aroused Congress to do something concrete and tangible about it. Many of the Task Force's recommendations were enacted into legislation. The Omnibus Crime Control Act of 1968 and Organized Crime Control Act of 1970, which came out of Task Force recommendations, (1) increased the numbers of, and funding for, organized crime intelligence and investigative units; (2) enacted wiretapping and other electronic eavesdropping laws; (3) set up the federal Witness Security Program*; and (4) passed RICO, which provided authority to the courts to impose extended sentences on organized crime leaders.

In 1983, the PCOC had as its mission the task of conducting a region-by-region analysis of organized crime by reviewing the nature of traditional organized crime and emerging criminal groups. It was directed by the president to identify sources and amounts of criminal income and to develop in-depth information on participants in organized crime activities. The mandate also included making recommendations to improve law enforcement efforts against organized crime.

The PCOC conducted many public hearings around the country, as had its predecessor in 1967, but unlike the Task Force, the President's Commission was mired in disputes. Although the PCOC produced four topical reports on money laundering and two on business and labor unions and drug trafficking as well as a summary report on the impact of organized crime, these efforts revealed little that was not already known. Noteworthy, however, was the Commission's attention to emerging, nontraditional criminal organizations. In addition, the PCOC did identify a heretofore neglected issue, the involvement of attorneys who specialized in defending organized crime figures. "Mob lawyers" testified and came under scrutiny regarding their roles as advisers to crime enterprises and the sources of their fees.

The PCOC emphasized the involvement of Asian and African American organizations in organized crime and outlined the operations of the Colombian drug cartels.* Motorcycle gangs were also highlighted as part of the new breed of organized criminal.

It became apparent that the investigation of organized crime is not limited solely to law enforcement agencies and that commissions can be a useful adjunct to traditional law enforcement tools. Because commissions are not interested or empowered to make specific criminal cases, they are able to take a long view and assess trends and impacts of law enforcement strategies. *See also* CONGRESSIONAL INVESTIGATIONS OF ORGANIZED CRIME

**SUGGESTED READING:** Charles Rogovin and Frederick Martens, "The Role of Crime Commissions in Organized Crime Control," in *Handbook of Organized Crime in the United States*, ed. Robert J. Kelly, Ko-lin Chin, and Rufus Schatzberg. 1994.

**CRIME FAMILY.** A subunit of Italian organized crime. At one time it was widely believed that 24 organized crime families divided the United States into territories of control. The crime families together form a nationwide confederation of criminals called La Cosa Nostra.*

Each family is headed by a boss* (see Figure 5). Families are organized much like legitimate corporations, with a pyramid-type system of authority. The boss is the supreme authority figure, served by an underboss (sottocapo)* and con-

**Figure 5**
**An Organized Crime Family**

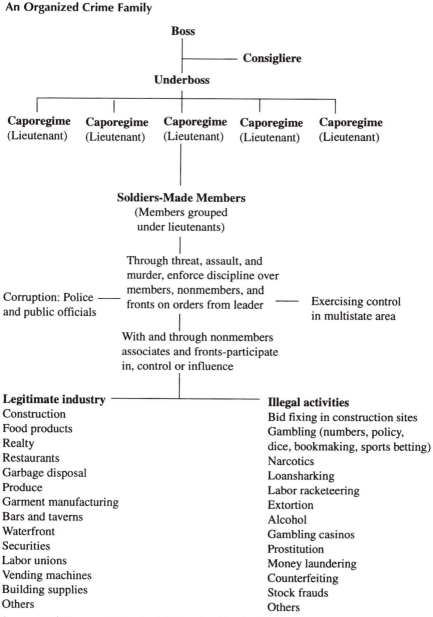

*Source:* Task Force on Organized Crime, President's Commission on Law Enforcement and Administration of Justice. Washington, D.C.: U.S. Government Printing Office, 1967; p. 9.

sigliere.* In the second tier of authority and power are the caporegimes (captains) who supervise crews* of ten or more members known by various names such as soldiers,* button men, and wise guys.

The wealthiest and most powerful families operate in New York, New Jersey, Missouri, Illinois, Louisiana, Florida, Michigan, and Rhode Island. The family is the most significant level of organization and the largest unit of criminal organization in which allegiance is owed to one man, the boss. Not every Cosa Nostra group is known as a crime family. In Chicago the Cosa Nostra organization is known as the Chicago Outfit* and has historically included nonmafia members. In Kansas City, the criminal apparatus is called "The Clique"; in other locales, such as New York City, Cosa Nostra crime families are named after their founders or very powerful bosses who established their identities. *See also* BOSS (DON); CAPO; LA COSA NOSTRA; MAFIA

**SELECTED READING:** Joseph Albini, *The American Mafia: Genesis of a Legend.* 1971.

**CRIPS AND BLOODS.** During the spread of minority gangs in the mid-1980s, the United States was caught in a pincer movement: The Los Angeles street gangs moved east, and the Jamaican posses moved west from the East Coast: and between them, by the end of the decade, they had introduced much of the rest of the country to crack.

The chief Los Angeles gangs are the Crips (approximately 30,000 strong now) and the Bloods (about 9,000), composed of Latinos and African Americans. Their expansion to other parts of the country took off in 1986. The Crips gang moved into Seattle and Oklahoma City in 1988. In 1991 the Justice Department placed the Crips and Bloods in 32 states and 113 cities. Some experts think that Los Angeles–based gangs now control up to 30 percent of the crack trade. Neither gang is rigidly hierarchical. Both are broken into loosely affiliated neighborhood groups called "sets," each with 30 to 100 members. With all the initial violence associated with crack, many gang members left southern California to avoid police. As the crack epidemic exploded, others simply moved to other areas and set up branch operations in places where friends or family were located.

Compared with Los Angeles, other cities have been easy pickings, especially for "rollers" or "Ogs" (original gangsters) and others who are in their twenties and have a thirst for more serious cash. Some "Ogs" have established connections with Colombian suppliers.

Crips and Bloods are reflections of a demographic bulge where its members tend to be in the most criminally prone age cohorts—adolescence to adulthood. Coupled with the exceedingly high unemployment rate among young males (36 percent), the conditions for the rapid expansion of minority crime are present.

Although the study of street gangs is emerging now as a vast cottage industry, virtually little has been written about Los Angeles's sociologically destructive gang culture. What is known is that the first generation of African American street gangs emerged as a defensive response to white confrontations in the schools and streets during the late 1940s. Until the 1970s these gangs tended to be defined mainly by school-based turf rather than by microscopically drawn neighborhood territories. Besides defending African American teenagers from racist attacks, the early gangs were also the architects and defenders of social space in new and usually hostile settings where new African American neighborhoods developed.

The decimation of the Black Panthers (a politically active street gang that emerged in Oakland, California, and spread to many African American communities) led directly to a renewal of gang activity two decades ago. "Crippin" was a bastard offspring of the Panthers' former charisma, which filled the void when the Panthers were crushed by law enforcement groups across the country. The legends about the Crips agree on certain particulars: The first "set" incubated in the social wasteland caused by the clearance for the Century Freeway, the traumatic removal of housing, and the destruction of neighborhood ties in Los Angeles. One legend has it that *Crips* stands for "continuous revolution in progress." However apocryphal this may be, it best describes the phenomenal spread of Crip sets across the ghetto between 1970 and 1972. Under incessant competitive pressure from the Crips, independent gangs federated as the red-handkerchief Bloods. The Bloods have been primarily a defensive reaction formation to the aggressive emergence of the Crips.

This was not merely a gang revival but instead a radical permutation of gang culture. The Crips inherited the Panther aura of fearlessness and transmitted the ideology of armed vanguardism, and "Crippin" often represents an escalation of intraghetto violence to *Clockwork Orange* levels (murder as a status symbol). The Crips have also blended a penchant for ultraviolence with an overweening ambition to dominate the entire ghetto. The Crips achieved a "managerial revolution" in gang existence. If they began as a teenage substitute for the fallen Panthers, they evolved through the 1970s into a hybrid of teen cult and proto-mafia.

In 1972, at the height of Crip mania hysteria, a conference gave a platform to the gangs, which produced a document of their grievances. To the astonishment of officials, the "mad dogs" outlined an eloquent and coherent set of demands: jobs, housing, better schools, recreation facilities, and community control of local institutions. It was a bravura demonstration that gang youth, however trapped in their own delusionary spirals of vendetta and self-destruction, clearly understood that they were the children of deferred dreams and defeated ambitions. Young African Americans have seen their labor market options virtually collapse as the factory and truck-driving jobs that gave their fathers and older brothers a modicum of dignity were replaced by imports or relocated to white areas far out on the galactic spiral arms of the Los Angeles Megalopolis. The deteriorating labor market for these young males is a major reason the counter-economy of drug dealing and youth crime has burgeoned.

It is a misnomer to call them "gangs" because the Crips and Bloods are really federations made up of dozens of independent gangs that each claim a territory much like the La Cosa Nostra* crime families*. Though a Crip is always a Crip, they do go to war with each other—unlike the Bloods. Crips wear blue colors, and the Bloods red to identify their affiliations. Bloods gangs can go under any name, but the Crips usually carry the term "Crips" after the street or neighborhood with which they identify.

Another feature of the African American underworld that developed in Los Angeles is that no particular individual gang leaders stand out as heads or bosses of the larger federation. Perhaps because of the mortality rate and imprisonment of so many gang members, a durable command structure cannot settle in.

As they move out of Los Angeles and establish a presence in other African American communities, the Crips and Bloods simply appear and then recruit local gangs into their drug dealing and aura of celebrity. As the gang members migrate, the potential for broader syndication spreading out from the mother gangs in Los Angeles poses a real threat.

The tacit expendability of African American and Hispanic youths in gang violence can be directly measured by the steady drainage of resources, with minimum outcry from elected officials, from the programs that served their most urgent needs. Job alternatives for gang members have been almost nonexistent, despite widespread recognition that jobs are the most potent deterrents to youth crime. The school system, meanwhile, has been traveling backward at high speed. At the state level the educational system has been in steep decline.

The specific genius of the Crips has been their ability to insert themselves into a leading circuit of the international drug trade. Through crack they have discovered a vocation for the ghetto in the ghetto's new world city economies. Peddling the imported, high-profit rock to a bipolar market of final consumers, including rich whites and poor street people, the Crips have become as much capitalists as outlaw proletarians.

In an age of narco-imperialism, they have become modern analogues to the "gunpowder states" of West Africa, those selfish, rogue chieftains who were middlemen in the eighteenth-century slave trade, prospering while the rest of Africa bled. The contemporary cocaine or crack trade is a stunning example of what some economists call "flexible accumulation." The rules of the game are to combine maximum financial control with interchangeable deployment of producers and sellers across variable markets.

The appearance of crack has given the Crips subculture a terrible, almost irresistible allure. There is little reason to believe that the crack economy of the new gang culture will stop growing, whatever the scales of repression, or stay confined to African American ghettos. Although the epicenters remain in the Watts-like ghetto zones of hard-core youth unemployment, the gang mystique has spread into middle-class African American areas where parents are close to panic or vigilantism. *See also* EL RUKNS; JAMAICAN POSSE GROUPS

**SUGGESTED READINGS:** Leon Bing, *Do or Die.* 1991; Kody Scott, *The Autobiography of an L.A. Gang Member.* 1993.

# D

**DALITZ, "MOE."** (b. Morris Barney Dalitz, 1900, Boston, MA—d. Aug. 30, 1989, Las Vegas, NV). Cleveland syndicate boss and Las Vegas, Nevada,* casino entrepreneur.

His criminal career began in Detroit as part of the "Little Jewish Navy" that smuggled liquor during Prohibition from Canada across the border into the United States. Dalitz then moved to Cleveland and became part of the "Cleveland Four," a quartet of Jewish racketeers that included Morris Kleinman, Louis Rothkopf, and Samuel Tucker, who formed an alliance with the Mayfield Road Gang in gambling and alcohol distribution.

Dalitz had the talent, much like his New York counterpart Meyer Lansky,* of forming durable alliances with non-Jews; in Cleveland his criminal enterprises were jointly conducted with the Polizzi Mafia family.

With the end of Prohibition, Dalitz and his cronies set up illegal gambling* operations in Newport, Kentucky, West Virginia, and Indiana. Las Vegas beckoned in the late 1950s and Dalitz, with partners in the Teamsters and La Cosa Nostra* families, took over the Desert Inn and several other casinos. Their racket was the "skim," taking gambling profits off the top before they were counted and audited.

Toward the end of the 1960s the Desert Inn Casino/Hotel was sold to billionaire Howard Hughes in order to avoid the Internal Revenue Service, who was closing in on the practice of skimming casino profits to beat taxes.

With loans from the Teamsters Pension Fund and with the political influence he accumulated over the years, Dalitz became involved in luxury hotel and recreational developments in southern California. The La Costa Hotel and Country Club, just north of San Diego, managed by Dalitz, accommodated the wealthy and powerful in the upperworld as well as the underworld. Indeed, in Dalitz's case, crime did pay and pay well. *See also* PROHIBITION AND ORGANIZED CRIME

**SUGGESTED READING:** Ed Reid and Ovid Demaris, *The Green Felt Jungle*. 1991.

**DECARLO, ANGELO.** ("Gyp") (b. 1902, Sicily—d. Oct. 20, 1973, Mountain-side, NJ). New Jersey loanshark and Genovese crime family* capo.*

Wiretaps in Angelo DeCarlo's headquarters in northern New Jersey revealed that an extensive political-criminal nexus including organized criminals, politicians, law enforcement officials, and businesspeople existed for many years and operated in a way that systematically defrauded the public. Some officials such as Congressman Peter Rodino were able to explain away the "Gyp's" references to him; others, such as Newark Mayor Hugh Addonizio and Hudson County political boss John J. Kenny, saw their political careers snuffed out.

Angelo DeCarlo was a career criminal associated with the Genovese Cosa Nostra family who offered no excuses for what he was, nor did he seek to hide the fact that he was, in his own words, a "hoodlum." Yet this self-declared thug managed to get a presidential pardon even after tapes of the lurid details of murders he committed and vicious beatings he administered were widely circulated by the FBI.

In 1970 he was sent to prison for 12 years on an extortion conviction, but within a year and a half, his sentence was commuted by President Richard Nixon. The rumor mill had all sorts of stories involving Vice President Spiro Agnew (who would later resign because of bribe-taking in construction projects when he was the mayor of Baltimore) and Frank Sinatra's interventions on behalf of this Mafia killer. DeCarlo's final act of criminal defiance occurred when he avoided paying the $20,000 fine his sentence carried by dying five days before it was due.

**SUGGESTED READING:** Henry A. Zeiger, *The Jersey Mob*. 1975.

**DECAVALCANTE, SAM "THE PLUMBER."** (b. Simone Rizzo DeCavalcante, 1919—    ). New Jersey crime family* boss.

His brief career as a La Cosa Nostra* crime lord may have been no more than a hobby in the larger, less exciting context of DeCavalcante's legitimate occupation as a plumbing supply salesman. But the FBI wiretapped his offices for four years and may have unwittingly created a mafia chief. Sam the Plumber's "family" represented a loosely structured constellation of soldiers* on the margins of northern New Jersey's other mafia groups who were linked to the Genovese,* Bonanno,* and Gambino crime families,* in New York City.

DeCavalcante operated a plumbing and heating firm in Kenilworth, New Jersey, where the FBI recorded his conversations between 1961 and 1965. When Sam the Plumber went to trial on extortion charges in 1969, 13 volumes of transcripts were filed by the prosecution. The 13 volumes of transcripts, the "DeCavalcante Tapes," as they became known, confirmed much of Joseph Valachi's* 1963 revelations about the structure and operations of the Cosa Nostra.

The DeCavalcante crime family consisted of not more than 60 members, and much of the boss's time in this period was occupied with personal romantic affairs, his assumption of leadership in 1964 after his predecessor Nick Delmore's death, and the crisis in the Mafia's Commission* over Joseph Bonanno* and his family war.

Sam the Plumber was convicted in 1969 on an extortion-conspiracy charge and sentenced to 15 years. He served his term in the federal prison in Atlanta, Georgia, and retired to Florida. His crime family simply dissolved, and his career as a mafia boss ended abruptly.

**SUGGESTED READING:** Henry A. Zeiger, *Sam the Plumber.* 1970.


**DELLACROCE, ANIELLO.** ("O'Neill," "Mr. Neil") (b. 1914, Manhattan, NY— d. Dec. 2, 1985, New York City). Powerful underboss of the Gambino crime family.*

Born in Manhattan in 1914, the son of Sicilian immigrants, Dellacroce dropped out of school in the eighth grade. In his early twenties, Aniello Dellacroce (translated the name means "little lamb of the cross") joined Vincent Mangano's* gang and then faithfully served when Albert Anastasia* assumed leadership of the crime family. Later, when Carlo Gambino* became boss, Dellacroce was part of the top echelon of the family; he served as underboss (sottocapo)* with a great deal of autonomy, operating crews* of soldiers* loyal to him alone. His reputation for violence was ferocious, and his dependability as a mafioso who would never break his vow of silence ensured his personal survival but also meant that he could be taken for granted to some extent.

Under Carlo Gambino's rule, Dellacroce served as underboss, and with Gambino's death, speculation was rife within the family that Carlo's experienced and ruthless underboss was going to take over. However, Gambino made it clear before his death that his cousin Paul Castellano* would become the boss. This occurred in 1976 while Dellacroce was in prison, as was his protégé John Gotti* thus he was not in much of a position to challenge Castellano even if he had been inclined to do so.

Dellacroce had to be offended by Gambino's decision not to make him his successor, and to placate the faithful underboss, the new boss confirmed O'Neill's control over some of the family's most lucrative rackets and money-making crews in Queens and Manhattan, a control that Gambino had awarded him before his death. These concessions may have seemed to appease the veteran Dellacroce, but in reality, they had not. As second in command under Gambino, Dellacroce, according to the Cosa Nostra's unwritten code, should have succeeded Gambino as boss. But Gambino had engaged in flagrant nepotism in naming his cousin. Since the 62-year-old Dellacroce was a mobster of the old school, believing that a boss should never be challenged, that his orders should always be obeyed and respected, he swallowed his pride at being passed over, but the slight nevertheless rankled him and embittered his relations with Big Paul. Gambino's favoritism for his cousin also irritated most of Castellano's capos* and soldiers. They were suspicious that Castellano might indulge in nepotism himself, showing favoritism to his three sons or to Carlo Gambino's son Tommy. An ambitious young soldier like John Gotti wanted to rise in the family on his own merits and not have to worry about some relative of Big Paul's being promoted over him.

Agreements as fragile as the Castellano-Dellacroce division of spoils and authority in a crime family seldom stay glued together. Sooner or later, power would lay in the streets, up for grabs. Dellacroce had all the prerequisites, including the cool toughness and mercilessness to get the job done, and the loyalty of many street criminals cut off from Castellano's "briefcase mafia." Except for the fact that Dellacroce was in ill health, it seemed he would eventually take over even if it meant a war in the family. Only Dellacroce could stop a rebellion of young ambitious soldiers like John Gotti, so when the underboss died in December 1985, the stage was set for a mutiny against Castellano. Castellano added fuel to the fire by not attending Dellacroce's funeral ceremonies. Gotti and other capos interpreted this breech of protocol as an insult and planned revenge. Three weeks after Dellacroce died, Castellano was murdered in the streets of Midtown Manhattan. *See also* CASTELLANO, PAUL; GAMBINO, CARLO; GOTTI, JOHN

**SUGGESTED READING:** John H. Davis, *Mafia Dynasty: The Rise and Fall of the Gambino Crime Family.* 1993.

**DEWEY, THOMAS E.** (b. Mar. 24, 1902, Owosso, MI—d. Mar. 16, 1971, Bal Harbour, FL). Prosecutor and rackets buster.

Dewey began his career as a Wall Street lawyer. But it was in the role of special prosecutor against gangsters that his reputation soared. He served as U.S. attorney, as district attorney in New York City, and as a special prosecutor appointed by the governor of New York State in the 1930s. His innovative investigation strategies put in prison top mob chiefs including Charles "Lucky" Luciano* and "Waxey" Gordon* and culminated in the executions of Mendy Weiss and Louis Buchalter* in 1944.

Before he rose to national prominence as the Republican candidate for president in 1948 and as governor of New York State, his gang-busting activities against the leaders of the New York City crime syndicate almost cost him his life. Prior to the investigation, prosecution, and conviction of Luciano, Dewey was after Dutch Schultz,* the "Beer Baron" and policy rackets king in Harlem. Schultz was extremely intelligent but also extremely volatile emotionally—even unstable, according to many gangsters and law enforcement officials who had contact with him. When Dewey's investigators and prosecutors began to focus on the Dutchman, who had just managed to fend off two tax evasion prosecutions, he attempted to get permission from the crime syndicate to assassinate Dewey. Without exception, the crime bosses rejected Schultz's appalling suggestion. They believed that killing Dewey would only arouse public anger to a higher pitch and promote a lynch mob climate that would eventuate in their downfall. The Dutchman was rebuked by his mob associates but made it clear that if the syndicate would not sanction a hit* then he, Schultz, would personally arrange for Dewey's murder.

In October 1935, Luciano, Meyer Lansky,* and other mob bosses were shocked to discover that Schultz had a murder contract planned against Dewey. The Fifth Avenue apartment of Dewey had been staked out; his routines and comings and goings with bodyguards were noted. Fearing his home phone might be tapped, each morning Dewey went to a neighborhood drugstore and used the telephone booth to call his office. Schultz's plan was to place a gunman, equipped with a silencer, and disguised as a parent strolling with a baby carriage, in the drugstore; the gunman would shoot Dewey as he entered the phone booth and calmly melt into the crowd as the chaos mounted.

The crime bosses responded instinctively by putting a murder contract on Schultz. Before the plan could be carried out, Schultz was shot in a Newark, New Jersey, steakhouse before the murder plot against Dewey could be put into action.

It wasn't until years later in 1940 when Dewey learned that the syndicate thwarted Schultz and killed him. By then, he had successfully prosecuted Luciano, who was serving a 30- to 50-year sentence for compulsory prostitution.

The special prosecutor's campaign against the mob was not solely focused on racketeers but also on politicians who acted in collusion with gangsters. In 1937, he publicly accused Albert Marinelli, a Tammany Hall leader of the Second Assembly District and County Clerk of New York, of being an associate of racketeers. Dewey charged that through Marinelli's help, important gangsters including James "Jimmy Doyle" Plumeri and Johnny Dio* had seized control of the trucking industry in downtown Manhattan. Marinelli's connection with Luciano was noted, as were the identities of many individuals appointed by Marinelli as election inspectors who had criminal records.

After World War II and an unsuccessful bid for the Republican nomination for president in 1944, Dewey as governor of New York State faced a dilemma. The War Department urged that Luciano's sentence be suspended in view of his services to Naval Intelligence during the war. Luciano had helped secure the eastern seaboard waterfront against sabotage and espionage and assisted the Allies through his Mafia contacts during the invasion of Sicily. The man who put Luciano behind bars now backed his release. Dewey's importance is in the successful methods he developed to combat organized crime.

**SUGGESTED READING:** Thomas E. Dewey, *Twenty Against the Underworld.* 1974.

**DIAMOND, JACK "LEGS".** (b. 1897, Philadelphia, PA—d. Dec. 1931, Albany, NY). New York racketeer and gunman.

It was Jack Diamond's dancing skills that earned him the nickname "Legs." The American-born son of Irish immigrants, Diamond grew up in Philadelphia and in his adolescence got into trouble. When his family moved to Brooklyn in 1913, Legs joined a gang on the Lower East Side of New York headed by "Little Augie" Orgen.* Before he was drafted into the army in 1918, Diamond had accumulated an extensive criminal record of robberies and burglaries.

After World War I, Diamond resumed his criminal career and worked as a strong-arm goon and gunman for Arnold "The Brain" Rothstein* in Prohibition rackets. With Rothstein's murder, Diamond freelanced in bootlegging and narcotics. His criminal career was marked by frequent attempts on his life because of his double-dealing and betrayals of associates. When Little Augie was assassinated in 1927 partly in revenge for his murder of Kid Dropper* (whom Diamond killed), and because other gangsters sought control of the labor unions Little Augie dominated, Diamond did not turn his guns on Jacob "Gurrah" Shapiro* and Louis Buchalter,* whose men wounded Diamond during the street killing of Orgen.

From those events, Diamond became a big shot on Broadway, opening a nightclub, the Hotsy Totsy, which became an underworld playground and meeting place. It was in the club that Diamond and an associate killed a mobster in full view of customers. They decided to clear themselves and did so by killing the witnesses—the bartender and three customers. Four others, including the hat-check girl, mysteriously disappeared. Diamond and his partner were not prosecuted.

War broke out in 1928 between Legs Diamond and Dutch Schultz,* who attempted to take over Diamond's rackets while he was in hiding over the nightclub murder. After killing five mobsters from the old Rothstein gang and two of Dutch Schultz's henchmen in 1930, Diamond was shot in the head but miraculously survived. In 1931, he was ambushed in upstate New York and shot four times in the back, lung, liver, and arm. The doctors said he had no chance, but he survived again.

After an acquittal on a liquor law violation in December 1931, Diamond was shot in the head while sleeping by two gunmen who had access to his "safe house." This time he was finally murdered, proving that Legs Diamond was no "Teflon gangster" after all.

**SUGGESTED READING:** Gary Levine, *Jack "Legs" Diamond: Anatomy of a Gangster.* 1995.

**DIGREGORIO, GASPER.** (b. Gasperino DiGregorio, 1905, Castellammare del Golfo, Sicily—d. 1970, New York City). Bonanno crime family* capo* and interim boss (don).*

Gasper DiGregorio was closely associated with Joseph Bonanno* throughout most of his criminal career, from their boyhoods in Sicily to the dangerous streets of New York City during the "Banana War" in 1966.

DiGregorio's legitimate interests included ownership of some garment factories, but his real career was as a capo (a boss) in the Bonanno crime family.

When Joe Bonanno disappeared rather suddenly in 1964 and did not reappear until May 1966, DiGregorio assumed control of the crime family in opposition to Joseph Bonanno's wishes that his son Salvatore (Bill) Bonanno should succeed him. The conflict over the leadership of the family divided it into a factional struggle known as the Banana War. DiGregorio's supporters and those loyal to Joe and his son Bill fought a gun battle in Troutman Street, a Bonanno stronghold in the Red Hook section of Brooklyn. There were no casualties then, but the war continued in 1966 after Joe Bonanno's return and reclamation of the leadership.

DiGregorio, who was already ill, was summoned to give evidence before a New York grand jury and had a heart attack. DiGregorio's career in La Cosa Nostra* ended, but so had Joseph Bonanno's, who was removed from his seat on the Commission* and forced into retirement in Tuscon, Arizona.

SUGGESTED READING: Gay Talese, *Honor Thy Father*. 1971.

DIO, JOHNNY. (b. John Dioguardi, 1914, New York City—d. Jan. 16, 1979, federal hospital facility, PA). Labor racketeer.

In 1956, crusading New York journalist Victor Riesel,* who wrote about labor and trade union affairs, was blinded by acid in a vicious attack. Riesel had been criticizing Jimmy Hoffa's* shadowy connections with underworld figures in his newspaper column when two men assaulted him in the street. The attack on Riesel, which left him permanently disabled, had allegedly been ordered by Johnny Dio of the Luchese crime family.*

Dio began his criminal career in Murder, Inc.,* under the tutelage of Louis Buchalter* and Jacob "Gurrah" Shapiro.* By the age of 24 he had become a capo* in the Luchese crime family and a specialist in labor racketeering; his technique was simple and crude but effective: instill fear in everyone; even when he spoke politely, it could bruise and intimidate others.

Knowledge of Dio's ability to manipulate unions and businesspeople spread widely in the underworld, and Dio was sought out by Jack Dragna* in Los Angeles for advice on how to terrorize locals of the International Ladies Garment Workers Union so that mob business could operate "sweatshops" without fear of union protests.

Trucking and textiles were not the only areas in which Johnny Dio exercised his skills. In the 1960s he became involved in meat wholesaling and attempted to gain control of Iowa Beef, which had contracts with fast-food businesses such as McDonald's and Burger King.

He was finally convicted in 1973 on a stock fraud charge and sentenced to 15 years in prison. He died in 1979, completely forgotten.

SUGGESTED READING: Jonathan Kwitny, *The Mafia in the Marketplace*. 1997.

DOMINICAN DRUG TRAFFICKING. With Cubans entering Florida in large numbers in the 1970s, and with tumultuous political conditions in many Central

American countries including Mexico, Nicaragua, Guatemala, and El Salvador pushing thousands of impoverished peasants and urban slum dwellers into the migratory streams flowing into the United States, hundreds of thousands of Dominicans overwhelmed the Washington Heights section of New York City in the 1980s. They, too, were fleeing from the grinding poverty of their Caribbean island, hoping for a chance of a better life in America.

Washington Heights was a quiet, working-class neighborhood three decades ago, unlike Harlem and other economically depressed communities in northern Manhattan. The arrival of Dominican immigrants (legal and illegal) dramatically transformed this community that thrives in the shadow of the Washington Bridge, which spans the Hudson River and connects New York City to the rest of the country.

But the wealth of the community is not just testimony to the hard work and determination of the newcomers; prosperity is also tangible proof that crime often pays: The cocaine trade is alive and well in Washington Heights. It is difficult to hide the fact that Washington Heights is one of the busiest drug trafficking markets in the entire country and that the Dominican gangs are at the center of the cocaine distribution network in the northeastern states.

"Mules" (drug couriers) working for the Colombian drug cartels* haul the cocaine north to the wholesale markets the Dominicans operate in New York City, where drug dealers from every ethnic group obtain supplies to meet the demand for crack in the streets of Philadelphia, Boston, Providence, Hartford, Newark, and many other cities in New Jersey, Connecticut, Massachusetts, New York, Pennsylvania, and Delaware.

Drug dealing is a business that leaves palpable evidence of its presence in any community. The obvious clues are violence, corruption, and homicides as the competition for markets becomes fierce. Washington Heights is no exception: Homicides in the local police precinct that covers the community rose dramatically from 57 per year to 122 in 1992; in 1994, more than two dozen police officers were arrested on a variety of charges connected with Dominican drug trafficking.

The drug economy of the community is the largest employer of young men and has effects on local retail business. Many of the neighborhood bodegas (small grocery stores) function as laundering operations and fronts for drug sales.

The drug underworld in Dominican neighborhoods is not organized in ways familiar from experience with La Cosa Nostra* or Sicilian Mafia operations. For example, many of the gangs have no leadership hierarchies with a "boss" perched at the top of the pyramid. It appears that every local drug network has its own power structure.

Several factors played a part in creating the Dominican drug trade. In terms of its political economic status, the Dominican Republic, which shares the island of Hispaniola with the wretchedly poor nation of Haiti, is itself crippled by poverty and corruption. Second only to Haiti, it is the poorest country in the Western Hemisphere, with an average income per person slightly more than

$1,000 a year. High-ranking government employees, including army officers, earn minimum wages, which makes them vulnerable to corruption by the drug traffickers. For decades the Dominican government was subject to civil wars, coup d'états, crooked elections, and military dictatorships. When Rafael Trujillo, who ruled the country for 30 years, was overthrown in 1961, his successor, Joaquin Balaguer, brought about no reforms but ruled to plunder the country for the benefit of his ruling-class supporters. The fervent hope of the beleaguered Dominican who is not born to privilege is for a better life in the United States. Thus, over the past decade the legal and illegal immigration of Dominicans to the United States has been a torrent of people finding any means, however perilous, to get out. Estimates put the total of Dominican immigrants at 500,000; they settled in Queens, Brooklyn, Washington Heights, Paterson, New Jersey, and Lawrence, Massachusetts. With so many illegals, their gravitation into the drug trade was inevitable, as so many of them arrived in the United States at the height of the popularity of cocaine; the Colombian cartels also needed trustworthy partners to get their drugs on to the streets.

For the Colombian drug traffickers the situation in the streets of American cities was volatile and very risky for retail operations. In the 1970s the Medellín cartel took over the cocaine trade in south Florida by waging war against the Cuban traffickers; by the mid-1980s, the Cali cocaine cartel* had secured New York as a wholesale cocaine racket, concentrating on importing bulk shipments and relying on the Dominicans to handle distribution. As their connections with the Colombians consolidated around profits, many Dominican criminals graduated from retail street dealing to wholesale distribution, acting as middlemen between the Colombians and other ethnic groups. Soon, Washington Heights became a major drug outlet serving the tristate area. Entire streets were lost to drug gang activity; in some buildings, dozens of apartments would be under the control of a drug gang, with various dwellings assigned different purposes: storage of drugs, a weapons cache, money counting, or drug transactions with buyers. Many facilities were equipped with state-of-the-art electronic devices to provide early warning of drug raids and secure safes for cash and weapons. As the Dominican drug gangs amass wealth and power, there are no signs of its underworld declining. *See also* COLOMBIAN DRUG CARTELS; DRUG TRAFFICKING AND ORGANIZED CRIME; JHERI-CURL GANG; WILD COMBOYS

**SUGGESTED READING:** James Inciardi, *Handbooks of Drug Control in the United States.* 1990.

**DON.** *See* BOSS (DON)

**DRAGNA, JACK.** ("Antonio Rizzoti") (b. 1891, Coreleone, Sicily—d. 1957, Los Angeles, CA). Los Angeles crime family boss.

Law enforcement officials would sarcastically refer to Jack Dragna as the "Al

Capone of L.A." and his organization as the "Mickey Mouse Mafia." For most of his career, Jack Dragna was upstaged by Chicago-based gangsters like Mickey Cohen* and John Roselli* or "Bugsy" Siegel* from New York. And when Las Vegas, Nevada,* inaugurated casino operations, Dragna failed to establish a foothold there even though he was friendly with Gaetano Luchese* and Joseph Profaci*—powerful mafia bosses in New York.

Dragna was a parochial, old-country Sicilian who had come permanently to America at the age of 23. To be fair, his capacity to establish a solid mafia crime family in the Los Angeles area was blunted by the absence of a real city government. With no political machine in place, he had few politicians to corrupt. Racketeering in the movie industry was firmly in the grip of Chicago and New York gangsters who were unwilling to share the wealth the movie industry generated. On many occasions, Dragna appealed to Meyer Lansky* and others in Chicago for a piece of the Las Vegas and Hollywood action, but to no avail. Indeed, the repeated failed attempts on Mickey Cohen's life relegated Dragna and his crew to third-rate status, and they were not to be taken seriously. His incompetence was also apparent in dealings with Meyer Lansky. According to Jimmy "The Weasel" Fratianno,* who would become, briefly, the acting boss of the Los Angeles family, Dragna personally assaulted Joseph Stacher,* a Lansky partner in Las Vegas, in order to persuade Lansky that Dragna wanted a piece of the Las Vegas action. Lansky agreed for a price—$125,000—which Dragna could not obtain. Dragna was thereafter ignored.

After his death in 1957, a succession of bosses followed who, like Dragna, appeared passive and benign. In the late 1970s Louis Dragna, the nephew of Jack, served as acting boss while Dominick Brooklier,* the sitting boss, served a prison term. Louis Dragna was convicted in 1980 on extortion of bookmakers and pornographers and, after serving a two-year sentence, drifted off into obscurity as a small-time dress manufacturer.

**SUGGESTED READING:** Ovid Demaris, *The Last Mafioso: The Treacherous World of Jimmy Fratiano.* 1985.

**DRUG TRAFFICKING AND ORGANIZED CRIME.** Drug trafficking is the most serious organized crime problem in the world today. The drug trade, according to major government and research organization studies, was estimated in 1994 at nearly $350 billion per year and imposes incalculable costs on individuals, families, communities, and governments worldwide. According to the President's Commission on Organized Crime study of drug trafficking (*America's Habit* [1986]), it is the primary activity of organized crime groups nationwide. Drug trafficking accounts for almost 40 percent of all organized crime activity across the country and generates not only huge profits for dealers but a great deal of violence as well. The menace of drugs is no longer restricted to a particular segment of society but is now of such a scope and severity that it is a threat to our national security and is, therefore, a legitimate national security issue.

The crime families* of La Cosa Nostra* as well as an array of more recently identified groups such as the Sicilian Mafia, outlaw motorcycle gangs,* Colombian drug cartels,* Dominican drug trafficking* groups, Chinese Triads,* and African American street gangs are involved in the illicit drug market. While the LCN has historically been involved in narcotics trafficking, newer organizations, in many ways quite different from the LCN, now play a major role in the drug trade. Generally, these newer groups develop solely around drug trafficking operations and are activity specific, dependent only on drug-related criminal activity for income. These groups from Latin America, Africa (Nigeria), the Caribbean, and Asia are more fluidly organized than LCN and are not as self-contained but are marked by a degree of violence and corruption unsurpassed by any other criminal activity.

Organized crime groups involved in drug trafficking, however, share some common features irrespective of their ethnic composition, global region, or particular illicit product. All contain a core criminal group and a specialized criminal support designed to facilitate illicit activity.

Despite denials by organized crime figures that they issued edicts against drug dealing in 1948, 1957, and 1960, these were largely ignored. In his autobiography, Joseph Bonanno,* head of the Bonanno crime family* of the LCN, reported that some activities were considered out of bounds: "I do not tolerate any dealings in . . . narcotics" (Bonanno and Lalli, *A Man of Honor*. 1983, p. 130). Yet officials of the Bureau of Narcotics testified in 1964 before the Senate Permanent Subcommittee on Investigation that "95 percent of the heroin smuggled into the United States since World War II has been controlled by Mafia gangsters" (p. 56).

Because drug trafficking and abuse are the most serious organized crime problems in America today, they need to be addressed at the highest levels of government where interdiction strategies and demand reduction policies are formulated, where resources are generated and disseminated to control and treatment agencies. Precisely what strategies are effective—whether it is supply curtailment in source countries or the demand for drugs in the United States—are hotly debated issues that have not been settled. The illicit trafficking can be attacked in several ways. The basic aim of enforcement activities is to immobilize or destroy the trafficking networks. In the past, enforcement agencies tended to view this problem as getting "Mr. Big"—arresting and convicting the upper-level leadership of trafficking organizations, the kingpins like Pablo Emilio Gavoroa Escobar* Jorge Luis Vasquez Ochoa,* Leory "Nicky" Barnes,* Gene Gotti, Gaetano Baldalementi, and Tommaso Buscetta,* who, it was assumed, controlled an organization's capacity to distribute drugs. If such persons could be arrested and eventually imprisoned, the network would fall apart.

More recently, the law enforcement community has become less certain that this strategy can succeed. Actually, as the record shows, even when "Mr. Big" is in prison, he can continue to manage the distribution of drugs. Moreover, and more important, the drug traffickers seem less dependent on the influence of single individuals than enforcement officials once assumed. Finally, the whole drug distribution system is less centralized than was once assumed. Relatively small and impermanent organizations—freelance entrepreneurs—supply a large proportion of illicit drugs.

To deal with decentralization, enforcement aims have shifted from stopping individual dealers to destroying whole networks. Federal investigators have been granted special powers to seize drug dealer assets, including boats, cars, planes, houses, bank accounts, and cash.

The main problem with attacking illicit trafficking organizations is that it is enormously expensive. Convincing evidence can be produced only through sustained efforts to recruit informants, establish electronic surveillance, and infiltrate undercover agents. *See also* AFRICAN AMERICAN ORGANIZED CRIME; ASIAN ORGANIZED CRIME; COLOMBIAN DRUG CARTELS; DOMINICAN DRUG TRAFFICKING; MATTHEWS, FRANK; MEXICAN ORGANIZED CRIME IN THE UNITED STATES; PIZZA CONNECTION

**SUGGESTED READINGS:** Joseph Bonanno and Sergio Lalli, *A Man of Honor: The Autobiography of Joseph Bonanno.* 1983; President's Commission on Organized Crime, *America's Habit: Drug Abuse, Drug Trafficking, and Organized Crime.* 1986; Senate Committee on Governmental Affairs, *Organized Crime and Illicit Traffic in Narcotics.* 1965.

# E

**EASTMAN, MONK.** (b. Edward Osterman, 1873, Brooklyn, NY—d. Dec. 20, 1920, Manhattan, NY). Leader of the Eastman gang in New York City.

A fearsome-looking character with numerous knife scars on his face, cauliflower ears from head battering, an unkempt appearance, always carrying a truncheon, Monk Eastman ruled an assortment of Jewish gangs in Manhattan's Lower East Side at the turn of the century. He operated brothels and engaged in extortion among street vendors, and he maintained close ties with Tammany Hall political leaders, who utilized his gangs during election campaigns. His protection rackets became a prototype for the kind of extortion schemes that became standard criminal methods for other immigrant gangsters throughout the twentieth century. He was among the first of the city's gangsters and racketeers to supply violence and muscle to both trade unions and employers in the labor struggles in various industries.

The political connections of street brawlers like Eastman are indeed interesting. At the election polls, Eastman's gangs supplied repeat voters and were quite persuasive at intimidating citizens. For such services, public officials allowed gang-sponsored rackets in various communities.

It was with the Eastman gang that Louis Buchalter* learned the arts of criminal violence that he would later employ with great skill in the garment industry.

In 1904, Eastman killed a Pinkerton detective and served a ten-year prison sentence in Sing Sing. When released, his power was gone; he enlisted in the army during World War I, served honorably in France, and returned to his old ways. In a failed shakedown with a bootlegger* in 1920, he was killed. *See also* KELLY, PAUL; ROTHSTEIN, ARNOLD "THE BRAIN"

**SUGGESTED READINGS:** Herbert Asbury, *The Gangs of New York.* 1927; Jenna Joselit, *Our Gang: Jewish Crime and the New York Jewish Community.* 1983.

**ECOCRIME.** The environment and organized crime.

Ecological crime is organized crime that results in major harm to the environment. It is a threat to the quality of life in North America and Europe and is particularly devastating in many developing regions of the world. In northeast and southeast Asia, Latin America, and Africa, criminal elements are flouting environmental protocols, agreements, and concerns; dumping waste and hazardous materials; and illegally destroying rain forests for profit or trafficking in endangered species.

The profits from environmental organized crime are not as large as those from drug trafficking, but they are substantial. Trafficking in hazardous materials that may be radioactive is very profitable, but it can have grave health consequences. Illegal trade in endangered species results in ecological damage and undermines biodiversity. Atmospheric damage from illegal timber harvesting has outcomes beyond the immediate destruction of a local area. And long-term damage occurs when toxic wastes are indiscriminately dumped without proper chemical controls.

In the developed world, the focus of ecological crime now is primarily in two areas: the disposal of trash and hazardous waste and the importation of products of endangered species. Organized crime groups based in developed countries either dispose of wastes illegally within their own countries or ship the materials overseas, usually to less developed nations. Trafficking in CFCs (chlorofluorocarbons) is probably the second largest illicit import into the United States after drugs.

In the developing world, ecocrime is often a major source of income, particularly in commodities that are regulated by international agreements. Overfishing of sturgeon in the Caspian Sea and illegal harvesting of teak (a rare hardwood tree) in Southeast Asia are examples of this phenomenon. The Russian "timber mafias" in the Far East, in Siberia and Pacific Russia, arrange for the purchase and delivery of expensive wood products in Asia.

The ecological crime groups tend to operate with the same methods that organized crime groups use in vice businesses. They have not hesitated to use violence against officials who try to combat smuggling rings or illegal waste disposal activities. Officials of state environmental commissions and agencies in the United States have been threatened by domestic crime groups, and law enforcers who challenge the La Cosa Nostra's* hold on garbage disposal in New York have been brutally attacked.

Environmental crime is rarely integrated into discussions of organized crime. While many environmental groups have published extensive reports on the general problem of environment degradation, systematic studies on the costs of organized criminality in this area have not been a focus of research. Moreover, many law enforcement agencies lack specifically trained personnel with the requisite expertise in environmental crime.

**SUGGESTED READING:** Frank Scarpitti and Alan A. Block, "America's Toxic Waste Racket: Dimensions of the Environmental, Crises," in *Organized Crime in America*, ed. T. Bynum. 1987.

**EGAN'S RATS.** St. Louis, Missouri, Prohibition mob.

During Prohibition (see PROHIBITION AND ORGANIZED CRIME*), Egan's Rats emerged as the most powerful gang in St. Louis, Missouri. The Rats were linked to the Purple Gang* of Detroit and in Chicago with Alphonse Capone* and his huge bootlegging empire.

The gang was founded at the turn of the century by "Jellyroll" Egan, whose small army of street thugs specialized in strikebreaking activities. After World War I, bootlegging became the main criminal enterprise, with the irony that roles were reversed for gang members: Now, they paid the police and politicians for protection, whereas before the Volstead Act (Eighteenth Amendment, which brought about Prohibition), the gang earned its living off businessmen and their political cronies.

There is speculation that Capone used some members of the gang in handling delicate Chicago problems. Leo Brothers, an Egan Rat, may have been the killer of Capone's newspaper connection "Jake" Lingle,* who, it was discovered, was informing on the Chicago gang's operations.

Repeal of Prohibition effectively ended the gang's criminal activities. Egan's Rats could not make adjustments to the post-Prohibition world. The successor to Egan, Dinty Colbeck, was assassinated in the 1930s when other criminal elements feared a revival of the gang's activities.

**SUGGESTED READING:** Dennis J. Kenney and James O. Finckenauer, *Organized Crime in America.* 1995.

**EL RUKNS.** One of the largest and most powerful African American organized criminal groups in the Chicago area has been El Rukns, a group that openly and contemptuously defied the Chicago mafia known as the Chicago Outfit.* El Rukns has been accused of narcotics dealing and assorted extortions and shake-downs in its communities. It evolved out of a street gang, the Blackstone Rang-ers, and has participated actively in local political campaigns. The group has even petitioned for status as a nonprofit charity organization while its key leaders are under indictment or imprisoned. This gang of toughened street youths, now adult, although engaging in serious crime, also worked within the ghetto to help the indigent. Mafia organizations have done the same thing; they simultaneously exploit and help, but always to their advantage. *See also* AFRICAN AMERI-CAN ORGANIZED CRIME; FORT, JEFF

**SUGGESTED READING:** Howard Abadinsky, *Organized Crime*, 5th ed. 1997.

**ENG, JOHNNY.** ("Onionhead") (b. 1951, Hong Kong—   ). Leader of the Fly-ing Dragons, drug trafficker.

Johnny Eng is a squat man with a fiery temper and a gangster's flare for expensive clothing and fancy jewelry. With new opportunities for heroin smug-gling attracting Chinese smugglers, a conflict emerged within the Hip Sing Tong and Flying Dragons, the enforcement arm of the Tong.* In the 1980s, police pressure and casino gambling in Atlantic City, New Jersey,* forced many Chinatown gambling houses to close. The heroin market was just waiting to be tapped. Drugs were nothing new to Chinatown: Tongs had been smuggling opium into American Chinatowns since the 1800s. From Hong Kong the Chinese Triads* were moving it into the country, and the mafia was buying it up. Anyone prepared to function as a middleman stood to make a fortune. Under the leader Michael Chen, who had no stomach for drugs, Johnny Eng was eager to jump into the business. In scenes reminiscent of Alphonse Capone* and Johnny Torrio* plotting against their boss Big Jim Colosimo, who refused to get involved in bootlegging, Eng had to remove Chen, who was an obstacle. Chen was found murdered in early 1983.

"Onionhead" thrived in the drug business. By the mid-1980s, Triad heroin flooded New York's ghettos, with most gangs and criminal Tong members involved in the trade. Eng emerged as the dai lo the top leader of the Flying Dragons. In May 1988, federal authorities indicted Eng on drug trafficking charges. In another case, he was charged with importing 186 pounds of heroin from Hong Kong into Boston, concealed in a bean sprout machine especially equipped to hide drugs. Soon after the discovery by police, Eng fled to Hong Kong, where he was arrested and extradited to the United States in October 1991. In September 1993, Johnny Eng was sentenced to 25 years in prison.

**SUGGESTED READING:** Ko-lin Chin, *Chinatown Gangs: Extortion, Enterprise, and Ethnicity.* 1996.


**ESCOBAR, PABLO EMILIO GAVOROA.** ("The Godfather") (b. Dec. 1, 1949, Rionegro, Colombia—d. Dec. 2, 1993, Colombia). Founder of the Medellín drug cartel.

In December 1993, Pablo Escobar, leader of the Medellín Colombian drug cartel,* was killed in a shootout with police officers. He had escaped from a prison he had built to ensure his own safety and comfort prior to surrendering to authorities on drug trafficking charges. Dissatisfied with prison restrictions, Escobar escaped and was the subject of a countrywide manhunt that ended with his death.

One of the most powerful drug traffickers in the world, heading an organization capable of manipulating the national state through bribes and intimidation, Pablo Escobar and his cartel partners operated a government within a government in Colombia during the 1970s and 1980s.

Physically unimposing, Pablo Escobar was a short man, overweight, with a mustache and a shock of black, curly hair. He was not born in abject poverty, nor was he as underprivileged as his apologists and image-makers suggested. He in fact graduated from high school and had some university training.

His criminal career began in adolescence when he stole headstones from local graveyards and engaged in stealing and fencing (illegal resale) of stereo equipment and auto parts. He was first arrested in 1974 on auto theft, and it was not until 1976 that Escobar was arrested on drug smuggling charges. He would later emerge during the marijuana smuggling days of the late 1970s with a reputation in the Medellín underworld not only as a cold-blooded killer but also as a master schemer and evader of justice.

Pablo Escobar was only one of Colombia's many cocaine traffickers who expanded their operations in the late 1970s. The men who became the leaders and biggest allies of the Medellín cartel were, like Escobar, all born between 1947 and 1949 during a chaotic political period in Colombia's history; Jorge Luis Vasquez Ochoa,* José Gonzalo Rodriguez Gacha,* and Carlos Lehder-Rivas* would come together to create one of the world's most powerful drug trafficking syndicates. Escobar's involvement as a cocaine trafficker occurred when he began as a middleman, obtaining small amounts of coca paste from Ecuador and selling it within Colombia. Then, after buying it from newly established laboratories in the Colombian Amazon that converted the paste into cocaine, he started to employ "mules" (couriers) who moved it to traffickers in Panama. In order to earn serious money, Escobar had to make the business vertical: He needed enough money to buy bulk direct from Bolivia and Peru, and he needed enough access to consumer markets abroad. Mustering up the cash brought him into partnerships with the Ochoa brothers, whose high-society links ensured a ready supply of investors (Figure 6).

Marijuana smuggling was such that many American groups could deal directly with suppliers in Mexico, Panama, Colombia, and the Caribbean basin islands like Jamaica. With cocaine, Americans never had a chance. They were too far away from its source and, aided by the sudden boost of Latin American migration during the 1970s, the Colombians were already developing their own U.S. distribution networks among Cubans and Dominicans. Escobar's first priority was to gather enough capital in order to impact Bolivian and Peruvian coca paste himself—Colombian coca leaf was as yet too low a quality—and to create cocaine in his own laboratories. By the mid-1970s, his criminal activities in car theft, kidnapping, fencing stolen goods, and drug trafficking yielded sufficient profits to establish his own labs and smuggling routes.

The cartel dramatically improved its capacity to move cocaine into the United States when Carlos Lehder bought Norman's Cay, an archipelago in the Bahamas. Lehder equipped the narrow strip of coral reef with electronic equipment and airport facilities for the transport of cocaine. Larger shipments of cocaine began to make their way into the Florida Everglades and locations in the Southwest via Mexico. To operate with minimum interference from authorities, Escobar and Lehder paid bribes to Lynden Pindling, the governor-general of the Bahamas, and Panama's dictator, Manuel Noriega.

Like other Colombian traffickers, Escobar poured his money into land and buildings. Construction in Medellín quadrupled in the 1980s with money from the cartel drug mafia. Escobar's pride and joy was his 8,000-acre ranch equipped with five swimming pools, man-made lakes, a jet aircraft runway, and animal

**Figure 6**
**A Cocaine Collaboration: The Ochos/Escobar Joint Venture**

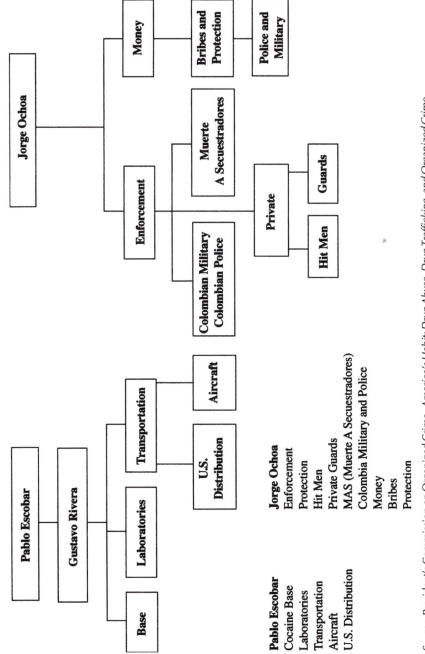

*Source:* President's Commission on Organized Crime, *America's Habit: Drug Abuse, Drug Trafficking, and Organized Crime.* Washington, D.C.: U.S. Government Printing Office, April 1986.

parks and zoos accommodating elephants, lions, buffaloes, zebras, rhinoceroses, and hippopotamuses. The clever Escobar used his zoo animals in his smuggling operations very effectively: Animal dung masked the smell of contraband cocaine.

Along with growing political pressure from the United States, internal unrest in Colombia created serious threats to Escobar's drug empire in the late 1980s. Cocaine and its derivative "crack" saturated American cities, and the outcry that Colombia stop the trade mounted steadily; within the country, competition and violence among narcotraffickers was heightened by left-wing and Communist terrorists such as M-19 and FARC (Revolutionary Armed Forces of Colombia), who demanded either ransom for kidnapped cartel members or a share of the drug profits.

Escobar would have none of it. He mobilized his enforcement squads, and the Medellín mafia declared war on the guerrillas. Dozens of top Colombian cocaine traffickers—including those from Cali, Medellín's chief competitor—gathered to develop a strategy of resistance. One Sunday in early December 1981, the cartels bared their teeth. At a soccer match in Cali, leaflets fluttered down from a small aircraft announcing the formation of Muerte a Secuestradores (Death to the Kidnappers). The leaflet indicated that Colombian "businessmen" had formed a defense group against the kidnappers, who would be subject to immediate execution and hung from trees in public parks. Within two months assassins killed dozens of M-19 leaders and militants; other guerrillas were turned over to Colombian security forces. The kidnap threat ended in 1982.

Escobar's problems were not over, however. The pressure from the United States increased on the Colombian government for his extradition on drug trafficking charges. Many within the cartels thought that Escobar could be a sacrificial lamb to appease the Americans and relax the pressure on the government and the mafias. "The Godfather" had a different approach to the problem: He arranged for an attack on the Ministry of Justice, where his hit men sought out judges who were marked for death and proceeded to destroy incriminating files. With his private army of 1,000 men, Escobar could easily kill rivals, politicians, police, and informers. During the struggle with the government it is estimated that he was responsible for 400 deaths. Extradition on drug charges to the United States would become an irrelevant issue for the likes of Escobar.

In 1988, an attempt was made on Escobar's life by the Cali cartel. The "War of the Cartels" ended shortly thereafter with 80 people murdered, more than 60 from Cali. Escobar had much to defend. He put together a highly sophisticated operation with its own security force, air network, export outlets, mechanics, chemists, and hit men. The trafficking network operated across the United States and Canada and was making inroads in Europe through the Sicilian Mafia. In 1988, when Escobar faced threats from the government and drug competitors, the Medellín cartel was taking in $10 billion a year.

The Colombian government faced a dilemma with traffickers as powerful as

Escobar. The U.S. government demanded their extradition, and the traffickers insisted that Colombia assert its independence and ignore American pressure. Bribes, threats, election frauds, and other forms of intimidation persuaded the Colombians to decide to punish their own and not extradite cartel bosses. Escobar acceded to government decisions and surrendered on condition that he build his own jail.

In late November 1993, Escobar escaped from the prison facility he built and was shot dead on December 2, 1993, in a fire fight with police and army units. There were indications in the press that members of the rival Cali cartel helped police locate Escobar. The question facing Colombians who had experienced most directly the ravages of the drug trade as well as Americans, many of whose people suffer greatly from cocaine and crack, is whether the elimination or incarceration of the leaders of criminal organizations are enough to frustrate narcotics trafficking. So far, the evidence suggests that a kingpin strategy focused on the leaders has not dramatically affected the availability of cocaine on the streets of American cities.

**SUGGESTED READINGS:** Guy Gugliotta and Jeff Leen, *Kings of Cocaine*. 1989; Simon Strong, *Whitewash*. 1996.

**ETHNIC SUCCESSION.** The ethnic component of organized crime.

For many individuals, organized crime operates as a ladder of social mobility and advancement in America. Social history documents the successive movement of a number of ethnic groups in and out of organized crime. Cut off from socially acceptable routes out of poverty, powerless in the ghetto, some ethnic youngsters learn on the streets of those ghettos that crime offers a quick, if perilous, way out. Ethnic succession is part of the American social process by which some members of minority groups struggle for a place in society and, as new and more socially acceptable avenues of mobility and advancement open, move on, into respectability.

Daniel Bell, a prominent American social scientist, described ethnic succession as the transfer from one wave of immigrants to another a "queer ladder of social mobility" that has organized crime as its first few rungs of the means of escape from the slums. The Irish came first, and they formed street gangs with colorful names like the "Bowery Boys" and "O'Connell's Guards" and eventually came to dominate crime as well as big-city politics at the beginning of the twentieth century. As they came to control the politics of the inner cities of large metropolitan areas, where they settled in great numbers, the Irish immigrant population achieved respectability and acquired wealth in construction work, trucking, and public utilities as well as on the waterfront. By the 1920s with the era of Prohibition and speculation in the money markets and real estate, the Irish were being replaced in organized crime by Jews. Arnold "The Brain" Rothstein,* Louis Buchalter,* Jacob "Gurrah" Shapiro,* and Meyer Lansky* participated in gambling and labor racketeering for over a decade. The Italians came next, and La Cosa Nostra* emerged as the most powerful type of organized criminal activity in the United States to this day.

It is important to emphasize that the great bulk of immigrants to the United States, who came from every corner of Europe, Latin America, Asia, and Africa, made their way into the American mainstream and middle-class legitimately through hard work, thrift, and an honest way of life. While virtually every race and ethnic background is represented within the ranks of organized crime, it is the image of the Italian gangster that has come to embody the popular perception of organized crime because they have prevailed for so long. Italian dominance in organized crime cannot be adequately explained by ethnic succession alone; the tight kinship structures and communal attitudes of southern Italians created a sense of group loyalty and solidarity along with a suspicion of outsiders, which was especially useful in criminal activity where silence and loyalty to the group are crucial for survival.

Ethnic succession is a perspective about organized crime that predicts other, "nontraditional" groups rising to power in the criminal underworld. According to the thesis that groups of successive immigrants experience difficulties in making social adjustments to a new and inhospitable environment, to which some newcomers react by innovative activity (crime), the rise of Russian, Chinese, and Latino groups is consistent with the perspective's predictions. Those who became involved in organized crime are not necessarily abnormal or committed to a deviant subculture but are merely using available, albeit illegal, opportunities to achieve economic success.

**SUGGESTED READINGS:** Daniel Bell, "Crime as an American Way of Life," in *The Crime Society*, ed. Francis A. J. Ianni. 1973; Francis A. J. Ianni, *Black Mafia: Ethnic Succession in Organized Crime*. 1974.

**EXTORTION.** Extortion is an offense regarded by many scholars and law enforcement officials as the essence of the culture of organized crime. It is the obtaining of property or objects of value, including money, from another using future threats of force, intimidation, physical injury, and/or property damage.

Extortion is not robbery; it may be distinguished from robbery in that robbery is theft using threats of immediate harm or injury. A robber usually has a weapon or makes threats of harm to a person (the victim) that accompany an actual theft of goods, money, or property.

If a citizen has something that criminals want—a business, for example—then a confrontation may be forced to surrender the business through threats of violence, disruption of the business's functioning, and so on. Chinese street gangs have been especially adroit at forcing tribute from businesspeople in the communities in which they operate, from taking free meals in restaurants to weekly payoffs from merchants under the threat of violence.

**SUGGESTED READING:** Stephen Fox, *Blood and Power: Organized Crime in Twentieth Century America*. 1989.

# F

**FENCING.** Fencing is the illegal processing of the proceeds of property crimes. It is a service industry connected with the underworld of thieves, robbers, and burglars who commit hijackings or crack safes in homes, rob jewelry stores, hold up trucks, and so on, and then take their stolen goods to a "fence" who has the capability and connections to store the goods and/or sell them off to willing buyers. For a percentage of the retail value of the goods, the fence agrees to serve as a middleman, to move the stolen property from the thieves' hands to someone willing to pay, usually in cash, a reduced price for stolen merchandise. Or a fence may funnel stolen goods to mob-run legitimate businesses, which will inconspicuously mix the stolen goods with legitimate goods. The unknowing consumer pays retail prices for stolen property, and the huge markup goes to organized crime.

**SUGGESTED READING:** Carl B. Klockars, *The Professional Fence.* 1974.

**FERRO, VITO CASCIO** ("Don Vito") (b. 1862, Bisaquino, Sicily—d. 1932, Ucciardone Prison, Palermo, Sicily). Capo di tutti capi (boss of bosses) of the Sicilian Mafia.

Vito Cascio Ferro was head of the Sicilian cosche (groups) around Palermo in the late nineteenth century. In 1900 he went to the United States and became one of the major exponents of La Mano Nera (The Black Hand*). But he was expelled from America after he left New York City and fled to New Orleans to escape police, who suspected him in a murder in the Harlem section of New York. Back in Sicily, he resumed his ordinary criminal activities involving counterfeiting and extortion of the latifundi as (large agricultural estates) and retail commercial markets in Palermo.

In 1909, the tall, distinguished-looking, scholarly Don Vito established his reputation as Sicily's greatest mafia capo* (chief) with the murder of New York police detective Joseph Petrosino,* who happened to be in Palermo searching police files for mafiosi who had emigrated to America. In 1927, Don Vito, who considered the United States a land of unlimited criminal opportunities, sent Salvatore Maranzano* to the United States so that he could evade Mussolini's antimafia campaign and organize the quarrelsome mafiosi in New York under one single leadership. Before that could be accomplished, however, Cascio Ferro was arrested in 1929 by the Fascist government, whose antimafia police chief Cesare Mori may have manufactured the evidence to convict the mafia boss. Don Vito was sent to the Ucciardone Prison in Palermo, where he died of natural causes in 1932.

In the United States, Maranzano was suddenly on his own and was unsuccessful in his efforts to wear the crown of "Boss of all bosses." He was murdered by the Americanized mafiosi he was sent to discipline.

**SUGGESTED READING:** Pino Arlacchi, *Mafia Business*. 1986.

**FIXER.** In many corrupted urban political machines the role of the fixer is vital for maintaining the smooth functioning of the system. The police, the politicians, the local business elite, and organized crime cannot be seen in open contact with each other, so another party who appears independent of each of these elements becomes the linchpin, the individual who can interact with each group without arousing too much suspicion. The fixer is like a thumb, able to touch the other fingers on a hand, enabling it to function. He (or she) is technically independent of government, an attorney in private practice, perhaps, who is intimately knowledgeable about the law enforcement community, the district attorney's office, the courts, the leading business groups and entrepreneurs in the community, and the organized crime bosses with vested interests in all sectors of the local society's power structure.

In New York during the 1930s, Jimmy Hines,* the head of the Democratic Party machine in Bronx County, New York City, functioned as an influential fixer and go-between for the Dutch Schultz* mob, the police, and the Democratic Party, which dominated the city's politics. In Louisiana, Carlos Marcello* a New Orleans La Cosa Nostra* boss, utilized local attorneys to arrange graft, bribes, contributions to political campaigns, and secret business ventures. Sometimes a gangster will clean up his image and mix in with legitimate society, as in the case of Frank Costello,* known in the mafia crime scene as the "Prime Minister of the Underworld." The public image of Costello was that of a philanthropist and charity organizer with powerful connections in politics and the judicial system. Over time many judges and politicians would owe their careers to Costello's influence. That influence (known as "juice") was used to secure court appointments of jurists and swing elections on behalf of mob-friendly political figures. For any durable crime organization, a fixer is a vital activity for the organization's security.

SUGGESTED READING: Donald R. Cressy, *Theft of the Nation: The Structure and Operations of Organized Crime in America.* 1969.

**FONG, JOE.** (b. 1955, Macao—    ). Founder of the Joe Boys San Francisco gang.

As with many Chinese gang members, Joe Fong was born in the slums of a large Asian city and found difficulty in adjusting to the new world in the United States. On Labor Day weekend (September 4, 1977) at 2:40 A.M., three masked gunmen of the Joe Boys gang entered the Golden Dragon restaurant and killed 5 persons and wounded 15. None of the victims were members of rival gangs. The gruesome episode took one minute; the killers used a sawed-off shotgun, .38 caliber pistols, and .45 caliber semiautomatic rifles known as "grease guns" because of their rapid fire. The speculation at the time was that the Joe Boys were hunting their rivals the Wah Ching (Chinese Youth). The massacre was set up by Joe Fong, head of the Joe Boys, in retaliation for an attack on three of his gang members on July 4 in San Francisco's Chinatown. In that incident 1 Joe Boy was shot dead and 2 others wounded.

When he arrived in the United States, Joe Fong and his brother Glen, who were "FOBs" (Fresh off the Boats), banded together with other immigrant youths to form a gang that was independent, with no Tong* affiliation. That caused trouble. The Chinatown communities of San Francisco and New York City are built upon a complex system of overlapping businesses and criminal corruption that binds businesspeople, district associations, and Tongs to the establishment.

By staying independent and not attaching his gang as a paramilitary enforcement group to a Tong, Joe Fong became a loose cannon who defied tradition much like Joseph Gallo* in New York City's La Cosa Nostra* families.

The Joe Boys survived numerous shootouts in the streets of San Francisco and developed skills in extortion of businesses by creating a flexible organizational structure for their 200 members. The gang was divided into cells, with each operating independently in areas within the larger geography controlled by the group. The average age of these street racketeers at the height of their power was 18 years old.

After the Golden Dragon bloodbath, Joe Fong and his lieutenants were arrested, and the gang was all but finished. *See also* ASIAN ORGANIZED CRIME; TONGS

SUGGESTED READING: Ko-lin Chin, *Chinese Subculture and Criminality: Non-Traditional Crime Groups in America.* 1990.

**FORT, JEFF.** (b. 1947, Mississippi—    ). Leader of a Chicago African American criminal organization.

Throughout the 1980s, El Rukns* was the major African American crime group in Chicago. It began as a coalition of street gangs formed by Jeff Fort. Fort's career fits into the traditional pathway of an organized crime leader, similar to that of Leroy "Nicky" Barnes* and Frank Lucas, and ending (momentarily) with incarceration. Fort was born in 1947 in Mississippi and arrived with his mother in Chicago in 1955, settling in the Woodlawn area of the city. Leaving school after the fourth grade, Fort was semiliterate and destined to a street life. As a teenager he began his criminal leadership as the head of Woodlawn's Blackstone Rangers in a long and bloody war of survival against rival groups. Fort grew up in a ghetto where the only stable businesses were those dispersing drugs, alcohol, junk food, and cheap entertainment.

By the time he was 18, Jeff Fort transformed the Blackstone Rangers into the Black P. Stone Nation, a coalition of 21 gangs ruled by a commission of gang leaders known as the "Main 21," with Fort at its head. His criminal career from the start was marked by a flair for the melodramatic. His original gang nucleus, the Blackstone Rangers, was identifiable by the red berets they wore in 1962—a defiant act that challenged the police and other gangs. In each of the succeeding years through 1965, when the great gang consolidation came together, Fort's Stones tripled its membership through ingenious and forcible recruitment tactics: In the Woodlawn streets one became a Stone, or else. The gang spread across the city of Chicago and impressed other gangs with its size and power. By 1966, Fort's control and influence over African American street gangs in large sections of Chicago had been achieved. By 1968 the Black P. Stone Nation began to evolve into an organized crime entity. Segments of the Stones operated throughout black communities, in the infamous Cabrini-Green Housing Projects on the north side and all the way to the southern-most portion of the city. Fort's first effort at putting his power to work was by shaking down pupils in school, charging a quarter a day in grammar schools and a dollar in high schools.

From schoolyard shakedowns, the gang proceeded to extort money from the street prostitution trade. The cost of doing business was $50 a day per hooker. To make it unmistakably clear that they fully intended to exercise control over street prostitution as "protectors" in 1971, a prostitute who refused to pay was viciously murdered.

In the same period, Fort cleverly linked himself with social activists and community organizations and went so far as to apply for a federal grant designed to train gang members in marketable, legitimate job skills. Under the auspices of the Woodlawn Organization, the Black P. Stone Nation received federal funding from the Office of Economic Opportunity in the amount of $1 million. The rationale for the grant made sense; some white clergymen and community activists were interested in channeling gang violence into constructive learning programs. But the mayor of Chicago was outraged by what he believed was the coddling of gangsters, so by 1969, a U.S. Senate investigation was convened at which Fort, who was subpoenaed, appeared before the Senate Permanent Subcommittee on Investigations, introduced himself, and walked out. He was imprisoned for contempt of Congress and the embezzlement of $7,500 in federal funds. The embezzlement bore the hallmarks of a racketeering scheme: Lower-level leaders of the Stones were hired as program instructors and recruited adolescents to enroll as students, for which they received weekly stipends to participate in the program. When checks were disbursed, they were endorsed over to Fort's lieutenants, with each enrollee receiving a nominal compensatory amount. After serving two years of a five-year sentence, Fort was paroled, and his organization came to dominate large areas of Chicago's African American community.

With his strength solidified through murder and intimidation, Fort moved beyond extortion activities into prostitution and local neighborhood business. By 1971, the Black P. Stone Nation took on narcotics dealers and made them pay a "street tax." These events precipitated a warning from the Chicago Outfit,* Chicago's La Cosa Nostra,* which played a major role in the organization of local drug dealing. La Cosa Nostra in Chicago was not involved in the street distribution and wholesaling of drugs but offered its protection for a price. When the Stones imposed their extortion fees on bags of dope, the Outfit sent a warning, but Fort was not impressed. Two associates of the Outfit were found slain in front of its headquarters shortly after Fort had participated in a "sit-down"* with Cosa Nostra bosses.

Chicago's Cosa Nostra, the Outfit, by this time was no longer actively participating in the street crime but retained the streets as protection markets over which they murdered a rival gang member (Willie Bibbs) in 1981. Bibbs, a member of the Titannic Stones, was murdered because he had failed to heed the El Rukns warning to share the proceeds of his drug dealings. *See also* AFRICAN AMERICAN ORGANIZED CRIME; EL RUKNS

SUGGESTED READING: George Seibel and Ronald Pincomb, "From the Black P. Stone Nation to the El Rukns," *Criminal Organizations* 8, nos. 3–4 (1994): 3–9.

FRANZESE, MICHAEL. (b. May 27, 1951, Brooklyn, NY—    ). Yuppie mafioso in fuel tax scam.

One of the youngest capos* in the Colombo crime family,* Michael Franzese, son of John "Sonny" Franzese, a tough capo in the same mafia group, represented a new type of criminal in the American underworld. He was educated and articulate, had a legitimate career in the film industry, sold and merged construction firms, and seemed to shed the mafia stigma of his father. But a federal indictment told another story.

Michael Franzese was deeply involved in multimillion-dollar tax fraud involving fuel taxes, insurance claims, and auto dealerships. The gas tax scam carried on through a "daisy chain" of gasoline wholesale and retail distribution companies where sales of petroleum products would be arranged among a large number of firms until the tax bill was owed by one firm known as the "burnout company." The "burnout firm" consisted of a mailing address, a telephone number, and a principal owner who was an illegal alien no one could locate. The burnout company, in turn, sold the gas with an invoice marked "all taxes paid." Then it would declare bankruptcy, and Franzese would create another daisy chain to evade taxes.

In spite of his clean-cut image, Mike Franzese inherited his father's business tactics and violent ways. But despite threats against potential witnesses against him, which were credible because of his mafia rank and affiliations, in March 1986, Franzese pleaded guilty to racketeering and conspiracy charges; he also accepted a prison term of ten years and agreed to forfeit assets worth $4.8 million. The deal with the government required him to pay an additional $10 million to the states defrauded in the gasoline tax scam (in which he had Russian organized criminals as partners).

He was able to persuade the Justice Department that he could not come up with the $14.8 million if he was stuck behind bars—not even after selling his properties and movie rights. An extraordinary agreement was struck: Franzese was permitted limited freedom under the guard of U.S. marshals. The surveillance was to be paid for by Franzese, who would do business (legitimate) to earn enough money to defray the expenses of the U.S. marshals' protection and generate enough cash to pay court-imposed fines and penalties. However, Franzese reverted to form, passed bad checks to the U.S. Marshals Service, and was sent off to prison.

The investigation of Franzese's affairs revealed another crooked business he was involved in along with mafia members from the Genovese,* Gambino,* and Colombo crime families.* It involved operating a 700-member union of private security guards whose members worked in sensitive spots as diverse as nuclear power plants and gambling casinos. The Allied International Union was originally a creation of the Genovese crime family, which then sold it off to a private builder who, along with Franzese as a partner, bilked union funds for private use. Further, by threatening strikes against nuclear power plants such as Three Mile Island and Atlantic City, New Jersey,* casinos, Franzese and his partner were able to obtain extortion payments. Franzese's career illustrates a dangerous side of organized crime—its ability to penetrate legitimate business and blur the distinctions between the underworld and upperworld. Franzese is currently out of prison and has become a Born Again Christian—who owes the government money.

**SUGGESTED READING:** Michael Franzese and Don Masters, *Quitting the Mob.* 1992.

**FRATIANNO, JIMMY "THE WEASEL."** (b. Aladena James Fratianno, Nov. 14, 1914, Naples, Italy—d. July 1, 1993). Los Angeles crime family informer.

Along with Joseph Valachi* and Vincent Charles Teresa,* Jimmy Fratianno became known to the public through a best-selling book about his life in the underworld. *The Last Mafioso* described his criminal career and his willingness to inform on his criminal associates in order to gain personal advantage in the mob and immunity against arrest by eliminating competitors.

Fratianno began his life of crime in Cleveland, where he committed 11 murders ordered by mob leaders. He won admiration and his nickname, "The Weasel," by outrunning and evading policemen who chased him in the streets.

When he left Cleveland's Little Italy, Fratianno had a reputation as a boxer and a strong-arm thug. He affiliated with the Chicago Outfit* and went to California, where he joined Jack Dragna* and Dominic Brooklier,* La Cosa Nostra* bosses on the West Coast during the 1940s and 1950s. Internal conflicts within the Los Angeles Mafia and trouble with Mickey Cohen* and his gang helped Fratianno rise to the position of acting boss of the Los Angeles crime family.

However, threats against his life persuaded him to become an informer, and when a contract was placed on his head by mob bosses in Chicago and Florida, he agreed to go into the Witness Security Program.* His testimony in various trials helped to convict a Teamster official in San Francisco and Mafia bosses in Los Angeles and New York. Fratianno testified effectively against Frank Tieri,* head of the Genovese crime family* in New York City.

**SUGGESTED READING:** Ovid Demaris, *The Last Mafioso* (1981).

**FULTON FISH MARKET.** A racketeering stronghold in legitimate business.

A million pounds of fish are processed every day through the Fulton Fish Market in lower Manhattan, New York City. Not all of this perishable food comes off fishing boats: Over the past five years the Fish Market has served as the focal point for preparing and distributing seafood products arriving by aircraft from Iceland, Norway, and Finland, among other places.

The Market existed for a century before criminals began exploiting it. Beginning in the 1920s, Joseph "Socks" Lanza* played a significant role in organizing the workers and the work of the Market.

Fish were unloaded from oceangoing boats and freshwater catches from as far as the Great Lakes. Once the workforce was Irish, but by the 1920s and 1930s, the fish handlers were mostly Italian. Lanza put together a union local by 1923, and from that power base, he turned the Market into his own empire.

Under Lanza's rules the crews of fishing vessels were not allowed to unload their own catches. For a fee, Market workers unloaded the fish. In addition, Lanza charged each boat $10 for the union's "benevolent fund"; if a captain refused, a bucket of fish might be accidentally dumped into the harbor.

Criminal control extended beyond the confines of off-loading docked ships: The Market's security force operated a watchman's service for retail shops and vehicles located on the margins of the Market waterfront—all of which is city-owned land; and fish processing plants paid the Sea Worker's Union thousands of dollars to keep their shops nonunion.

As a caporegime in the Genovese crime family,* Lanza's extortions knew few bounds and raised the cost of fish products in the consumer marketplace. Because of criminal control, many seafood firms seeking to avoid the high prices that extortion entails have fled to Philadelphia, Boston, and Newark. The exodus

New York, NY, May 1943. A scene at the Fulton Fish Market showing the dock where New England fishing boats unload their cargo. Reproduced from the Collections of the Library of Congress.

of fish industry businesses has cost New York City $2 billion in lost sales annually.

In the 1990s, the mayor of New York City asserted control over the crime-ridden Market through his powers of regulation, licensing, and investigation. In early 1995, the city evicted six unloading companies affiliated with the Genovese crime family and hired an outside firm to replace them. Then in October 1995, in response to the city's aggressive moves against the mob, a wildcat strike threw the Market into chaos.

Again in 1996 more sudden, disruptive strikes were orchestrated by the mob. Still, the city held onto its resolve to recover the economic resource of the Market for the citizens of New York City. The results have been mixed: Reforms have reduced but not eliminated organized criminal influence, but this is seen as a mixed blessing by the Market's firms, who complain about the bureaucratic red tape city involvement entails. Similar criticisms have occurred in the construction industry when the mob's "brokering" activities as middlemen facilitating the work process were dismantled by prosecutions and vigilant law enforcement activities.

**SUGGESTED READING:** Robert J. Kelly, *The Upperworld and the Underworld: Case Studies of Racketeering and Business Infiltrations in the United States.* 1999.

# G

**GALANTE, CARMINE "THE CIGAR."** (b. 1910, Sicily—d. July 12, 1979, Brooklyn, NY). Boss of the Bonanno crime family*/1970s.

As an underboss (sottocapo)* in the Bonanno crime family, Galante specialized in drugs. He began his career as "button man" (La Cosa Nostra* soldier), carrying out murders and expanding the reach of the Bonanno crime family into Canada, Arizona, and the Caribbean. In the 1960s he was sentenced to 20 years on a drug trafficking charge. Out on parole in 1974 after 12 years in Lewisburg prison, he plunged back into the heroin trade, becoming partners with Sicilians with whom he formed a close alliance.

Galante was soon challenging the power of the other New York dons. In 1978, on his orders, several members of the Genovese* and Gambino crime families* were gunned down. His ambitions became intolerable to the other bosses, and they began conspiring against him. By 1979 a plot had been hatched to assassinate him. On board were Frank Tieri,* Paul Castellano,* Jerry Catena, and Santos Trafficante, Jr.*—heads of Cosa Nostra crime families.

In one of the more spectacular hits* in mob history, Galante was taken out in broad daylight while eating lunch in the open-air garden of Joe and Mary's Restaurant in the Bushwick section of Brooklyn. He was finishing his meal and lighting his cigar, his trademark, when three masked gunmen erupted into the place and blasted him to death with two shotguns. He died with his cigar in his mouth. Later it was discovered that two of the men implicated in the murder, Baldo Amato and Cesare Bonventre, both Sicilians and Bonanno cousins who were members of the Bonanno crime family, helped to set up the murder on behalf of Philip Rastelli,* a contender for power in the family. Amato and Bonventre were later found murdered.

**SUGGESTED READING:** Virgil W. Peterson, *The Mob: 200 Years of Organized Crime in New York.* 1983.

Carmine "The Cigar" Galante. Reproduced from the
Collections of the Library of Congress.

**GALLO, JOSEPH.** ("Crazy Joe") (b. Apr. 1929, Brooklyn, NY—d. Apr. 7, 1972,
New York, NY). Mafia rebel and innovator.

Considered headstrong and devious by many in the underworld, Joe Gallo
would not tolerate mafia traditions he saw as flawed, nor would he abide by
rules and customs of La Cosa Nostra* that seemed self-defeating and destructive.
As with many rebels and innovators who recognized the need for change and
acted on it, he may have paid with his life for his farsightedness.

As made members (sworn-in soldiers) of the Joseph Profaci* crime family,
Crazy Joe and his older brother Larry operated a large crew* of associates
around the Brooklyn waterfront, where they were involved in hijacking, gambling, extortion, and cargo theft and worked as a "hit* team" of enforcers for
family boss Joseph Profaci. It is widely believed that the Gallos carried out the
assassination of Albert Anastasia* in 1957 and murdered many enemies of the
Profaci family.

Some years later, in 1961, the Gallos (including their youngest brother, Albert
"Kid Blast" Gallo) went to war with their boss over the distribution of a gambling enterprise whose operator Frank ("Frankie Shots") Abbatemarco they murdered on orders from Profaci. The boss divided the enterprise of the murdered
Frankie Shots among friends and relatives. In retaliation for the insult, the Gallos
abducted four of Profaci's closest associates. The conflict cost a dozen lives on

both sides, but then Profaci agreed to be more generous and give the Gallos a fair share of the Brooklyn rackets. The agreement broke down when Profaci attempted to kill Larry Gallo shortly thereafter, when Crazy Joe was serving a prison sentence. The "Profaci-Gallo war" did not quiet down until August 1962, when the boss died of natural causes.

During this time, Crazy Joe attempted to shake down several businesses in order to improve the gang's war chest. He was arrested, convicted of extortion, and served a lengthy sentence (14 years) in Greenhaven State Prison. While in prison, Gallo befriended Leroy "Nicky" Barnes,* the legendary African American heroin kingpin. Gallo recognized the changes that were occurring in the underworld and realized that as the ethnic and racial compositions of ghettos were altered by demographics, so too, would organized crime that was ghetto oriented have to change as well, if it was to survive. Crazy Joe understood that more and more "street action" would be taken over by African Americans and Latinos. He also understood that mobsters who figured this out and acted on it would grow in power, compared to the "Mustache Petes,"* the old-timers committed to customs and rules that excluded anyone who was not Italian. Gallo and Barnes agreed to create a multiracial gang that could operate everywhere and that would represent a real rival to the Cosa Nostra. New York City's ghettos were filled with angry and hungry young hoodlums armed to the teeth who together constituted enough power to threaten and even depose the tradition-bound Cosa Nostra that Profaci symbolized. In a spirit of cooperation, Gallo sent released African American prisoners to work in crime operations controlled by his gang. None of this went unnoticed in the Profaci family, now headed by Joseph Colombo, Jr.*

It turned out that nothing substantial would emerge from the Gallo-Barnes connection, but other problems and opportunities absorbed the energies of Joe Gallo. Released in 1971, a new Joe Gallo reappeared on the Brooklyn streets. At the time that Gallo was moving in the company of theater people and intellectuals, becoming something of a celebrity, a journalist wrote a thinly disguised novel of the Gallo gang's misadventures, reigniting the Profaci/Colombo crime family war. Joseph Colombo decided to take on the FBI in a public relations war, organizing an Italian American Anti-Defamation League that demanded the end of the negative stereotyping of Italian Americans as gangsters and mafiosi. Initial successes in mobilizing the community soon faded; mob chiefs in the Cosa Nostra were also leery of media attention and tried to dissuade Colombo, demanding that he discontinue his campaign and rallies. Colombo ignored the advice, and in June 1972, he was shot down at a rally in Columbus Circle. He lingered in a vegetative state for seven years and then died. The murderer turned out to be African American, and Gallo was hauled in by the police for questioning. No legal evidence could tie him to the crime, but his enemies in the mob did not need legal proof.

Suspicions were heightened further with Colombo out of the way and acting boss Carmine "The Snake" Persico* in prison when Gallo's men moved in on Colombo activities and reclaimed the south Brooklyn waterfront as their territory.

On April 7, 1972, Joey Gallo was celebrating his 43rd birthday with his wife and daughter and theater and show business friends when he was attacked and killed outside Umberto's Clam House in Little Italy in lower Manhattan. Three Colombo gunmen entered the restaurant and opened fire.

**SUGGESTED READINGS:** Jimmy Breslin, *The Gang That Couldn't Shoot Straight.* 1969; Donald Goddard, *Joey: The Life of "Crazy Joe" Gallo.* 1974; Raymond V. Martin, *Revolt in the Mafia.* 1963.

**GAMBINO, CARLO.** "Don Carlo" (b. Aug. 24, 1900, Palermo, Sicily—d. Oct. 15, 1976, New York). Powerful La Cosa Nostra* family boss (don).*

Because he headed what many in law enforcement believed was the most powerful crime family in the American Cosa Nostra, Carlo Gambino was labeled "capo di tutti capi" (boss of all bosses). Generally soft-spoken and self-effacing, Gambino was also quite ordinary looking: small in stature, with a large nose, he resembled more a Sicilian immigrant peasant than the head of a powerful criminal organization, which at its height numbered nearly 2,000 "made" members, some 30 capos,* and thousands of "associates" operating through a variety of criminal syndicates and enterprises as well as many legitimate businesses that were woven into the orbit of crime activity. All in all, with the slight frame, droopy eyes, and protruding nose, he seemed the last thing one would expect in a mafia don. But Gambino's 19-year reign as a crime family boss was exceptional in its longevity. Under Gambino's stewardship, the family became a major force in the Italian American underworld.

After succeeding Albert Anastasia* (whose assassination it is believed he had a hand in), Gambino neutralized internal family unrest by appointing as his underboss one of Anastasia's most loyal followers, a tough-looking gangster from Little Italy, Aniello Dellacroce.* He also kept Anastasia's brother, Anthony Anastasio* (the original spelling of the name), in charge of Local 1814 of the ILA (International Longshoremen's Union), which enabled the crime family to control the Brooklyn docks. And when Anastasio died of natural causes, he appointed Anastasio's son-in-law, Anthony Scotto,* a capo in the family, and passed on to him leadership of the local.

Carlo Gambino wanted the crime family to move in new directions—he desired a "briefcase" mafia and wished to leave behind the "street" mafia of violence, mayhem, gang wars, and chaos.

Even though a segment of his personal family (known as the "Cherry Hill" Gambinos), cousins from Sicily, were deeply immersed in drugs in New Jersey and maintained ties abroad with the Sicilian Mafia, Carlo Gambino was adamant about narcotics and the unwelcome public attention it provoked. All he had to do was to look at Vito Genovese,* who died in prison while serving a lengthy sentence on what many crime family members believed was a trumped-up narcotics conviction. The message from Gambino was crystal clear: death for anyone in the family dealing drugs.

Although mob members, including Gambino himself, would not be likely to abandon such criminal standbys as loansharking,* illegal gambling,* hijackings, fencing stolen goods, and racketeering, Gambino favored a more sophisticated approach to crime: dominating the construction industry, trucking, food distribution, garbage disposal, along with the infiltration of the garment and seafood industries, health maintenance organizations, and so on. All these immensely lucrative businesses were available to mob influence and corruption and would not attract media headlines that more obvious and more dangerous mob activities usually did.

Another aspect of Gambino's leadership was his wariness about outsiders and reliance on personal family relationships. The family was replete with marriages of in-laws as well as cousins, reflecting his inbred, secretive ways. The Gambino and Luchese crime families* had shared power in New York's garment industry. In earlier times just before World War II, and after Louis Buchalter's* crime syndicate collapsed, Gambino and Luchese had extorted protection money from manufacturers to safeguard against hijackings. That had changed. Now control was exerted with a stranglehold on the industry's trucking. Nothing moved except in trucks owned by the two families through front companies. Garment manufacturers were comforted by this new stability in the industry and passed on the costs to unsuspecting American consumers. Don Carlo saw to it that a son, Thomas, received a good education and was then placed in the family's garment firms to keep an eye on family interests.

With illness and the end within sight, after repeated heart problems in the 1970s, Gambino chose Paul Castellano,* a capo in the family and a successful businessman in his own right in the meat provisions industry, as the new boss. Incidentally, Castellano was Gambino's brother-in-law.

The strategic error in dividing the family into two irreconcilable factions was committed by Gambino himself. The statesmanship that allowed him to die in bed of natural causes eluded him at a crucial moment when the future of the crime family hung on his decision as to a successor. Blood bonds that he relied on all his life might have clouded his judgment, perhaps reflecting a subconscious need to perpetuate a Gambino hegemony in his carefully constructed, quite formidable crime machine; that may have figured in the selection of his brother-in-law Castellano over the tough, popular, streetwise Dellacroce. As a result of his decision, the crime family developed a seam of distrust that ran right down the middle of it. Like King Lear, Gambino had uncharacteristically divided his strength while still alive.

Gambino's career in organized crime was launched during Prohibition (*see* PROHIBITION AND ORGANIZED CRIME*) in which he, like many others, engaged in bootlegging, gambling, and assorted vices. During World War II, he became a millionaire dealing in black market food ration stamps and gasoline. His talent for racketeering matured in the postwar period when he served as a capo and then underboss in the Anastasia crime family that eventually would be permanently identified with his name. Law enforcement officials connected Gambino with numerous legitimate businesses including meat vending, garment trucking, real estate, labor consulting, marine insurance, and alcohol manufacture. His skills in criminal enterprises included labor racketeering, loansharking, vending machines, and gambling, among others.

Gambino was confirmed as a boss at the Apalachin meeting* of crime bosses in 1957 after the murder of Albert Anastasia by members of the Profaci crime family. Gambino was believed to have been involved in a complex conspiracy with Vito Genovese to eliminate Frank Costello* (Genovese's rival for the leadership of the Luciano crime family*) and the murder of Albert Anastasia, who killed the Mangano brothers in 1957 and took control of that family. Gambino emerged as head of this family after Anastasia's assassination.

Gambino's manipulation of Cosa Nostra members knew few bounds. In 1961, he intervened in an internal dispute between the Gallo brothers and the boss, Joseph Profaci. When the war ended with Profaci's death from cancer, Joseph Magliocco took control and sought peace. Magliocco died shortly thereafter from tensions caused by the struggle and pressures from another powerful Cosa Nostra boss, Joseph Bonanno,* who with Profaci believed the Gallo faction rebellion was instigated by Gambino and Gaetano Luchese.* Bonanno arranged to have Gambino and Luchese killed by Joseph Colombo, Jr.,* who leaked the information to Gambino and Luchese. Magliocco was deposed, and Colombo was named his successor.

Colombo earned the wrath of Gambino in 1971 when, contrary to Gambino's belief in maintaining a low profile, which meant staying out of the newspapers and off television, Colombo organized a public protest group to fight what he complained was FBI harassment of his children and personal family. Colombo's grandstanding and many public appearances irritated the FBI and not least of all his mentor Carlo Gambino. At an Italian-American Unity Day rally in New York City's Columbus Circle in June 1971, Colombo was shot in the head and neck and never fully recovered. It was rumored that Gambino had approved the contract murder of Colombo. After the shooting of Colombo in 1971, the family was run for a long time by Vincent ("Vinnie Blue Eyes") Aloi, a godson of Gambino.

Carlo Gambino has left an enduring imprint on organized crime in the United states and in New York City. The criminal enterprise he had led for almost 20 years had become the largest and richest of all the nation's Cosa Nostra families, a force for corruption of incalculable dimensions. The mayhem and suffering that accompanied Gambino's rise to power, which continued unabated in the rule of his successors throughout the 1980s, cannot be adequately measured, only imagined. Gambino's legacy, in the end, was wholesale subversion of private business and public institutions and environmental havoc (with his control of waste disposal cartels) on a scale never before seen in New York City. His crime rule also meant countless ruined lives, decimated families, and legions of addicts enslaved to drugs. To combat this monstrous parasite the government had spent millions of dollars with regrettably few results. What Gambino left New York was a criminally imposed tax on commerce in general and a widespread anxiety among all of its citizens.

**SUGGESTED READINGS:** John H. Davis, *Mafia Dynasty: The Rise and Fall of the Gambino Crime Family*. 1993; Paul S. Meskil, *Don Carlo: Boss of Bosses*. 1973.

**GAMBINO CRIME FAMILY.** The Gambino crime family is believed to be under the leadership of John Gotti, Jr., the son of John Gotti,* who is imprisoned in the federal correctional facility in Marion, Illinois. Until Gotti's imprisonment, the Gambino crime network was considered to be the largest, most influential criminal organization in New York City. From 1957 when Carlo Gambino* took the leadership following Albert Anastasia's* murder, the crime family steadily extended its influence and power. At the height of its influence in the 1960s and early 1970s, the areas of its operation included the five boroughs of New York City, Nassau, Suffolk and Westchester Counties contiguous with New York City; New Jersey, Pennsylvania, Connecticut, Florida, and Las Vegas, Nevada.*

The crime family had a listed membership, "made" men, of nearly 350, with 28 capos* and nearly 3,000 close associates of the soldiers.* The network is not only involved in the usual criminal activities such as gambling, drug trafficking, and loan sharking*; but it is also entrenched deeply in legitimate business in the food, entertainment, construction, and jewelry industries. Also, Gambino crime family members are active in labor union affairs. In the late 1990s crime family associates without criminal records, "front men," have managed to penetrate other segments of legitimate businesses including recreational facilities, health clubs, and casino gambling businesses in Atlantic City, New Jersey,* and Connecticut.

Law enforcement intelligence assessments suggest that the organization is still trying to recover from the breakup of leadership in 1991 when John Gotti, the boss (don),* "Sammy the Bull" Gravano,* family consigliere,* and Frank "Frankie Loc" Locasio, the underboss (sottocapo),* were arrested and subsequently convicted of a number of RICO*-type crimes.

**SUGGESTED READING:** John H. Davis, *Mafia Dynasty: The Rise and Fall of the Gambino Crime Family*. 1993.

**GAMBLING.** Gambling includes a variety of games of chance and betting on sporting events. Some are legal, some not. Betting, or wagering, at state-licensed horse and dog tracks; government-operated offtrack betting parlors; state-sponsored lotteries; casino gambling in Nevada, New Jersey, Connecticut, Louisiana, Mississippi, on riverboats in Illinois, and on Indian reservations; and licensed gambling clubs and casinos in California—all are popular and growing forms of recreation across the country that produce millions in taxes and revenues.

Legal gambling activities have grown in the United States while at the same time low priority has been assigned to gambling enforcement, which only makes it more attractive to organized crime. While profits from drug trafficking are quite substantial, so are penalties and enforcement activities. Penalties for illegal gambling* are, by contrast, minimal. Indeed, arrests for illegal gambling have declined significantly during the 1990s, particularly in urban areas. Lack of enforcement resources attributable to competing demands for police services, combined with more sophisticated telephonic communication (mobile phones, for example) explain why gambling enforcement has declined. Most important, technology aside, there is currently little public pressure to improve gambling enforcement. *See also* ILLEGAL GAMBLING

**SUGGESTED READING:** Mark Haller, *Life Under Bruno: The Economics of an Organized Crime Family.* 1991.

**GANGSTER TALK.** While omerta,* the famous Sicilian code of silence, is really just a romantic way of saying that one does not cooperate and talk to the police, the fact is that organized crime did not discover the virtues of total silence until the early 1950s. Until that time, many prominent members—Frank Costello,* Joseph Adonis,* Gaetano Luchese*—had taken the stand and answered questions. True, they were often evasive and forgetful, but they did give some answers. The Kefauver Committee* hearings in 1950–1951 and the Joseph Valachi* hearings in 1963 put a stop to that. Today, gangsters have learned the words and phrases of the Fifth Amendment perfectly.

When talking to each other, organized criminals habitually talk in such an oblique and elliptical style that even if they are overheard, the conversation makes little more sense than silence would to a stranger.

There is a certain amount of skepticism in the upperworld about how organized criminals talk to one another. Many react with amused incredulity to what sounds to them like dialogue from a movie or video. The argot of organized crime has been a pungent blend of underworld slang ("swag" for stolen goods; "hit*" for murder), slang from Jewish ("goniff" for thief), and Italian ("compare" for Godfather), and ghetto language from African American street talk ("wasted" for killed; "strapped" for armed). It is also heavily laced with profanity, which punctuates virtually every sentence.

The police call this language "street talk," and many use it themselves. Gangsters and racketeers often speak this way, but when the situation calls for it— such as an appearance in court—most of them can speak English as well as the average citizen, thought it is not what might be called their native tongue. In street talk, females—except one's mother or sister—are "broads" or "bitches"; a "shylock" is a loanshark and the interest he charges is "vigorish" or "vig"; "heat" is police pressure. To be arrested is to be "busted" or "collared."

SUGGESTED READING: Nicholas Pileggi, *Wiseguy: Life in a Mafia Family*. 1987.

**GARBAGE AND WASTE COLLECTION.** Until the late 1990s in various metropolitan areas across the country, a significant number of garbage companies were enterprises owned, operated, or controlled by organized crime figures. Through outright ownership, labor union influence, control of trade associations, and the employment of organized crime's traditional tactics of fear and intimidation, racketeers had come to virtually control the garbage disposal business from the mid-1950s to the early 1990s.

The garbage collection business was characterized by small partnerships or family companies, which is attractive to organized crime: When enterprises in an industry are small scale, local, and family based, have low-status skill requirements for the labor work, and utilize comparatively simple technologies in the work environment, vulnerability to organized crime infiltration is enhanced. The solid waste collection industry met these criteria. It is because of its scale, workforce skills, technologies, and localization that it was an easy-entry enterprise, requiring some garbage trucks and a hardworking labor force.

Because intense competition that drove profits down was harming so many businesses, an association of carters formed, looking for market stability. With the help of Vincent Squillante,* a member of the Luciano crime family,* involved in labor racketeering and garbage collection in Westchester County, New York, a group of carters was formed in Suffolk and Nassau Counties, suburbs of New York City, around 1955. Squillante's role was to consolidate the carters, neutralize the union (the Teamsters) wage demands, and bring competitive bidding under control by suppressing competition. This required the use of violence and the corruption of local politicians.

All the carters were required to join the Greater New York Cartmen's Association. When in 1956 New York City required all commercial enterprises to arrange for their own garbage collection services, the need to organize the market was imperative. Within months cartels (a combination of independent businesses formed to regulate pricing, bids, customer allocations, and business territories) were created that restrained competition and set up customer allocation agreements built around the membership of the waste hauling trade associations the racketeers managed. In New York City alone, there were about 300 trash haulers servicing 250,000 businesses organized around four waste hauling associations.

The associations provided their members with benefits: stable market conditions for employers and profitable side ventures (ownership of some refuge dumps, truck servicing, and repair companies for mob-connected members). The losers were the employees and customers of the carting firms.

Rigging bids to haul municipal garbage and bribing public officials also appeared to have been common business practices for members of the New Jersey Garbage Contractors Association. More recently in 1996, a New York State grand jury indicted the executives of 12 carting companies who had formed a

Vito "Don Vitone" Genovese. Reproduced from
the Collections of the Library of Congress.

"bidding club" under the auspices of New York's crime families. It was revealed
that among the victims of overcharging and bid-rigging for trash removal were
14 federal buildings including courthouses where many organized crime figures
have been tried.

The cost of allowing organized crime to structure and dominate the waste
disposal industry can be measured in costs to customers and in a climate of
criminality that it creates. The illegal nature of so much of the business has
raised costs of waste collection and disposal for all customers victimized by
garbage company conspiracies. Estimates suggest that in New York City customer allocation agreements inflate the costs of collection by some 35 percent,
or about $60 million a year. The other costs are moral but equally harmful.
Criminal involvement in the industry has blurred distinctions between right and
wrong. Fraud, extortion, and corruption have weakened public confidence in the
integrity of law enforcement and regulatory agencies in the industry.

**SUGGESTED READING:** Alan A. Block and Frank R. Scarpitti, *Poisoning for Profit:
The Mafia and Toxic Waste in America.* 1985.

**GENOVESE, VITO.** ("Don Vitone," "Don Vito") (b. Nov. 27, 1897, Naples,
Italy—d. Feb. 14, 1969, Atlanta Federal Prison). Major crime family boss (don)*
and La Cosa Nostra* leader.

Three pivotal events in the history of American organized crime involved

Vito Genovese: the Castellammarese War,* the Apalachin meeting,* and the testimony of Joseph Valachi.* Genovese arrived in the United States at 15 and lived in the Italian ghetto called "Little Italy" in New York City's lower East Side. He became a street thief and eventually an associate of Charles "Lucky" Luciano.*

By the 1930s, Genovese was a powerful capo* in the Mafia* and participated in the Castellammarese War. Apart from his role in the vice industries and bootlegging, Genovese was known as a narcotics smuggler. When Luciano organized the crime families in the 1930s, Genovese was one of his top aides and emerged as a rival of Frank Costello* when Luciano was imprisoned on prostitution charges. A bungled murder in 1934 forced him to flee to Italy in 1937, where he managed to gain the confidence of Benito Mussolini, the Fascist leader who had organized a massive antimafia campaign that jailed hundreds of mafia members throughout Sicily and southern Italy in the 1920s. The always resourceful Genovese was able, nonetheless, to become a confidant of Il Duce and was reputed to have arranged as a friendly gesture the 1943 assassination of Carlo Tresca, an anti-Fascist newspaper editor in New York. When the Allies invaded Italy, Genovese won the confidence of American military authorities for whom he worked as an interpreter and informer. This role also enabled him to become familiar with black marketing operations throughout Italy and the Mediterranean drug trafficking countries.

After the war, Genovese, who had been identified as a fugitive, was returned to the United States to face murder charges, but all of the witnesses against him had been silenced or had disappeared. Charges were dropped, and Don Vitone embarked on an energetic campaign to take control of the Luciano crime family,* whose boss had been deported to Italy. Even with Lucky Luciano out of the way, Frank Costello and his partner Meyer Lansky* would have to be eliminated or neutralized in order for Genovese to realize his dreams of power.

Costello was a powerful capo in the crime family with influential political friends and was Genovese's first target. In 1957, Vincent "The Chin" Gigante,* who would later become boss of the Luciano/Genovese crime family, made an attempt to murder Frank Costello as he entered his apartment building in New York City. The shot merely grazed Costello's skull, but the message was clear that the Costello stewardship of the family was being openly challenged. Costello's power in the family had been steadily eroding: In 1951, Willie Moretti,* a New Jersey capo who supplied Costello with muscle and shooters, was murdered; and with Luciano gone Albert Anastasia,* a friend of Costello's, began moving in on Lansky's gambling operations in Cuba; so Lansky approved a hit* on Anastasia. On October 25, 1957, Albert ("Lord High Executioner") Anastasia was murdered in the barbershop of a Manhattan hotel, and with his death, Costello lost considerable power in the crime family. Informed sources in law enforcement concluded that Vito Genovese* would have the most to gain with Anastasia's elimination. It is believed that the Apalachin meeting in November 1957 was instigated by Genovese to tighten and approve his control of the crime family and obtain the approval of other bosses. The meeting, which had attracted more than 60 top bosses of the Mafia from around the country, ended in a fiasco when the state police discovered the meeting and sought to question dozens of Mafia figures who fled into the surrounding woods.

Two years later, in April 1959, Costello and Luciano (and perhaps Meyer Lansky) exerted their influence to set up Genovese for an arrest on drug trafficking. Even police experts believed that the case was questionable. Members of the Genovese crime family* were involved in drugs, but the individual who swore in court that he had personally met, talked to, and sold Genovese heroin was a small-time drug courier not connected with the family. To anyone familiar with the protocol and insulation of top bosses from common street criminals, the entire episode seemed scarcely credible. There are, therefore, good reasons to suppose that Genovese was set up—not by the police but by his enemies within the Cosa Nostra who feared and hated him.

One hypothesis suggests that Costello, Lansky, and Luciano concocted this frame-up that the federal government simply accepted on its face, not bothering to be too inquisitive about the improbable details. Genovese and two dozen of his associates were convicted, with the boss sentenced to 15 years in prison.

While in prison, Genovese continued to direct the activities of his crime organization. As time passed and information leaked about his conviction on drug trafficking, he became suspicious to the point of paranoia and ordered the death of one of his top capos, Anthony (Tony Bender) Strollo. He also suspected Joe Valachi, a low-level soldier in the family imprisoned with him in Atlanta of being an informer and a member of the conspiracy to destroy him. He ordered Valachi's death, but Valachi killed a man whom he thought had the contract on his life and, facing life imprisonment, decided to cooperate with federal authorities. Valachi would reveal the secrets of Cosa Nostra to the entire nation in sensational testimony before the McClelland Senate Committee on Labor Racketeering.

In 1969, ten years into his sentence, Vito Genovese died in prison of a heart condition. In 1970, statements attributed to Luciano and Lansky suggest that the drug arrest and conviction of Genovese was put into motion by underworld figures who felt threatened by his lust for power. The crime family continues to operate and still bears the name of Don Vito Genovese. *See also* MC-CLELLAND COMMITTEE

**SUGGESTED READING:** Ralph Salerno and John Tompkins, *The Crime Confederation.* 1969.


**GENOVESE CRIME FAMILY.** Charles "Lucky" Luciano,* the criminal who "Americanized" the Mafia* in the United States and helped to create the structure of the modern La Cosa Nostra,* originally headed the Genovese crime family. It was named after its most notorious and ambitious godfather, Vito Genovese,* who assumed leadership in 1957 after the assassination of his enemy, family boss Albert Anastasia,* and a failed attempt on Frank Costello,* who was serving as the head of the family in Luciano's exile in Italy. Costello retired quickly and quietly when he recovered from a head wound; the would-be assassin, Vincent "The Chin" Gigante,* a lowly soldier* and ex-prize fighter, would eventually rise to leadership in the 1990s, only to be deposed by the federal government after long court battles over Gigante's mental capacity to stand trial on racketeering and other criminal charges.

The crime family was born out of the internecine gang battles of the 1930s, the Castellammarese War,* which redesigned organized crime in the United States for the remainder of the century. The influence of the Genovese crime network is felt throughout the metropolitan area of New York City, extending from its "New York" branch headquartered in the Greenwich Village section of New York City to groups in New Jersey, Pennsylvania, Delaware, Maryland, and Connecticut. Its illicit enterprises in the carting and trucking industry, in liquor wholesale and retail, and in Times Square pornography strengthens the crime family's traditional criminal money-generating activities—gambling, narcotics, loansharking,* extortion, and labor racketeering.

The rise and fall of the tides of Genovese crime family power belies its durability and sophistication. Many police experts and observers consider the Genovese family, after Genovese's demise in 1969, to be the "Ivy League" of organized crime. Frank Tieri* put the criminal network back on the underworld's map in 1972; by 1976, after Gambino's death had ended the Genovese subordination to the de facto boss of bosses, Don Carlo, the crime family regained its prestige and power when it moved aggressively into Atlantic City, New Jersey,* casino gambling enterprises. By the late 1980s, Vincent "The Chin" Gigante became boss, but the size of the membership, the identity of individual members and bosses, and the types of businesses in which the group had interests and associates were closely kept secrets that enhanced the power of the Genovese crews.

It is estimated that the crime family has interests in seafood distributors, restaurants, the waste cartage and livery industries, and vending machine businesses. In 1997, it was determined that the boss, Vincent Gigante, was mentally competent to stand trial. He was convicted and sentenced for life. The leadership has now devolved to Frank Iliano and Laurence Dentico.*

**SUGGESTED READING:** Peter Maas, *The Valachi Papers*. 1968.

**GIANCANA, SAM.** ("Mooney," "Momo") (b. Gilormo Giangona, May 24, 1908, Chicago, IL—d. June 19, 1975, Chicago, IL). Chicago syndicate* leader and Mafia*/CIA conspirator.

The "42 Gang" of Chicago's notorious "Patch" ghetto was not unlike the equally infamous Five Pointers gang in New York City, which served as an incubator for future master criminals. Sam Giancana, like Charles "Lucky" Luciano,* was the child of immigrant parents who found themselves trapped in the unforgiving slums of a big city and were tied to a life of backbreaking

Sam "Momo" Giancana. Reproduced from the Collections of the Library of Congress.

manual labor. The experience of his parents' humiliation helped to produce in Giancana a contempt for legitimate work. But rather than become a political revolutionary or radical, he became a cunning criminal. The "42 Gang" was involved in politics, to some extent, but its primary activity was conventional crime, and Giancana involved himself completely in its activities, with numerous arrests for felonies including murder. By 1928, he had been arrested 50 times, although it was not until 1929 that his luck ran out, and he was sentenced to five years' imprisonment for burglary. During World War II, he was rejected for military service on the grounds that he was a "psychopath."

Momo Giancana came to the attention of Alphonse Capone,* the towering figure of the Chicago underworld who was something of a role model for aspiring young criminals. Giancana had a reputation as a "wheelman," an excellent driver who could be relied on in difficult circumstances. He served first as a chauffeur/bodyguard for Paul "The Waiter" Ricca,* a powerful gangster who, with Anthony Joseph Accardo,* Jake Guzik,* Joseph John Aiuppa,* and Frank "The Enforcer" Nitti,* represented the strength of the Chicago Outfit* that would ensure the rise of Momo Giancana up the ranks to boss.

Always resourceful and cunning, while serving a prison sentence in 1938 on a bootlegging conviction, Momo learned from another inmate, Eddie Jones, an

African American numbers* operator, just how profitable the racket was in Chicago's large African American community. Jones thought of Giancana as a friend during their years together in prison and helped finance Momo's entry into the jukebox racket. In return, Giancana double-crossed his prison mentor and had Jones kidnapped in 1946. Jones paid a $100,000 ransom and fled to Mexico. The individual replacing Jones was compliant, but when he held back protection payments on the racket's operations on Chicago's South side, Teddy Roe, Jones's protégé, was murdered in the street.

By the 1950s, as the old guard of the Chicago mob went into retirement or succumbed to old age, Momo Giancana's star began to rise. He had masterminded the takeover of African American numbers rackets whose profits enabled him to branch out into other enterprises including skimming money from Las Vegas, Nevada,* casinos and extorting money from the entertainment industry. His acquaintances with top comedians, singers, and movie actors in Hollywood and Las Vegas were widely known. Frank Sinatra and Phyllis McGuire were identified as close friends. And then there was the Kennedy connection.

In the controversies surrounding the Kennedy assassination, organized crime figures prominently. Many observers critical of the Warren Commission Report, which identified Lee Harvey Oswald as the lone assassin, have not only challenged that conclusion as absurd but have produced evidence of complex secret connections among the Kennedy election campaign in 1960, the anti-Castro movement, and the CIA/Mafia linkage. Giancana seems to have been deeply involved in all of these events. Apparently, a love/hate relationship existed between the Kennedys and the Mafia.

Before Robert F. Kennedy* was appointed attorney general of the United States by his brother John, Bobby went after Jimmy Hoffa,* the corrupt head of the International Teamsters Union, and led the effort to mobilize a war against the underworld by insisting that J. Edgar Hoover* FBI director, energize his agency in the fight. Kennedy played a role not only in revitalizing federal law enforcement by creating federal "strike forces," which combined the resources and expertise of federal and local law enforcement, but targeted specific leaders of the American Cosa Nostra—among them Carlos Marcello* of Louisiana, Giancana of Chicago, and Jimmy Hoffa, president of the International Teamsters Union. Hoffa was accused of allowing gangsters access to union pension funds, which were then invested in Las Vegas casinos. Hoffa's angry resistance to Kennedy served to deepen Kennedy's resolve to "get Hoffa." In the midst of this feud between the country's most powerful trade union boss and the top law enforcement officer of the United States was a sordid history of mob alliances with the Kennedy administration.

The Kennedys, through the patriarch of the family, Joseph Kennedy, had long affiliations with the mob. Frank Costello,* the "Prime Minister of the Underworld," often boasted that he and Joe Kennedy were bootleggers* together during Prohibition (*see* PROHIBITION AND ORGANIZED CRIME*). The 1960 election campaign was close, and rumors circulated that the Kennedy campaign, directed by Bobby, had reached out to the Mafia in key states and election districts including Cook County (Chicago) Illinois and New Orleans. Sam Giancana helped to carry Cook County for the Kennedys in spite of a preelection insult from Bobby Kennedy, who brought Giancana in to face the McClelland Committee* and humiliated him publicly with embarrassing questions.

The relationship between Giancana and the Kennedy administration was indeed strange. Judith Campbell, a prostitute and sometime lover of Giancana, also maintained a sexual relationship with President Kennedy and, according to her, passed messages between the two men.

Even with Bobby hounding hoodlums, the Kennedys still took favors from the Mafia. An arrangement began in 1960 where the CIA hired Giancana and John Roselli,* assisted by Cuban exiles in south Florida, to kill Fidel Castro, but the plot never materialized; many of the underworld participants, including Giancana and Roselli, were subsequently murdered before scheduled congressional hearings in 1975 and 1976 about the CIA/underworld connection.

Prior to his mysterious death in 1975, Giancana generated a great deal of attention with his public friendship with Frank Sinatra and open romance with Las Vegas entertainer Phyliss McGuire. Momo led a public life when confronting the law enforcement establishment: A lot of publicity was generated when he obtained an injunction against FBI-intensive surveillance of his home, business places, and recreational locations. After serving almost a year in prison, from July 1965 to May 1966, for refusing to testify before a federal grand jury after he had been granted immunity from prosecution, Giancana went into exile in Mexico and remained there until 1974. Apparently, the Chicago Outfit,* which had run smoothly without Giancana and his high profile, many romances, and battles with the government that attracted unwanted attention, had no need of him. In July 1974 Mexican immigration authorities forced him back into the United States, where he was wanted for questioning in the murder of a former Outfit member who worked as an informer for the Special Investigations Unit of the Cook County Sheriff's Office.

In 1975, as the details of the Mafia/CIA relationship were being disclosed, Giancana was subpoenaed to testify before a Senate committee. He had been replaced by Joey Aiuppa as street boss—a selection Giancana opposed. Just days before his scheduled appearance, on June 19, he was cooking dinner in his basement kitchen when he was murdered. It is believed that the person who was with him, a trusted acquaintance, no doubt, murdered him—probably someone Giancana would not have suspected. The irony is that Giancana's intimate knowledge of how the Mafia stalks and destroys its victims was of no help to him personally.

**SUGGESTED READINGS:** William Brashler, *The Don: The Life and Death of Sam Giancana.* 1977; Sam Giancana and Chuck Giancana, *Double Cross.* 1992.

**GIGANTE, VINCENT "THE CHIN."** (b. 1926, New York City—incarcerated). Head of the Genovese crime family* and mob enforcer.

Vincent "The Chin" Gigante. Reproduced from the
Collections of the Library of Congress.

Before his imprisonment in 1997, Vincent "The Chin" Gigante, reputed boss
of the Genovese crime family, would often be seen wandering the streets of
"Little Italy" in a bathrobe, muttering to himself or talking to trees and birds.
Many believed he was mentally ill and could not stand trial; others, primarily
law enforcement authorities, believed it was an act orchestrated to keep Gigante
out of jail. "He is sick," claimed his brother, Father Louis Gigante, a Roman
Catholic priest and former member of the New York City Council. Until 1997,
prosecutors and defense attorneys clashed over whether he suffered from a de-
bilitating disorder like schizophrenia or a dementia stemming from vascular
disease. But trials could not be put off when Salvatore "Sammy the Bull" Gravano,* the highest-ranking mob defector in history who put John Gotti* and
many others away for life, testified that Gigante's illness was a clever charade
designed to shield him from prosecution.

The Genovese crime family is considered by many experts to be the most
sophisticated among the five that operate in the New York metropolitan area.
Under Gigante's leadership, it has avoided major disruptions and infiltrations
that the other families have been vulnerable to because of inept security, internal
bickering, and the ever-present threat of law enforcement surveillance.

Gigante was born and raised in Greenwich Village, which was a bohemian
community but also an Italian ethnic neighborhood in New York City. He

dropped out of high school and pursued a career as a boxer. His occupation was listed as a tailor. Gigante's career in a Cosa Nostra* dates from 1957 when Vito Genovese,* a powerful boss in the Luciano crime family,* ordered Frank Costello,* another influential boss in the Luciano family, killed so that he, Genovese, could seize the leadership of the entire crime family. Until then, Gigante functioned as no more than a thug and strong arm on the fringes of the family. The rubout of Frank Costello was an opportunity to become a full-fledged member and acquire the wealth and power associated with being a "made man." The Chin practiced his marksmanship in anticipation of the hit.*

On May 2, 1957, Costello was entering his apartment building on Central Park West when a car pulled up to the curb; a huge man got out, rushed past Costello, and entered the building. When Costello got into the lobby, the big man appeared from behind a pillar and called out, "This is for you, Frank." Costello turned as a bullet grazed his scalp just above his right ear. But Costello survived what looked like a fatal head wound. The Chin was identified by witnesses in the lobby and quickly arrested. When the Chin surrendered to authorities, he had lost most of the 300 pounds he weighed when he attempted to kill Frank Costello. No one could identify him as the shooter, including Costello, who had the best look at him. Gigante was acquitted. Obviously, Costello adhered to the code of omerta* (silence). Gigante's attempted assassination was the opening event of major changes that were about to occur in the American underworld. The struggle for control of Cosa Nostra activities and families was ignited by the assassination of Albert Anastasia,* several lower-level bosses in the Anastasia family, and the debacle of the Apalachin meeting* in November 1957.

In 1959, Gigante was sentenced to a seven-year prison term for narcotics violations. By the 1970s, he was back in the folds of the crime family and had risen to the rank of consigliere* (adviser) under Frank Tieri.* It is believed that in 1987 when Anthony Salerno* was imprisoned in the "Commission* case" along with other bosses, Gigante became acting boss.

The Chin would appear in the streets of "Little Italy" apparently disoriented. He managed to avoid prosecution for years using this tactic and instructed his soldiers* (crime family members) never to use his name in conversations. The combination of feigned mental illness, extraordinary security measures against electronic surveillance, and a low-keyed profile enabled Gigante to stay out of jail and helped his crime organization to survive and emerge as the most powerful in the United States in recent years.

Indictment in 1990 on extortion and bid-rigging in the construction industry and in 1993 an indictment on a murder conspiracy charge that involved a plot to kill John Gotti, head of the Gambino crime family,* finally were heard in trial after appeals claiming Gigante was incompetent to stand trial were exhausted. He was convicted and imprisoned for life.

**SUGGESTED READINGS:** T. J. English, "Where Crime Rules," *New York Times*. June 26, 1995: 11; Selwyn Roab, "Crackdown on Mob Seen as a Mixed Blessing by Merchants of Fulton Fish Market," *New York Times*. March 31, 1996: 18.

## "GOOD FELLOWS." *See* SOLDIERS

**GORDON, "WAXEY."** (b. Irving Wexler, 1886, Manhattan, NY—d. June 24, 1952, Alcatraz Prison, San Francisco, CA). Major New York Prohibition bootlegger* and gangster.

Before Prohibition (*see* PROHIBITION AND ORGANIZED CRIME*), Waxey Gordon was a skilled street criminal, a "cannon" (pickpocket) whose deftness in picking pockets was so good that it was said the victim's purse or wallet was coated in wax. Gordon graduated from robbery when Prohibition became the law of the land. He married a rabbi's daughter and teamed up with members of Egan's Rats,* a St. Louis mob specializing in hijacking trucks. Financed by Arnold "The Brain" Rothstein,* Gordon emerged as a major bootlegger with a fleet of rum ships and breweries. By the 1920s, having perfected the art of the payoff to politicians and police, Gordon became a multimillionaire and lived extravagantly in New York City and southern New Jersey with a diverse portfolio of nightclub ownership, speakeasies, illegal gambling* joints, and a fleet of rum-running ships.

All of this wealth and influence put him into conflict with Meyer Lansky,* "Bugsy" Siegel,* Charles "Lucky" Luciano,* and Dutch Schultz* in a struggle for control of bootleg territory known as the "War of the Jews." Lansky reputedly fed information to the IRS about sources of Gordon's $1 to $2 million yearly income. By November of 1933 Gordon was brought to federal trial by Thomas E. Dewey,* then a chief assistant in the U.S. Attorney's Office. Waxey Gordon was convicted and served 7 years of a 10-year sentence for tax evasion. When released in 1940, he could not regain his former power in the underworld and resorted to small-time narcotics dealing for which he was arrested and sentenced to 25 years to life and shipped off to Alcatraz prison. At the age of 63, incarcerated in a prison designed for violent felons, he died of a heart attack, having served only six months.

**SUGGESTED READING:** Jenna W. Joselit, *Our Gang: Jewish Crime and The New York Jewish Community, 1900–1940*. 1983.

**GOTTI, JOHN.** ("Johnny Boy," "Dapper Don," "Teflon Don") (b. Oct. 27, 1940, Bronx, NY—   ). Boss (don)* of the Gambino crime family.*

In a career of just under seven years as the boss of the most powerful Mafia crime family in the United States, John Gotti seized the popular imagination as no other gangster since Alphonse Capone* more than a half century before. He grasped power by murdering the boss, Paul Castellano,* who allegedly had

John Gotti. Reproduced courtesy of AP/
Wide World Photos.

marked Gotti for death because of complicity in drug dealing and his rebellious
ways.

Because of the sensational nature of Castellano's execution, Gotti became the
object of press attention when authorities let it be known that he was a prime
suspect in the murder—and the new godfather. He rose to the occasion. Gotti
dressed and behaved the way he thought the public expected gangsters to look
and act. It was as if he studied gangster movies to shape his image. With his
diamond pinkie ring, meticulously styled silvery hair, a healthy tan from regular
sunlamp treatments, his wardrobe of $2,000 custom-made Brioni double-
breasted suits and $200 handpainted ties, the tabloids were soon labeling him
"the Dapper Don." Instead of skulking in the shadows, Gotti reveled in his new
celebrity. Always ready with a quip, flashing a smile, he took to the television
cameras.

All but unknown prior to Castellano's murder, his past was dredged up.
Gotti's career as a mafioso began as an avenger, the man assigned to retaliate
against the kidnapper and murderer of Carlo Gambino's* nephew. Identified for
the murder, he had taken the conviction and imprisonment in what gangsters
consider manly fashion.

In 1956, John Gotti dropped out of school and joined a tough street gang,
where he came to the attention of mafia strongman Carmine ("Charley Wagons")
Fatico, a hijacker in the Gambino crime family. Through Fatico, Gotti met An-

iello Dellacroce,* a powerful underboss (sottocapo)* in the family, and entered into a criminal way of strong-arm tactics, cargo thefts, and hijackings at Kennedy Airport in Queens, New York. In 1967, he was arrested in connection with a hijacking and served three years. In 1973, he was again arrested, but this time on a murder charge. This was Gotti's first big assignment for the Gambino family. A nephew of Carlo Gambino had been kidnapped and murdered despite payment of a $100,000 ransom. Gotti and an associate were involved in the shooting of the kidnapper and were later identified and arrested. Ray Cohn, a well-connected defense attorney, managed to get the charges reduced to a four-year term. When Gotti was released from prison, he became a "made man" (inducted as a member into the crime family) and appointed an "acting captain" of the Bergin, Queens crew.

Gotti's life took a personally tragic turn in 1980 when his 12-year-old son Frank was killed in an auto accident involving a neighbor. The mysterious disappearance, and presumed death, of the neighbor who had accidentally killed Gotti's youngest son evoked chilling fear. At the same time his regularly solitary vigils at the boy's crypt showed a man with inconsolable grief. Who could not sympathize with a father's pain and anguish? A complex villain had emerged who was telegenic and apparently immune from the clutches of law enforcement. The "Dapper Don" became the "Teflon Don" after winning acquittal after acquittal.

With Gambino's death in 1976, Paul Castellano was elevated to head of the family. "Big Paul," as he was known to his associates, thought of himself as a businessman who was burdened with some deplorable associates, such as John Gotti, whose violence and thuggery, however, were useful from time to time. Gotti had the swagger, garish dress, and toughness of the hip, cool gangster. In contrast, Castellano affected the image of a businessman. He said when asked that he was a butcher (of meat, not men). The tensions between Castellano and Gotti would shake the crime family and the entire New York underworld to its foundations.

The internal conflict between Castellano and Gotti began in 1981 when a telephone tap on one of Gotti's associates uncovered evidence of drug trafficking, which led to an indictment against Gotti's brother Gene Gotti and, by extension, implicated John. The Gambino family had a simple, brutal rule concerning drugs: Deal drugs and die. Fearful of being murdered by the boss because his close associates had defied the drug ban, Gotti struck first. For years the Gambino family was fractured by conflicts over its direction and areas of interest. Gotti's mentor and partner Aniello Dellacroce died in 1985, and Gotti's protection from Castellano's wrath vanished. The tensions within the family were complicated by the widespread suspicion that Castellano himself was disliked by many of his own street soldiers and was capable of making deals with federal prosecutors to save himself from prison. The stage for a rebellion was set.

After clearing it with the heads of the other families (except for the unpredictable Vincent "The Chin" Gigante,* of the Genovese crime family*), Gotti arranged for eight assassins to murder Castellano and his chief capo, Thomas Bilotti, as they arrived at a mid-Manhattan restaurant for a meeting. The hit went off as planned on December 16, 1985. A few weeks later, Gotti was anointed as the new boss of the Gambino family.

In 1986, Gotti faced more trouble with racketeering charges that could have meant a 20-year sentence. Before the end of the year, *Time* magazine featured him on its cover accompanied by the stark line "Crime Boss" in a painting by the pop artist Andy Warhol. Till then, the only other gangster to have graced a *Time* cover, a half-century before, was Al Capone.

After a year in trial, in March 1987, Gotti was acquitted. In 1989, another attempt to topple the new "godfather" also failed when a union leader who was presumably the target of Gotti's anger recanted his testimony, and the "Teflon Don" confounded the government once again. Investigation of the Castellano murder turned up nothing substantial that implicated John Gotti, though everyone including the mob knew he engineered the hits.

Money from the enormously profitable construction industry rackets, loan-sharking,* extortion, gambling, and tribute from the 28 capos* running their crews* brought large sums of cash into John Gotti's greedy hands. As fast as the cash rolled in, lots of it quickly rolled out. Gotti was what is known as a "degenerate" gambler—a constant loser who bets impulsively. As a money machine turning out a steady stream of cash, the Gambino crime family had no equal. But it would soon come crashing down when the FBI discovered a weakness in the mob's defenses. Bugs and sophisticated electronic surveillance devices were planted in an apartment above the Ravenite Social Club, the official headquarters of the Gambino family on Mulberry Street in Little Italy. Gotti and his chief lieutenants, "Sammy the Bull" Gravano* and Frank Locascio, used the apartment for discussions of sensitive mob business. The apartment belonged to an elderly widow of a deceased mob soldier, which the FBI stumbled across quite by accident in routine visual surveillances.

Without realizing that the government was eavesdropping, John Gotti talked himself into a life sentence without parole. In December 1990, the government considered that it had sufficient evidence to arrest Gotti, Gravano, and Locascio on multiple racketeering counts and murder. By early fall 1991, Gravano broke his mafia vows and became a government witness. His testimony against his boss was devastating.

On April 2, 1991, after 13 hours of deliberation a jury found Gotti guilty of all the racketeering and murder counts against him. He received a life sentence without parole, which is currently being served at the maximum security federal penitentiary in Marion, Illinois.

**SUGGESTED READINGS:** John Cummings and Ernest Volkman, *Goombata: The Improbable Rise and Fall of John Gotti.* 1990; Gene Mustain and Jerry Capeci, *Mob Star: The Story of John Gotti, the Most Powerful Criminal in America.* 1988.

Salvatore "Sammy the Bull" Gravano. Reproduced courtesy of AP/Wide World Photos.

**GRAVANO, "SAMMY THE BULL."** (b. Salvatore Gravano, Mar. 12, 1945, NY—    ). Underboss (sottocapo)* of the La Cosa Nostra* Gambino crime family* and defector.

In 1992 the highest-ranking member of La Cosa Nostra ever to defect broke his blood oath of silence and testified against his boss, John Gotti,* head of the most powerful crime family in the United States. Salvatore ("Sammy the Bull") Gravano served as underboss in the Gambino crime family,* second in command of its numerous criminal enterprises across the nation. Unlike his publicity-seeking boss, Gravano clung to the tradition of secrecy of La Cosa Nostra and avoided the limelight. He became a government witness in many mafia trials and helped to convict major figures in the Italian American underworld.

Gravano grew up in the Bensonhurst section of Brooklyn in a household of Sicilian immigrant parents. Through hard work, his mother and father provided him and his two older sisters with a decent life. A dress manufacturing shop in Brooklyn enabled the Gravanos to own their home and acquire a summer residence in Long Island—a suburb to the east of New York City.

Because of a severe case of dyslexia, Gravano was considered a slow learner in school and was often discouraged and humiliated from continuing. The ultimate humiliation occurred when he was denied promotion in grade school and in junior high school. He dropped out and began to associate with a vicious gang in the streets of Brooklyn. Those who were not concerned with Gravano's difficulties in reading were hoodlums who admired instead his fierceness in street fighting. The nickname "Sammy the Bull" was a label Gravano acquired as a boy and it stayed with him through a notorious career as a gangster, murderer, and then defector from the underworld, where he spent much of his adult life. His experiences in the Brooklyn street gang where he had his first brushes with law enforcement were a training ground for a criminal career.

In 1964, as an alternative to a jail term, Gravano joined the army. After two years he was honorably discharged and returned to a life of petty crime back in Brooklyn.

By 1968, Gravano "went on the record" with a made member of the Colombo crime family.* Going on the record meant being affiliated openly with a Cosa Nostra member who would be responsible for his conduct. Gravano began a period of recruitment and sponsorship for eventual induction into the mafia. After committing murders for Cosa Nostra members, he was officially made a soldier* in the Gambino crime family in 1975.

As soon as Gravano was officially baptized a Gambino family soldier, he was authorized to have associates. He formed a "crew"* (a gang of criminal and noncriminal associates who themselves were not made men*) and proceeded to engage in typical criminal activities but also expanded his interests into construction and its related industries and labor unions. Eventually, Gravano would amass millions for himself and his bosses in construction racketeering in the New York area. He also ventured into night clubs, bars, and discotheques— mainly through legitimate business partners who served as "fronts."

In the mid-1980s events unfolded in New York that permanently changed this underworld. Based on wiretap and informant information, the government launched the "Pizza Connection"* cases against four of the five Cosa Nostra bosses in New York City, who together controlled the Commission* of the American Mafia.* The cases were drug related, and this could mean life sentences without parole for men in their late sixties and seventies, who could then expect to die in jail.

By 1985, the Cosa Nostra and law enforcement reached a milestone. Family bosses across the country were convicted and received lengthy sentences for conspiracies in the casino industries and racketeering enterprises founded with union pension funds. In New England and Philadelphia the crime families were under enormous pressure from the FBI. Paul Castellano* as head of the most powerful crime family was indicted and faced multiple RICO* charges. More than this, he feared being connected to drug trafficking, for which several members and associates of the Gambino family has been indicted. Castellano invoked a strict rule about drug trafficking: Family members were forbidden to deal drugs; disobey it and die.

John Gotti's brother Gene, his cousin Angelo Ruggerio, and John Carneglia— all made members—had been convicted of drug trafficking. For John Gotti, the options were clear: Kill the boss, or be killed. Over the years, Castellano had done little to bring together the main factions in the family, and conspiracy against the boss festered among those crews who felt alienated from the "Administration." Gotti decided to exploit the clamoring unrest among the crime family members and assassinate the boss. In this, he managed to persuade Gravano to join in the murder plot. Castellano was shot down in December 1985 in the teeming streets of Midtown Manhattan by John Gotti and Salvatore Gravano, who engineered the murder.

In the aftermath of the murders of Castellano and Bilotti (his right-hand man), Gotti emerged as the boss (don),* and Gravano was made a capo.* Within two years, his indispensable talents at moneymaking, murder, and discipline within the ranks elevated him to consigliere* and then underboss—the number-two man in the crime family.

In December 1990, Gotti, Gravano, and Frank Locascio, the leaders of the crime family, were arrested in the family's headquarters in Little Italy—the Ravenite Social Club.

Gravano was charged with RICO racketeering counts that included illegal gambling,* loansharking,* obstruction of justice, conspiracy to murder, and murder. Later Gravano would blame Gotti's ostentatious style of leadership as contributing to their arrests and convictions. He soon realized that he was to be made the bad guy and positioned to take the fall on the murder counts for Gotti. In late October 1991, Gravano announced to government attorneys and FBI agents that he wanted to "switch governments." Gravano told his biographer Peter Maas that it became clear to him that Gotti intended to offer him as a sacrificial lamb to the government by arranging a defense that would cast the blame for the murders on Gravano.

Gravano became the government's star witness and helped to convict John Gotti and scores of other criminals within the ranks of La Cosa Nostra.

In 1994, Gravano was sentenced to five years, followed by three years of supervised release. After a short stay in the government's Witness Security Program* and some surgical work on his face, Gravano became a free man.

**SUGGESTED READING:** Peter Mass, *Underboss: Sammy the Bull Gravano's Story of Life in the Mafia.* 1997.


**GUZIK, JAKE.** ("Greasy Thumb") (b. 1886, Moscow, Russia—d. Feb. 21, 1956, Chicago, IL). Capone associate and financial adviser.

Guzik was neither a gunman nor a goon in Alphonse Capone's* organization. He was a brilliant bookkeeper and a bootlegger* with interests in prostitution. Guzik was the indispensable payoff man for the Capone organization; he dispensed bribes and payoffs to police officers, politicians, and businessmen.

During the 1940s and 1950s when Capone was gone, Guzik worked diligently for Frank "The Enforcer" Nitti,* Anthony Joseph Accardo,* and Paul "The

Waiter" Ricca*—the heirs to the Capone empire known as the Chicago Outfit.* His advice on syndicate* matters was sought by many organized crime figures including Joseph Adonis, Frank Costello,* and Meyer Lansky.*

His only serious legal problems occurred in the 1930s when he served five years for tax evasion. He died in bed of natural causes—one of the few Chicago Outfit leaders to do so.

**SUGGESTED READING:** Robert M. Lombardo, "The Social Organization of Organized Crime in Chicago," *Contemporary Criminal Justice*. December 4, 1994: 290–313.

# H

**HELL'S ANGELS.** The biggest, most original, and perhaps baddest motorcycle gang ever is the Hell's Angels. In the deviant subcultures of petty criminals, drifters, and rebellious personalities, an "Angel" symbolizes freedom and individualism; for law enforcement authorities, a Hell's Angel spells trouble.

Formed in California in 1947 by a group of ex-servicemen who had no desire to return to a humdrum nine-to-five life after their experiences in wartime, the Hell's Angels have spread to several foreign countries. Films romanticizing their lifestyles and subculture are numerous. Their nomadic values and rebellious streak have often led to major confrontations with law enforcement authorities. The Hell's Angels are now believed to represent a very serious criminal threat much like the traditional organized crime groups in the United States.

When they formed in San Bernardino, California, the Angels initially called themselves the "Pissed Off Bastards of Bloomington," (POBOB), which is a small town between San Bernardino and Riverside. They were dedicated to mocking conventional social values through acts of petty vandalism and rowdiness. It was only later in a police incident at a motorcycle rally in Hollister, California, that the term "outlaw" was used to describe the POBOB. They reorganized in Fontana, California, in 1948 under the name "Hell's Angels" and adopted the dress and symbols of black leather jackets, blue jeans, and boots that would become internationally known.

Because of their constant troubles with the police, by 1957 the Hell's Angels were on the brink of extinction. Having been in contact with people familiar with drugs, the Angels became involved in the distribution of methamphetamine, or "speed," also known as "crack." With drug dealing and the publicity stemming from films such as *The Wild One* (1954), with Marlon Brando, *Hell's Angels on Wheels*, with Jack Nicholson, and exaggerations of their dangerousness by the California attorney general, their ranks swelled. By the late 1960s, returning Vietnam veterans angry with their treatment also found a hospitable environment among the Hell's Angels.

From the hell-raising rascals of the post–World War II era, a number of clubs have become highly structured, disciplined organizations whose main source of income is no longer legitimate work but pure criminal activity.

The Hell's Angels are centered in California, with the "mother club" in Oakland. The Angels have a written constitution and bylaws; they have become so big that they are divided into East and West Coast factions. The structure of the motorcycle club is replete with the offices of president, vice president, road captains, sergeant at arms, treasurers, and enforcers.

Historically, the Hell's Angels have been all-white male in composition: no blacks, no Jews, no minorities; women typically are playthings and exploited in various criminal enterprises as prostitutes, drug couriers, and weapons carriers. The criminal activities include motorcycle and auto theft, prostitution, illegal weapons dealing, and drug trafficking. In addition, the Angels have operated as partners with traditional organized crime groups as enforcers and murderers.

The threat the Hell's Angels pose was described in the report of the President's Commission on Organized Crime in 1986. It stated that the outlaw motorcycle group evolved from a bunch of rowdy rebels into a genuine organized crime group. *See also* OUTLAW MOTORCYCLE GANGS

**SUGGESTED READING:** Yves Lavigne, *Hell's Angels: Taking Care of Business*. 1987.

**HERRERA-BUITRAGO, HELMER.** ("Pacho") (b. 1951, Palmira, Colombia— incarcerated). Colombian cocaine trafficking boss, Cali cocaine cartel.*

"Pacho Herrera's" surrender to the Colombian National Police is the result of their untiring efforts to bring the last of the Cali cartel kingpins before the bar of justice. While little is known outside of Colombian and American law enforcement circles, Herrera is one of the most influential and violent members of the Cali cartel leadership. His surrender in September 1996 after months of being on the run is additional proof that these gangsters are not invincible.

Herrera is one of the charter members of the Cali mafia and was the only remaining "kingpin" being sought by Colombian authorities. He had been the subject of an intensive manhunt by the Colombian National Police (CNP) and the Drug Enforcement Administration of the U.S. government for the past year.

Pacho Herrera started his criminal career selling relatively small amounts of cocaine in New York, where he was arrested in 1975 and later in 1979. He was a major supplier of cocaine for both New York and southern Florida. The Colombian charges against Herrera were based upon the seizure of 3,500 kilograms of cocaine in Tarpon Springs, Florida, in 1988. The violence and suffering caused by Herrera's criminal activities ranged from the jungles of Colombia to the neighborhoods of Florida and the streets of New York.

Herrera's organization was large and well organized. He had multiple sources for cocaine base from both Peru and Bolivia and an excellent transportation

Virginia Hill. Reproduced from the Collections of the
Library of Congress.

organization, which delivered cocaine base to numerous conversion laboratories
in Colombia. DEA intelligence reports indicate that Herrera had used his close
association with various guerrilla groups including M-19 and FARC for the
protection of remote laboratory sites. Herrera's organization staged multiton cocaine shipments from clandestine airstrips in Colombia or from north coast ports
through Central America and the Caribbean to various U.S. locations. To ensure
the rapid return of his cocaine distribution profits to Colombia, he operated one
of the Cali cartel's most profitable money laundering* operations in New York.

Pacho Herrera in 1995 become the subject of law enforcement investigations
in the Eastern District of New York and was indicted on drug-related charges
in Federal District Court in the Southern District of Florida in June 1995. *See
also* OCHOA, JORGE LUIS VASQUEZ

**SUGGESTED READING:** Francisco Thoumi, "Why the Illegal Psychoactive Drugs
Industry Grew in Colombia," *Journal of Interamerican Studies and World Affairs*. Fall,
1992: 37–63.

**HILL, VIRGINIA.** (b. 1918, AL—d. Mar. 1966, Salzburg, Austria). Mob witness
and syndicate* courier.

Hill left rural Alabama at the age of 16 and went to Chicago to make her way in show business. She found employment with a bookie, Joe Epstein, who introduced her to Alphonse Capone* big shots Frank "The Enforcer" Nitti* and Anthony Joseph Accardo* and New York gangsters such as Joseph Adonis* and Frank Costello.* Hill was a party girl but also had a specific function besides providing sex, which involved carrying a great deal of cash for various members of the crime syndicate to secret Swiss bank accounts.

But "Bugsy" Siegel* was Hill's true love and cause of her subsequent problems with the mob and the government. When Siegel launched his Las Vegas, Nevada,* project to build a casino/hotel in the desert using mob money, Virginia Hill was at his side assisting him in the interior design and layout of the construction. As the project proceeded and costs mounted alarmingly, suspicions grew that a double cross was in the making. In order to quell criticisms among mob investors, Hill went to Paris in June 1947 while Siegel stayed at her home in Beverly Hills, California. Siegel was murdered, and Meyer Lansky* told her to return the money Siegel gave her for the Swiss account. Fearing for her life, she returned it.

In 1951, she appeared before the Kefauver Committee* and entertained the senators and the nation with her jaunty televised testimony but did not reveal the secrets of mob operations. Untroubled by a reputation as a morally loose woman, Hill left the United States and wandered through Europe with her husband, an Austrian ski instructor. It was rumored that she provided funds to the exiled Charles "Lucky" Luciano* in Italy.

She attempted suicide several times and finally succeeded in 1966 in Austria, where she swallowed sleeping pills.

**SUGGESTED READING:** Dean Jennings, *We Only Kill Each Other*. 1967.

**HINES, JIMMY.** (b. James J. Hines, 1877, New York City—d. 1957, NY). Tammany Hall political leader and mob affiliate.

Jimmy Hines grew up in ward politics where politicians relied heavily on the services of gangsters to win elections. So it was no surprise that he staged his electoral campaigns at the turn of the century for aldermen with the help of hoodlums such as Spike Sullivan and Harry "Gyp the Blood" Horowitz in the upper west side of Manhattan. As his career matured, Hines developed relationships with a broader, more powerful group of New York racketeers including Arnold "The Brain" Rothstein,* Dutch Schultz,* Owney Madden,* and Frank Costello,* the last being the Mafia's emissary to the political machines.

The extent of the tie between local politics and the mob is illustrated by the fact that in 1932 when Hines attended the Democratic Party National Convention in Chicago that nominated Franklin Delano Roosevelt, Frank Costello shared his hotel suite. On Schultz's payroll alone, Hines received from $500 to $1,000 per week to protect the numbers* rackets in Harlem and Manhattan and the bootleg operations in the Bronx. Hines's principal duty as the political agent of the mob was to see to it that police did not interfere with their rackets.

In 1935, Thomas E. Dewey* became district attorney of Manhattan and targeted key racketeers such as Schultz, "Waxey" Gordon,* and Charles "Lucky" Luciano,* along with their henchmen and partners in legitimate society. Dewey, a Republican and future presidential candidate, went after Hines, who was at one time the most powerful Democrat in New York State and Roosevelt's primary patronage dispenser in New York City. The first prosecution on conspiracies involving bribes of the judiciary and police ended in a mistrial, but Hines was convicted on February 25, 1939, in a second trial and went to Sing Sing prison in 1940, where he served 4 years. Hines died in 1957, at age 80; he epitomized the political-criminal nexus that enables organized crime to exist.

**SUGGESTED READING:** James B. Jacobs, *Busting the Mob: United States vs. Cosa Nostra.* 1994.

**HIT.** (Mob murder). It is necessary to kill people in the underworld, but organized criminals attempt to do this on most occasions within the bounds of good public relations. When a member of the Mafia or some other criminal organization is marked for murder, the deed can often be engineered as a disappearance. The victim simply vanishes without a trace—no visible gunplay, no blood, no body, no noisy violence, no public outcry. In many cases, when the man and his car disappear, his family does not even report him missing. Even when they do, the technique is not only good public relations, but it helps ensure that the crime will never be solved: a missing person does not rate the same police attention as a murder. Take the case of Anthony C. Strollo ("Tony Bender," "Tony Banda"), a capo* in the Genovese crime family.* On the morning of April 8, 1962, Bender told his wife he was going out for a "few minutes"; he strolled out of his home and was never seen again. It is rumored that he is either part of a New York skyscraper or that he "sleeps with the fishes" (dumped in the river).

There are times when a murder, a hit, cannot be concealed, especially when, unlike Tony Bender who apparently was taken by surprise, a victim's suspicions have been aroused and he becomes careful about where he goes and who he is with, as Joseph Valachi* did in the Atlanta Prison. In retaliation for the contract hit on his life, which he discovered and avoided, Valachi talked and talked, unraveling the great secret history of La Cosa Nostra* on television before the McClelland Committee.*

A man who is aware of a threat against his life will have to be killed publicly ("cowboying it"), but it is important that innocent bystanders not be hit, as they were in the Alphonse Capone*–Charles Dion O'Banion* bootlegging wars in Chicago. The death of one waiter, child, or cab driver will cause more indignation than the murder of a dozen gangsters. The safety of bystanders is one of the reasons the machine gun is no longer used except in unusual circumstances. It is a difficult weapon to control. In the fall of 1967 during the internal warfare in the Bonanno crime family,* a special situation did occur, and a machine gun

Jimmy Hoffa. Reproduced from the Collections of the Library of Congress.

was used to hit three gangsters in a New York restaurant. If the enforcer had used a pistol, one of the men might have had enough time to shoot back. If he had used a shotgun, pellets might have hit other patrons. As it was, the hit man came out of the kitchen, walked close to the table where the victims were sitting, and killed them all with a single, expertly aimed burst of gunfire.

The need to discourage informers and rebels from defying the crime organization's authority can justify an exception to the rule to keep murder concealed and quiet. The old symbolism—mutilation of the sex organs, blotted-out eyes, a coin on the lips—is passé, but the disciplinary value of a headless or handless corpse makes the mob's point vividly.

**HOFFA, JIMMY.** (b. James R. Hoffa, Feb. 14, 1913, Brazil, IN—d. missing July 30, 1975, presumed dead, Detroit, MI). Teamsters Union president, associate of organized crime groups.

In 1924, Jimmy Hoffa moved with his family to Detroit, Michigan, where he would ascend in 1957 to the head of the largest, most powerful labor union in the United States—the International Brotherhood of Teamsters. The teamsters represented 1.6 million workers involved in trucking, transport, and manufacturing in the United States and Canada.

Plotting Hoffa's career on a chart of success and failure would describe a parabola. He organized his first strike at the tender age of 19 and soon after joined the Detroit local of the Teamsters. By all accounts, like the Reuther brothers, John L. Lewis and Harry Bridges, Hoffa was a natural in the labor union business. His curve crested just about the time of Senate hearings and his indictment, and he slid slowly into oblivion during his imprisonment. July 30, 1975, the day of his apparent abduction and murder, marked the end of a stormy, brilliant career.

Settling into his professional twilight like so many of his predecessors, Hoffa was accorded by the rank and file secular sainthood. But he was no sentimental hero, nor was he a romantic primitive. The legacy is more complicated and contradictory than that: He could be raw meat with adversaries and then shrewd and fair-minded with others; he believed, perhaps sincerely, in giving ex-cons a break, since so many of them were frozen out of any work at all. Unlike Dave Beck, Jackie Presser, and others, Hoffa was a half pint, but he compensated for the lack of physical size and brawn with swagger and toughness. Throughout his life he kept physically fit and made a fetish of his prowess; his bluster and explosive temper were calculated weapons expertly wielded to sustain an image of the bulldog with a tight-mouthed smirk and devastating glare.

Hoffa could hate as fervently and blindly as he could love. When President-Kenney was murdered, he ordered the flag at national headquarters in Washington, D.C. to fly topside in twisted, childish defiance of the national mourning. The two sides of his personality may not be mere cynical contrivances designed to instill fear and gain power as much as they are aspects of personal fears that hounded him throughout his life.

In 1941 his involvement with organized crime began after he had risen to the leadership of Local 299 in Detroit. Hoffa found himself in a battle not with the management of a business firm taking advantage of its drivers but with the CIO, the huge trade union organization that took up the slack of the AFL. The CIO competed with the IBT to represent Detroit Teamsters and employed a small army of goons that beat up IBT recruiters and organizers. In response, Hoffa also turned to the underworld and obtained the services of the Meli crime family. The CIO lost the battle, but so did the Teamsters and Jimmy Hoffa because the labor leader would become a pawn of the gangsters and in the process be transformed himself into a labor racketeer.

Gangsters like Anthony Provenzano,* a capo* in the New York Genovese crime family,* and a Teamster local president in New Jersey, would help to push Hoffa to the top, and Hoffa in return helped gangsters use their union position for personal moneymaking schemes, extortion from employers, loan-sharking,* and pension frauds.

For as long as anyone can remember, the Teamsters were joined at the hip with La Cosa Nostra.* LCN benefited from the pension funds and the legitimate veneer that Teamster employment afforded many of its members. At the same time, the Teamster links with the mob provided it with an image of toughness.

The real energy behind Hoffa was in the struggles and confrontations with Attorney General Robert F. Kennedy* against the backdrop of underworld intrigues. Curiously, it is in conflict with the government that Hoffa exhibits a defiant moral nobility; Jimmy thought Bobby Kennedy was an opportunist, a rich kid, who meddled in union affairs only to develop a reputation as a crime fighter at the expense of the working man.

At first, Kennedy had an abrasive history with Hoffa over the involvement of organized crime in the Teamsters. As counsel to the McClelland Committee* on Labor Racketeering before his brother's election as president and his appointment as attorney general, Bobby Kennedy saw the Apalachin incident (*see* APALACHIN MEETING*) in 1957 as a ripe event for maneuvering the "Mafia"* back into the public eye. Now the Committee could display its outrage at the invasion of dangerous gangsters and hoodlums into the unions. In 1958, the Committee reported that labor bosses were enriching themselves at the expense of honest union members. The First Interim Report of the Committee mentioned Jimmy Hoffa by name as backing racketeers who stole union funds, extorted money from employers, and sought to undermine union prerogatives in negotiating work conditions by arranging sweetheart contracts.

Added to this, the antagonism between the two became inflamed and bitter over the controversial 1960 Presidential election. The Teamsters supported Nixon not JFK and were instrumental in delivering Ohio into the Republican column. Despite heavy mob support for Kennedy in Illinois, Florida, Louisiana and Kentucky, among other states, the Kennedys made Hoffa their public enemy number one.

With Kennedy as attorney general, Hoffa became a top priority for the Administration. In 1962 Kennedy's efforts succeeded in bringing Hoffa to trial for employer extortion. The case ended in a hung jury, but then Hoffa was nabbed for attempting to bribe a juror. He was sentenced to eight years. In 1964 he was convicted of misappropriating $1.7 million in union pension funds. He appealed for three years and then served 58 months, having his term commuted by President Richard Nixon, whom the IBT supported, in 1971.

Though his release contained the proviso that he avoid union activity for ten years, he ignored it and sought to regain control of the Teamsters. The mob apparently had other ideas and had established a cozy relationship with its president Frank Fitzsimmons. Should Hoffa return to power—which was plausible, given his popularity among the rank and file—FBI surveillance could interfere with underworld operations. The entreaties to stay clear of the union from Cosa Nostra leaders like Provenzano, Anthony Salerno,* head of the Genovese crime family at that time, and "Tony Ducks" Corrallo,* head of the Luchese crime family,* went unheeded by Hoffa. On July 30, 1975, Hoffa went to a meeting in suburban Detroit with some labor bosses and mobsters. He was never seen again. *See also* INTERNATIONAL BROTHERHOOD OF TEAMSTERS

**SUGGESTED READINGS:** Steven Bull, *The Teamsters.* 1978; Dan Moldea, *The Hoffa Wars.* 1978.

**HOLSTEIN, CASPER.** (b. Virgin Islands—d. Apr. 9, 1944, New York City). Harlem policy rackets organizer.

No one seems to know exactly where or with whom the numbers* game originated, but the most authoritative sources suggest that it began with a West Indian black—Casper Holstein, who combined the traits of a financier with the imagination of a Midas. Before his rise to affluence he studied the financial press with feverish interest. Arriving in New York just before the old policy game was wiped out, he learned a rewarding lesson—that everybody everywhere desires to get rich quickly and that this desire could be profitably exploited. When he rose to wealth and position, he contributed to black education, donating annually a substantial literary prize, and arranged for hundreds of poor black children to enjoy summer recreational activities on the Hudson.

Holstein was considered by many to have been the foremost policy king in Harlem during the 1920s. In his 1926 novel *Nigger Heaven*, Carl Van Vechten depicted life in Harlem during the early 1920s. A character in the book, Randolph Pettijohn, the "Bolita King," is Van Vechten's fictional characterization of Casper Holstein. In real life, Holstein was the owner of a popular club in Harlem, the Turf Club, located at 111 West 136th Street. In September 1928, Casper Holstein was kidnapped by white gangsters who demanded a $50,000 ransom for his release. The event was widely reported in the media. After his release three days later, he failed to identify the five men who were arrested for his kidnapping. The case sparked national attention. It was the first time a wealthy African American was kidnapped and held for $50,000 ransom. The *New York Times* reported that Holstein, one of Harlem's wealthiest African Americans, had bet more than $30,000 on the races at Belmont Park in the week before his abduction. His notoriety suggested another dimension to Harlem: not engulfed in wretched poverty but also affluent, with criminal money flowing easily. A year later in Chicago, Illinois, Walter Kelly, an African American policy banker, was also kidnapped by white gangsters and held for $25,000 ransom.

In the early 1930s, when the Seabury Commission (*see* SEABURY INVESTIGATIONS*) investigated corruption in the Magistrate's Courts of the Bronx and Manhattan, Harlem's policy operators came under scrutiny. Holstein is alleged to have dropped out of the policy racket to avoid public notice. He was arrested for the first time in 1935 for a policy violation. He maintained that it was his aggressive involvement in Virgin Islands politics, his homeland, that led law enforcement authorities to investigate his alleged gambling activities in New York. He claimed that he was framed. He received a penitentiary term and remained in prison for nearly a year.

Although he may have ended his career ignominiously, Holstein was one of many criminal entrepreneurs who operated a large-scale policy bank in the Harlem ghetto, employing hundreds of policy workers. Apart from their chief purpose of generating money, numbers gambling banks created jobs for the unemployed and were a source of ready capital in African American communities. Those African Americans who were gainfully employed outside the Harlem community and brought their salaries back to Harlem, using part of it to play numbers, added to the economy of the area. In addition, a usury industry sprang up to serve the clientele of the numbers game. This species of an illegal enterprise* may have broadened its scope beyond the gambling needs of the minority community, taking on a life of its own. The extent to which numbers became an integral part of the economy in African American communities is suggested by African American writer Saunders Redding, who characterized the pervasiveness of numbers gambling as "the fever that has struck all classes and conditions of men." *See also* AFRICAN AMERICAN ORGANIZED CRIME; SCHULTZ, DUTCH; ST. CLAIR, STEPHANIE

**SUGGESTED READINGS:** James B. Johnson, *Black Manhattan*. 1968; Allan H. Spear, *Black Chicago: The Making of a Negro Ghetto*, 1890–1920. 1967; Saunder J. Redding, "Playing the Numbers," *The North American Review*. December 1934: 533–42.

**HOOVER, J. EDGAR.** (b. Jan. 1, 1895, Washington, D.C.—d. May 2, 1972, Washington, D.C.). FBI director from 1924 to 1972.

For a long time, indeed ever since the 1920s, J. Edgar Hoover refused to admit the reality of interstate organized crime. "They're just a bunch of hoodlums," he would say as if that settled the matter. By rights, the war on organized crime should have been directed by Hoover. He virtually invented the FBI. Hoover was in the Department of Justice in 1924 when the Bureau was created; as its director, he defined its mission and activities through the 1960s.

It took a new administration in Washington, D.C. in 1961 with a brash, young attorney general, Robert F. Kennedy,* to galvanize the director into action. Kennedy demanded that Hoover take steps to control and eventually crush La Cosa Nostra.* Hoover's critics in looking for an explanation of his frequent denials that a mafia existed in the United States found that his social contacts included associations that gratified his gambling compulsions, which they took to mean that he had close ties with people on the edge of the underworld. There is at least some truth to this theory. But Hoover may have had less sinister, more practical reasons to ignore big-time gangsters and Mafia racketeers. His reputation was to play it safe in the volatile atmosphere of federal bureaucracy, so in the 1930s he took the politically easy path of chasing bank robbers like "Baby Face" Nelson, John Dillinger, "Machine Gun" Kelly, and Communists. On the other hand, to confront the national underworld would have meant expending major resources and committing agents to investigations with no certain outcome. Moreover, going after organized crime meant exposing his agents to significant corruption hazards. Whatever Hoover's reasons, no one was happier than the mob.

J. Edgar Hoover. Reproduced from the Collections of the Library of Congress.

It has been rumored that the mob manipulated the director through his horse-
racing mania. Frank Costello* and Frank Erickson, top kingpins in syndicate*
gambling operations, would pass "tips" on horses to Walter Winchell,* a New
York gossip columnist, who would pass these along to Hoover as sure things.
Duly compromised, Hoover would be unlikely to initiate an attack against the
syndicate.

The director's deliberate blindness toward organized crime ended abruptly in
1957 when a major incident occurred in Apalachin, New York. A national Cosa
Nostra conference was discovered and broken up by New York State police.
The state troopers managed to round up nearly 60 mob bosses. Leading newspapers in the country were critical of the FBI because the Apalachin meeting*
was uncovered by accident, by a curious local state police officer. Editorials
wondered, Where was the FBI? Not even Hoover would dare to deny the existence of organized crime after this embarrassment.

Hoover quickly responded, demanding that his agency get up to speed after
nearly three decades of denial and indifference. While some FBI agents now
felt unshackled to go after the mob, Hoover placed responsibility for gathering
intelligence data with the Bureau's research and analysis division. Hoover soon
tired of the chase and would have eased back had not Bobby Kennedy, the new
attorney general in 1961, intervened and insisted as Hoover's boss that the FBI
keep up the pressure on the Mafia. Perhaps because of his background as chief

counsel with the McClelland Committee* investigating labor racketeering, Kennedy had no compunctions about tangling with Hoover. Kennedy told Hoover to go after the Cosa Nostra. With Kennedy's prodding the FBI became the major law enforcement agency combating traditional organized crime. *See also* APALACHIN MEETING

**SUGGESTED READINGS:** William B. Brever, *J. Edgar Hoover and His G-Men.* 1995; Sanford Unger, *The FBI.* 1975.

**IANNIELLO, "MATTY THE HORSE."** (b. Matthew Ianniello, 1920, New York City—incarcerated). Genovese caporegime in vice and sex industries.

On April 17, 1972, Joseph Gallo* was celebrating his birthday with members of his family when he stopped at Umberto's Clam House in "Little Italy." The restaurant was frequented by members of the Genovese* and Colombo crime families* and owned informally by "Matty the Horse"—a Genovese capo.* Gallo was murdered there by three Colombo gunmen, and although Matty was present, no one could implicate him in the assassination plot.

His real business was not murder but sex. He supervised a broad network of Midtown Manhattan sex establishments—gay, topless, and transvestite bars. Also, he played a role in the large pornography industry and is believed to have controlled many of the porno shops and massage parlors in the Times Square area.

His only conviction came in 1971 when he was fined and given a suspended one-year jail term for refusing to answer questions before a Manhattan grand jury looking into police corruption. In 1985, "The Horse" (he was a hulking 220-pound bouncer in his youth) was arrested on racketeering charges and accused of skimming profits from his New York sex businesses and restaurants. In 1986 he was convicted of racketeering and extortion and is currently serving out his sentence in a federal correctional facility.

**SUGGESTED READING:** Peter Diapoulos and Steven Linakis, *The Sixth Family*. 1976.

**ILLEGAL ENTERPRISE.** Defined as the sale of illegal goods and services to customers who know that the goods or services are illegal, illegal enterprise has long been a central part of the American underworld, but it has received little attention as a separate criminal category. Although such activities are relatively short term and small scale when compared with legal businesses, three major factors explain the cooperation that emerges among illegal entrepreneurs. The first is *systematic corruption*, which permits police or politicians to bring order to illegal activities within a political jurisdiction. Police function as "referees" and discipline purveyors of illegal goods or services. A second factor is *overlapping partnerships* by which illegal businessmen launch and maintain illegal businesses. Hijackers cooperate with fences in stealing items (cars, utility goods, etc.), which a fence can sell quickly because there is a market for such items. A third factor concerns the *internal economic characteristics* of illegal businesses, which shape the manner in which they operate. Thus, it matters little if Mafia* members or Dominican drug gangs operate a drug retail distribution network: The nature of the commodity, law enforcement policies, and the price structure of the product possess a dynamic that shapes the illegal operation. Moreover, enterprises that involve illegal goods (illegal alcohol during Prohibition [*see* PROHIBITION AND ORGANIZED CRIME*] or cocaine/heroin trafficking today) often have at least three levels of operation. First, goods must be manufactured or imported; second, they need to be processed and wholesaled; third and finally, they are peddled to consumers. Both the distribution of bootleg liquor in the 1920s and the distribution of illegal drugs more recently have generally involved entrepreneurs (individuals who organize, operate, and assume the risk for a business venture) who specialize at different levels. Indeed, syndicates* (an association of business people in an illegal venture) in illegal alcohol or drugs rarely involve a single group engaged at all three levels. This fact, that illegal entrepreneurs have generally operated at separate levels, necessarily requires continued business dealings among individuals with different specializations in manufacture, transport, security, distribution, and so on.

**SUGGESTED READING:** Mark H. Moore, "Organized Crime as a Business Enterprise," in *Major Issues in Organized Crime Control*, ed. H. Edelhertz. 1987.


**ILLEGAL GAMBLING.** Second only to drugs, gambling remains the huge moneymaker for organized crime. Gambling includes a wide array of games of chance and sporting events on which bets are made. Some of these are legal, such as betting at state-licensed horse- and dog-racing tracks or at state-sponsored lotteries or betting in games of chance featured in casino gambling establishments licensed by certain states. At the same time, there are unauthorized (illegal) gambling operations, and these compete with legalized, licensed gaming in terms of the dollar amount played or the number of people who bet with local bookmakers.

Illegal gambling attracts customers because credit is usually extended to players, the odds tend to be better than their legal counterparts, gamblers take bets on sports and international events, and if someone is lucky enough to win, the IRS will not be informed of the winner's tax liability. Also, the low priority given to gambling enforcement adds to its attractiveness for organized crime. Where profits from drug trafficking are quite substantial, so are the penalties compared to the light sentences and fines for illegal gambling. In fact, arrests for illegal gambling have declined significantly during the 1990s. Lack of enforcement resources attributable to competing demands for police services in other areas, combined with more sophisticated telephonic communications—the mobile cell phone, for example—help to explain why enforcement has declined. Further, public pressure to stamp out gambling is minimal because patrons of bookies seldom think of their bets as supporting more sinister and harmful organized crime activities. Bettors either do not realize or simply ignore the fact that their losses (the bookie's profits) ultimately find their way into money laundering,* pornography, or drugs. Most customers see no evil in betting illegally; after all, it is the bookie, not the bettor, who occasionally goes to jail. But the gambling business is neither so straightforward nor as harmless as most pretend.

Estimates of the amount of money bet illegally and the percentage of profits derived by organized crime from this activity are difficult to come by because measuring the aggregated volume of money bet illegally is not reliable. A comparison with statistics from legal gambling enterprises provides a crude frame of reference for speculating about the numbers of dollars waged illegally. By 1993, gambling in some form had been legalized in 47 states and the District of Columbia. Through these legitimate outlets alone, some $30 billion was gambled in 1992.

**SUGGESTED READING:** S. Walker, *Sense and Nonsense About Crime and Drugs: A Policy Guide.* 1994.

**IMMUNITY.** The Fifth Amendment provides important protection for the individual against the coercive power of the state when it stipulates that no persons shall be compelled in a criminal case to be a witness against themselves. But even this protection can be partially neutralized by a grant of immunity. There are two types of immunity: (1) *transactional immunity*, which provides blanket protection for crimes about which individuals may be forced to testify; and (2) *use immunity*, which prohibits the information provided by a person from being used against him or her, but the person can still be prosecuted using evidence obtained independently of his or her compelled testimony.

In the federal system and in the criminal justice systems of many states, the courts or prosecutors may grant immunity of the two types described to reluctant witnesses. Legislative or administrative bodies such as congressional committees, state or federal task forces, or commissions can also request grants of immunity. A witness who after being granted immunity refuses to testify can be subjected to civil or criminal contempt and imprisoned for the duration of an investigative grand jury's term.

A proceeding is summary in nature and relatively simple. Upon refusing to answer in a grand jury or other authorized body, the witness appears before the courts. The prosecutor makes application, and the court instructs the witness to testify. If recalcitrant, the witness appears before the court; the prosecutor explains how the witness is disobeying the court order. The witness is given the opportunity to be heard, and thereafter the court decides whether the witness is in contempt and should be remanded. The remand order ordinarily specifies that the witness shall remain confined until he or she is willing to comply by agreeing to testify or remain in jail for the life of the grand jury. In 1970, as a result of his refusal to testify, Jerry Catena (a capo* in the New Jersey faction of the Genovese crime family*) was imprisoned for contempt where he remained imprisoned for five years, never testifying. It should be noted that a criminal contempt proceeding is different than a remand order, since the contempt is an offense that requires a formal trial and the full array of due process rights enjoyed by any criminal defendant. Being found guilty of criminal contempt can result in a substantial sentence of imprisonment.

When granted immunity from prosecution, the result has a favorable impact on a jury. It renders a defendant's testimony more credible in that a prosecutor can point to a witness like "Sammy the Bull" Gravano,* whose criminal record is sordid, and say to the jury that the witness has no reason to lie because his immunity is assured and if he lies he will be prosecuted for perjury on each charge for which immunity was granted.

Immunity has loosened the tongues of many mafia members who swore oaths of silence. When faced with long prison terms or immunity and guarded freedom, the temptation to cooperate is often irresistible. Government success in persuading gangsters to cooperate has broken the backs of many organized criminal groups.

**INTERNATIONAL BROTHERHOOD OF TEAMSTERS.** Organized crime has had a negative input on American labor by its involvement in two unions, the International Longshoremen's Association, the dockworkers, and the International Brotherhood of Teamsters (IBT), the truck drivers of the country. With some 500,000 members in 1940, the Teamsters made up the biggest union in the AFL (American Federation of Labor), second only to the CIO (Congress of Industrial Organizations) and United Mine Workers among all labor organizations. The combination of union power and criminal influence created serious problems for the country.

Because almost every industry used trucks, the Teamsters organized workers in poultry, construction, laundries, taxicabs, freight terminals, and so on. On the waterfronts, trucking is a fluid commodity that cannot be stored up, as coal, wheat, oil, or steel can be, against the possibility of a strike. Trucks have to roll—otherwise, products and produce would spoil; strikes could, and did, wipe out small-scale industries, and that fact gave the Teamsters enormous power.

The union was formed in 1903 and was organized from the bottom up. Locals were locals, as it were, organized by local people. As the depression lifted in the 1930s, unions swelled in size and militancy, including the Teamsters, whose reputation was one of violence and strikes, but often with good cause. During the period of its expansion in the New Deal era of Franklin Roosevelt, gangsters fought against the Teamsters as they had against garment workers in New York, steelworkers in the Midwest, and dockworkers on both coasts. But gangsters also fought with the Teamsters. The mafiosi Jimmy "The Weasel" Fratianno* and Babe Triscaro of the Cleveland Mafia were strikebreakers and also union goons, often with both sides at the same time, the same union local and the company resisting union organizing. Their services went to the highest bidder and the side they thought would win.

With their history of violence, the Teamsters made accommodations with the underworld. If the gangsters played dirty, so did the strikebreakers, employees, and cops. All over the country, gangsters and Teamsters worked out arrangements where either the thugs supported Teamsters during strikes or they stayed out of the conflict altogether. Officially, the International Brotherhood of Teamsters denounced gangsters that got in the union locals: Joey Glimco (Local 777) and Joseph John Aiuppa* (Local 450) in Chicago, and Anthony Provenzano* (Local 560) in New Jersey were all big men. A factor that should not be ignored in explaining criminal infiltrations into the Teamsters and other unions is that Communist penetrations of unions rarely occurred when the union was mobbed up: The two conspiracies could not coexist.

The most tumultuous period in Teamster history occurred during the presidency of Jimmy Hoffa,* whose career began in the Detroit local. Senate investigations of labor racketeering made Hoffa and the Teamsters the prime villains. Testimony before the McClelland Committee,* whose chief counsel was Robert F. Kennedy,* who would become Hoffa's main antagonist, showed a pattern of stolen or misappropriated union funds, "sweetheart" contracts with employers who paid off union officials, denial of democratic processes in union elections, and intimidation of union members by thugs. The Committee laid the blame at Hoffa's doorstep, but the truth was that Jimmy took cues, not orders, from gangsters. The congressional hearings showed his dealings and connections with major underworld figures such as William Bufalino and Peter Licavoli of Detroit; Babe Triscaro of Cleveland; Johnny Dio,* "Tony Ducks" Corallo,* and Vincent Squillante* of New York; and Anthony Provenzano* and Angelo DeCarlo* of New Jersey. Most of these men were mafiosi and union officials.

Hoffa eventually would be imprisoned, but the Teamsters retained their tainted connections with the underworld mainly because the Teamsters and gangsters needed each other. The unions needed mob muscle, and the mob needed union pension funds—this secret convenant had become something of a legacy and tradition.

**SUGGESTED READING:** Victor S. Navasky, *Kennedy Justice.* 1977.


**IVANKOV, VYACHESLAV.** ("Yaponchik") (b. 1938, Vladivostok, Russia—). Russian criminal boss of "thieves-in-law."

Known to the Russian police as "Little Japanese," it is believed that he was smuggled into the United States in January 1993 after a long criminal career in the former Soviet Union. In 1980 he formed the Solontsevskaya gang in Moscow, whose members often posed as police officers and robbed the homes of wealthy Russians. Having been sentenced to 14 years in a Soviet prison after a conviction for one of these crimes, he bribed a judge and was released from Tula prison in Siberia in 1991. Two years later, he fled the country and headed for New York. Apparently, the idea was to use his reputation in the former Soviet empire to bring together the loosely organized Russian gangs in the United States into a crime syndicate.* Ivankov established a base in Brighton Beach, a section of New York City known as "Little Odessa" because of the concentration of Russian residents. By 1995 his gang had about 100 members and was acknowledged as the strongest Russian crime group in New York.

In June of 1995, Ivankov was arrested with eight other accomplices and charged with attempted extortion. Wiretap information identified him as the principal player in an effort to extract $3.5 million from two Russian-born businesspeople who owned a Manhattan investment firm. The plot failed but revealed the ability of Russian gangsters to reach beyond the Russian ethnic enclaves and operate on an international scale. The extortion scheme involved a threat of death, which was carried out, against the father of one of the New York victims. The father was killed on a Moscow subway platform as part of the threat and intimidation. *See also* AGRON, EVSEI; RUSSIAN ORGANIZED CRIME

**SUGGESTED READING:** Stephen Handelman, *Comrade Criminal: Russia's New Mafiya.* 1995.

**JAMAICAN POSSE GROUPS.** The term *posse* was adapted by Jamaican gangs from Hollywood westerns. The gangs evolved as an informal mechanism in gaining local community control. Posse maturation in Jamaica has its underpinnings in both political nationalism and the Rastafarian movement, which emerged in the late 1950s and 1960s. Neighborhood street gangs aligned themselves with either of the two leading political parties, the Jamaica Labor Party (JLP) and the People's National Party (PNP). These groups interacted closely with activist Rastafarians in various violent endeavors and drug and weapons trafficking. What have become known as criminal "posses" in the United States originated with Jamaican street gangs, and many active organizations in the United States still bear the names of streets or neighborhoods in Jamaica's cities. The first U.S. posses were the Untouchables from Tecks Lane in the Racetown section of Kingston and the Dunkirk Boys from the Franklin town area of Kingston. The Shower and the Spangler posses are two of the largest and the best organized of the posses operating in the United States.

Jamaican criminals use several methods to infiltrate a community. A common tactic is to select an African American female and lavish her with gifts, money, cocaine, or crack. She in return permits the Jamaican criminals to use her home for their drug trafficking operation. Another method is to pay selected individuals rent for apartments from which the posse operates. The Jamaican posses also establish "gatehouses" for their drug distribution. Gatehouses are usually vacant or abandoned buildings that are fortified to make their operation less vulnerable to police raids and robberies by competitors. Their illicit drug organizations are composed of individuals who serve as wholesalers, packagers of drugs, retailers, lookouts, and carpenters, whose jobs are to operate and protect the gatehouses.

Although Jamaican organized crime activity in the United States dates back to the 1970s, it was not until the 1980s that Jamaican posses emerged as a significant criminal threat in the United States. These groups are primarily involved in drug trafficking, especially cocaine and marijuana, and increasingly in illegal arms traffic and other weapons violations. Jamaicans have been successful at organizing and competing against other drug groups. A strong vertical structure enables Jamaican posses to control costs and offer lower prices than existing local criminal groups. Their aggressive marketing strategies enable them to expand rapidly. The posses have a strong propensity for violence and use it to acquire and maintain territories. Some have a multilayered structure; however, other less-structured Jamaican groups also exist, including some with family-based associations. In 1991 an estimated 40 Jamaican posses, with 20,000 members, were alleged to be involved in illicit operations in the United States.

The two largest posses, the Spanglers and Showers, have been whittled away by successful prosecutions in New York and Florida. But their street operations have quickly been taken over by new groups: The Dunkirk Boys in Queens, New York, has some 2,000 members; Jungle Posse of Brooklyn's East New York section has 2,500 members; and Samokan Posse, also of Brooklyn, has 1,000 members.

A gang of illegal aliens from Jamaica, known as the Gulleymen, operated a network of crack houses and heroin dealerships, while transporting illegal handguns purchased in southern states to the North. Federal agents allege that the gang made $60,000 a day in profits and believe that the Gulleymen take that name from a neighborhood in Kingston, Jamaica, called McGregor's Gully. Agents allege also that the gang has sold franchises to street-level dealers, supplying them with crack and protection for a set fee. Most of their murder victims have been rival drug dealers and former gang members. Profits from drug and arms dealing have gone into real estate in Brooklyn and Long Island or have been returned to Jamaica to boost the campaign war chests of Jamaican politicians.

What is the future of the Jamaican posses? Various law enforcement investigations estimate that they have come up faster than any other organized crime group now active in the United States. The fact that they maintain close ties with the Colombian drug cartels* and are expanding their contacts with African American gangs such as the Crips suggest that the posses will be a continuing problem. *See also* CRIPS AND BLOODS; COLOMBIAN DRUG CARTELS

**SUGGESTED READING:** U.S. Department of Justice, *Attacking Organized Crime—National Strategy.* 1991.

**JHERI-CURL GANG.** Dominican drug traffickers.

A pioneer of the Dominican drug trade in the Washington Heights section of New York City was a young Dominican born in Santiago, Dominican Republic, named Luis Polanco-Rodriguez, known on the streets as "Yayo." Yayo's claim to fame had to do with his skill in promoting the sale of "crack." His gang was the first to move the drug in quantity in New York City and the surrounding metropolitan area. He sold his drug under the name "Based balls," and for a time, his network was the largest in New York. But then the DEA caught up with him, which prompted his return to the Dominican Republic. Yayo introduced sales techniques in drug dealing that worked miracles. There were gimmicks from mass marketing—such as two-for-one sales and ladies' day specials—that caught on. Crack was being sold as if it were perfume or cologne.

Yayo's group was succeeded in the 1990s by others who relied on violence more than sales imagination to push their products. Especially notorious was the Jheri-Curl gang. Led by the five Martinez brothers, the gang maintained a $5 million a year crack business in Upper Manhattan for nearly three years. Rafael Martinez, the founder of the gang, deliberately made his gang members easily identifiable in order to intimidate residents and discourage competitors. The gang members were required to sport distinctive haircuts—shaved close on the sides with a pile of jheri-curls on top; and their cars were painted in a bright gold color.

The Jheri-Curls were a vicious gang that openly threatened the residents on West 157th Street. Women were assaulted in the street, weapons were fired into the air, and people kept their children off the streets. Anyone who resisted the gang's antics risked his or her life. Finally, an outraged community refusing to succumb to fear cooperated with a criminal task force of state and federal law enforcement officers to put most of the gang behind bars. *See also* DOMINICAN DRUG TRAFFICKING; WILD COWBOYS

**SUGGESTED READING:** William Kleinknecht, *The New Ethnic Mobs.* 1996.

**JOHNSON, ELLSWORTH.** ("Bumpy") (b. 1906, SC—d. July 1968) African American drug trafficker, gambling racketeer.

Ellsworth Raymond "Bumpy" Johnson, a Harlem underworld figure (a bump on the back of his head gave him his nickname), worked as a middleman and enforcer from 1940 to 1968 between the Italian syndicate* (the Genovese crime family*) and African American gangsters operating in Harlem. If an African American drug dealer wanted to buy a large quantity of drugs, Johnson arranged the sale. Italian gangsters knew him as a "persuader," one who could settle underworld quarrels before they erupted into violence. As such, Johnson was assigned to a place that for an African American in those days was considered high in the ruling circles of organized crime. When he was not in jail (where he spent 25 years of his adult life), millions of dollars in syndicate funds passed through his hands. He died in July 1968 while free on $50,000 bail following a 1967 indictment by a federal grand jury on charges of importing narcotics from Peru to be sold in Harlem.

Johnson was the model for the Harlem kingpin depicted in the "Shaft" films of the 1970s and, together with Stephanie St. Clair,* presented as a major figure within the Harlem gambling rackets in a film entitled *Hoodlum*. He was articulate, well dressed, and suave—able to function as a bridge between the larger white crime syndicates and the Harlem criminal network.

His close alliances with leading La Cosa Nostra* figures and the power they projected enabled Johnson to operate not merely as a vassal of the Italian American underworld but as a resourceful power broker in the black world. *See also* HOLSTEIN, CASPER; ST. CLAIR, STEPHANIE

**SUGGESTED READING:** Francis A. J. Ianni, *Black Mafia*. 1975.

**JUNIOR BLACK MAFIA.** As the drug trade came under the control of violent African American gangs in the 1980s, Philadelphia saw the rise of the Junior Black Mafia (JBM). When the gang began in 1985 in West Philadelphia, selling marijuana and cocaine, Aaron Jones and his lieutenants were planning to create a syndicate* modeled on the American Mafia.*

For two years the gang expanded, unleashing a reign of terror in the ghettos of Philadelphia. Its slogan, which was not an idle threat, was "Get down or lay down"—either join the gang or die. Murder victims included independent drug dealers, disloyal members of the JBM, and often, innocent bystanders.

The gang's objective was to take over the city's drug trade. The JBM developed a fearsome reputation as it spread into various sections of Philadelphia. Links were formed with Mexican suppliers, and as the JBM increased its power and size, members began sporting diamond-encrusted rings engraved with the initials "JBM."

In 1988, the JBM became entangled with a large South Philadelphia drug organization headed by John Craig Haynes, who refused to "get down" with the JBM. Haynes's organization was a multimillion-dollar drug distribution network that emerged out of the poor, underclass communities of South Philadelphia and was not very likely to be easily intimidated by gunplay. After several attempts on Haynes's life, where gang members on both sides and innocent people were killed or wounded, the fighting died down as authorities pressed investigations. For the JBM, federal racketeering indictments in 1991 led to the arrest and convictions of the leader and 25 other JBM members.

**SUGGESTED READING:** Pennsylvania Crime Commission, *Organized Crime in Pennsylvania: A Decade of Change*. 1990.

# K

**KEFAUVER COMMITTEE.** Senate investigation of organized crime (May 1950–May 1951).

The Special Committee to Investigate Organized Crime in Interstate Commerce, known generally as the Kefauver Crime Committee, began its work in May 1950 with Senator Estes Kefauver of Tennessee as its chair. The Committee came to life and got its impetus from the highly publicized findings of several urban crime commissions that were made up of private citizens as well as government authorities. The disturbing findings of the Chicago Crime Commission investigations and the murder of Charles Binaggio,* a mob figure linked closely with the top political echelon in Missouri, helped push through government authorization for the Committee's work. Naturally, bosses (dons)* of big-city political machines worried that an investigation might look into their activities. Senator Pat McCarren of Nevada and Senator Joseph McCarthy of Wisconsin opposed the Special Investigation Committee for their own reasons, but public pressure ensured its funding and investigative activities.

The Kefauver Committee was broadly charged with investigating whether organized crime exploited interstate commerce in violation of federal or state laws, and it was authorized to look into the nature and extent of such criminal operations. The hearings were made all the more dramatic by extensive television coverage, which seized public attention in an unexpected manner. For the first time, millions of Americans (some 20 million by one estimate) observed the drama (and boredom) of a congressional hearing as it unfolded. Bookies, crime bosses, gun molls, pimps, police chiefs, slippery lawyers—all marched across the television screens and entertained and appalled an enthralled television audience.

Before Kefauver's term as chair of the Committee ended in May 1951, the Committee heard more than 600 witnesses in New York City, Chicago, Miami,

Tampa, New Orleans, Cleveland, Kansas City, Detroit, St. Louis, Las Vegas, Los Angeles, San Francisco, Philadelphia, Boston, and Washington, D.C.

In its findings the Committee reported that much of crime, especially vice activities, is organized to a substantial degree in many big cities around the country. It identified two major crime syndicates, the Anthony Joseph Jake Accardo*–Charles Guzik*–Fischetti crime organization in Chicago and the Frank Costello*–Joseph Adonis*–Meyer Lansky* syndicate in New York City. The Committee's most sensational claim was that a sinister criminal organization known as the Mafia* operated throughout the United States with ties in other nations. Finally, the Committee found unsurprisingly that widespread political corruption allowed the syndicate to flourish.

The Committee's most constructive work had been its documentation of widespread corruption at the local and state level and the exposing of attempts by law enforcement officials to conceal their malfeasance, incompetence, or complicity in criminal activities.

**SUGGESTED READING:** Estes Kefauver, *Crime in America.* 1951.

**KELLY, PAUL.** (b. Antonio Paolo Vaccarelli, 1859, Naples, Italy—d. New York City, n.d.). Five Points gang boss.

One of the most treacherous and resourceful gang leaders in the early twentieth century, Paul Kelly was an immigrant boxer who headed the Whyos, a huge street gang in the slum tenements of New York's Lower East Side. Kelly, a Neapolitan, was fluent in several languages and involved with the political bosses of the powerful political machine called Tammany Hall before World War I.

Many modern-day gang leaders came out of the "Five Points gang" and its allied organizations including Johnny Torrio,* Alphonse Capone,* Charles "Lucky" Luciano,* and Ciro Terranova, "the artichoke king."

The Five Pointers succeeded the Dead Rabbits, the Plug Uglies, and the Whyos and could muster 1,500 members when needed for turf wars and election campaigns. The gang was named "Five Points" because its territories were defined by the intersections of Broadway, the Bowery, Canal Street, Fourteenth Street, and City Hall park in Manhattan.

Its members included Irish, Italians, and Jews. The only requirement was that a member remain loyal to Kelly. This urbane gangster managed to survive the era of reforms that swept through New York City in the decade preceding World War I. He organized waterfront unions and consolidated his political influence with the leaders of the Democratic Party in New York City. Kelly was an important leader of the underworld in New York City and one of the first criminal bosses to form a durable connection and working relationship with government authorities. *See also* EASTMAN, MONK; ROTHSTEIN, ARNOLD "THE BRAIN"

Robert F. Kennedy (with brother, John F. Kennedy). Reproduced from the Collections of the Library of Congress.

**SUGGESTED READINGS:** Herbert Asbury, *The Gangs of New York*, 1927; William Balsamo and George Carpozi, *Under the Clock: The True Story of the First Godfather*. 1988.

**KENNEDY, JOHN F.** *See* KENNEDY, ROBERT F.; MAFIA AND THE KENNEDY ASSOCIATION

**KENNEDY, ROBERT F.** (b. Nov. 20, 1925, Brookline, MA—d. June 6, 1968, Los Angeles, CA). Attorney general of the United States, organized crime rackets buster.

As attorney general of the United States, Robert Kennedy devoted more time and resources to the pursuit of organized crime than all his predecessors put together. Because of his zeal in prosecuting mobsters, many believe that both Robert and his brother John F. Kennedy,* president of the United States, were assassinated by the underworld. In a dying declaration to his attorney Frank Ragano, Santos Trafficante, Jr.,* head of the Tampa La Cosa Nostra,* is alleged to have accused Carlos Marcello,* Jimmy Hoffa,* and others associated with Sam Giancana,* boss of the Chicago Outfit,* of conspiring to murder President John Kennedy in the hope of silencing and destroying the power base of Bobby Kennedy, who was hounding them and interfering with mob operations across the country. Whether they attempted to assassinate the president is unclear.

Bobby Kennedy's role as an anticrime crusader is complicated by his brother's political career and his father's shadowy past with the mob. As the patriarch of the family, Joseph Kennedy was believed to have numerous ties to the underworld through bootlegging, gambling, show business, and Hollywood. He was also a major force in Massachusetts politics and served as ambassador to the Court of St. James (United Kingdom) in the pre–World War II Roosevelt administration.

Through his father's influence, Bobby Kennedy joined the staff of the McClelland Committee,* investigating labor racketeering. In 1956, despite his father's (and brother Jack's) opposition, Bobby put together for Senator Mc-Clelland the most thorough exposure of organized crime that Congress had undertaken since the Kefauver Committee* hearings. Kennedy identified the Teamsters Union as a major supporter of organized crime and its presidents Dave Beck and James Hoffa as supportive of labor racketeering.

With John Kennedy's election in 1960, Robert Kennedy was appointed attorney general, head of the Department of Justice. The presidential campaign of 1960 apparently utilized mob influence in key states—especially Illinois—to ensure victory. Organized crime figures were thought to be influential in turning out the vote for a Kennedy victory, so it came as a shock when Bobby launched a major anti–organized crime campaign across the nation. Understandably, many mobsters felt betrayed; and those who were hounded by Kennedy's Justice Department (which forced a reluctant J. Edgar Hoover* to mobilize the FBI) swore vengeance. James Hoffa, head of the Teamsters, was subject to intense surveillance, as were Sam Giancana, boss of the Chicago Outfit, and Carlos Marcello, boss of the Louisiana Cosa Nostra. The word in the underworld was "double cross."

The final provocation from the Kennedy administration occurred when Joseph Valachi,* a soldier* in the Genovese crime family,* talked publicly before McClelland's investigative subcommittee in the fall of 1963—months before the dreadful event in Dallas on November 22, the assassination of President Kennedy.

Robert Kennedy resigned as attorney general in the summer of 1964. During 1963 the Justice Department under his leadership tallied up 615 indictments and 288 convictions of mobsters. Kennedy's hope that Valachi's testimony would shake the Congress out of its lethargy worked: Within four years a Presidential Task Force would recommend laws and strategies that would put the Cosa Nostra on the run, permanently.

**SUGGESTED READINGS:** C. David Heymann, *RFK: A Candid Biography of Robert F. Kennedy.* 1998; Robert F. Kennedy, *The Enemy Within.* 1960.

**KID DROPPER.** (b. Nathan Kaplan, 1891 or 1895, New York City—d. Aug. 28, 1923, New York). Gang leader and labor racketeer.

With the opening of the "Roaring Twenties," Kid Dropper was among the top gangsters in New York City. Before World War I, he had been a member of the Five Points gang headed by Paul Kelly.* Kaplan began his criminal career as a thief using the dropped-wallet scam—where a wallet filled with counterfeit cash is found and sold to the victim on the spot because the finder (thief) can't spend the time locating the owner for the reward.

In 1911, the Kid went to prison for seven years on a robbery charge. When released, he formed a gang of labor sluggers. His main rival in this new criminal field that emerged in response to trade union agitation was "Little Augie" Orgen.* A gang war developed between the Kid and Little Augie. Prior to that, Kid Dropper's gang dominated the labor racket in New York City, working sometimes for the unions, sometimes for employers. Between 1920 and 1923, Kid Dropper is believed to have been responsible for at least 20 murders.

Encouraged by the success of Kid Dropper, Little Augie organized a small group of sluggers known as the "Little Augies" that included Louis Buchalter,* Jack Diamond,* and Jacob "Gurrah" Shapiro.*

Soon a war developed between the two gangs for control of the wet wash laundry workers. Orgen ordered Louis "Lepke" Buchalter and "Gurrah" Shapiro to get the Kid. In August 1923, Kid Dropper was arrested on a weapons charge, and during his transfer to court, a hoodlum named Louis Cohen shot him dead. Cohen, alias Kushner, was defended by James "Dandy Jim" Walker (a future mayor of New York), who managed to get the charge reduced to manslaughter and a light sentence. Little Augie would meet a similar fate at the hands of the men whom he entrusted to destroy Kid Dropper.

**SELECTED READING:** Albert Fried, *The Rise and Fall of the Jewish Gangster in America.* 1980.

**KISS OF DEATH.** A mafia cultural practice where an enemy is informed by a kiss that he is destined for death. It goes against the underworld's customary practice of hiding and shielding their activities from public scrutiny as much as possible. However, the kiss can also be construed as a warning: A deadbeat who owes a loanshark money might be inspired to pay up; a witness in a criminal proceeding might forget crucial details in their testimony.

Charles "Lucky" Luciano* treated this Sicilian Mafia ritual with contempt not because he was so Americanized but because it was counterproductive in America: Kissing publicly called attention to individuals and identified them as mafiosi when the organization did everything imaginable to maintain secrecy and protect one's identity.

Sometimes among mafiosi themselves, the kiss of death backfired and failed to strike terror in the victim or seal their lips. Vito Genovese* gave Joseph Valachi* a kiss when both were imprisoned in the Atlanta, Georgia, federal penitentiary. Rather than cringe in fear and beg for his life, Valachi talked and became one of the most important informers in underworld history.

**SUGGESTED READING:** Peter Maas, *The Valachi Papers.* 1968.

**LABOR RACKETEERING.** Labor racketeering refers to the intrusion of members of criminal groups into positions of authority or power within labor unions. Once entrenched in unions, they misuse pension and health funds by illegally investing in high-risk ventures or obtain loans that are never paid back. The International Brotherhood of Teamsters* union pension fund is a classic example of how the process works.

Unions are attractive to racketeers for a number of reasons, and many unions in the construction field, transport, waterfront, building maintenance, electrical, carpentry, garment, cement, and foundation engineering have been infiltrated or controlled by criminals who have exploited union members or used the union to intimidate employers and legitimate business firms.

Obviously, not all unions offer criminals the same opportunities. The occupational structure, the nature of the membership, and the employers play an important role. Unions with low-skill workers who are less aware of their rights and perhaps less competent at exercising them provide the best targets. Similarly, industries consisting of numerous small firms selling essentially similar goods or services, using the same technology, are particularly vulnerable to labor racketeering. Each firm is more seriously affected by a strike, given the availability of alternative supplies.

The ability to organize criminal interests to infiltrate the construction industry in New York City was promoted by a combination of these factors. Unlike most industries, the employment of construction workers lies in the hands of the union rather than the employer. In the construction marketplace itself, there are a large number of contractors and subcontractors with many small firms among them locked in intensive competition. This makes legitimate businesses vulnerable to extortion. Racketeers can coerce payoffs by threatening loss of labor or of supplies, delays in deliveries, or property damage to equipment or structures. Likewise, businesses can be easily corrupted when offered competitive advantage on bids for jobs made available by powerful racketeer elements who also organize the builders in cartels and "clubs" where favored members obtain lucrative building contracts for a small piece of the action. In brief, allocating contracts to favored firms depends on a racketeer's capacity to control building trades unions. *See also* GRAVANO, "SAMMY THE BULL"; RACKETEERING

**SUGGESTED READING:** New York State Organized Crime Task Force, *Corruption and Racketeering in the New York City Construction Industry, Final Report.* 1988.

**LA COSA NOSTRA.** (American Mafia) (1931–   ).

In 1931, warring factions of the Italian underworld, primarily Sicilian and Neapolitan, came together to form La Cosa Nostra (literally, in English, "Our Thing"), which is the name of the American Mafia. This union emerged out of the bloody Castellamarese War,* and it came to dominate organized crime, both ethnic and the homegrown American variety, throughout the country during the next two decades. By the end of World War II in 1945, La Cosa Nostra consisted of 24 crime families* from coast to coast, each with a similar organizational structure of boss (don),* underboss (sottocapo),* consigliere,* caporegimes, soldiers,* and associates in a pyramidallike structure. Above the crime families was a National Commission* of the most important LCN bosses who determined policy, enforced rules, and settled interfamily disputes. LCN flourished in cosmopolitan New York City as well as cow-town Kansas City. Two resort cities were ordained to be "open" to the activities of any family—Las Vegas, Nevada,* and Miami, Florida.

In 1957, the LCN was wracked by a series of internal convulsions. After Charles "Lucky" Luciano,* one of its original architects, had been deported to Italy, Vito Genovese,* an important and ambitious capo in the family, sought control by attempting to assassinate the acting boss, Frank Costello.*

Costello decided to step down, and the Luciano crime family* became the Genovese crime family*—a name by which it is known today. Still, Genovese feared retaliation from another family boss and Costello ally, Albert Anastasia,* one of the most notorious bullies in all of La Cosa Nostra. Genovese conspired with an Anastasia capo, Carlo Gambino,* to do away with Anastasia. In October 1957, Anastasia was murdered in a Manhattan barbershop. The Anastasia family was now the Gambino crime family.*

To deal with all the violence and mayhem and the threat of an internal war that could only be self-destructive, a national conclave of Cosa Nostra's leadership was scheduled for November 1957 in the small upstate New York village of Apalachin (*see* APALACHIN MEETING*), where a capo in the Magaddino crime family of Buffalo, New York, lived. The idea was that a meeting in such an out-of-the-way rural area would go unnoticed. Just the opposite happened. Alert New York State police spotted almost 100 strangers converging on the residence of Joseph LaBarbera and set up roadblocks. Soon, many of the nation's top mobsters were scampering through the woods to avoid detection.

Many of them were arrested and convicted of obstructing justice by refusing to explain their presence in Apalachin. These convictions were later reversed on the ground that merely meeting as they had was not by itself a crime. However, the disclosure in the press effectively ended any more national Cosa Nostra Commission get-togethers. If crime families around the country had to communicate with one another, emissaries were dispatched. Only in New York City, where five crime families uniquely rubbed shoulders, did the Commission system continue to function.

At the Apalachin crime conference, both Vito Genovese and Carlo Gambino were officially recognized as family bosses. And to regain some measure of stability, because of the sale of memberships by Anastasia, the membership books of the New York crime families were closed.

In testimony before a Senate committee, Angelo Lonardo, an underboss in the Cleveland crime family, claimed that two Commissions operated after Apalachin: a Commission on the East Coast representing most of the families east of the Mississippi and a Commission in Chicago representing western interests.

In the fall of 1963, the McClelland Committee* investigating racketeering in labor unions heard testimony from a convicted criminal who was also a lowly member of the Genovese crime family. Joseph Valachi* outlined for a nationwide television audience the structure and operations of La Cosa Nostra. The Valachi confessions and disclosures are ranked next to Apalachin as the greatest single blows ever delivered to organized crime in the United States matched only, perhaps, by "Sammy the Bull" Gravano's* revelations of criminal operations among the powerful New York families in the 1990s.

Both Valachi and Gravano were threats to the LCN on several levels. In the case of Valachi, his television appearance and discussions were shocking because they were fresh and startling; Gravano's testimony in trials and appearances before congressional committees created a powerful spectacle of a man who was not taking the Fifth Amendment (a constitutional protection where one refuses to answer all questions because of self-incrimination) who implicated himself and others in a whole series of crimes—in crime as a way of life. If much of the material and disclosures were not new to law enforcement professionals, it was novel and shocking to millions of young people. If it had no other impact, Valachi and then Gravano reminded the public that there was something more to organized crime than the "godfather": There was the sinister business of narcotics peddling, muggings, and murders in the street.

At another level, the defectors undermined LCN's discipline by violating the vow of silence (the code of omerta*) and not getting killed for it. For Valachi, his fate was a life of protection and solitary confinement; for Gravano, five years' imprisonment, life in the Witness Security Program,* and eventual freedom but a lifestyle of caution. Both men should have been killed or silenced by intimidation but were not despite the fact that open "contracts" (a fee paid for their murder) were put on the lives of both men. So far, no one has collected the $500,000 offered for Gravano's life.

Fiorello La Guardia. Reproduced from the Collections of the Library of Congress.

Most dangerous of all to LCN is that law enforcement intelligence now realizes that the way Valachi and Gravano were treated by their criminal associates and bosses made them vulnerable and ready to defect. The RICO* statutes were designed precisely to encourage defection, which means in the case of Mafia members breaking the code of silence. Long prison terms without the possibility of parole coupled with the despotism characteristic of LCN leaders apparently creates dissatisfied members willing to face the risks of talking. Today, LCN leadership, the celebrity of being a boss, is also something of a curse: It means close surveillance, arrest, and long jail terms.

**SUGGESTED READINGS:** Donald Cressey, *Theft of the Nation: The Structure and Operations of Organized Crime in America.* 1969; Peter Maas, *Underboss: Sammy the Bull Gravano's Story of Life in the Mafia* 1997; Peter Maas, *The Valachi Papers.* 1968.

**LA GUARDIA, FIORELLO.** ("The Little Flower") (b. 1882, New York City— d. 1947, New York City). Reform New York City mayor and rackets buster.

In 1933, following decades of heavy criminal influence in the city's politics, Fiorello La Guardia stood astride the city. He was the squat "Little Flower" whose public stance was an uncompromising war against gangsters, racketeers, and those who protected them: The very first day that the Little Flower occupied the mayor's office, he declared open warfare against the underworld. During the first week of January 1934, La Guardia sent word to Lewis J. Valentine, who was to become chief inspector, the second-highest rank in the police department, to "be good or be gone." The Little Flower demanded a clean, corruption-free department and a leadership determined to eradicate the underworld. Valentine would become police commissioner and serve for 11 years during La Guardia's three terms as mayor.

La Guardia's prime target was the slot-machine industry ruled by Frank Costello.* To give his crusade the necessary publicity, the mayor posed for newspaper photographers as he smashed slot machines with a sledge hammer before they were dumped into the East River. The "clean up" campaign also included the roundup of firearms—5,000 of which were taken from criminals in 1934 and dumped in Long Island Sound along with all sorts of gambling devices. In 1935, La Guardia issued an unprecedented public warning that New York City had no room for Dutch Schultz,* the violent, notorious Bronx beer baron of Prohibition (*see* PROHIBITION AND ORGANIZED CRIME*) and Harlem numbers* racket king.

Together with special prosecutor Thomas E. Dewey,* La Guardia established an excellent record as a crime fighter and honest politician. Accustomed to being ripped off by one corrupt city administrator after another, almost every branch of government had been improved under La Guardia. In three electoral campaigns the public rallied to the Little Flower and returned him to office.

La Guardia was a New Yorker endowed with a gift for language. Prior to the mayoralty, he worked for U.S. consulates in Austria-Hungary, Italy, and at Ellis Island as an interpreter in the immigration offices. In 1916, he was elected to Congress as a progressive Republican and fought for major reforms in child labor, the protection of labor unions (the Norris-La Guardia Act forbade the use of injunctions in labor disputes), and women's rights. His flamboyant career as New York City mayor occurred at a time of serious social and economic unrest in the United States; the aftereffects of Prohibition and the enormous underworld structures it helped to create were felt in every corner of the economy; the depression left millions jobless and desperate and a thriving underworld led by Louis Buchalter,* Frank Costello, Charles "Lucky" Luciano,* Meyer Lansky,* and Dutch Schultz. La Guardia was unusual in his open and fearless opposition to the gangsters; his city government unfailingly cooperated with major investigations such as the Seabury* probes that did much to neutralize political corruption and inspire other politicians to openly advocate anticrime issues.

**SUGGESTED READING:** Fiorello H. La Guardia, *The Making of an Insurgent: An Autobiography, 1882–1919.* 1948.

**LANSKY, MEYER.** (b. Maier Suchowljansky, July 4, 1902, Grodno, Byelorussia—d. Jan. 15, 1983, Miami, FL). Major underworld figure best known for his financial skills in international money laundering* and gambling enterprises.

Lansky, a brother Jacob, and a sister were brought to the United States in

Meyer Lansky. Reproduced from the
Collections of the Library of Congress.

1911. As a youth, he lived on the Lower East Side of New York City, where
in public school he was considered a good student.

Until his first arrest for assault in 1918, Lansky was an honest craftsman. The
victim of his attack was Salvatore Lucania who, years later, as Charles "Lucky"
Luciano,* became a leading figure in the American Mafia and close friend and
associate of Lansky's in numerous criminal enterprises including offshore gambling casinos in Cuba and the Bahamas.

It was the volatile streets of the Lower East Side that lured Lansky into crime.
He was adept at numbers, and after he quit school at the age of 16, he became
an enforcer for labor unions and brutalized strikebreakers. At about this time he
forged a friendship with another Jewish hoodlum, "Bugsy" Siegel,* and created
the "Bug and Meyer Mob" that engaged in hijacking, robberies, burglaries, and
extortion.

In 1921, Lansky met Arnold "The Brain" Rothstein,* who was mentor to
many infamous criminals and racketeers. Rothstein's success was largely dependent on the highly sophisticated legitimate business techniques he brought
to the rackets and vices. Gambling, fencing, and political corruption were the
hallmarks of Rothstein's legacy. Lansky was a student of Rothstein's methods
and absorbed many important lessons; he also picked up that sinister silkiness
of manner that became his trademark.

During his seven years with Rothstein in vice rackets, Lansky met important gangsters who would later emerge as "Founding Fathers" of the National Crime Syndicate. Rothstein played the role of "broker" not only between New York City's political machine, Tammany Hall, and the gamblers and bootleggers* but also between two of New York's powerful political-criminal factions: one, headed by Jimmy Hines* with ties to Dutch Schultz*; the other, also with a Tammany link, involved Italian gangsters such as "Joe the Boss" Masseria,* Frank Costello,* Lucky Luciano, and Salvatore Maranzano.* Rothstein was tied to both groups and did favors for each—pistol permits, bail bonds, fencing, and fixing.

With Rothstein's assassination over a gambling debt in 1928, Lansky and his partners took over his businesses and his connections. Lansky's speciality was gambling. In the same year as Rothstein's murder, Lansky became a naturalized citizen and launched new criminal enterprises with Frank Costello and Lucky Luciano. Known as "lakehouses," these forerunners of hotel/casinos in Florida, Havana, and Las Vegas, Nevada,* were gambling establishments set up in Saratoga, New York, in the fashionable lake resort area, which featured a famous racetrack. The Piping Rock Casino and Cafe in Saratoga was an immediate success, earning Lansky a reputation for operating a fair establishment with no tricks or hustles.

On May 9, 1929, Lansky married Anna Citron, a religious woman who had no connections and very limited knowledge of her husband's nefarious reputation and shadowy occupation. They were to have three children, one of whom, Paul, went on to distinguish himself with a West Point appointment and career as a successful businessman. The marriage did not survive: In 1947 Lansky was divorced, and his wife entered a mental institution, where she remained for the rest of her life.

By 1930, the Italian underworld was in chaos. Lansky offered his services to his partners Luciano and Costello during the bloody Castellamarese War,* which involved a struggle between two factions of the Sicilian Mafia. Luciano had betrayed his boss to bring about peace and feared that his new master Salvatore Maranzano distrusted him. Maranzano did plan to assassinate Luciano as a precaution against another betrayal. But Lansky, anticipating a double cross, arranged for the murder of Maranzano. The plot succeeded, with Luciano emerging as the most powerful mafioso in New York. Because he was not Italian, Lansky could never be part of La Cosa Nostra,* but he did establish himself as a partner of Luciano and others in a number of powerful criminal rackets.

The 1930s were a busy time for Lansky: He was a central figure in the creation of a National Crime Syndicate that consolidated fragmented gangland empires into a flexible crime confederation, one of whose more gruesome aspects was Murder, Inc.*—a squad of professional assassins on payroll who were prepared to commit murder anywhere in the country at the behest of syndicate bosses. Lansky also arranged casino gambling in Cuba and in Hallendale, Florida. By the mid-1930s he had good reason to relocate his business out of

New York: Luciano and other crime bosses had been prosecuted and convicted by Thomas E. Dewey,* a crusading district attorney, dedicated to crushing the crime syndicate. Lansky headed south, joined by his brother Jacob and Cosa Nostra member Vincent "Jimmy Blue Eyes" Aloi, who protected his operations.

When World War II began, Lansky dutifully registered for the draft but was not called. However, his contribution to the war effort involved secret maneuverings and negotiations with Naval Intelligence and the help of Lucky Luciano and waterfront racketeers to ensure that Nazi sabotage and spies would be cleared off the docks of eastern seaports. After the war years, Lansky concentrated on his investments in Cuba and Nevada, where his former associate Bugsy Siegel pioneered casino gambling.

The Kefauver Committee* hearings in 1950 and 1951 put Lansky, Costello, and many other racketeers into the living rooms of millions of Americans. The unprecedented televised hearings conferred a kind of celebrity on Lansky, who always lived quietly, dressed conservatively, and never sought the limelight of public attention, as had other gangsters. Lansky predictably took the Fifth Amendment and said nothing. In 1953 he was indicted on illegal gambling* in New York State and served a three-month jail term.

Throughout the 1950s Lansky concentrated on his interests in Cuba, which turned sour when Castro came to power in 1959. The Nacional, Lansky's plush casino in Havana, was seized along with its substantial assets when the revolutionary leaders banned gambling.

The 1960s were a mixed blessing for Meyer Lansky. According to law enforcement sources, his skimming operations in Las Vegas yielded enormous profits for himself and his partners. He was able to attract partners, even legitimate investors, because he built many businesses, even high-risk enterprises, solely on the strength of his word, fairness, and honesty. Indeed, it was rumored that he was so successful that he had to maintain a full-time money manager in Switzerland to look after his accounts. The Department of Justice evidently took the rumors of Lansky's vast criminal wealth seriously and created a "Lansky Strike Force" in 1962 to monitor his activities. It was at this time that the FBI overheard one of the most widely quoted remarks Lansky uttered to a confederate in a telephone conversation: "Organized Crime is bigger than U.S. Steel." This remark was widely circulated by law enforcement officials as indicative of the potential threat that organized crime posed.

The relentless government surveillance finally unnerved Lansky, and in June 1970, fearing an indictment for tax evasion, he fled to Israel, where he claimed citizenship as a Jew under Israel's "Law of Return." The United States requested his extradition, and after a drawn-out legal battle, Israel declared Lansky a "threat to the state" and denied his application for citizenship.

Denied permission to stay, in 1972 Lansky left for Paraguay but was refused permission to even leave his plane. Seven countries rejected his incredible offer of $1 million for sanctuary. Returning to the United States, the aging crime figure was arrested in Miami in 1972 for income tax evasion and contempt of court. Ironically, his only conviction was for illegal gambling—not a very serious offense—yet his reputation as a master criminal followed him to the grave.

Back in the United States, Lansky lived in seclusion in Miami, or at least tried to. In 1973, a New England gambler and Cosa Nostra associate, Vincent Teresa, alleged that he regularly delivered casino skim money from establishments in London and Las Vegas to Lansky. Lansky went to trial on the charge but was again acquitted. After 1973, it became clear that he was, as he insisted, retired. Still, Lansky's name would routinely surface in government hearings concerning mob influence in Atlantic City, New Jersey,* and other gambling venues or in connection with illegal loans from Teamster pension funds. At his death, none of the millions believed to be stashed away surfaced. On his deathbed, Lansky proudly said he never killed a man he did business with. But the fact remains that he made his living through men who murdered.

**SUGGESTED READINGS:** Robert Lacey, *Little Man: Meyer Lansky and the Gangster Life*. 1991; Hank Messick, *Lansky*. 1973.

**LANZA, JOSEPH "SOCKS."** (b. 1904, Palermo, Sicily—d. Oct. 11, 1968, New York City.) Racket boss of New York Fulton Fish Market.*

By controlling a space not more than three feet between a fishing boat and a New York dock, Joey "Socks" Lanza exercised tight control over one of the most lucrative seafood and maritime markets in the entire country.

As a young man Lanza worked in the Fulton Fish Market in Lower Manhattan as a handler, and by 1923, he became an organizer for the United Seafood Workers (USW) union. During this time, he was inducted into the Luciano crime family* (later the Genovese crime family*) and gained control of Local 359 of the union. Because wholesalers depend on speed for unpacking and delivery of their product, which is perishable, they are vulnerable to delays. In this way, Lanza was able to extort money from wholesalers who wanted competitive advantages that Lanza could bestow—for a price. It is estimated that through Socks Lanza the crime family most closely associated with the Fulton Fish Market was able to extract $20 million a year.

Lanza acquired his nickname because he wore thick, colorful socks around the fish market. He was physically tough and large, and few dared challenge him. In 1938 he was convicted of racketeering* and then emerged during the early phases of World War II as a key figure in government wartime plans to protect the waterfront from enemy espionage activities. In 1942, the Office of Naval Intelligence determined that the Third Naval District, which included the harbors and waterfront area of New York and New Jersey, might be vulnerable to sabotage and espionage. Naval Intelligence suspected that information dealing with convoy war material and ship movements was being leaked and that some ships in the commercial fishing fleets might be providing fuel, supplies, and information to enemy submarines that were known to be stalking the area.

Lanza was contacted for help. He was asked to persuade dockworkers to help the navy and suggest that fishing smacks might be equipped with special communication devices to report submarine sightings. The understanding was that the navy would thereafter discreetly intervene on his behalf when the district attorney and the courts considered the criminal charges against him. Lanza was instrumental in bringing Charles "Lucky" Luciano* into the operation, an event that greatly enhanced the collaboration between the navy and organized crime. Luciano's influence was, after all, much greater than Lanza's, especially with Italian-born stevedores and fishermen. As a result of Lanza's efforts, Naval Intelligence agents were able to obtain strategic positions in key waterfront installations and effectively monitor and counter espionage activities. The waterfront racketeer helped secure the ships and docks for the country's war effort.

In 1943, Lanza was convicted of extortion and sentenced to 7.5 to 15 years, but he was released in 1950 and resumed his place in the thriving Market. Arrested again in 1957 on parole violation, he was released when political pressure was placed on the parole board. He again returned to the Market and maintained his tight grip on its operations until his death in 1968.

**SUGGESTED READING:** Alan A. Block, "A Modern Marriage of Convenience: Organized Crime and U.S. Intelligence," in *Organized Crime: A Global Perspective*, ed. Robert J. Kelly. 1986.

**"LARRY FAB"** (b. Laurence J. Dentico, 1923, Brooklyn, NY—  ) and **ILLIANO, "PUNCHY."** (b. Frank J. Illiano, 1928, Brooklyn, NY—  ). Genovese crime family* street bosses.

With the imprisonment of Vincent "The Chin" Gigante* in 1998 after a long battle to declare him mentally competent, the Genovese crime family* found itself leaderless. The replacement for Gigante, Dominick V. Cirillo, who had been running the crime family for the past year, suffered a heart attack in May 1998.

Two members of the crime family, Laurence ("Larry Fab") Dentico and Frank ("Punchy") Illiano, have emerged as interim, street bosses. Dentico, in his late seventies, and Illiano, also in his seventies, have been linked to Mafia* activities for more than three decades. Both men, who are seasoned soldiers* in La Cosa Nostra,* supervise 20 capos* who control the criminal activities of 250 soldiers and more than 1,000 associates involved in illegal gambling,* loansharking,* fencing, pornography, and labor racketeering.* As elder statesmen in the Genovese crime family, Dentico and Illiano are responsible for keeping things running until a boss (don)* is selected. On the other hand, a multiheaded leadership similar to the Chicago Outfit* and Sicilian Cosa Nostra may be the wave of the future for the New York Cosa Nostra. In recent years, the federal government has concentrated its control efforts against individual bosses and succeeded thereby in disrupting crime family operations.

Dentico has a criminal career that goes back 40 years. In the 1950s he worked for Vito Genovese* and served a prison sentence between 1949 and 1952 for heroin trafficking. As late as 1981 he was convicted on charges of attempting to bribe officials in Union City, New Jersey, on public construction contracts and served a six-year prison term.

Illiano was a member of the notorious Joseph Gallo* gang during the war between Joseph Profaci* and the Gallos and then between Joseph Colombo, Jr.* and Joe Gallo. In the mid-1970s, Illiano joined the Genovese crime family after being wounded in the internal gang warfare. He was arrested many times on charges including rape, assault, and bookmaking but was acquitted on most of them. Throughout his career he has been active in gambling and loansharking rackets and is believed to have siphoned off funds from Italian street fairs in Brooklyn that are controlled by the Genovese crime family.

**SUGGESTED READING:** Donald Goddard, *Joey.* 1974.

**LAS VEGAS, NEVADA.** Casino gambling complex and organized crime.

The legend is that until "Bugsy" Siegel* had a "vision" about Las Vegas as a gambling mecca in the desert, it would remain no more than a water stop on the rail line between California and the Midwest. After World War II, the Nevada desert town was seen by some as a mob "profit center." Las Vegas could be a perfect setting for mob business because Nevada had lax laws in many of its counties, which had been passed as a Depression-fighting tool, permitting gambling and even prostitution because the state desperately needed development. It could be expected that many of its politicians who were eager for investment money might turn a blind eye, no matter the source of the funds, to build up Las Vegas. "Bugsy" Siegel, a New York gangster associated with Meyer Lansky* and other powerful underworld figures, was authorized to build a gambling casino in the desert town. Siegel had relocated to California before the war to organize mob interests and came upon Las Vegas quite by accident. His enthusiasm for the project enabled him to obtain $6 million in mob money to construct a casino/hotel. The Flamingo turned out to be a bust. Siegel was murdered in 1947 because he skimmed huge sums from the construction of the casino. Reorganized, the Stardust hummed; so did the Desert Inn (sponsored by "Moe" Dalitz* and the Cleveland syndicate), the Thunderbird (Lansky), and the Sands (Abner Zwillman,* Joseph Stacher*). With these successes another wave of casinos was constructed, funded by the mob and monies drawn from the International Brotherhood of Teamsters* Central States Pension Fund. The Riveria (under the auspices of the Alphonse Capone* outfit), the Dunes (Raymond L. S. Patriarca* and the New England Mafia), the Stardust (Tony Cornero and Chicago), and the Tropicana (Frank Costello,* Phil Kastel, and the New York Cosa Nostra) were all mob financed. The casinos were very profitable for the underworld: The "skim" (stealing gambling profits before they are counted) became a major source of illegal income.

By 1955, Las Vegas was an "open town," controlled by no single criminal group. Until Lansky assumed a role as an informal overseer of operations, the casinos were crooked, but then their operations were made businesslike, and they soon became profitable. Hollywood celebrities and entertainers such as Frank Sinatra, Dean Martin, George Raft, and Elvis Presley were brought in to add to the glamour and appeal of the gambling spots.

What the Las Vegas experience meant for the American organized underworld was as important perhaps as Prohibition (*see* PROHIBITION AND ORGA-NIZING CRIME\*). The underworld became more organized, with lines between states and regions, between various ethnic groups, obliterated by the lure of money. At the same time, issues of turf and territory became more complex. Fear of criminal infiltrations prompted state officials in Nevada to set up strict rules governing licensing and participation in casino operations, which were really aimed at keeping the Mafia out. It didn't work. Fronts and straight men were used to conceal secret mob involvement, and the syndicates took over.

By the 1960s, legitimate businesspeople showed interest in Las Vegas. How-ard Hughes, the multibillionaire, began buying up hotels, collecting as many as 17 in Nevada alone. But by the 1970s, Hughes was in the hole, probably because many mob employees were kept in their positions, given their experience and expertise and skimmed profits. Finally, Hughes got out, but his legacy was important. He showed that legitimate people could run casinos and could operate profitably if the underworld influence with its "skimming" operations could be eliminated.

In the past two decades, as Nevada gaming officials have at last taken a closer look at the casinos, the participation of legitimate people and investors in the casino industry has revived interest in the business. With mob influence checked, legalized gambling in the state has been a major mechanism for raising new tax dollars and serves as a strategy underpinning economic development.

**SUGGESTED READINGS:** John Dombrink and William Y. Thompson, *The Last Resort.* 1990; Ed Reid and Ovid Demaris, *The Green Felt Jungle.* 1964.

**LATIN KINGS.** (Latino street gang and racketeering enterprise.)

With its beginnings dating back to 1940 in Chicago, Illinois, the Latin Kings are the oldest and perhaps largest Hispanic street gang in the United States. The gang formed in self-defense against predatory attacks from non-Hispanic rivals. Out of self-protection, the gang expanded and grew, developing a reputation for violence that earned it respect in the streets.

Known formally as "The Almighty Latin Kings and Queens Nation," the gang has chapters across the country in Illinois, New York, Connecticut, Florida, New Mexico, and California, and it appears to be spreading in areas where the Hispanic-speaking population is densely settled.

The gang has established hierarchy and chain of command, which enforces strict adherence to a charter of detailed rules governing gang member admission, behavior, and etiquette. As with other gangs, the Latin Kings have "colors"—black symbolizing death and gold representing life. Leaders are known by elaborate titles—"King Blood," "First Supreme Crown," "King Tone"—and rituals that are accompanied by language that is a mix of blunt street talk and arcane vocabulary.

In the 1980s the gang established itself in prison facilities in several states where many of its members were serving terms for narcotics trafficking, extortion, weapons smuggling, and so on. At its height in the 1980s the gang had more than 2,000 members, and as it grew in size, disciplinary problems developed so that in the early 1990s, the then King Blood, Luis Felipe, a Cuban refugee from the Cuban Mariel exodus staged by Fidel Castro, who is serving a life sentence in a federal correctional facility in Connecticut, ordered executions of members guilty of filching gang money and otherwise breaking the rules. Street lieutenants were instructed to "T.O.S." (terminate on sight) some members or, for less egregious offenders, "B.O.S." (beat on sight).

Despite the violence that still defines the gang, there are indications that as the Latin Kings matured into sophisticated criminal enterprises, they do seem to substantiate the ethnic succession* theory about organized crime where for some minorities crime becomes the means to climb the social ladder into eventual middle-class respectability.

**SUGGESTED READING:** C. Ronald Huff, ed., *Gangs in America.* 1990.

**LATINO ORGANIZED CRIME.** Latino or Hispanic organized crime in the United States has grown significantly over the past 30 years. It has spread across American cities as the population of Spanish-speaking peoples in the United States has grown in size. Where most criminal groups historically depended on traditional vices such as gambling, prostitution, and bootlegging to get a foothold in the underworld, Latino groups have been successful mainly because of drugs. During the 1980s and 1990s the distribution of cocaine has been one of the biggest sources of income for organized crime groups in general and one of the most important products Latino groups handle. Typically, Colombian manufacturers will deal with Mexican and Caribbean groups who transport and distribute cocaine in the United States, leaving street sales and retail selling to African Americans and local traffickers. Cubans, Dominicans, and Jamaicans serve as middlemen between Colombian importers and the street gangs dealing cocaine and its potent derivative, crack.

Not all Latino crime organizations have developed in the same ways. Where Dominicans have dominated drug trafficking in New York, New Jersey, Pennsylvania, and Connecticut, Cubans have concentrated on drug trafficking in the Southeast and developed powerful gambling syndicates. Mexicans have a virtual monopoly on drug trafficking on the West Coast and in the Southwest and influence in the Chicago metropolitan area. Compared to these, Puerto Ricans, who have a long history in the mideastern area of the United States, have remained relatively small players in organized crime. Still, street gangs such as the Latin Kings* have attracted thousands of young Puerto Ricans into their

ranks in New York and Connecticut. *See also* BATTLE, JOSÉ MIGUEL; CO-
LOMBIAN DRUG CARTELS; DOMINICAN DRUG TRAFFICKING; LATIN
KINGS

**SUGGESTED READING:** Rensselaer W. Lee III, *The White Labyrinth.* 1990.

**LEHDER-RIVAS, CARLOS.** (b. 1949, Colombia—incarcerated). Medellín cartel
drug lord.

Carlos Lehder-Rivas was born in Colombia but lived for almost ten years in
Detroit, Michigan, where he acquired English and a knowledge of American
culture. In 1973 he became involved with car thieves and was arrested. He
skipped bail but was later arrested in Miami on drug possession charges. When
he was released in 1975, he was deported. By 1980, he was smuggling cocaine
into the United States. Business was so profitable that planeloads of cocaine
were being shipped into the United States, provided in part by Pablo Emilio
Gavoroa Escobar,* a leader of the Medellín cartel.

Success in drug trafficking resulted in Lehder moving into Norman's Cay in
the Bahamas, where he bought a luxurious home and constructed an airport to
facilitate drug smuggling operations into the United States. It has been alleged
that Lehder bribed the Bahamian prime minister Lynden O. Pindling to ignore
the smuggling operation. Other members of the Medellín cartel, namely, Pablo
Escobar and Jorge Luis Vasquez Ochoa,* utilized the airstrip for their shipments
of cocaine to America. The close relationship among Lehder, Escobar, and
Ochoa would develop into a coalition that would rule the cocaine trade and set
the terms of its organization during the period of its greatest expansion.

In 1981, Lehder was indicted by a Jacksonville, Florida, federal grand jury
for drug trafficking and income tax evasion. His extradition was requested, but
first he had to be found and arrested.

Lehder was obsessed by fantasies of political power and had become violently
anti-American. He founded a youth movement and supported candidates for
political office in Colombia. While a fugitive in 1985, perhaps because he felt
hounded by American law enforcement pressure for his arrest and extradition
to the United States for trial, Lehder appeared on Colombian television appealing
to Colombian revolutionary organizations, such as the Marxist group known as
M-19, to participate in the "cocaine bonanza" in an effort to resist American
imperialism. Lehder explained to his stunned audiences that marijuana and cocaine could be the weapons of revolution against the power of the North American colossus. His party newspaper printed articles condemning the DEA (Drug
Enforcement Administration), and his drug apparatus distributed leaflets in the
countryside, urging the peasants to join the guerrillas and traffickers.

In a shootout in 1987, Lehder was finally arrested and extradited to the United
States. He may have been betrayed by others in the drug cartel who feared the
public attention Lehder attracted with his antics. The following year he was
convicted of cocaine trafficking and sentenced to life without parole in a federal
correctional facility.

**SUGGESTED READING:** Paul Eddy, Hugo Sabogal, and Sara Walden, *The Cocaine Wars.* 1988.

**LICAVOLI, JAMES T. "BLACKIE."** ("Jack White") (b. 1904, St. Louis, MO— d. 1985, Oxford, Wisconsin, federal correctional institute). Cleveland Cosa Nostra crime family boss, 1970s and 1980s.

James Licavoli came from a prominent family in organized crime in Detroit, St. Louis, and Cleveland. Licavoli came to Cleveland in 1938 and established himself in gambling rackets in Youngstown and Warren, Ohio. "Moe" Dalitz,* a top Prohibition bootlegger* and leader of the Mayfield Road gang in Cleveland, formed an alliance with the Licavolis in Detroit and St. Louis; when Dalitz and his associates moved on to Havana, Miami, and Las Vegas, Nevada,* the cities of Detroit and Cleveland were left to the Mafia.*

With the death of John Scalish of the Cleveland Cosa Nostra in 1976, Licavoli expected to become boss (don)* but was challenged by another ambitious mafioso, John Nardi. Combining the power of his position in the Cleveland Teamsters Union and affiliation with Danny Green's Irish gang, Nardi sought to push Licavoli aside and take the coveted position of boss. A mafia war began in Cleveland. Soldiers* on both sides began to disappear, were found murdered, or were blown up in car explosions.

Other crime families became concerned and impatient when bodies of mobsters were found in streets and off roadways in Akron and other Ohio cities. Frank Tieri,* head of the Genovese crime family* in New York, offered to help Licavoli, who refused outside assistance. Joseph John Aiuppa* of the Chicago Outfit* was a cause for concern: He ordered Chicago Outfit members who might be sympathetic to Licavoli to stay out of the fight. Licavoli battled effectively and successfully despite the intimidation of larger crime families outside Cleveland. Both Nardi and Greene were eventually killed in car bombings.

Licavoli proved to be a cunning boss as well as a good street general: He managed to turn the tables on the local FBI by infiltrating a female into a clerk's job to provide information on informers. Still, in 1982 he was convicted of RICO* charges, the first mafia boss to have that distinction; he died in custody three years later.

**SUGGESTED READINGS:** Hank Messick, *The Silent Syndicate.* 1967.

**LINGLE, "JAKE."** (b. Alfred Lingle, 1892, Chicago, IL—d. June 9, 1930, Chicago). Police reporter and mob retainer.

Jake Lingle made a small salary as an ordinary police reporter for the *Chicago Tribune* in the 1920s. He was not born into wealth, yet he owned a house in Chicago and a summer home in Indiana; he took winter vacations in Florida and gambled excessively—often betting a thousand dollars on a race.

Lingle was on the payroll of Chicago crime boss Alphonse Capone,* functioning as a middleman between the Chicago mob and the police commissioner, bartering favors from the police for cash and influence within the underworld.

In the aftermath of his murder in broad daylight on a crowded train station, Jake Lingle became a folk hero and symbol for a crusading profession of journalists who risked their lives to inform the public. However, when Lingle's dubious criminal connections with the mob and the corrupted law enforcement establishment were revealed, the rewards totaling nearly $60,000 for information leading to the arrest of the perpetrators were quickly and quietly dropped. Apparently, Lingle was killed not because he was a "first-line soldier," as the American Newspaper Publishers Association eulogized him, but because he had the nerve to double-cross Capone by promising favors for hefty bribes from political leaders that never materialized. Lingle did not enjoy the "diplomatic immunity" of most journalists, which criminals respected because he, Lingle, was a corrupt "player." *See also* RIESEL, VICTOR; RUNYON, DAMON; WINCHELL, WALTER

**SUGGESTED READING:** Laurence Bergreen, *Capone: The Man and the Era.* 1994.

**LOANSHARKING.** Loansharking, also referred to as "usury," is the lending of money at a rate of interest that exceeds the legal limits. At one time—and still in many situations—loansharking and gambling were tightly linked together. A loser in a gambling situation compounds his (or her) problems by turning to loansharks: The predators attach a heavy interest to an instant loan.

Usury laws place a limit on interest rates at about 25 percent per year. Loansharks may charge as much as 20 percent per week. Typically, the borrower is a high-credit-risk customer who cannot turn to legitimate lending institutions such as banks for a loan. In return for the risk, loansharks charge "6 for 5"—that is, for every $5 borrowed, $6 must be repaid every week, which amounts to an annual interest rate of 1,004 percent! In underworld argot or slang, the principal (amount borrowed) is called "the nut" and the interest, "the vig."

By some business standards, loansharks have the best jobs in organized crime. They have little operating overhead: no office, no written, incriminating records, no regular employees or office operating expenses, and no special equipment or skills—just the ability to intimidate customers into paying. A loanshark can run his affairs out of his wallet and from a prodigious memory. Unlike other types of crime, the loanshark possesses no special tools nor leaves incriminating evidence beyond unmarked cash in which he deals. Seldom bothered by police, the loanshark has little reason to bribe them. While lending money informally at astronomical interest rates many not equal gambling in dollar volume or, in terms of the bottom line, net profit as to risk, loansharking is much better business than illegal gambling.*

Loansharks are sometimes referred to as "shylocks"—Shakespeare's Jewish moneylender in *The Merchant of Venice*; "shark" is a vernacular corruption of "shylock," and "shark" became "loanshark," which is accurately descriptive of the practice.

Today, a loanshark runs a business that is not only profitable but an avenue to other opportunities as well. While it is true that anyone can operate their own informal money-lending business, without a reputation for toughness one would quickly fail to retrieve their money. However, individuals connected with organized crime groups have diverse threats to coerce repayment.

The loansharking business is typically hierarchical: At the top is an investor who provides the money to be loaned. This may be a major organized crime figure able to commit many thousands of dollars for circulation as "street money." At the second level are the money middlemen who are entrusted to do the work of lending. For their role, middlemen pay a "vig," or interest, or about 1 percent per week on the money they receive for distribution. In exchange, they have the freedom to lend it as they see fit. Often the middle-level lenders distribute the money to a third level of lender who actually makes loans. They in turn pay 1 percent to 2.25 percent for use of the money, and they can make loans at any interest rate the market will bear.

Borrowers come to loansharks with a variety of needs: drug dealers needing a huge amount of cash for a buy and a quick deal; those desperate to pay a long overdue gambling debt; and otherwise honest citizens cut off from legitimate credit and lending institutions such as businessmen in need of large amounts of ready cash to meet supplier demands or payrolls. The garment manufacturing industry was often plagued by cash flow problems, and many manufacturers would reach out to loansharks to help them through a crisis or periodic cycles of boom and bust.

Loansharks do not wish to use violence because that attracts law enforcement and ruins their reputations as "reasonable people." Actually, the loanshark is interested in the "vig," and if that is not available, the debt is leveraged as a way to acquire a business (for laundering money) or other financial assets.

However loans are satisfied—and the options to indefinite vig payments are numerous—loansharking is a profitable enterprise. Estimates of its profitability range up to $2 billion annually among the established crime families.

**SUGGESTED READING:** M. Haller and J. Alvitti, "Loansharking in American Cities: Historical Analysis of a Marginal Enterprise," in *Prostitution, Drugs, Gambling and Organized Crime—Part 1*, ed. E. Mankkomen. 1992.

**LOMBARDOZZI, CARMINE "THE DOCTOR."** ("The King of Wall Street," "The Italian Meyer Lansky") (b. 1910, Sicily—d. May 10, 1992, Brooklyn, NY). Gambino crime family* capo,* securities fraud specialist.

When he died of a heart attack in May 1992, at his mansion-type home in Brooklyn, New York, with a Rolls-Royce in the driveway and a yacht in the boat basin, "The Doctor" was known as the financial wizard of the Gambino crime family. For years, the elegantly dressed, well-groomed capo was the biggest loanshark in New York's financial district, making usurious loans to scores of brokers and hundreds of Wall Street back-office personnel who needed funds with which to speculate in the stock market. Carmine Lombardozzi eventually became the biggest earner in the Gambino family.

His loansharking* provided entry to Wall Street. Lombardozzi's crew specialized in securities fraud, theft, and stock market swindles. His stature in the Gambino family was evident from his attendance at the Apalachin meeting* in 1957, where representatives from the major La Cosa Nostra* families in the United States met to discuss problems and policies of national significance.

In 1960, Lombardozzi and his associate, Arturo Tortorello, also known as "Artie Todd" or "Joey Grasso," were charged with several stock swindles; in 1963 both men were convicted and served prison terms for probation violations connected with previous convictions. Earlier in 1962, the financial world was rocked by a theft of $1.3 million in negotiable securities from the prestigious brokerage house Bache and Company. Arrests of employees connected with the theft included a company stock record clerk who simply walked out of the company's offices with the stolen stocks tucked under his shirt. Among those arrested for attempting to dispose of the stolen securities was John Lombardozzi, Carmine's brother. Subsequent information disclosed that Carmine had distributed some of the stolen securities, which found their way to Swiss banks.

In testimony before a U.S. Senate investigative subcommittee witnesses connected with stock frauds pointed to Lombardozzi as someone who had Wall Street clerks under his influence because they were trapped by gambling debts or other financial problems. Lombardozzi trafficked in stolen securities and stocks the way drug dealers handled cocaine and heroin. An ex-convict who fenced stolen stocks indicated that between 1958 and 1963, $40 to $50 million in stolen securities came through Carmine Lombardozzi. Though stocks were his chief criminal interest, Lombardozzi was also known as a powerful loanshark in the Gambino family whose advice was widely sought.

**SUGGESTED READING:** Humbert Nelli, *The Business of Crime.* 1976.

**LOUIE, NICKY.** (b. Yin Poy Louie, 1951, Kowloon, Hong Kong—    ). Founder of the Ghost Shadows Chinatown gang.

Nicky Louie was Chinatown's first violent crime boss since the Tong wars of the 1920s. Before he arrived on the scene, Chinatown gangs were little more than ruffians, nuisances engaged in muggings of pedestrians and petty shakedowns of merchants. Louie turned this around by transforming the street gangs into a criminal enterprise, as the Irish, Jewish, and Italian immigrants had done earlier in the century when they arrived penniless, ignorant, and fearful. His gang, the Ghost Shadows, became as important in Chinatown as any of the community's Tong or family associations.

His story was typical: Born in the slums of Kowloon, Hong Kong, he emigrated at age 15 with his family to New York City. Louie and his family were part of the first great wave of Chinese immigration following major changes in the 1965 Immigration Act, which gave preference to Asian, African, and Latin

American immigration over European quotas. Both of his parents were hard-working, but Nicky was impressed by the neighborhood gangs on Hester Street in Chinatown.

In 1970 he formed a gang called the Sing Yee On, which was renamed the Ghost Shadows. Modeled along Tong structures, the gang had a chairman, trea-surer, and an English and Chinese secretary. Louie never looked the part of a tough guy, like Alphonse Capone*; he was slightly built and boyish looking but renowned for his cunning and willingness to use violence.

By 1975, as the Ghost Shadows expanded their territories and encroached on the turf of other gangs, warfare erupted. By 1976 intergang wars among the Chinese gangs over extortion territories and gambling dens spilled over into the streets of Chinatown, Queens, and Brooklyn—wherever a Chinese community was settled. The chief protagonists were the Flying Dragons, associated with the rival Hip Sing Tong, and the White Eagles, affiliated with the Chinese Consol-idated Benevolent Association. Several assassination attempts against Louie by rival gang members and from within his own gang failed. He was on the run and sought to establish new contacts in Chicago and Toronto. By 1985, 25 members of Louie's Ghost Shadows were convicted on RICO* racketeering* charges. His cooperation with the government reduced his sentence to nine years. In 1994 he was released and pursues interests in producing films. *See also* CHINESE STREET GANGS; CHINESE TRIADS

**SUGGESTED READING:** Ko-lin Chin, *Chinese Subculture and Criminality*. 1990.

**LOVETT, WILLIAM.** ("Wild Bill") (b. 1892, New York City—d. Oct. 31, 1923, New York City). Irish waterfront racketeer, leader of the White Hand Gang.*

"Wild Bill" Lovett led a group of Irish hoodlums and gangsters on the New York waterfront in the early decades of the twentieth century. He was a slightly built man of considerable cunning and courage. During World War I, he served with the 11th Infantry Division and won the Distinguished Service Cross. On the home front, the Brooklyn docks around the Brooklyn Bridge and Red Hook section, life could be as precarious as the trenches in France. Lovett managed through stealth and cleverness to gain control of the White Hand Society*—an Irish extortion gang and pack of waterfront thieves who came together to con-front The Black Hand (La Mano Nera)*—Italian criminals who threatened Irish dominance on the piers.

Wild Bill's approach to waterfront racketeering* was direct and simple: Ship-pers, dock owners, or dock hands who refused to pay tribute to the gang were warned, sometimes with a gunshot wound; should they still refuse or resist gang demands, they would be killed. With these brutally straightforward tactics, Lov-ett temporarily ejected the mafia from the docks. For all his violent skirmishing, Lovett spent only seven months in jail. He also had a talent for surviving bullet wounds: He was shot in January 1923 twice in the chest, just above his heart, but recovered. What he did not recover from was an attack in October 1923, when several mafiosi attacked him while he was intoxicated. He was shot three times and killed with a cleaver that fatally fractured his skull.

With Lovett's assassination, Italian gangsters such as Joseph Adonis,* Vincent Mangano,* and Albert Anastasia* moved to take over the waterfront.

**SUGGESTED READING:** Richard Hammer, Playboy's *Illustrated History of Organized Crime*. 1975.

**LUCHESE, GAETANO.** ("Three-Finger Brown," "Thomas," "Tommy Brown"). (b. Dec. 1, 1899, Palermo, Sicily—d. July 14, 1967, Lido Beach, NY) Cosa Nostra* crime family boss.

Thomas Luchese immigrated to the United States in 1911 but did not become a naturalized citizen until 1943. In 1921, he was convicted of grand larceny (auto theft) and served a short prison sentence. Later in the 1920s, Luchese moved into the garment center, where he hired labor goons to intimidate businesspeople into extortion payments. He also found time to involve himself in the Italian lottery. He continued to diversify and mix illegal and legal interests. His California Dried Fruit Importers company also functioned as a front for illegal alcohol manufacture.

During the 1930s, Luchese became a powerful force in the garment industry. In his capacity as a mafioso, he worked as a labor consultant and prevented the "sweat shops" on Seventh Avenue in New York City from becoming unionized. During World War II, the Gagliano crime family of Cosa Nostra, of which Luchese was then underboss (sottocapo),* was heavily involved in the black marketing (illegal sale, manufacture, and distribution) of sugar, gasoline ration stamps, and meat. Along with Carlo Gambino,* a capo* at that time in the Vincent Mangano*/Albert Anastasia* crime family, through his clothing business, Luchese was not only able to secure government contracts to make uniforms for the armed services but was also able to sell manufactured civilian clothing in the vast black markets that he had helped to create.

Luchese moved up in the ranks of La Cosa Nostra after the war. He got deeper in the garment industry and started a construction firm to build tract housing for veterans. His considerable influence with the trade unions in the construction industry enabled him to frustrate his legitimate competitors.

In 1953, Gaetano Gagliano died of natural causes, and Luchese succeeded him as boss (don)* of the crime family. Because of his power and wealth, he managed to virtually wipe out his criminal past. His son received a congressional appointment to the U.S. Air Force Academy at West Point, but his daughter married a son of Carlo Gambino.

By the 1960s he was believed to be a multimillionaire. At the time the government levied $162,000 against him for unpaid taxes between 1947 and 1951. He had been investigated by the New York State Crime Commission, the Waterfront Commission, and the McClelland Committee* on labor racketeering.* In the 1970s, members of his crime family were implicated in the widescale hijacking and theft at Kennedy International Airport.

Luchese acquired his nickname "Three-Finger Brown" from a policeman who fingerprinted him in 1921. He lost his right index finger in a machine-shop accident in 1919, and after an arrest in 1921, a policeman who was a fan of Mordechai (Three-Finger) Brown, a pitcher with the Chicago Cubs baseball team, wrote that name down under the alias section of the arrest card. His role in the formation of La Cosa Nostra was vital, and it is for that reason, more than anything else, that his criminal career warrants attention. *See also* GALLO, JOSEPH

**SUGGESTED READINGS:** Howard Abadinsky, *Organized Crime*, 5th ed. 1997; Joseph Bonanno, with S. Lalli, *A Man of Honor: The Autobiography of Joseph Bonanno*. 1983.

**LUCHESE CRIME FAMILY.** The crime family headed by Gaetano Luchese,* also known as "Tommy Brown" and "Three-Finger Brown," originated with the Salvatore Maranzano* Mafia network that was fighting with "Joe the Boss" Masseria's* gang in the Castellammarese War* of 1930–1931. When Tom Gagliano, the boss of the family until 1953, died, his underboss (sottocaro)* Luchese became the boss (don).*

Under Luchese's command, the crime family prospered in many lucrative rackets (drugs, gambling, loansharking,* hijacking) and legitimate businesses, especially in construction, garments, and trade waste removal, according to law enforcement sources. Luchese did not remain aloof and secretive, as Carlo Gambino* did. In the 1950s, Luchese was a prime supporter of Mayor Vincent Impellitteri, who replaced a disgraced William O'Dwyer, forced to resign in the face of charges of mob connections and cover-ups.

In 1967, Luchese died of natural causes. Leadership of the crime family passed to Carmine Tramunti, whose drug trafficking and racketeering in East Harlem led to a long prison term in 1974. A more resourceful and wily boss, "Tony Ducks" Corallo,* took control with Salvatore "Tom Mix" Santoro and Christy "Christy Tick" Furnari, as underboss and consigliere,* respectively. He was approved as boss by the Commission* of La Cosa Nostra* in 1978.

The Luchese crime family is the smallest of the five New York families. According to law enforcement estimates (1992), the crime family consists of 100 to 115 members, with a support group of associates numbering approximately 500.

Under Corallo, who was sentenced in 1986 to a 100-year prison term for being a member of the LCN Commission, the crime family, which had a reputation as sophisticated and peaceful, found itself embroiled in a major political scandal in New York City with Mayor John V. Lindsay's Commissioner of Water, Gas and Electricity, James Marcus. Marcus had enormous gambling debts that Corallo agreed to eliminate if Marcus could arrange a cleaning contract in a New York City reservoir for a preferred firm. The plot was discovered, and all the principals were punished. Corallo served 2 years in the 1967 case.

In recent years, like other crime families, the Luchese group has been racked

Charles "Lucky" Luciano. Reproduced from the Collections of the Library of Congress.

by rebellion, betrayal, and prosecution. Internal warfare and defections into the government's Witness Security Program* have destroyed the leadership to the point where violent, psychopathic Anthony "Gaspipe" Casso* assumed the boss position in 1991. In 1994, an indication of the weakness of La Cosa Nostra crime families, Casso himself agreed to become a government witness.

**SUGGESTED READING:** Ernest Volkman, *Gangbusters.* 1998.

**LUCIANO, CHARLES "LUCKY."** ("Charley Lucky," "Charles Ross") (b. Salvatore Lucania, Nov. 24, 1897, Sicily—d. 1962, Naples). Major crime syndicate* architect and La Cosa Nostra* boss (don).*

Charles "Lucky" Luciano is best known for transforming brawling gangs of thugs into smooth-running crime syndicates. He was the original "dapper don" in the New York underworld without the loutishness of an Alphonse Capone* or John Gotti.*

With the possible exception of Al Capone, Charles "Lucky" Luciano, sometimes known as "Charley Lucky" or "Charles Ross," was the most influential Italian American gangster in the twentieth century. In 1931, Luciano played an important role in "Americanizing" organized crime. With Meyer Lansky,* Owney Madden,* "Moe" Dalitz,* and other underworld figures around the country, Luciano helped create a national gambling syndicate and a Mafia* Commission* to resolve disputes and conflicts among mafiosi.

Salvatore Lucania was born in Sicily at the turn of the century. In 1906 his family immigrated to the United States. He rarely attended school, and in 1907 he was arrested for shoplifting. Luciano began working legitimately for a hat manufacturer, but his life in the slums of the Lower East Side of Manhattan also equipped him with a set of criminal skills and values that pushed aside the ethic of hard work his family and many other immigrants were committed to.

Before he was 18 years old, Lucky had been charged and convicted of heroin possession and served a prison term of six months. By 1916, he was a leading member of the notorious "Five Points gang." Apart from its routine criminal activities, the Five Pointers worked for the Tammany Hall political machine and enjoyed its protection.

By 1920, Luciano had emerged as a power in the bootlegging rackets and was closely tied to Meyer Lansky and "Bugsy" Siegel.* Through Lansky and Siegel, Luciano expanded his network of friends and associates to include other ethnic gangsters like Dutch Schultz,* Big Bill Dwyer, Arnold "The Brain" Rothstein,* Dandy Phil Kastel, Frank Erickson, and Frank Costello,* who more tradition-bound mafiosi called "the dirty Calabrian" because of his affiliations with Jews and other non-Italians. Lucky was impressed by Costello's ability to buy protection from city officials, which was an important ingredient in the success of big-time racketeering and vice.

Ignoring the warnings of the old time mafiosi about associating with non-Italians, Luciano maintained these ties, believing instead that the "Mustache Petes"* (the Old World gangsters) were the problem. At the same time, he became a boss in New York's largest Mafia crime family led by "Joe the Boss" Masseria,* for whom he felt contempt but whom he feared—at least until the Castellammarese War* erupted between Joe the Boss and his Sicilian immigrant rival, Salvatore Maranzano.* Luciano was not enamored by Maranzano's dictatorial style of leadership either but tolerated it until Maranzano threatened Luciano and his associates who favored "Americanization"—more cooperation between Italian and non-Italian ethnic gangsters.

Masseria was the main obstacle but was removed by a plot in which Luciano played a central role: He lured Masseria to a Coney Island restaurant along the Brooklyn coastline, where he was assassinated while Lucky was conveniently in the men's room. For this decisive act, which ended the Castellammarese War, Maranzano selected Luciano as his number-two man in his Mafia empire. Maranzano anointed himself "capo di tutti capi" (boss of bosses) and set up the crime family structure of La Cosa Nostra, which endures to this day. But Maranzano's plans, though grandiose, were also lethal for Luciano and others who had betrayed Masseria. The new boss of bosses was not paranoid but had to think shrewdly in a business where misjudgment of character can mean one's life. If Luciano and his supporters could deceive Masseria for mere business advantages, then their loyalty and trustworthiness had to be considered questionable. Luciano and his associates were seen as threats to the Mafia kingdom Maranzano envisioned. Maranzano began planning Luciano's death as well as that of another potential rival: Al Capone. But Maranzano failed to act quickly enough, and Luciano learned of his murder plans. With Lansky's aid, Luciano arranged for Maranzano's murder in his office while Maranzano himself awaited the arrival of Luciano to kill him.

Maranzano's execution ended the Sicilian factional war and left a leadership vacuum in the Italian Mafia in the United States. Actually, the "Old World" Mafia lost its foothold in America with the end of the Castellammarese War. Luciano with his non-Italian cohorts formed a National Crime Syndicate that included Meyer Lansky, Dutch Schultz, and Louis Buchalter* as well as Mafia associates of Luciano such as Frank Costello, Gaetano Luchese,* Albert Anastasia,* and Joseph Adonis.*

The crime syndicate realignment meant the elimination of the "boss of bosses" position in the Mafia; Maranzano's idea of a crime family setup across the United States was retained; and a Commission was established to avoid endless warfare and settle crime family disputes in a businesslike manner. With a well-organized Mafia and a multiethnic larger syndicate engaged in vice activities in many key urban areas around the country, the underworld became a durable, profitable enterprise.

Luciano was at the pinnacle of criminal power. Not only did he enjoy the protection and support of La Cosa Nostra crime families (he headed one of several in New York), but his alliances with Jews, Irish, and other ethnics enabled him to accumulate additional power that ensured his virtual domination of American organized crime.

Lucky led an affluent life as a crime czar. He lived luxuriously in New York's Waldorf Astoria under the name "Charles Ross" and was a neighbor of such distinguished individuals as General Douglas MacArthur and the former president of the United States, Herbert Hoover.

In 1935, Thomas E. Dewey,* a rackets-busting special prosecutor, launched a campaign against the big crime bosses in New York including Dutch Schultz, Lepke Buchalter, "Waxey" Gordon,* and Luciano. A year later, Luciano was convicted of compulsory prostitution and was sentenced to 50 years' imprisonment. The sentence was a cruel twist of fate for Luciano because he had been the protector of Dewey without the prosecutor knowing that his life had been threatened but saved by Luciano's interventions. Dutch Schultz was threatened by Dewey; he had just managed to beat tax evasion charges and was in a nasty mood, demanding that Dewey be killed. Luciano intervened, fearing public outrage similar to what occurred against Capone in Chicago. Schultz spurned the syndicate's decision against killing Dewey and promised to go ahead without syndicate approval. Luciano stopped Schultz by obtaining a murder contract on his life, which was then carried out.

With Luciano in prison, Lansky relocated to Miami, Florida, and Bugsy Siegel went to California and then Las Vegas, Nevada,* to set up mob-controlled casino gambling operations. Although he was imprisoned, Luciano continued to exercise active leadership of his crime family through Frank Costello and also play a role in syndicate affairs.

During World War II, German U-boats and agents posed a threat to the waterfront facilities on the East Coast of the United States. Shipping war supplies to the British and Russians was vital for the Allies, and German submarine operations and espionage activities were very active in vital port areas from Newfoundland to the Caribbean. U.S. Naval Intelligence approached Luciano for help. Meyer Lansky was contacted, and through Joseph "Socks" Lanza,* Luciano instructed his associates in the International Longshoremen's Union to cooperate with the U.S. Navy in reporting incidents of sabotage and by providing information on suspected enemy agents.

In another effort to help his adopted country in 1943, Luciano through his underboss Vito Genovese* (who left the United States before the war to avoid a murder indictment) alerted the Sicilian Mafia bosses to help the Allied invasion of Sicily. As a result of his services to the United States during the war, in 1946 Luciano was pardoned by Governor Thomas E. Dewey but was deported to Italy with the provision that he would not be able to return to the United States. Eight months after his departure to Naples, Luciano traveled to Havana, Cuba, and set up a major syndicate meeting in 1947 where drug trafficking and the status of the mob's investment in the Las Vegas Flamingo Hotel construction (being handled by "Bugsy" Siegel) were on the agenda. In June 1947, Siegel was murdered for looting the syndicate's money. When Luciano's presence was discovered by U.S. government agents, he was forced to return to Italy, where he continued to issue orders. With protests from the Federal Narcotics Bureau, the Italian government forced Luciano to take up residence in Palermo, Sicily, which, however, did not deter his efforts to set up a heroin pipeline to the United States.

Several events spelled the decline of Luciano as a force in the American and international underworld. With the assassination of Albert Anastasia in 1957, the attempted murder of Frank Costello by a Vito Genovese gunman, and the debacle of the Apalachin meeting* of Cosa Nostra bosses in upstate New York, Luciano's influence began to erode. He was believed to be marked for death by Genovese, who wanted control of the crime family (which he subsequently achieved). Before his decline, Luciano, with Carlo Gambino,* Meyer Lansky, and Frank Costello, managed to frame the bloodthirsty Genovese on drug charges, which led to his imprisonment in Atlanta, where he died. By 1959, Luciano suffered physically from heart problems and organizationally when his income from mob sources in the United States was significantly reduced. Sensing that there was not much time left, Luciano wanted to make a film about his life and began talking to journalists and movie producers. The New York mob rejected the idea and warned Lucky not to cooperate.

In January 1962, Luciano died of a heart attack while meeting some filmmakers at the Naples airport. He managed several interviews, but nothing came of the project except a controversial book based on several interviews with him.

**SUGGESTED READING:** Martin Gosch and Richard Hammer, *The Last Testament of Lucky Luciano*. 1974.

**LUCIANO CRIME FAMILY.** *See* LUCIANO, CHARLES "LUCKY"

# M

**MADDEN, OWNEY.** ("The Killer") (b. 1892, Liverpool, England—d. Apr. 24, 1965, Hot Springs, AR). New York racketeer and bootlegger.

Madden began his career as head of the Gophers, a Hell's Kitchen gang on New York's West Side that operated from basements and tenement cellars. It was widely feared because of the violence of its gang members. In 1915, Madden served a term in Sing Sing prison on a murder charge. Upon his release on parole in 1923, he began hijacking liquor trucks and became a partner of Vincent ("Bill") Dwyer, a major bootlegger,* and George Jean ("Big Frenchy") de-Mange, a bootlegger and speakeasy operator who would become partners with Madden in the famous Cotton Club in Harlem. By the time he was 23, Madden had personally killed five men and participated in murder conspiracies of many others. "Owney the Killer" was an appropriate nickname. However, his affiliations with Big Frenchy, Bill Dwyer, and even Dutch Schultz* matured him; his gruff, tough-guy image underwent a metamorphosis as he acquired some polish, finesse, and respectability as the operator of a nightclub catering to wealthy patrons from the affluent classes of New York society.

During Prohibition (*see* PROHIBITION AND ORGANIZED CRIME*), Madden's bootlegging enterprises thrived, and as he ascended into the higher regions of the New York underworld, he associated with major racketeers including Charles "Lucky" Luciano,* Frank Costello,* Louis Buchalter,* "Bugsy" Siegel,* and Meyer Lansky.* Madden became involved in legitimate businesses including laundry services and coal delivery and secured the protection of Jimmy Hines,* a major Tammany Hall political boss with influence in the police department. He continued his operations in bootlegging until 1932 when he was arrested for parole violation and returned to prison. In 1933 Prohibition ended; Madden was paroled and headed south to Hot Springs, Arkansas, a town with a notorious reputation for illegal gambling* and corrupt politics. Madden took his bootleg millions and bought the Hotel Arkansas, a spa and casino that would become a gangster hideout and getaway. Gangsters on the lam took the train to Hot Springs and stayed in big, well-kept rooms, took the waters, and lost fortunes to Madden's casino.

In 1935, Lucky Luciano found temporary refuge in Hot Springs from Thomas E. Dewey's* pursuit. Eventually, the police discovered Lucky's hideout and extradited him back to New York City to face prostitution charges and a long prison sentence.

Madden settled down in Hot Springs despite the notoriety of his past and his dangerous associates. He married the postmaster's daughter and became a naturalized citizen in 1943. Madden died of natural causes in 1965.

**MADE MAN.** *See* "MAKING YOUR BONES"; SOLDIERS

**MAFIA.** There are two meanings of the term "mafia"; they are related and dependent upon one another but also distinct. In one sense, "Mafia" refers to a secret criminal organization that originated in Italy specifically in Sicily during periods of domestic and foreign oppression. In another sense "mafia" is a state of mind, a spirit of mistrust and suspicion that pervades personal and public life among Sicilians and other southern Italians. Mafia (organizations) could not flourish without the cultural and historical energy of mafia (a psychology of solidarity and protection based on kinship relationships). Transported to the United States with the influx of Sicilian and southern Italian immigrants, La Cosa Nostra,* the modified versions of Mafia and mafia, emerged among Italians living in the ghettos and "Little Italies" within American cities.

New York City was the cradle of the American Mafia; five of the most powerful crime families* of the 20-odd across the nation were located and operated in New York City since the 1930 Castellammarese War,* which consolidated control of organized crime in the hands of mafiosi and their non-Italian associates.

As an organization, Mafia, or La Cosa Nostra, is built around a cosca, which refers to the leaves of an artichoke. At the center of the plant, at its heart, is the "capomafioso;" the "padrino"—the boss (don).* The structure of the organization may resemble a business corporation, pyramidlike, where its activities involve vice activities that require centralized, coordinated management; in other respects personal relationships are more or less patron/client ties based on kinship, friendship, and the exchange of favors. In Italy, a typical cosca has no more than 15 or 20 members; the mafioso at the center commands these "networks," who act on his behalf as power brokers, intermediaries, providing services, entree, or making indirect threats—which is the essence of mafia power. In return for services rendered, the mafioso may expect reciprocal favors in kind, or money, jobs, political and police influence, protection of vices and rackets, and so on—all fitting under the label of "rispetto" (respect). Carlo Gambino,* an unassuming "capomafioso" at the head, or in the heart of, the most powerful Mafia crime family in America, would often hold court in a neighborhood cafe and grant favors: a job for a child, a lawyer for a troubled youth, support for a pregnant daughter, and so on; in return for information and silence, no matter what one may witness in the street. *See also* CAMORRA; COMMISSION; CRIME FAMILY; LA COSA NOSTRA; OMERTA

**SELECTED READING:** Jay S. Albanese, *Organized Crime in America*, 3rd ed. 1996.

**MAFIA AND THE KENNEDY ASSASSINATION.** What was the relationship between the Kennedys and the Mafia*? After the 1963 assassination of John F. Kennedy on November 22, speculation raged, but it was not until 1979 when a congressional committee looking into the assassination of both John F. Kennedy and Martin Luther King reached a disturbing conclusion: It pointed the finger at the mob as a participant in Kennedy's death.

Joseph P. Kennedy, the family patriarch, made money with gangsters during Prohibition (*see* PROHIBITION AND ORGANIZED CRIME*); Frank Costello* alleged that he and Joe Kennedy were partners in bootlegging, but Kennedy, Sr. managed to retain a sanitized image such that in 1938 he was appointed ambassador to the Court of St. James (England) by President Franklin D. Roosevelt.

In 1960, John F. Kennedy won the presidency in a closely contested election with Richard Nixon; earlier, from 1957 to 1960, John F. Kennedy and his brother Robert F. Kennedy* served on the McClelland Committee,* which investigated the Teamsters and their underworld connections. Among those investigated were Carlos Marcello* of New Orleans and Sam Giancana* of the Chicago Outfit.*

But John F. Kennedy was imperiled by the political debts he incurred with the Mafia despite his anticrime crusading image. In West Virginia, the Mafia, in exchange for votes, allegedly arranged to get Joseph Adonis* back into the United States. And in precincts in Chicago, it is widely believed that the mob produced the votes needed to carry Illinois for Kennedy.

In February 1960, John F. Kennedy started an affair with Judith Campbell, who was in contact with Sam Giancana. It is alleged that she acted as a courier for John F. Kennedy, bringing cash to Giancana for voter corruption.

In office, John F. Kennedy incurred another political debt. Three Mafia bosses, Santos Trafficante, Jr.,* John Roselli,* and Sam Giancana, were hired by the CIA to kill Castro (*see* OPERATION MONGOOSE). The CIA/Mafia plot continued under John F. Kennedy until the Bay of Pigs failure. Understandably, Cuban dissidents were enraged by John F. Kennedy.

Then, in 1960, Robert Kennedy became attorney general and declared war on organized crime. It was the number-one priority of the Department of Justice. The paradox was that the Kennedys were going after the people who allegedly helped them into office.

FBI transcripts in 1961 between Roselli and Giancana disclose that the mob believed that the Kennedys betrayed them. The mob felt hounded by the men who they had helped.

Robert F. Kennedy put together a "hit list" of mafia chiefs to try to prosecute. Carlos Marcello,* Sam Giancana, and Jimmy Hoffa* were at the top of the list.

In 1978, testimony before the House Assassination Committee indicated that the La Cosa Nostra had plans to hit* (murder) the president because of Bobby Kennedy's harassment.

Some critics assert that Lee Harvey Oswald, the alleged assassin of John F. Kennedy, may have been an instrument of the Mafia in a time-honored tradition of murder: The actual killer would have no direct connection with the mob.

An angry and defiant Oswald insisted, after his arrest, on his innocence, claiming he was a "patsy," and steadfastly denied his guilt. Oswald dropped hints of his associates being involved. If he was a patsy, who was using him? The men around Oswald, David Ferrie and Guy Banister, were also connected to Carlos Marcello in small time criminal and vice activity.

On November 22, 1963, Marcello was in court when John F. Kennedy was shot. Oswald was arrested shortly after. Within 48 hours, however, Jack Ruby, a former low-level Chicago hoodlum, killed Oswald. Later, suspicions arose that Ruby was linked to the Dallas underworld and the Chicago of Alphonse Capone.* Ruby allegedly made mob-connected trips to Cuba to help Trafficante, and most important, Ruby claimed he had access to police. Jack Ruby died in 1967 in custody and suggested on his deathbed that no one will ever know the true facts.

Thereafter, Robert Kennedy left the Justice Department, and the war on the Mafia ground to a halt.

**SUGGESTED READINGS:** William Breuer, *Vendetta: Castro and the Kennedy Brothers.* 1997; Seymour Hersh, *The Dark Side of Camelot.* 1997.

**MAGADDINO, STEFANO.** ("Steve") (b. 1891, Castellammare, Sicily—d. 1974, Buffalo, NY). Buffalo Cosa Nostra crime boss.

Magaddino truly exemplified the old mafia bosses whose greed, self-absorption, and refusal to Americanize encouraged younger mobsters to refer to them as "Mustache Petes"* from the old country. Magaddino is believed to have entered the United States in 1903 and settled in Brooklyn until the Mafia vendettas that originated in Sicilian feuds forced him to leave and head for Buffalo, where he remained until his death from natural causes at the age of 82.

His crime family operated throughout western New York, parts of Ohio, Pennsylvania, and Canada. Bootlegging, extortion, racketeering, gambling, and labor racketeering were the major illicit sources of income, of which Magaddino took a sizable portion from his soldiers.* The first Department of Justice strike force operation in the 1970s infiltrated Magaddino's family, and the demoralization of its soldiers, attributable to their boss's tight-fisted greed, splintered the family when he died.

Magaddino and Joseph Bonanno* were cousins. Relations between them were not cordial, and during the crisis of the "Banana War" among the godfathers of

New York City's La Cosa Nostra* crime families, Magaddino was instrumental in kidnapping Bonanno at the behest of the national Commission.* For almost two years Magaddino kept Bonanno on a leash until he agreed to step down as boss of his family and retire to Arizona.

**SUGGESTED READING:** Joseph Bonanno (with Sergio Lalli), *A Man of Honor: The Autobiography of Joseph Bonanno.* 1983.

**"MAKING YOUR BONES."** (Crime family entrance requirement).

Committing murder "making your bones," considered a prerequisite for induction into La Cosa Nostra,* is no longer a uniform rule of admission. Murder on demand, at the behest of a made man, was the linchpin of Cosa Nostra—for control and discipline, to achieve and maintain power. For made members and associates, it was an everyday, accepted fact of life. The code that could trigger a "hit*" was very clear. If someone broke the rules, he would be "whacked" (murdered). Murder was the means of proving that one had the courage and determination to be part of Cosa Nostra, and it was the means to bring some semblance of order into an organization that could be chaotic.

In theory, a Cosa Nostra "hit" (murder) required a precise procedure. A case had to be made to justify a killing. It then had to be sanctioned by the family boss (don)*. A murder that had not been so authorized invited immediate retribution. Yet time after time, transgressions against the rules occurred out of fear, jealousy, greed, or desperation.

To "make one's bones" shows that the aspirant is prepared to accept the authority of the family without question, without hesitation, without even personal consideration of the risks. It also screens out weak individuals and law enforcement undercover infiltrators who cannot commit murder under such circumstances because they are sworn peace officers.

Not everyone who is recruited into La Cosa Nostra or other criminal organizations must meet this supreme test of courage and obedience today. Paul Castellano,* Vincent Charles Teresa,* and others were exceptions; they were inducted into the Mafia for other reasons: blood relations of high standing in the family (Castellano); the capacity to earn money (Teresa); or the practical need for manpower (Joseph Valachi*).

**SUGGESTED READING:** Joseph Pistone, *The Ceremony: Mafia Initiation Tapes.* 1992.

**MANGANO, VINCENT.** (b. 1888, Trapani, Sicily—1951, missing, presumed dead). Cosa Nostra* crime family* boss (don), New York City, 1940s.

In the chaotic aftermath of the Castellammarese War,* five crime families were formed, with Vincent and Philip Mangano as heads of gangs closely associated with Brooklyn waterfront rackets. Over time as the crime families evolved or were transformed by war and violence, the Mangano crime family would eventually become the Gambino crime family,* after its most infamous boss.

Vincent Mangano* and his brother Philip concentrated on the waterfront, while their underboss (sottocapo),* Albert Anastasia,* moved closer to other crime bosses Charles "Lucky" Luciano* and Louis Buchalter,* whose criminal enterprises extended over many vice activities and rackets in numerous industries. This disloyalty of Anastasia's led to conflict with the Manganos. Hatred between them welled up and often ended in physical assaults.

On April 19, 1951, Philip Mangano's body was found in a marshland in Brooklyn—obviously a mob hit.* Vincent could not be found for questioning. Clearly he, too, had been murdered. Anastasia was questioned but had an airtight alibi. At a meeting of the New York crime bosses, Anastasia was confirmed as the new head of the family. Had they decided against him, he, too, would have been listed as "missing," presumed dead.

**SUGGESTED READING:** Stephen Fox, *Blood and Power: Organized Crime in Twentieth Century America.* 1989.

**MARANZANO, SALVATORE.** ("Little Caesar") (b. 1868, Castellammare del Golfo, Sicily—d. Sept. 10, 1931, New York City). Capo di tutti capi (boss of bosses) of the American Mafia,* 1931.

When the Castellammarese War* ended in 1931 with the murder of "Joe the Boss" Masseria,* Salvatore Maranzano, an immigrant mafioso who had once considered becoming a priest, arranged a meeting in the Bronx that would have profound consequences for the course of organized crime in the United States for the rest of the century. To the 400 or 500 mafiosi attending the meeting, Maranzano explained the shape of the new organization he planned: he would be "boss of bosses"; the "men of honor" (mafiosi) would be realigned in "families" (gangs) with their own capos* (captains), answerable to their bosses and ultimately to Don Salvatore himself. The organization would be know hereafter as "Cosa Nostra" (Our Thing), and rituals for admission and membership (omerta*) would be rigorously enforced. Five families were created.

But Maranzano did not trust Charles "Lucky" Luciano,* Vito Genovese,* Alphonse Capone,* and others who were instrumental in deposing Masseria—Maranzano's deadly rival. Pursuing his instincts and acting on his fears, he arranged the murders of these men through a professional gunman, Vincent "Mad Dog" Coll.* But the plot failed when Luciano and his partners decided to eliminate Maranzano. He was murdered by killers masquerading as federal tax officers who wanted to inspect his books. Maranzano was slain by gun and knife in his offices in Midtown Manhattan only months after Masseria was killed.

Maranzano came to the United States and settled in 1927. He was probably the only Mafia chief to have a college education. He was a protégé of Sicilian Mafia Capo Vito Cascio Ferro* and a serious student of Julius Caesar's military campaigns. His mission in America was to organize the local mafiosi into a branch of the Sicilian Mafia under Cascio Ferro. But they were already "Americanized" and had other plans that did not include being subordinated to a distant foreigner.

**SELECTED READING:** John H. Davis, *Mafia Dynasty: The Rise and Fall of the Gambino Crime Family.* 1993.

**MARCELLO, CARLOS.** (b. Calagero Menacore, Feb. 6, 1910, Tunis, North Africa—d. Mar. 2, 1993, New Orleans, LA). Boss of the New Orleans Cosa Nostra.

Ever since the assassination of President John F. Kennedy, there has been constant speculation about the involvement of organized crime—especially the roles played in the plot by Carlos Marcello, crime boss of Louisiana and a long-standing member of La Cosa Nostra.* Conspiracy theories often cast Marcello along with Santos Trafficante, Jr., crime family boss of Tampa, Florida, and Jimmy Hoffa,* convicted Teamster boss, as the principal architects in the as-sassination. Marcello and Hoffa nursed grudges against Robert F. Kennedy,* the president's brother and attorney general of the United States who declared war against the underworld. Kennedy's feud with Hoffa went back to his days as chief counsel of the McClelland Committee* on Labor Racketeering when he harassed Jimmy Hoffa and accused the president of the International Broth-erhood of Teamsters* as being a "front" for the mob. Kennedy publicly charged that Hoffa had made enormous loans available from the Teamsters' Central States pension funds to Chicago gangsters as well as Carlos Marcello and Santos Trafficante, Jr. When Kennedy became head of the Department of Justice, he created a special unit to "get Hoffa" and Marcello.

Marcello was known as hot-tempered and vengeful when crossed. He was also known to hire hit* teams from other Mafia families, far removed from Louisiana, to perform contract murders in his realm. Vincent Teresa, in his book *My Life in the Mafia*, describes an episode when Marcello recruited a group of killers from Teresa's own crime family, the Patriarcas of Providence, Rhode Island.

The case for Carlos Marcello's participation in the president's assassination appears strong on the surface but is largely circumstantial. The question that can be posed is, Did the killing of President Kennedy fit the traditional pattern of a Mafia execution? And if it did, would a powerful Mafia leader choose the crew he did to accomplish a major execution? The answer is yes. Kennedy's murder was a public execution, so it was clear that this was no spontaneous madman—it had to be planned. The Mafia often kills in public, in plain sight to "discourage others." But why would he run such risks? On this question, the recollections of Santos Trafficante, his longtime associate, are informative. Frank Ragano, Trafficante's lawyer for many years, reports a conversation he had with Traffi-cante in the former's confessional book *Mob Lawyer*, published just months before his death. Trafficante said, "Carlos [Marcello] fucked up. We shouldn't have killed Giovanni [John Kennedy]. We should have killed Bobby [Kennedy]." Ragano interpreted these cryptic comments to mean than Trafficante and Marcello were part of a Cosa Nostra conspiracy to assassinate President John Kennedy. Trafficante told Ragano this in 1987, months before his death. Trafficante was doomed by a bad heart, and Marcello was in prison, suffering from Alzheimer's disease and strokes. Marcello would be paroled in 1989 and unable to speak. He was never again seen in public.

Until his death in 1993, Carlos Marcello was one of the toughest crime family bosses in the United States. New Orleans and Louisiana were ruled by the Marcello organization as if they were independent nation–states. Few fellow mafiosi would venture into Louisiana without first getting permission to do so.

Marcello was born Calagero Menacore in Tunis, North Africa, in 1910 of Sicilian parents. He was brought to the United States as an infant by his immigrant parents. He was just 20 years old when he was first arrested; the charge was bank robbery, but it was dismissed. Over the years, police records would show charges including illegal gambling,* drug trafficking, robbery, extortion, income tax evasion—none of which led to his imprisonment. Clearly, the New Orleans family enjoyed a cozy relationship with many local and state officials in Louisiana.

In the 1930s, Marcello took up the reins of the New Orleans crime family when its boss, Sam Carrola, was imprisoned. He assumed command and helped to arrange the shipment of slot machines from New York City into New Orleans after negotiating with powerful gangsters in New York such as Charles "Lucky" Luciano,* Meyer Lansky,* and Frank Costello.* The political figure behind the invitation to the New York underworld to send it gambling equipment was Senator Huey "Kingfish" Long; Marcello deftly arranged for the New York crime syndicate* to supply the capital, Long would furnish the political protection, and the New Orleans Cosa Nostra crime family would supervise operations and draw off a good percentage of the profits.

Because he was not a citizen, Marcello drew the attention of the Immigration and Naturalization Service and was subjected to deportation proceedings, none of which proved successful because of his political connections. On numerous occasions, the U.S. government tried to interest Italy, France, and Tunisia in taking Marcello, but he had bribed officials in each country, who then declared him a noncitizen.

At the McClelland Hearings in 1959, Robert Kennedy, then chief counsel of the committee, described Marcello as head of the underworld in the southeastern part of the United States. A year later, Bobby Kennedy solicited Marcello's help with the Louisiana delegation at the Democratic Party National Convention. Marcello, however, was committed to Lyndon Johnson.

Kennedy promised to get even. When the Kennedys won the White House in 1960, Bobby Kennedy, the attorney general, moved quickly to expedite deportation proceedings that had hung over Marcello since the 1950 Kefauver Committee* hearings. Not a U.S. citizen, Marcello held only a dubious Guatemalan passport issued on a forged birth record. In 1961, he was seized by U.S.

Giuseppe "Joe the Boss" Masseria. Reproduced from the Collections of the Library of Congress.

government agents, zipped off to an airport, and dumped in Guatemala. The
unhappy Guatemalan government deposited Marcello in a jungle village in El
Salvador. He was then shunted out of the country into Honduras. The most
feared man in Louisiana found himself stranded but eventually flew back (illegally) to New Orleans, where he found a tax lien for more than $800,000 await-
ing him. Outraged, he contacted Sam Giancana,* a top boss in the Chicago
Outfit* (syndicate), who had close contacts with the Kennedy administration,
including Frank Sinatra. It didn't help.

According to one thesis about the Kennedy assassination, the mob's real target
was Bobby Kennedy, and the best way to tame him was to eliminate the president. Throughout the years following the assassination, Marcello denied the
charges.

**SUGGESTED READINGS:** John H. Davis, *Mafia Kingfish*. 1989; Frank Ragano, *Mob
Lawyer*. 1994; Gino Russo, *Live by the Sword: The Secret War Against Castro and the
Death of JFK*. 1998; Vincent Teresa and Thomas Renner, *My Life in the Mafia*. 1973.

**MASSERIA, "JOE THE BOSS."** (b. Giuseppe Masseria, 1880, Palermo, Sicily—
d. Apr. 15, 1931, Brooklyn, NY). Mafia leader in New York, 1920–1930.

In the 1920s Joe the Boss had become the dominant player in New York's growing illegal liquor trade and had amassed a huge fortune in the process. A stocky five-foot-two-inch gunman, he fled a murder charge in Sicily in 1903. Within a few years in New York City he joined the Morello gang, the city's first important Mafia* group. With murders and imprisonment taking its toll of the Morellos, Masseria took control in 1913. Working for Masseria in the 1920s were Carlo Gambino,* Joseph Adonis,* and Albert Anastasia*—future gang leaders.

Masseria had a reputation as a glutton, as coarse and unkempt. His principal talents were evading murder attempts and being a tough, resourceful street fighter. It was not long before a powerful rival challenged Masseria's dominance in New York. Salvatore Maranzano,* a Sicilian mafioso, arrived in New York to rally his kinsmen and Castellammarese under the flag of Sicilian Mafia chief Vito Cascio Ferro.* Thus began the Castellammarese War.*

Fighting broke out as the New York mafiosi took sides in the struggle. By 1928, Masseria was demanding tribute from the Castellammarese, who, if they refused to pay, were murdered. The war dragged on, with heavy casualties and loss of revenue from lucrative bootleg rackets.

Around this time, Charles "Lucky" Luciano,* Meyer Lansky,* "Bugsy" Siegel,* Frank Costello,* and Vito Genovese,* joined Masseria, but these alliances proved very unstable. Before long, Masseria was outgeneraled, and as the war ground on, Luciano and Genovese decided to destroy Masseria if Maranzano would guarantee them protection after Joe the Boss was eliminated.

In April 1931, Luciano lured Masseria to lunch at a Coney Island (Brooklyn) restaurant. After a heavy meal, Luciano excused himself and went to the men's room. When he returned he found Masseria's blood-spattered body lying on the floor, surrounded by terrified waitresses and customers. Four gunmen shot Joe the Boss: Bugsy Siegel, Joe Adonis, Vito Genovese, and Albert Anastasia—all friends of Lucky Luciano and future targets of their sponsor Maranzano.

**MATTHEWS, FRANK.** ("The Black Luciano") (b. Feb. 13, 1944, Durham, NC—missing, presumed dead). African American drug trafficker.

Frank Matthews migrated from Durham, North Carolina, to New York when he was a young man. In the 1960s, he worked in Bedford-Stuyvesant as a collector for an Italian-owned numbers* operation before becoming a drug trafficker. As the Mafia's* grip on African American neighborhoods in New York loosened, narcotics distribution in Brooklyn's minority areas was being taken over by the people who lived there. They were no longer content to remain in the pay of La Cosa Nostra* importers and wholesalers. Many were now customers, looking to their former employers not just for supplies but for working capital and management expertise as well. African American drug dealers were organizing, much as the Italian American gangs had done in the 1920s and 1930s, with the purpose of ratifying one another's territorial claims and spheres of interest and eliminating competition.

Seeing narcotics rather than the more modest rackets in gambling and prostitution as the gold mine of quick millions, Frank Matthews examined the Brooklyn drug markets, took inventory of what was required to gain control of some territory that could function as a supply base for out-of-town networks, and approached Cosa Nostra drug dealers for supplies and finance. The standard terms of Cosa Nostra drug deals were 30 percent down and the balance on the delivery of heroin—in cash. Only a handful of African Americans possessed the resources to transact business with the Mafia on credit consignments—and then only at the risk of their lives. Matthews had contacts in both the Bonanno* and Gambino crime families,* but they declined to help.

The Mafia crime families may have had a monopoly on heroin—for the moment—but they had no such import control on cocaine or over the Cubans who brought it into the United States. Undaunted, Matthews changed his tactics and made contact with "Spanish Raymond" Marquez in the policy business, who introduced him to some of the important cocaine traffickers in New York.

Within a year, Matthews built an organization, mainly of "home boys" with connections in a dozen eastern and southern cities. The former chicken thief from North Carolina soon impressed the Cosa Nostra, who reconsidered selling him heroin, partly, to preclude his dealing directly with the Corsican mafia, the main suppliers of the American mafia, and partly to retain some sort of influence over Matthews's rather reckless business methods. Quickly thereafter, he created a drug mill for processing and would pay premium prices to any kilo supplier in order to keep his business flourishing. Many of the principals in Matthews's organization worked behind a legitimate front that shielded them from police surveillance.

From 1969 to 1971, Matthews expanded his narcotics business in city after city, state after state. Where no dealers were operating, he established a business, and where one did exist, he absorbed it, making offers that no local dealers could refuse. He established headquarters in Atlanta, Georgia, and sank millions into local real estate but maintained his New York base of distribution, which enabled him to fan out in the Northeast in Connecticut, Rhode Island, and Massachusetts. Through a partner, he serviced wholesale drug outlets in Detroit, Chicago, and Los Angeles. By 1972, Matthews formed alliances to prevent costly wars with competitors.

Sometime toward the end of 1971, Matthews put together a national conclave in Atlanta of top African American and Hispanic drug dealers. The main business item of the meeting was to discuss ways and means of breaking the Mafia's stranglehold on heroin imports. Preferably, it should be done peacefully, so that existing supply arrangements would not be interrupted or jeopardized. The need for an independent source was critical, because in the minds of these narcotics racketeers, a competitive alternative to Cosa Nostra drug supplies might achieve several desirable goals. It would remove the brake on expansion and keep Cosa Nostra wholesale prices reasonable. It would also provide a margin of safety in the event that Cosa Nostra traffickers were arrested, which always loomed as a real possibility as the country's fears and concerns over drug abuse put pressure on the government to do something to control trafficking.

The discussions concluded with Matthews exploring Corsican drug sources though Cuban networks. The Cosa Nostra was still the principal source of supply but tolerated the fact that African American traffickers sought multiple wholesale sources. The Corsican connections temporarily turned wholesale drug dealing into a buyer's market. As African Americans consolidated their hold on distribution territories and sources, Cosa Nostra crime families astutely plugged into the expanding drug networks as investors and advisers.

The racial deténte and fragile alliance between the two underworlds could easily have unraveled because of Matthew's sensitivities and his threat of gang violence, should Cosa Nostra soldiers* continue to insult his people. Intimidation came not only from the Cosa Nostra, police, and other drug enforcement agencies but from African American competitors and opponents of narcotics. Matthews could and did make credible threats against Cosa Nostra soldiers who interfered with his associates, but with African American extortionists, the tactics in coping were complicated.

In New York, Philadelphia, and several other cities, the Matthews organization—indeed, the drug trade as a whole—was under attack by self-styled Black Muslim commando groups seeking to collect a 10 to 15 percent "tax" on sales. By preying on dealers in no position to holler "cop" when victimized by kidnapping and extortion, these so-called Muslim groups were out to get rich on narcotics without even having to handle them—and without forfeiting the goodwill of a black community appalled by the drug problem and inclined, like the police, to blame atrocities on narcotics gang warfare.

But the Black Muslim commandos were in no position to resort to police protection either. Matthews declared open season on Muslims and the "Black mafia" of Philadelphia. This latter group, according to the Pennsylvania Crime Commission Report of 1990, was an outgrowth of 1960s street gangs in Philadelphia's impoverished African American neighborhoods. They controlled narcotics sales and distribution and engaged in extortion.

Its most infamous incident occurred on Easter Sunday, 1972, when the elite of Philadelphia's African American underworld converged at Club Harlem, a brassy nightspot in Atlantic City, New Jersey.* Some of Frank Matthews's key people in Philadelphia were assassinated, along with five others, in an auditorium packed with 600 people. The official explanation for the audacious act that produced the carnage was that Tyrone Palmer, one of Matthews's men, was murdered in fulfillment of a "contract" worth $15,000, issued by the associates of Palmer's underboss (sottocapo),* who had been murdered on Palmer's orders for some slight or indiscretion.

In New York, the main threat to Matthews and others were street-level vigilantes who could not be bought off and who were not susceptible to violent countermeasures. Often, these self-righteous individuals were frustrated by lack of law enforcement activity in their communities or by corruption of the police and had no other motive but to clean up their neighborhoods. Along with similarly committed Black Panthers and genuine Black Muslims, they had taken to shooting pushers on sight. But pushers were expendable. So the war of attrition instigated by otherwise upstanding citizens petered out from sheer exhaustion.

In July 1973, the world came crashing down on Frank Matthews. He was due in Brooklyn Federal Court to plead to an indictment superseding one of six on narcotics trafficking already handed down against him. He failed to appear and has not been seen or found since—nor has an estimated $20 million in cash. Police forces all over the world continue to search for him. *See also* AFRICAN AMERICAN ORGANIZED CRIME; BARNES, LEROY "NICKY"

**SUGGESTED READING:** Donald Goddard, *Easy Money.* 1989.

**McCLELLAND COMMITTEE.** Senator John McClelland (Democrat, Arkansas) was appointed chair of the Permanent Subcommittee on Investigation (1963–1964), which investigated labor racketeering* in the nation's trade unions. Its chief counsel, Robert F. Kennedy,* focused the committee's work on the Teamsters Union and its president, Jimmy Hoffa,* inquiring into the role of pension fund loans to organized criminals and the infiltration of La Cosa Nostra* into the union's locals.

In 1963, the McClelland Committee held televised hearings on organized crime with Joseph Valachi,* a onetime Genovese crime family* member, as its star witness. Valachi's appearance was historic. He revealed the internal structure of La Cosa Nostra, its organizing principles, and the extent of its criminal power and influence across the United States. Because of Valachi and the McClelland Committee, the mystique of the Mafia* had been shattered forever. Giving him the opportunity to talk and live after revealing the secrets of La Cosa Nostra—emboldened others to come forward after Valachi and McClelland led the way.

**SUGGESTED READING:** John McClellan, *Crime Without Punishment.* 1962.

**MEDELLÍN.** *See* CALI COCAINE CARTEL; COLOMBIAN DRUG CARTELS; ESCOBAR, PABLO EMILIO GAVOROA; OCHOA, JORGE LUIS VASQUEZ

**MEDIA.** *See* ORGANIZED CRIME AND THE MEDIA

**MEXICAN ORGANIZED CRIME IN THE UNITED STATES.**     According to the President's Commission on Organized Crime (PCOC), about a dozen major Mexican criminal organizations supply heroin and cocaine to the United States. Generally, the groups are extended family organizations with most members related by blood and marriage. The organizations that are involved in opium cultivation are made up of village middlemen, brokers, and distributors. In the United States the organizations, like their Colombian counterparts, control wholesale distribution but steer clear of street action, which is too high risk and often very violent.

For years the Herrera family dominated Mexican heroin trafficking. From the first laboratory in Mexico established shortly after World War II, the Herreras shipped heroin to relatives living in Chicago. The family consisted of several subfamily groupings, so that the Herreras were a cartel-type drug trafficking organization long before the Colombians came on the scene.

The head of the Herrera family is Jamie ("Don Jamie") Herrera, born in 1924 or 1927. For a time he served as a police officer in the city and state of Durango. The organization is estimated to have nearly 5,000 members, of whom 2,000 are related by blood or marriage.

In the United States, the Herreras use Chicago as their national headquarters. Chicago has a very large Mexican presence, and from the city, Mexican heroin is shipped to dealers in New York, Philadelphia, Boston, Detroit, and other locales. Overall management is in the hands of several directors and their representatives in various American cities. Don Jamie periodically visits Chicago to supervise American operations but otherwise remains in his native state of Durango.

The business skill of the Herrera family became evident in the 1980s when it successfully established cocaine contacts throughout Latin America. But in the 1990s other Mexican drug barons such as Juan Guerra and Juan Garcia Abrego* had emerged. The Mexican traffickers have also been innovative and expanded their drug portfolio: While latecomers to the trade, they have become dominant in the manufacture and distribution of "speed" (methamphetamine). They import precursor drugs from Asia and Europe and convert them into "speed" or "crack" in Mexican-based labs. Mexican involvement with the substance apparently began when the U.S.-based Hell's Angels* turned to them in order to avoid problems associated with the manufacturing processes.

"Speed" was once the domain of outlaw motorcycle gangs,* but now since the Mexicans have improved the methods of manufacture, the bikers are buying speed from Mexican drug families in the rural belt around San Diego County in California. *See also* ABREGO, JUAN GARCIA; LATINO ORGANIZED CRIME

**SUGGESTED READING:** President's Commission on Organized Crime, *America's Habit: Drug Abuse, Drug Trafficking, and Organized Crime.* 1986.

**MOB NICKNAMES.** Many gangsters were and are often known by special identifiers beyond their real names. These descriptive additional names often replace a criminal's actual name as his (or her) public identity. Newspapers love these nicknames because they make flashy headlines: "Legs Diamond" and "Dutch Schultz"* sounded more like gangster names than John T. Nolan (Legs Diamond) or Arthur Flegenheimer (Dutch Schultz). And on occasion the imagination of a journalist would sometimes create an identity for a gangster: When

Vincent "The Mad Mick" Coll accidentally killed a child who was an innocent bystander, he became Vincent "Mad Dog" Coll* in the newspapers, and it stuck. Gaetano Luchese,* a La Cosa Nostra* godfather, also known by his alias, Tommy Brown, was called "Three-Finger Brown" after a baseball pitcher who also lacked some fingers. Luchese insisted that no one else ever call him "Three-Fingers."

In some instances, nicknames come from childhood that carry over into adult life. "Lepke" is a Yiddish derivative of "Louis" that Louis Buchalter* acquired as an adolescent in his neighborhood, and it stayed with him. Abner Zwillman* a powerful racketeer in New Jersey, was always tall for his age as a kid; hence, his nickname "Longy."

Names have been used as ethnic disguises. Jewish hoods might take Italian or Irish names. Vincenzo Demora became "Machine Gun" Jack McGurn, and Francesco Castiglia became Frank Costello;* John Dioguardi cut his name down to Johnny Dio* to make it easier to pronounce. It is worth noting that while many Jews took other names, no non-Jews ever assumed a Jewish name.

Mob nicknames most typically describe certain physical or personal characteristics. "Sammy the Bull" Gravano* was short, squat, and physically tenacious; "Scarface" Alphonse Capone* had a facial scar acquired in a street fight; Ernest "The Hawk" Rupolo* wore a patch to cover an eye destroyed in a gunfight; and Vincent "The Chin" Gigante* possesses a rather prominent jaw. Nicknames that are personally descriptive include: Charlie "Lucky" Luciano* (who miraculously survived a mob beating and slashing); Anthony Anastasio* ("Tough Tony"), a rough-and-tumble ILA waterfront boss; Joseph Gallo ("Crazy Joe"), an eccentric rebel in the Profaci-Gallo crime family; "Bugsy" Siegel,* an explosive, unpredictable tough guy; Carmine "The Cigar" Galante,* who always had a cigar in his mouth—even when he was murdered. Anthony, Benjamin, and Theodore DeMartino of the Luciano crime family* were known ignominiously as Tony the Bum, Benny the Bum, and Teddy the Bum.

Nicknames might also convey a man's criminal specialty or status. "Joe the Boss" Masseria* was a mafia boss; "Killer" Burke was a bloodthirsty hit* man; "Kid Twist" Reles* was an expert in strangling people; Trigger Mike Coppola* was good with guns and fond of using them; and despite his efforts to manage a good self-image, "The Killer" Owney Madden* never lived down the reputation he earned as a young man in his hell-raising days.

Nicknames are common in closed societies like criminal gangs, college fraternities, and military units. They function primarily as symbols of trust and comradeship.

For the outside world of law-abiding citizens, gangster nicknames may indeed seem funny and colorful and may, unfortunately, encourage the delusion that these individuals are too amusing to be dangerous.

**MONEY LAUNDERING.** Money laundering is the concealment of the source and/or destination of funds gained through illegal activities. The activity generally occurs in and through four methods: currency smuggling, bank and corporate transactions, nonbank financial institution transactions, and commodity acquisition.

Currency smuggling is used where territorial borders lack rigorous shipment and luggage checks. Couriers can carry the currency, or it can be hidden in legally shipped goods, much like drugs. Some estimates indicate that nearly 80 percent of illegal monies generated in the United States are smuggled overseas. Currency smuggling is only the first phase in "cleaning" or "washing" money. Once moved, cash and other currency instruments must then be transferred either into a banking system or into legitimate businesses as part of their cash flows. The currency can also be put to work by buying goods or exchanged for higher, "clean" denomination currency. In 1991 several individuals from Lebanon and Argentina were convicted of laundering $1 billion in Colombian drug profits through the purchase and sale of gold using jewelry firms in Miami, New York City, Houston, and Los Angeles as fronts.

In money laundering schemes involving bulk cash the first step is to convert large quantities into cashier's checks. Such checks are attractive because they are difficult to trace: They do not bear the receiver's name or address. In drug trafficking transactions where there are large amounts of cash in small denominations, the idea is to convert the small bills into large ones—$1 million in $20 bills weighs 110 pounds; $1 million in $100 bills weighs only 22 pounds. To avoid IRS reporting requirements under the Bank Secrecy Act,* cash transfers must be under $10,000 or conducted through banking officials who agree to waive completion of a Currency Transaction Report (CTR), which is required for each deposit, withdrawal, or exchange of currency or monetary instruments (bank checks, etc.) in excess of $10,000. Likewise, a Currency and Monetary Instrument Report (CMIR) must be filed for cash or specified monetary instruments exceeding $10,000 in value that enter or leave the United States.

In 1985, the Bank of Boston, one of the oldest and most respected financial institutions in the city, unwittingly helped to launder money for the underboss (sottocapo)* of the Raymond L. S. Patriarca La Cosa Nostra* crime family of New England. From 1979 to 1983, Gennaro Angiulo* and his brothers converted paper bags stuffed with tens of thousands of dollars in small bills into $100 bills and more than $7 million in cashier's checks. None of the transactions was reported to the IRS, as legally required. Two real estate companies controlled by the Angiulos in Boston's Italian neighborhood, the North End, had been placed on the bank's "exempt" list of selected firms (much like food supermarkets that handle large quantities of cash in small denominations on a daily basis) such that cash transactions exceeding $10,000 did not have to be reported to the IRS.

Along the Texas-Mexico border, currency exchanges (casas de cambio) have sprung up to service drug traffickers, smugglers, and those dealing in consumer products. The exchange businesses are poorly regulated on both sides of the border and routinely accept large amounts of illegal cash without fear of government regulation or monitoring. Typically, a currency dealer will create large accounts that pool funds that are then deposited in a domestic or foreign bank. When a drug trafficker sends money to his own country, the casa operator wires the funds from its bank to the trafficker's foreign accounts. And even when an American bank completes a CTR, it names the casa as the owner of the funds, not the actual owner.

In other schemes, money launderers use lots of people ("smurfs") to convert cash into money orders and cashier's checks that do not specify payees.

Before the passage of the Money Laundering Control Act of 1986 (Title 18 U.S.C. sections 1956 and 1957), money laundering was not a federal crime in itself; the Department of Justice used a variety of other statutes—RICO,* Bank Secrecy Act, Illegal Money Transmitting Businesses, and so on—to prosecute money laundering cases. Money laundering was made a separate federal offense punishable by a fine of $500,000, or twice the value of the property involved, and a prison sentence of 20 years. Legislation enacted in 1988 strengthened the provisions of the Money Laundering Control Act of 1986 by allowing the government to file suit claiming ownership of all cash funneled through financial and banking operations intending to disguise its illegal source. Also, the courts have been empowered to issue orders freezing all contested funds unless and until a case is adjudicated (determined or decided by judicial procedure). Similarly, law enforcement responses to the cash nexus that is the lifeblood of organized crime include an amendment to the Drug Abuse Act of 1988 that requires that "offshore" banks (banks located outside the territorial boundaries of the United States) record any U.S. cash transactions in excess of $10,000 and permit U.S. officials access to such records. Offshore banks that fail to comply can be banned from holding accounts in U.S. banks and denied access to U.S. dollar–clearing and money transfer systems. To further stiffen the defenses against the cash circuits of criminal enterprises, in 1995 the president of the United States issued a directive under the International Emergency Economic Powers Act requiring financial institutions to search for and freeze accounts held in the name of persons or companies determined by the government to have assisted or to have played a significant role in international drug trafficking. The Presidential Directive also forbids American businesses and officials from trading with those identified as drug traffickers and their front firms. *See also* BANK SECRECY ACT

**SUGGESTED READING:** Barbara Webster and Michael S. McCampbell, *International Money Laundering: Research and Investigation Join Forces.* 1992.

**MONTANA, JOHN C.** (b. 1893, Montedoro, Sicily—d. 1964, Buffalo, NY). Mafia leader in the Magaddino crime family.

Until the Apalachin meeting* fiasco and the McClelland Committee* hearings in 1957, John Montana was a model citizen, respected in the city of Buffalo. He owned the largest taxicab fleet in western New York, which operated a virtual monopoly at the airport, train station, and better hotels. In 1956, he had been named "Man of the Year" by a local civic group of Buffalo.

But then his carefully contrived cover was blown when he was arrested at Apalachin, New York, in 1957 along with many other godfathers and underworld chiefs. For decades he had been a high-ranking member of the La Cosa Nostra* crime family* headed by Stefano Magaddino.* Born in Sicily, Montana came to the United States in 1907; in the 1920s he was a bootlegger* and later owned a liquor distribution business with his mafia cronies. His rise in the Cosa Nostra was evident in 1931 when he attended a national meeting of mafiosi in Chicago.

Appearing before the McClelland Committee on labor racketeering* was an embarrassment for Montana and a revelation to many who believed he was a hardworking, honest, community-minded citizen who immigrated to America and made good through honest, hard work.

The lame excuse he offered for his presence at the crime conclave in upper New York State in November 1957 was not credible. He claimed he was on his way to a business meeting in Philadelphia and experienced car trouble; so he decided to stop at the home of his friend, Joseph Barbara, and have his car repaired. To compound his humiliation, he was demoted to the rank of a simple "soldier"* in the Magaddino crime family. The public humiliation and loss of prestige in the Mafia* destroyed the once influential and effective labor racketeer and political fixer.

**SUGGESTED READING:** William Brashler, *The Don: The Life and Death of Sam Giancana.* 1977.

**MORAN, GEORGE "BUGS."** (b. 1883, MN—d. Feb. 1957, Leavenworth Penitentiary, KS). Chicago North Side gang boss.

Of all the hoodlums in Charles Dion O'Banion's* North Side gang, George "Bugs" Moran was the most violent and unstable. He was called "Bugs" to his face because of his ferocious temper and irrational outbursts. Moran took to a life of crime in his youth on Chicago's North Side, and by the time he was 21, he had participated in 26 known robberies and had served several jail sentences. Whenever there was a beer war slaying, the police routinely hauled "Bugs" in for questioning.

He rose to power in the O'Banion gang because of the conflict with Alphonse Capone.* In 1924, Capone murdered O'Banion, and in 1926, he killed Earl "Hymie" Weiss.* And then Schemer Drucci, another North Side gang boss in 1927, was killed by the police. All these events propelled Moran to the top position in 1927.

Killing Capone was a task that would preoccupy Moran for the next couple of years, culminating in the 1929 horrendous St. Valentine's Day Massacre.*

Like Hymie Weiss and Dion O'Banion, Moran was a regular churchgoer and had moral scruples about prostitution even though he was an accomplished cold-blooded murderer. Moran's hatred for Capone bordered on the pathological. When he made peace treaties with Capone, he would deliberately break them just to antagonize the "Big Fellow."

Moran narrowly escaped his appointment with death at the St. Valentine's Day Massacre and lived on and on, although his career was much diminished. When questioned by reporters about the mass murder, he uttered a comment that became famous: "Only Capone kills like that," he said. After the murders, he joined forces with Capone's enemies, but all their plots failed. After that, with his mob destroyed, he reverted to the petty burglaries of his youth, and in 1956, the FBI finally caught up with him for a bank robbery he had committed years before. Moran died in Leavenworth Penitentiary of lung cancer in 1957 and was buried in the prison's cemetery. He outlived his nemesis Al Capone by ten years.

**SUGGESTED READING:** Robert J. Schoenberg, *Mr. Capone.* 1992.


**MORETTI, WILLIE.** (b. 1894, Sicily—d. Oct. 4, 1951, Bergen, NJ). Mob enforcer and racketeer, 1940s–1950s.

Willie Moretti had a reputation as a tough gangster who also enjoyed nightclub life and entertainment. He operated in northern New Jersey and was involved in extortion, gambling, and drugs and functioned as the boss of a group of 60 enforcers that protected the vice and racketeering* interests of Abner Zwillman.* Moretti's interests were also linked with Charles "Lucky" Luciano,* Frank Costello,* and Joseph Adonis* of New York.

In the late 1940s, Moretti exhibited the early signs of mental illness probably caused by an untreated syphilitic infection. This worried gang bosses, who feared he might unintentionally or unknowingly reveal mob secrets. Then in 1950, Moretti was subpoenaed by the Kefauver Committee,* but his appearance turned into a circus of irrelevant, incoherent, humorous responses to Committee questions about criminal activities in New Jersey and New York. At one point he said in answer to a question about the Mafia* that he was not part of it because he did not have a membership card. He blathered on, endlessly. Though his appearance was harmless to his criminal partners, his mental capacities had so deteriorated by 1951 that he started to talk with journalists and police. A decision was made: A "mercy killing" would solve the problem. On October 4, 1951, Moretti met four men in a New Jersey restaurant near his Riveria nightclub/casino in Palisades, New Jersey; four shots were fired and Moretti lay dead. For the mob his killing was a sign of respect.

**SELECTED READING:** Robert Rudolph, *The Boys from New Jersey.* 1992.


**MOTORCYCLE GANGS.** *See* HELL'S ANGELS; OUTLAW MOTORCYCLE GANGS

**MURDER, INC.** Professional assassins organized by crime syndicates.

As the major gangs expanding around vice and racketeering* enterprises in the 1930s consolidated, some top crime syndicate* bosses believed that specialists in violence or "muscle" would always be needed to maintain order and discipline. In the businesslike atmosphere of organized crime in the 1930s where Prohibition (*see* PROHIBITION AND ORGANIZED CRIME*) and an economic depression affected millions of workers and their families, lawlessness and social unrest appeared to be enveloping the nation—even threatening the crime syndicates. Setting up teams of experts in murder would afford protection of criminal enterprises. "Rubouts" (contract murders) could be planned carefully using professional "hit men" (killers) paid directly by, or arranged by, crime groups from around the country. The idea of a unit or division of crime enterprises specializing in mayhem and murder epitomizes the concept of "cold-blooded."

Syndicate hit men could be brought in to do a murder or a beating from out of town, thus leaving law enforcement authorities with few suspects and even fewer motives. Witnesses, if there were any, could hardly be expected to make identifications.

When the grisly facts of Murder, Inc. were revealed in 1940, a new vocabulary describing criminal behavior stunned the public and law enforcement community. Professional killers fulfilled "contracts" (orders to commit murder or violence) to "hit*" (kill or maim) "bums" and "mutts," "canaries," "stoolies," and "rats" (victims who betrayed criminals to the police or failed to satisfy their commitments to pay loans or perform services for underworld partners). The language of business disguised the violence and in some ways put crime on a businesslike level of activity. Murder became an aspect of routine business. However, the terms used to define and describe the victims have psychological features that insult and demean them in much the same way that Nazis depicted their victims in the death camps as "subhumans" and "vermin" who deserved to die.

Aside from this dark, impersonal technique of murdering people, the enforcement arm of the multiethnic syndicates operated in an orderly fashion, meaning that it operated within a set of prescribed rules. Individuals were killed strictly for business reasons—there was nothing personal involved—or so it was claimed. Certain individuals were untouchable: political figures, journalists, prosecutors, and police so long as they were straight and had no corrupt relationships with the underworld. Also, ordinary citizens were immune, too. Rubbing out "civilians," as noncriminal citizens were called, could backfire (as it did in Capone's Chicago beer wars) and stir up the public, producing "heat" against the underworld. Also, a vital ingredient in all syndicate operations could be jeopardized—cooperation from bribed police—should bloodletting become too indiscriminate and harm the innocent public.

Like any legitimate enterprise, Murder, Inc. had a structure, bosses, and employees. The head and chief executive officer of the crime syndicate's enforcement group was the notorious Albert Anastasia,* known as the "Lord High Executioner." Anastasia took orders from Louis Buchalter,* a major labor racketeer involved in the garment industry and its unions, and Joseph Adonis,* a waterfront racketeer, gambler, and associate of top syndicate bosses. None of the several hundred murders committed by the members of Murder, Inc. occurred without the consent of other key crime bosses.

Notable members of Murder, Inc. below Anastasia who assigned "hits" and selected individuals to carry them out included Mendy Weiss, an associate of Buchalter in garment industry rackets; Louis Capone (no relation to Alphonse Capone* of Chicago); and "Kid Twist" Reles,* a skilled assassin with an ice pick. The execution gang used a convenience store and coffeeshop in a rundown neighborhood in Brownsville, Brooklyn, as a location to meet and obtain instructions on new jobs and contracts. Assorted criminals much as "Pittsburgh Phil" Strauss,* Vito "Chicken Head" Gurino, "Happy" Maione, Bugsy Goldstein, "Blue Jaw" Magoon, and Frank "The Dasher" Abbandando were the workhorses of the syndicate's killing machine.

The Brooklyn District Attorney's Office finally obtained evidence of the existence of Murder, Inc. and its shocking activities in 1940 when one of its members, "Kid Twist" Reles, decided to talk. Fearing for his life, Reles revealed details on some 200 murders in which he participated or shared knowledge of. The indictments against "Pittsburgh Phil" Strauss and Frank "The Dasher" Abbandando alone involved 108 murders.

One of the most infamous concerned the assassination of Dutch Schultz,* a major crime boss in the Bronx and Manhattan with powerful political connections in the New York Democratic Party. After Schultz became a prime target of the crusading rackets buster, special prosecutor Thomas E. Dewey,* Schultz wanted Dewey murdered. But this violated the operating rules of the crime organizations never to kill clean law enforcement officials. Schultz insisted even after his associates voted against the hit, and he swore that he would take care of Dewey himself. Schultz's fate was sealed. Several gunmen of the Murder, Inc. gang assaulted Schultz's headquarters in a Newark, New Jersey, restaurant and killed him and some of his henchmen.

The information provided by Reles on Murder, Inc. led to the convictions and death sentences of Pittsburgh Phil, Mendy Weiss, Bugsy Goldstein, Happy Maione, and Dasher Abbandando. Lepke Buchalter, a syndicate boss—the only one ever to face the electric chair—was executed in Sing Sing Prison in 1944.

The effectiveness of Reles's testimony threatened other mob bosses such as Albert Anastasia, Meyer Lansky,* Charles "Lucky" Luciano,* and "Bugsy" Siegel,* among others. In November 1941, Reles fell to his death while under protective custody in a Brooklyn hotel. No one believed that Kid Twist accidentally fell from a sixth-floor window. Whether his death was a suicide or murder, however, has never been established. It was rumored at the time that important political and law enforcement officials were threatened by Kid Twist's revelations and cooperated with mob bosses in arranging his death.

**SUGGESTED READING:** Burton Turkus and Sid Feder, *Murder, Inc.: The Story of the Syndicate.* 1951.

**MUSTACHE PETES.** Old-fashioned Sicilian Mafia* members operated in the United States during the Prohibition (*see* PROHIBITION AND ORGANIZED CRIME*) era. They earned their nickname by wearing huge mustaches in accordance with Sicilian/Italian cultural norms. They are sometimes referred to sarcastically today as zips* or "geeks."

It was some of the immigrant generation of Sicilian mafiosi who sought to retain the exclusivity of the Mafia, allowing only Sicilians to join the secret society. Younger, more Americanized Italian gangsters considered this ethnic segregation preposterous and resisted it. Charles "Lucky" Luciano,* for example, resented both "Joe the Boss" Masseria's* and Salvatore Maranzano's* demand that he sever his associations with his Jewish partners Meyer Lansky* and "Bugsy" Siegel.* In fact, Alphonse Capone's* organization in Chicago and the Detroit and Cleveland Mafias cooperated with other ethnics, especially the highly organized Jewish gangsters in the Purple Gang* of Detroit, Murder, Inc.* in New York City, and the Mayfield Road Gang in Cleveland.

In New York and other cities, the Mustache Petes had to be eliminated violently. Even men like Joseph Bonanno,* who was steeped in Old World tradition, realized that the ways of the old Sicilian dons would not work in America. After the Castellammarese War,* which saw the end of the old Mafia as a force in the United States, a more powerful new Mafia emerged with broader alliances poised to reach beyond the confines of the Little Italies.

**SUGGESTED READING:** Raimondo Catanzaro, *Men of Respect: A Social History of the Sicilian Mafia.* 1992.

# N

**NESS, ELIOT.** (b. Apr. 19, 1903, Chicago, IL—d. May 16, 1957, Cloudersport, PA). "The Untouchables" law enforcement unit chief.

Now part of American folklore about Prohibition (see PROHIBITION AND ORGANIZED CRIME*) and its gangsters such as the larger-than-life Alphonse Capone,* Eliot Ness achieved celebrity as a lawman when in 1928 as a University of Chicago graduate the 26-year-old was put in charge of a special federal unit whose job was to harass Capone. The exploits of the unit—dubbed "Untouchables" because they were allegedly incorruptible—has been captured in a very successful television series, books, and several films. Many of the exploits depicted in the media of Ness and his unit were, if not fictitious, then gross exaggerations of their role in destroying Capone.

His most impressive achievement in law enforcement occurred after the Capone era in Chicago. In 1935 Ness was appointed public safety director for Cleveland—a city ravaged by the mob, police, and political corruption. Violence was a common occurrence in the streets as gangs battled for territory. His first step was to reform the police department, which he did through transfers and dismissals of corrupt and derelict officers.

The notorious Mayfield Road Gang was crushed by 1941 when its leaders "Moe" Dalitz* and others decided that other cities and counties in northern Kentucky were less dangerous because their sheriffs were less zealous.

During World War II, Ness served as a federal director of the Office of Defense, which sought to control prostitution rackets around military bases and war factories. After the war, he went to work for the Diebold Safe Company in Canton, Ohio; it was there that he developed a serious alcohol problem. In the early 1950s he devoted his time to recollecting about his past with TV producers and editors. In 1957, he died of a heart attack after years of alcohol abuse.

**SUGGESTED READING:** Oscar Farley and Paul Robsky, *The Last of the Untouchables.* 1988.

**NICKNAMES.** *See* MOB NICKNAMES

**NITTI, FRANK "THE ENFORCER."** (b. Francisco Nitto, 1884, Naples, Italy—d. Mar. 19, 1943, Chicago, IL). Alphonse Capone* mob boss, 1940s.

Nitti was a cousin of Al Capone, as were numerous other associates of the "Big Fellow." Nitti began in a legitimate career as a barber but quickly got involved with Capone gangsters as a fence* during Prohibition (*see* PROHIBITION AND ORGANIZED CRIME*). He also peddled bootleg alcohol with frightful efficiency and in time rose in the ranks of the Capone organization.

After "Big Al" went off to prison on tax evasion charges, Nitti was identified as one of the top bosses in the Chicago Outfit.* When the mob began to expand its operations into legitimate businesses such as the movie industry, Nitti backed Willie Morris Bioff* and George Brown in shaking down the Hollywood studios. However, when Bioff began talking to save himself from a lengthy prison term on extortion and racketeering,* Nitti was implicated. Chicago mob bosses Paul "The Waiter" Ricca,* Anthony Joseph Accardo,* and Joseph John Aiuppa* ordered Nitti to plead guilty and take the heat off them. The idea did not appeal to Nitti, who had a tough time in prison in 1932 on an income tax charge. The mob bosses suspected that Nitti might talk rather than face prison. Awaiting trial anticipating a hostile response from his mob associates, he became despondent and shot himself in the Chicago stockyards.

**SUGGESTED READING:** John Kobler, *Capone: The Life and World of Al Capone.* 1971.

**NUMBERS.** The numbers gambling racket has been called the "poor man's insurance policy." The term "policy" is used synonymously with numbers. In numbers gambling a player selects one, two, or three digits from 0 to 9 in any combination thereof. If the player picks the correct digits and their sequence, the payoff is 600 to 1.

The structure of this illegal lottery was dramatically transformed by an African American gambler who managed to eliminate the manipulation and fraud in the game where numbers were picked from the results of parimutuel wagering at certain racetracks that could be fixed. Casper Holstein* used the Clearing House totals of the New York Stock Exchange, which could not be tampered with by gangsters, ensuring the honesty of the outcome. *See also* GAMBLING; HOLSTEIN, CASPER; ILLEGAL GAMBLING; ST. CLAIR, STEPHANIE

**SUGGESTED READING:** Rufus Schatzberg and Robert J. Kelly, *African-American Organized Crime: A Social History.* 1997.

**O'BANION, CHARLES DION.** ("Deanie") (b. 1892, Chicago, IL—d. Nov. 10, 1924, Chicago). Chicago gang boss and enemy of Alphonse Capone.*

At first, Chicago's two main bootleggers* were Dion O'Banion and Roger Touhy.* O'Banion grew up in a rough Irish immigrant neighborhood in Chicago's North Side. Although he spent four years as an altar boy, he ran with a juvenile gang, the Market Streeters. They were hired as sluggers in a newspaper circulation war by the Chicago *Herald-Examiner*. In his late teens he served two brief sentences for assault and burglary, his only time in jail.

At the outset of Prohibition (*see* PROHIBITION AND ORGANIZED CRIME*) (1920), O'Banion—known as "Deanie"—was well established as a powerful hoodlum in Chicago. His gang included a few Italians (such as "Schemer" Drucci), some Jews (the Gusenberg brothers), and Poles (Earl "Hymie" Weiss*) as well as Irishmen (George "Bugs" Moran*). They hijacked the bootleg shipments of lesser gangs, which brought them easy money and many enemies. As a hobby, O'Banion ran a floral shop and had a good eye for arranging flowers for elaborately ostentatious gangland funerals. His political connections were finely tuned, which enabled him to survive: In 1924 he was a guest at a testimonial dinner attended by top police department officials.

With Prohibition in full swing, conflict developed between O'Banion and the Al Capone-Johnny Torrio bootleg syndicate, which would not tolerate hijackings and thefts of their beer trucks and smuggled liquor. A truce and partnership were arranged that divided Chicago into territories, the violation of which meant swift and deadly reprisals from the other syndicate members. Torrio's plan did not work out, however. O'Banion tipped federal agents of Torrio's purchase of his illegal brewery: When Torrio discovered O'Banion's treachery, war erupted. Three men appeared in his florist shop to buy flowers for the funeral of a local political boss and mafioso Mike Merlo. Instead, they murdered "Deanie" right in his shop. He had one of the biggest funerals Chicago ever saw. The war between O'Banion's gang and Torrio-Capone did not end there: It was led by Hymie Weiss and Bugs Moran and eventuated in Hymie Weiss's death, Torrio's retirement, and the tragic St. Valentine's Day Massacre.*

**SUGGESTED READING:** Robert M. Lombardo, "The Organized Crime Neighborhoods of Chicago," in *Handbook of Organized Crime in the United States*, ed. Robert J. Kelly et al. 1994.

**OCHOA, JORGE LUIS VASQUEZ.** ("El Gordo" [The Fat Man]) (b. 1949, Medellín, Colombia—    ). Principal leader of the Medellín cocaine cartel.

Along with Pablo Emilio Gavoroa Escobar,* Jorge Luis Ochoa Vasquez, known as "The Fat Man," was one of the original members of the Medellín cartel. After being on the run for years, Ochoa surrendered to authorities in Colombia in January 1991, as did his brothers Fabio and Juan David. All pled guilty, confessed to a few narcotics-related crimes, agreed to pay nominal fines, and went to jail. Ochoa was released in July 1996 after serving five and a half years in custody. He is believed to be one of the world's wealthiest men, probably worth more than $10 billion.

For years prior to their arrests, the Ochoas presided over *la mafia criolla*, the Colombian version of La Cosa Nostra.* Medellín was the boiler room of the international cocaine trade, and Ochoa and his family were among a handful of families that dominated it.

Jorge Ochoa and his relatives and friends, including Pablo Escobar and José Gonzalo Rodriguez Gacha,* controlled a loose federation of underground corporations they called "la compania" (the company), known to the outside world as the Cartel. It is well structured and highly organized. With it were groups specializing in obtaining the raw materials needed for the production of cocaine and delivering them to clandestine laboratories throughout Colombia, Panama, Venezuela, Brazil, Argentina, and even the United States. There were groups responsible for security and, if necessary, for subverting law enforcement agents, the military, politicians, judges, and even presidents. There were yet other groups that handled transportation of the cocaine to markets around the world.

As the cartel grew in wealth and power, Ochoa wanted more including a stake in distribution in the United States. In the early phases of trafficking, the cartel wholesaled cocaine to retail distributors in the United States. In the late 1980s the Ochoas set up thousands of Colombians in "cells," which were small distribution groups in key markets in American and European cities including places like Madrid, Paris, London, Rome, Hamburg, and Rotterdam. The cells were organized by special envoys from Medellín and worked under a strict code of discipline. Under Ochoa's leadership, the Medellín cartel emerged as a sophisticated and ruthless multinational conglomerate dealing in dope. Ochoa brought Colombia to its knees through violence and corruption and had an impact on other countries far beyond Colombia's borders.

In 1984, Ochoa was arrested in Spain on a conspiracy to distribute cocaine.

The DEA pressed the Spanish government to extradite him to the United States. After a year of legal battles, Ochoa was sent back to Colombia on charges of illegal bull smuggling—the U.S. extradition petition having been denied. The appeal was lost by the American government, as was the chief witness against Ochoa, Barry Seal, a former air smuggler in the employ of the Medellín cartel who was assassinated in New Orleans.

Ochoa managed to stay free in Colombia on the bull smuggling charges through the shrewd manipulation of his lawyers. On November 21, 1987, he was arrested by a traffic cop not far from Cali. The Fat Man tried to bribe the police, offering at one point 100 million pesos ($400,000), but they would have none of it. The government decided to hold him on the bull smuggling charge and then consider extradition to the United States, but the cartel reacted to Ochoa's capture almost immediately. Within 24 hours, 12 gunmen attempted to assassinate Gomez Martinez, editor of Bogotá's biggest daily newspaper, in his home. The attempt failed, but the cartel made clear it did not want Ochoa extradited to the United States and threatened total war against the country's political leaders. On January 18, 1988, a candidate for mayor of Bogotá was abducted; a week later, Carlos Mauro Hayos, attorney general of Colombia, was attacked, abducted, and executed.

After hiding out while the war between Colombian authorities and the cartel continued, Ochoa surrendered and served a sentence in Colombia. He was not extradited.

**SUGGESTED READING:** Paul Eddy, Hugo Sabogal, and Sara Walden, *The Cocaine Wars*. 1988.


**OMERTA.** Mafia code of silence.

The rule of silence as a protection strategy of the mafia and the American La Cosa Nostra* is quite simple and brutal. It is a grave mistake to talk to law enforcement authorities about anything that would harm the organization. If a rival gang murdered a man's father before his eyes, he would be forbidden to inform the police. If an individual was mortally wounded, even then he would be forbidden to talk to the police. If one's wealth was stolen, or one's child molested, one could not confide in the authorities. The Mafia and the crime family were the only avengers.

The code of silence is a disciplinary mechanism that the Mafia employs to control its members. By threatening death for its violation, mafia leaders are able to maintain loyalty and avoid prosecution. That is the chief reason for the enforcement of the rule, but it also serves another preservative function. When Mafia members and their associates refuse to divulge what they know, it is a way of telling their victims and witnesses to their criminal acts that they, too, are bound by omerta. If victims or witnesses talk, the harsh penalties against betrayal will be invoked. In this way the rule that binds the Mafia together also seals the lips of witnesses and victims.

Anticrime strategies designed by law enforcement have attempted to under-mine omerta and turn organized criminals into informers, ready and willing to testify for the state against their fellow criminals. The Witness Security Pro-gram* and immunity provisions in the law have encouraged many mafiosi and others to cooperate with the government. *See also* VALACHI, JOSEPH; WIT-NESS SECURITY PROGRAM

**SUGGESTED READING:** Raimando Catanzano, *Man of Respect: A Social History of the Sicilian Mafia.* 1992.

**ONG, BENNY.** ("Eng," "Uncle Seven") (b. 1907, Hong Kong—d. Aug. 1994, New York City). Hip Sing Tong* boss. Chinatown "godfather."

Benny Ong personified the two sides of life in Chinatowns throughout Amer-ica. He lived in both the underworld and upperworld, that invisible line between the legitimate and the illegitimate, between what tourists see on the colorful streets and what goes on behind the Chinatown storefronts. Many of the Tong leaders who make up the legitimate power of community leaders, merchant associations, district family associations, and burial societies are also sponsors of illegal gambling* halls and prostitution services.

When Benny Ong died in 1994 there was a funeral procession in the streets of New York's Chinatown. Thousands of people lined the sidewalks as his 120-car funeral procession made its way through the humid, narrow streets. A large photo of his smiling face, decked in white carnations and red roses, was mounted in a flower limousine. The words "Big Bucks, Benny Ong" were displayed on flowerpots in keeping with the Chinese tradition of wishing the dead prosperity in the afterlife.

"Uncle Seven," as he was known to Chinatown, was well known for his temper and energy even in his old age. As "adviser for life" of the Hip Sing, a powerful Chinatown Tong (fraternal and business association), Ong was con-sidered one of Chinatown's most important elders. His influence was enormous: Uncle Seven could help an immigrant get a job, settle a dispute between businessmen, secure loans for merchants, and so on. In 1991, a U.S. Senate subcommittee identified Benny Ong as the "godfather" of organized crime in Chinatown. He allegedly took a percentage of gambling,* loansharking,* and extortion money in the Hip Sing territory, which covered scores of restaurants and retail businesses along the Bowery, Pell, and Hester streets. His real claim to power lay in his influence with the Flying Dragons, a vicious street gang affiliated with the Hip Sing for more than two decades. The Flying Dragons protected the Tong's gambling establishments and exacted extortion payments from businesses in the Tong's territory—only sparing those with close ties to Uncle Seven. Anyone daring to question Ong's power did so at great risk.

One individual was taught that lesson in the early 1980s. Herbert Liu, a former Hip Sing member, left the Tong to form his own association. It opened a gambling den and was to be a chapter of another Tong, the Chinese Freemasons. Liu also made the mistake of recruiting former members of the Flying Dragons to protect his gambling enterprise. Ong saw it as an open challenge to his authority. On December 23, 1982, several members of the Freemasons and the White Tiger gangs were in the Golden Star bar on East Broadway when several masked gunmen stepped in and opened fire. Three gang members were killed outright and eight others were wounded. Ong was never officially tied to the killings but was quoted in a newspaper article as saying that he spent 60 years building up respect, and no one should think that he could topple him from power overnight. *See also* ASIAN ORGANIZED CRIME; CHINESE TRIADS; TONGS

**SUGGESTED READING:** Martin Booth, *The Triads*. 1990.

**OPERATION MONGOOSE.** CIA-Mafia conspiracy to kill Fidel Castro.

"Operation Mongoose" was the code name for the CIA-Mafia* assassination plot against Fidel Castro of Cuba. The CIA advocated the murder of Castro in 1959, and it was Meyer Lansky* who saw that for the mob to resume its gambling enterprises in Cuba Castro would have to be killed. Meanwhile, "Moe" Dalitz,* a former Cleveland syndicate* boss (don)* and partner of Lansky in Las Vegas, Nevada,* casino skimming operations, brought this proposal to Howard Hughes, who encouraged Robert Maheu, his associate and former CIA operative, to proceed with a murder scheme. John Roselli* and Sam Giancana* were recruited into the conspiracy, and they persuaded Santos Trafficante, Jr.* to get involved.

Various zany murder schemes were proposed by the CIA (which has never officially admitted complicity in the plot) including a poison pill in Castro's soup, an ambush through a machine gun attack, infecting his clothes with dangerous fungi, injecting psychedelic substances into his cigars, and so on. Nothing happened. Apparently, Trafficante misled the CIA into believing that his people in Cuba were busy preparing Castro's demise when he did nothing substantial to enable Mongoose to succeed.

Giancana, according to Roselli's testimony before the secret Senate Committees, was angry at Trafficante because he believed that if the mob destroyed and deposed Castro, its power and leverage in the United States would be unprecedented and unstoppable. The government could not afford the scandal of being compromised by the threat of public disclosure of its collaboration with criminals in an illegal international political act.

The plot to kill Castro involving an unholy alliance between the CIA and the Mafia was kept secret until both Sam Giancana and John Roselli were murdered within a year of each other in 1975 and 1976, respectively. Each man met his death just before they were scheduled to testify before Senate committees about their role in CIA activities abroad.

**SUGGESTED READING:** Charles Rappleye and Ed Becker, *All-American Mafioso: The Johnny Roselli Story.* 1991.

**ORGANIZED CRIME AND THE MEDIA.** In the 1930s and 1940s, the Italian gangster had to share the Hollywood screen with his Irish and Jewish counterparts. In the succeeding decades as television and video technologies became more sophisticated and available to millions of viewers, series like *The Untouchables*, and movies like *The Godfather* trilogy, the Italian gangster became the stereotypical image.

Organized crime has been associated with the big city and the swarthy foreigner. With the help of the media, a few thousand hoodlums in the organized rackets who are of Italian origin, representing a tiny fraction of the Italian American population, became, in the eyes of many, representative of an ethnic group. There have been Irish, Jewish, African American, Latino, Italian, and even Anglo-Protestant mobsters in American history. But none of these gangsters is considered representative of the larger ethnic formation from which they happen to originate. Needless to say, few of the movies dealing with such characters have ever provided an authentic rendition of the rich cultural heritages and working-class histories of these groups.

Partly in response to protests launched against the gangland shows, Italian surnames began appearing in movies and television dramas attached to characters other than mobsters and thugs; they were mostly police, criminal lawyers, and private investigators such as "Colombo," "Baretta," and "Petrocelli." The Italian crime buster, however, is still closely associated with crime and violence; and like all media lawmen, his or her operational methods are sometimes difficult to distinguish from those of the criminals against whom he is pitted.

Of the various Italian stereotypes in the media, the Mafia* image is the most enduring. By 1985, *Prizzi's Honor*, a major film, offered a new twist in gangster depravity, a romance between a mafioso and a lovely lady who herself turns out to be an efficient gangland "hit"* woman—a killer for hire. Almost 40 years after television first featured the Italian mobster in *The Untouchables*, Mafia characters continue in abundance in films and TV series. As if to demonstrate that nothing changes, in 1990 alone, Hollywood offered the public *The Freshman*—a spoof on *The Godfather* films; *My Blue Heaven*, about the foibles of a Mafia gangster in the Witness Security Program*; *King of New York*, a tale of drug dealing and violence in the big city; *Miller's Crossing*, which chronicled the history of ethnic mob wars in the 1930s; *Godfather III*—the continuing history of the Corleone crime family in the international setting of high finance, political intrigue, and hypocrisy; and *Goodfellas*, a portrait of petty thieves and their excessive violence in an Italian American community. In all these films, Italian mobsters either are the central characters or play important supporting roles. *King of New York* manages, amid the constant violence and murder, to offend women, African Americans, Chinese, Latinos, and Irish—as well as Italians. *Godfather III* is a dreary imitation of the two previous *Godfather* films in which the Mafia don is elevated to a kind of admirable patriarchal deity after having arranged the murder of his brother, numerous other mafiosi, corrupt politicians, businessmen, and clergy.

The image of the Italian as a gangster even permeates movies about other groups. *Once Upon a Time in America* (1984), a film about Jewish mobsters, and *Year of the Dragon* (1985), about Chinese racketeers and drug traffickers, were amply offensive to these respective groups. Each film also included Italian racketeers as a sort of basic ethnic criminal element that competes with the Jewish and Chinese mobsters. Only the remake of *Scarface* (1983), which presents the rise and fall of a Cuban exile from a dishwasher with a petty criminal record to a top cocaine trafficker in Miami, excluded Italians even though the original film made in 1932 was a thinly disguised portrayal of Alphonse Capone's* criminal career in Chicago.

The hero in *Year of the Dragon* is an obsessive Polish American police captain and Vietnam veteran who describes himself as a "polack." In the film, he refers to the Chinese legacy of a "thousand year history" of crime—which the Chinese have now brought to America. The film deals in other stereotypes as well. The Chinese mobsters are especially brutal with their own people and have nothing but contempt for "white devils."

It is well to be reminded in the face of this media onslaught of negative images that not all Italians are gangsters, and not all gangsters are Italian or emulate Mafia styles.

A good example of media power is the career of John Gotti,* now imprisoned for life, who rose to the top of La Cosa Nostra in 1985 after the assassination of Gambino crime family* boss Paul Castellano.* As recently as 1984, the would-be mob boss retained many of the characteristics of a street thug. That year, he got himself involved in a felony assault over a double-parked car. After Castellano's murder, Gotti became boss and dramatically refined his act.

Hollywood makes myths. For a decade, *The Godfather* epics—and the Mafia—had eclipsed westerns in popular culture, fulfilling America's mythic needs. The fictional *Godfather* was mythmaking at its most compelling. It took an intricately structured "other" world that was in fact without the slightest hint of social redemption and reinvented it, but with people audiences could root for and against. Its protagonists were flawed, not superhuman projections of good and evil, caught in destinies not of their own making. That loyalty and honor mattered for little in the actual Cosa Nostra and were simply an irritating fact to be ignored in the interests of dramatic effects; perceived reality was what mattered. *The Godfather* saga contained everything that concerned and excited mass audiences of ordinary people: family, romance, power, lust, betrayal, greed, even salvation. And it all played out on an epic stage with death, inevitable and often violent, waiting in the wings.

The problem was that there were no nonfiction equivalents. All the media had left to contend with was the gray corporate image of Paul Castellano, erstwhile business executive; the visage of a dour "Tony Ducks" Corallo*; a cigar-chomping Runyonesque Anthony Salerno*; a loony Vincent "The Chin" Gigante*; and finally, the oily, unappetizing Carmine "The Snake" Persico.*

**SUGGESTED READINGS:** Randall Miller, *Ethnic Images in American Film and Television*. 1978; Michael Parenti, "The Media and the Mafia," *Monthly Review*. March 1979: 20–26.

**ORGEN, "LITTLE AUGIE."** (b. Jacob Orgen, 1894, NY—d. Oct. 15, 1927, NY). Labor racketeer.

"Little Augie" Orgen was a garment industry racketeer just prior to the formation of the New York syndicate.* He had been a member of "Dopey" Benny Fein's gang, the foremost labor gangster in the pre–World War I period. With Fein put out of action by law enforcement, Orgen created his own organization and murdered his rival, Kid Dropper.* The Little Augies, as they were known, included Louis Buchalter,* Jacob "Gurrah" Shapiro,* and Jack Diamond.*

In time, Little Augie's tactics would no longer work. Beating union workers into compliance with garment industry manufacturers and managers led to arrests and jail terms. Lepke, Shapiro, and others preferred infiltrating unions rather than intimidating them and beating them into submission. But Orgen insisted on sticking to the old ways; he also broke away from labor racketeering* to get into narcotics on his own. However, he was tempted back into the labor extortion racket when the painters' association offered him $50,000 cash to keep the painters' union from striking for better wages. Without clearing the deal with Lepke, who wished to stay clear of the painters' dispute, Little Augie refused to return the cash and intervened in the labor management dispute using Jack "Legs" Diamond as a bodyguard and enforcer who carried out orders, making sure that the painters' union did not strike. Lepke and Shapiro decided to act, and on October 15, 1927, they murdered Orgen on a Manhattan street. Diamond's life was spared. Thereafter, Lepke and Shapiro went on to dominate the garment industry rackets.

Little Augie came from a family of deeply religious Jews who listed his age on his coffin as 25 years old when in fact he was 33 at the time of his death. The family had considered him dead since 1919, when he had embraced a life of crime.

**SUGGESTED READING:** Robert A. Rockaway, *But—He Was Good to His Mother: The Lives and Crimes of Jewish Gangsters*. 1993.

**OUTLAW MOTORCYCLE GANGS.** Outlaw motorcycle gangs appeared after World War II as millions of young men left the military and returned to the uncertainties of civilian life. Many were rebellious and deeply alienated from a society they defended but that in the postwar period seemed indifferent and hostile to their readjustment.

The gangs or clubs formed in California and spread out across the country. Today, some gangs such as the Hell's Angels* and the Outlaws are international with chapters in Europe, Australia, and Latin America. For a time the motorcycle clubs symbolized romantic rebellion against the stifling conformity of the 1950s: Popular films such as *Angels on Wheels*, *The Wild One* with Marlon Brando, and in the 1960s, *Easy Rider* with Peter Fonda personified a sense of freedom and individualism that the subculture of the motorcycle group with its distinctive mode of dress and lifestyle came to represent. However, over the last 25 years this perception has changed with motorcyclists affiliated with these "clubs" that are really gangs perceived as common criminals rather than nomadic rebels on the road.

Today, it is estimated that there are between 800 and 900 motorcycle gangs in the United States, ranging from small, loosely organized groups of a few adventurous riders to sophisticated multiple chapter gangs with branches in many states and cities and even in other countries. The largest gangs have engaged in murder, extortion, arson, drug manufacturing, car theft, and drug trafficking. Drugs are their principal source of income, and in this activity, the gangs have been known to cooperate with other organized crime groups.

Motorcycle gangs have structures of organization that are bureaucratic, with particular roles defined for each position. For example, the Hell's Angels, and groups that imitate them, have written constitutions and bylaws, presidents, regional vice presidents, sergeants at arms, road captains, and enforcers for "runs" (club trips on public roads).

The symbol of membership is gang "colors." These are typically denim or leather jackets with embroidered identification patches sewn on the back. The patch displays a gang logo and sometimes slogans or initials that stand for the gang's chapter or home city. The most famous "colors" are those of the Hell's Angels—a winged death's head wearing a leather pilot's helmet. Initiation ceremonies are not as rigorous as mafia induction techniques but do require that prospective members serve an apprenticeship and commit murder, if asked, to be voted in.

Law enforcement authorities have identified the types of criminal enterprises outlaw motorcycle gangs engage in on a regular basis. These include motorcycle and auto theft on a large scale where, in western states such as California and Arizona, Texas, and New Mexico, repair shops operated by the gang serve as cover operations for shipping and selling stolen vehicles and parts. The gangs also participate in prostitution using female associate members performing in gang-owned massage parlors, bars, and nightclubs. They also have been charged with transporting and selling stolen firearms. Crimes such as contract murder and extortion have been carried out for La Cosa Nostra* crime families.

The biggest illegal moneymaker for the gangs is drugs. They manufacture LSD, PCP ("Angel Dust"), and "crank" (methamphetamines). Along with heroin, cocaine, and marijuana, the gangs market their own products, from manufacture to street distribution. Some gang members are millionaires because of their drug enterprises, but there is also a great deal of violence associated with the trade and a great deal of corruption that the motorcycle gangs share with more traditional organized crime groups. According to the President's Commission on Organized Crime (1905), outlaw motorcycle gangs represent a very serious threat to the country, and there are no signs that their numbers will diminish in the future.

**SUGGESTED READINGS:** Yves Lavigne, *Hell's Angels: Taking Care of Business*. 1987; Hunter S. Thompson, *Hell's Angels: A Strange and Terrible Saga*. 1966.

**PATRIARCA, RAYMOND L. S.** (b. Mar. 17, 1908, Worcester, MA—d. July 11, 1984, Providence, RI). Organized crime figure, head of the New England Cosa Nostra family for more than 25 years.

Raymond Patriarca was the son of Italian immigrants. He lived all his adult life in Providence, Rhode Island, but exercised influence over the organized criminal activities throughout the New England region and played a role in Mafia activities across the United States.

He left school at the age of eight to work as a shoeshine boy and bellhop but eventually gravitated toward criminal activities, finding armed robbery and illegal alcohol smuggling in the Prohibition (*see* PROHIBITION AND ORGANIZED CRIME\*) period far more lucrative than menial labor. In the 1930s, the Providence Board of Public Safety referred to Patriarca as "Public Enemy Number 1" and ordered the police to arrest him on sight. By 1938, he had apparently cultivated important political connections: Having been convicted of armed robbery, Patriarca served less than six months of a long prison term and so outraged government officials that a Massachusetts state legislator demanded an investigation into the pardon granted by Governor Charles F. Hurley.

Just before America's entry into World War II, Patriarca consolidated his power and brought together numerous gangs engaged in gambling operations. In the hearings of the Senate Subcommittee on Labor Racketeering in 1963, Joseph Valachi,\* a Mafia\* turncoat who introduced the term "La Cosa Nostra"\* to the American public, more or less confirmed Patriarca's rise to power in the American underworld in his testimony about the structure of the national syndicate.\*

In 1972 more notoriety surrounded New England's "godfather." Serving a prison term for a murder conviction in Atlanta, he was subpoenaed to testify before the House Select Committee on Crime concerning alleged investments made by Frank Sinatra in a racetrack in Hanover, Massachusetts, which was under suspicion of infiltration by criminals. Patriarca denied any knowledge of the track or its owners. He further claimed that he never met Mr. Sinatra even though the singer had invested more than $50,000 in the venture. Years earlier, Robert F. Kennedy,* a young counsel for a Senate committee looking into mob infiltration and corruption within the Teamsters Union,* questioned him very aggressively about a jukebox business believed to be connected with the Teamsters and their underworld cronies. Patriarca falsely but coolly claimed that the capital required to launch his business came from his mother's inheritance.

In the course of a criminal career that stretched across a half century, he was arrested more than 30 times, for which he served several prison sentences on charges ranging from bootlegging in the 1920s to conspiracy to murder in the late 1960s. Even while in prison, however, the New England crime boss maintained a firm grip on the organization. He continued to direct the affairs of his criminal enterprises so well that his time away from "the office" seems scarcely to have been noticed. His businesses were a web of legal and illegal activities that he shrewdly mixed together in order to confuse and deter law enforcement investigations. In the last part of his life when his power and notoriety were at their height, Patriarca insisted that he was a legitimate businessman in Providence. In 1981, three years before his death, he was indicted by a grand jury in Miami, Florida, on charges of labor racketeering*; he bitterly observed that government harassment would follow him to the grave. Federal and local law enforcement suspected Patriarca of loansharking,* operating illegal numbers* lotteries, trafficking in marijuana and cocaine, and smuggling immigrants into the United States.

When questioned about the veracity of *The Godfather*, the 1969 novel that is the best-selling book on crime ever published, Patriarca told the congressional committee members that he thought it was a good book—but nothing more than fiction. Turning the tables on the committee, he brazenly averred that the public's scandalous interest in the underworld should be laid at the doorstep of the government, which publicized and glamorized organized crime.

He never admitted to being a member of the Mafia, although FBI wiretaps would reveal frequent references to his important role in the high councils of the American Mafia.* Time after time, Patriarca—referred to in government-monitored telephone conversations as "Raymond"—would play important roles in solving major disputes among Cosa Nostra members and families. In 1963, Patriarca was instrumental in bringing the Joseph Gallo*–Joseph Profaci* crime family war to a satisfactory conclusion and intervened again in 1964 as a Cosa Nostra Commission* agent in the settlement of the Bonanno crime family* dissolution after its founding boss, Joseph Bonanno,* had threatened the lives of two other Mafia leaders.

Patriarca's influence extended beyond the Italian American underworld. In 1961, a war erupted in Boston between two Irish American groups—the McCleans and the McLaughlins. Patriarca intervened and brokered a peace

treaty, and when the truce broke down, he "declared war" on the McLaughlins—
a move that brought the conflict to a swift end.

Patriarca as a boss was the central figure in the New England Cosa Nostra.
Typically, he operated his vending machine business, the National Cigarette
Service, from a fixed location in the "Little Italy" of Providence, Rhode Island,
until he died of natural causes in 1984 at age 76. The entire area around Patriarca's headquarters was an armed camp, where it was impossible to move
through the neighborhood without being spotted. Such was his reputation that
no upstart gangster would venture to challenge him on his home turf.

**SUGGESTED READINGS:** Gerard O'Neill and Dick Lehr, *The Underboss: The Rise and
Fall of a Mafia Family.* 1989; Vincent Teresa, with Thomas C. Renner, *My Life in the
Mafia.* 1973.


**PATRICK, LEONARD.** (b. Oct. 13, 1913, England—d. ?). Chicago mob fig-
ure/informant.

Leonard Patrick was an extortionist and a bookmaker affiliated with the Chicago Outfit.* He grew up on the West Side of Chicago, the Jewish community
(his parents were English Jews who adopted an Irish surname), and became a
partner/associate of Gus Alex,* a loanshark* and extortionist who operated on
Chicago's North Side and suburbs. Patrick served time in the 1930s on an
Indiana bank robbery and later admitted participation in at least six murders.
His West Side restaurant was a center of bookmaking throughout the 1950s and
1960s; he also controlled some legitimate businesses, mainly laundry companies
that provided a useful front for his gambling,* loansharking, and extortion activities.

In 1952, Patrick pled guilty to racketeering* charges and became a government witness. His testimony resulted in the convictions of Gus Alex and several
others in the Outfit extortion rackets. It is believed that Patrick talked to federal
authorities because he feared a long prison term, which at his age meant dying
behind bars.

**SUGGESTED READING:** Howard Abadinsky, *Organized Crime,* 5th ed. 1997.


**PERSICO, CARMINE.** ("The Snake") (b. 1937, Brooklyn, NY—incarcerated).
Colombo crime family boss (don).*

In the early 1960s, Larry and Joseph Gallo* continued to complain that their
power and wealth in the Profaci crime family* had not improved since Joseph
Colombo, Jr.* became boss. For all the services the Gallos rendered, including
murders, extortions, and general violence, they demanded reparations that Colombo rejected. Gallo's threats found sympathetic ears among some crime family members. One was Carmine "The Snake" Persico, a major capo* who agreed
with the Gallos that things had to improve. However, Profaci cleverly lured
Persico away from the Gallo faction with promises of more power. Persico's

failed attempt to kill Larry Gallo created more internal violence in the family. When Colombo came to power, his preoccupation with confronting the FBI led to his shooting in 1972. Within three years Persico emerged as the boss. Most of his reign as head of the family, however, was spent behind bars on convictions for hijacking and racketeering.* In 1987, Persico was convicted in the "Commission"* case and sentenced to a 100-year prison term. His power is not completely diminished even behind bars. His son Alphonse functions as a messenger and carries messages and instructions to the soldiers.*

**SUGGESTED READINGS:** Peter Diapoulos, *The Sixth Family.* 1981; Donald Goddard, *Joey: The Life of "Crazy Joe" Gallo.* 1974.

**PETROSINO, JOSEPH.** (b. 1860, Padua, Italy—d. Mar. 12, 1909, Palermo, Sicily). New York City Police lieutenant, head of the "Italian Squad."

"Pay or die." That expression whispered in the teeming Italian ghettos of New York City, Chicago, Philadelphia, New Orleans, and San Francisco terrorized immigrants who thought they had left behind the dreaded The Black Hand (La Mano Nera)* of mafia cutthroats and predators. At the turn of the century with immigrants from Sicily and the Italian southern regions flowing into America, extortion, murder, and robbery rose dramatically in their communities. Police were befuddled by the newcomers who spoke little or no English and seemed to fear the Irish policemen as much as the Black Hand thugs.

In 1883, when Joseph Petrosino joined the New York City Police Department, it desperately needed Italian-speaking officers to make contact with the 500,000 new immigrants in the city. His assignment was to uncover the Black Hand and destroy it so that the Italian communities could feel confident in the police and help them to curb crime. Petrosino was appointed head of the "Italian Squad" in 1905. It was a 27-man unit trained to investigate Black Hand crimes. In the four years that Petrosino led the squad, Black Hand crimes, including bombings, kidnappings, murders, rapes, and arsons, dropped by 50 percent. In one of his most famous cases, Petrosino arrested the Black Handers who threatened the life of opera star Enrico Caruso, who was performing at the Metropolitan Opera House in New York City.

In 1909, Petrosino went to Palermo, Sicily, to gather information about criminals believed to have emigrated to the United States. While waiting for a tram in the Garibaldi Gardens, he was shot dead. A rumor circulated that Vito Cascio Ferro,* the most important capo mafioso in Sicily at that time, presumably executed Petrosino. Cascio Ferro's alibi was airtight, however.

The streets of New York City were jammed with mourners. Unfortunately, Petrosino's death protected many mafiosi from deportation—a fate that would haunt American law enforcement in years to come.

**SUGGESTED READING:** Arrigo Petacco, *Joe Petrosino.* 1974.

**PISTONE, JOSEPH D.** ("Donnie Brasco") (b. 1938, Philadelphia, PA—    ). FBI undercover agent, Mafia* infiltrator.

For six years FBI agent Joseph D. Pistone assumed the identity of a jewel thief and "wise guy" (an associate of underworld criminals). He managed to reach and secure the trust of major La Cosa Nostra* soldiers* and bosses (dons)* in several crime families.* Exposure would have meant instant death.

He entered his undercover role in 1976 after some experience with organized crime investigations in Philadelphia and Jacksonville, Florida. With his knowledge of intelligence and the street life of gangsters, he became a jewel thief and managed to meet "Lefty Guns" Ruggiero, a Bonanno "made guy" who introduced him to the bosses in the Bonanno crime family.*

Being a "wise guy," which means living by one's wits most of the time, is not a routine, 9-to-5 job at the office. Pistone/Brasco was on call from his Mafia associates around the clock, on weekends and holidays. Indeed, he missed his daughters' growing up, almost destroyed his marriage, and alienated many of his colleagues in the FBI who witnessed Brasco's "going native" where his intense involvement with mafiosi began to rub off and affect his personality.

Pistone ended his undercover role as Donnie Brasco in July 1981 when he was on the verge of being inducted into La Cosa Nostra as a full-fledged member. His testimony in the Pizza Connection* and the "Mafia Commission"* cases resulted in more than 100 convictions of organized criminals around the country.

His knowledge and testimony were so effective that a $500,000 murder contract was put on his life. FBI agents in New York had to forcibly persuade Paul Castellano,* head of the Gambino crime family,* to have it removed. Ironically, Pistone and his family had to go into the Witness Security Program,* which was originally designed for criminal defectors in order to ensure their safety. A major film, *Donnie Brasco*, was produced in 1995 about Agent Pistone's incredible career.

**SUGGESTED READING:** Joseph D. Pistone, with Richard Woodley, *Donnie Brasco: My Undercover Life in the Mafia.* 1987.

**PIZZA CONNECTION.** International Mafia drug trafficking.

In 1987 a sensational trial was concluded in New York City. It involved the drug trafficking activities of a Mafia group numbering 22 defendants headed by Gaetano Badalamenti, an ousted capo* mafioso from Cinisi, Sicily, that supplied $1.6 billion of heroin to a group headed by Salvatore Catalano, a capo in the Bonanno crime family.* Catalano arrived in the United States in 1961 and headed a crew of "zips"* in the Knickerbocker Avenue section of Brooklyn; they conducted legal and illegal activities on the margins of the American Mafia (La Cosa Nostra).*

The operation was truly international in scope: Morphine base was purchased in Turkey and processed in Sicilian laboratories controlled by Mafia families. Badalamenti in South America and Catalano in New York would arrange for pickups and shipments to pizza parlors in the United States owned by the mafiosi. The pizza parlors would serve as distribution centers for the drugs and collection areas for payments. The Pizza Connection trial was the biggest drug case ever to come before an American judge and jury.

One of the important Zip drug organizations was led by several Gambino cousins who were headquartered in Cherry Hill, New Jersey. Although related to Carlo Gambino* of New York, the "Cherry Hill Gambinos" operated independently of the New York crime family. Eventually, as the government investigation proceeded, most of them were arrested and charged with heroin and cocaine trafficking and sentenced to long jail terms.

**SUGGESTED READING:** Shana Alexander, *The Pizza Connection: Lawyers, Money, Drugs, and Mafia.* 1988.

**POLITICAL CORRUPTION.** The corrupt manipulation of political parties, officials, and bureaucracies is best illustrated by the activities of Alphonse Capone's* criminal syndicate* in the Chicago area during the after Prohibition (*see* PROHIBITION AND ORGANIZED CRIME*). Capone subverted the functions of government in order to facilitate the operation of his criminal enterprises, which he did with skill, deftness, and brutal cruelty.

American cities have a long history of corrupt relations between illegal enterprises* and local police and politicians. For organized criminals, payments to politicians and police may be seen as normal business expenses in return for services to the enterprise or as extortionate demands that absorb some of the profits of the enterprise. For police and politicians, levying regular assessments on illegal activities has provided a source of extra income as well as a way to oversee neighborhood enterprises that could not be legally controlled. Oversight by local political organizations (or the police) has been the most important source of coordination for illegal enterprises in American cities.

At the turn of the century, a number of factors combined to facilitate corruption. First, urban political organizations (called "political machines" by their opponents) would accept payments to do favors for various interests or individuals including suppressing an arrest, obtaining a job for a voter, and so on. Second, certain structural characteristics of city government enhanced the role of local politicians. Throughout the nineteenth and well into the twentieth centuries, the main political unit in American urban life was the local ward or district. Wards were not simply electoral units but also administrative units. It was common for ward boundaries and police precincts to overlap and also for each ward to have its own police court. Because ward politicians (who were, incidentally, often local saloon keepers and gamblers) selected the local police captain and because police magistrates (judges) were cogs in the ward's political machine, the criminal justice system was a major resource available to politicians for doing favors that might strengthen the political organization.

With the passage of time, control by local politicians, particularly in large cities, weakened; corruption became more centralized in large political units and regulatory agencies. On the one hand, bribes and payoffs to local police and government agents continued, but larger flows of cash and electoral support gained momentum as the principal organizing factor in the political-criminal nexus.

This gave rise to "clean graft" where an entire police unit, a precinct, will create a "pad," a fixed general payoff on a monthly basis from racketeers to all members of a precinct—from the patrolman up through sergeants, lieutenants, detectives, captains, inspectors, and chiefs and even, in larger urban areas, division and borough commands. Moreover, bribes can be disseminated to other government officials that regulate trade, commercial licensing, building and fire codes, labor union activities, and commercial practices.

At still another level, large criminal syndicates may contribute significant amounts of money or other resources to political figures in higher offices: to gubernatorial campaigns, to federal political offices in the Congress, or to appointees of top agency positions that can have an impact on law enforcement. Carlos Marcello,* head of the Cosa Nostra in New Orleans, supported candidates quietly with large contributions for statewide office in Louisiana; the 1960 presidential campaign of John F. Kennedy was scandalized by rumors of mob support from the Chicago Outfit*; Capone in Chicago and Gaetano Luchese* and Frank Costello* in New York City poured millions into mayoral races during their careers.

For many organized criminals, the distinction between legal and illegal business activities is blurred. Their own careers move from one to the other, and their ventures often bridge the two worlds. They know that many retailers will buy stolen goods, that some bankers will make loans with stolen securities as collateral, that businesses ranging from the garment industry to antique dealers borrow from loansharks, and that many business people will eagerly launder the funds from illegal enterprises.

Gangsters operate within a world of illicit moneymaking, deals, and favors; all "wise guys" have rackets, and they see little difference between their rackets and the rackets of the "straight" society that looks down on them.

Finally, without political corruption, organized crime could not operate over time. It is a vital component of criminal activities.

**SUGGESTED READING:** William Chambliss, *On the Take: From Petty Crooks to Presidents.* 1978.


**PROFACI, JOSEPH.** ("The Old Man") (b. Oct. 2, 1897, Sicily—d. June 7, 1962, NY). Cosa Nostra crime family boss.

Like other "founding fathers" of La Cosa Nostra* (Charles "Lucky" Luciano,* Gaetano Luchese,* Joseph Bonanno,* Vincent Mangano,* Frank Costello,* Vito Genovese,* Gaetano Gagliano), Profaci was born in Italy and came to the United States in 1922 as a young man. He never served time in prison on a felony conviction which is rather remarkable for a man who had a crime family* named

Joseph Profaci. Reproduced from the Collections
of the Library of Congress.

after him. Profaci was appointed as a crime family boss by Joseph Maranzano*
at the end of the Castellammarese War* in 1931. Commonly referred to as the
"Old Man," Profaci served as boss for over 30 years until his death in 1962 of
natural causes. According to Joseph Bonanno, another Mafia boss, in the aftermath of the "Joe the Boss" Masseria/Salvatore Maranzano Castellamarese War,
Profaci sided with Maranzano (the eventual victor), but his family did not participate in the conflict. Indeed, "Maranzano urged Profaci to remain neutral and
to act as an intermediary with other groups" (Bonanno 1983, 85).

Profaci's daughter would later marry Bonanno's oldest son, which strengthened the ties between the two, as had intermarriage woven strong bonds between
Luchese and Carlo Gambino.*

Profaci was known among the younger and more modern members of the
Cosa Nostra as a "Mustache Pete"* because of his reticence and insularity in
interpersonal matters—preferring the company of his family relatives and old
country comrades to that of his criminal associates. He was a devoted family
man, devoid of any extramarital interests—unlike many of his criminal colleagues. Another positive trait was his churchgoing, but this, too, proved to be
a foreboding commitment and somewhat dismaying when expensive jewels dec-
orating a religious statue were stolen from a church in Bensonhurst that Profaci
helped to build. His reaction to the theft was swift and deadly. The jewels were

recovered, and the thief was found dead with a string of rosary beads wrapped around his neck as a warning to others.

Profaci owned many legitimate businesses and was the largest single importer of olive oil into the United States. He ruled his crime family with an iron hand, and eventually his coolness toward his criminal soldiers* and his practice of nepotism, where relatives and personal friends enjoyed the fruits of crime, produced an open rebellion in the family. Profaci was the only don of a Cosa Nostra family in America to levy a $25 tax monthly on each member. Allegedly, the tax was meant to build a legal defense fund for soldiers.* The miserly Profaci pocketed the paltry "soldier's tax" and alienated his soldiers even more with his pettiness. When the Joseph Gallo* faction within the family successfully carried out dangerous executions for their boss, Profaci failed to reward them appropriately. Instead, he ruthlessly murdered a member of the hit* team as a warning.

In 1961, the Gallos decided to act. Larry Gallo and his brothers Joe ("Crazy Joe")* and Albert ("Kid Blast"), along with a caporegime in the family, Nicholas (Jiggs) Forlano, went to war with Profaci. Five members of Joseph Profaci's real family were kidnapped.

After some negotiation, Profaci agreed to be more generous with the Gallo faction in distributing the spoils of crime. But he double-crossed the Gallos; and the attempted murder of Larry Gallo was by sheer luck interrupted by police intervention. The attempted hit on Larry Gallo set off a war within the crime families.

Casualties of the Gallo-Profaci war were numerous. Between 1961 and 1963, nine persons were murdered; three were reported missing, presumed dead. Scores of gangsters and innocent victims were assaulted or wounded by gunfire. The war was still in full swing when Profaci died in 1962. Joseph Magliocco (whose sister was married to Profaci) became boss. He was indecisive as a wartime leader, and his weakness led to his death in 1963 from a heart attack. In the time that Magliocco ran the family, he relied on Joseph Bonanno for help. Bonanno was suspicious of Luchese and Gambino, fearing that they wished to extend their power by absorbing the Profaci crime family. A plot was hatched to assassinate Luchese and Gambino, but it was foiled when Joseph Colombo,* who was contracted to murder the top Mafia chiefs, leaked the scheme to Gambino and Luchese. Colombo emerged as head of the Profaci family. The conflict between the Gallo faction and Profaci leadership was temporary resolved, only to flare up again between Joe Gallo and Joseph Colombo some years later.

**SUGGESTED READINGS:** Joseph Bonanno, with S. Lalli, *A Man of Honor*. 1983; Peter Diapoulos and Steven Linakis, *The Sixth Family*. 1981; Raymond V. Martin, *Revolt in the Mafia*. 1973; Virgil W. Peterson, *The Mob: 200 Years of Organized Crime in New York*. 1983; Gay Talese, *Honor Thy Father*. 1971.

**PROHIBITION AND ORGANIZED CRIME.** (January 1920–December 1933). As outlined in the Eighteenth Amendment, passed by Congress in 1919, an alcohol control policy forbidding the export, import, manufacture, and sale of alcoholic beverages in the United States.

Before 1920, in a world unsettled by rapid urbanization, industrial modernization, and massive immigration, the campaign against alcohol began. In reality, it was a response to huge and frightening challenges posed to traditional white, rural, predominantly Anglo-Saxon and Protestant America. The "new Americans" included whisky-drinking Irish, beer-drinking Germans, wine-drinking Italians, and vodka-drinking Poles and Slavs. During World War I, conservative and romantic impulses, which harked back nostalgically to a wholly mythical, sober, pastoral, pioneer arcadia, combined to ensure the passage of Prohibition legislation. The fact that the wide popular support for the measure was based more on emotional factors than any clear analysis of practical policy undoubtedly contributed to its ineffective enforcement.

The Women's Christian Temperance movement, along with the Anti-Saloon League, led the campaign against what one leading activist called "the beastly, bloated bastard of Beelzebub, the liquor traffic." Significant support for the Prohibition movement came from women who took to it with exceptional vigor. An early campaigner was the celebrated Carrie Nation who toured Kansas at the turn of the century, chopping up kegs of strong drink and entire saloons, accompanied with the stirring slogan "Smash! Smash! For Jesus' sake, Smash!" The extravagances of the Temperance movement and the exhilarating days of Prohibition itself are often easier to describe than explain.

One overlooked outcome of Prohibition was that it was an albatross that poisoned the political life of America. The proponents of Prohibition saw it as the cure for all the social ills in America. Instead, it produced new problems without getting rid of the old. In the end, Prohibition was the major force in the formation of organized crime in the United States as we know it.

With the passage of the Volstead Act in 1920—enacted to enforce the provisions of the Eighteenth Amendment, prohibiting the manufacture, distribution, and sale of alcohol for consumption—200,000 "speakeasies" (illegal drinking establishments, as they were called) sprung up across the country and with them were large bootlegging organizations that met the needs of the underground liquor industry. In New York, 15,000 saloons closed during Prohibition, and more than 30,000 speakeasies replaced them.

Speakeasies were illegal, and cities like New York became enveloped in corruption and bribery. And if bribing the police and politicians did not work, bootleggers* used violence to get their way. Bootleggers brought in liquor from Europe and Canada through intricate smuggling routes, and to further satisfy the unquenchable demands of a thirsty public, the manufacture of alcohol in the country emerged as a major cottage industry.

When the Eighteenth Amendment took effect in 1920, it became a principal factor in shaping the structures of modern organized crime in the United States long after its repeal in 1933. Prohibition created many criminal opportunities for Jewish, Irish, Italians, Polish, WASP, and other ethnic gangsters who often cooperated with each other in the interests of profits. At first, however, during the "Roaring Twenties," vicious competition emerged as the gangs battled for control of the illegal alcohol business. With an enormous consumer market in place, with practically no public disapproval attached to the consumption of liquor, Prohibition was a golden criminal opportunity that energized criminal groups.

In Detroit, the Purple Gang,* which specialized in robbery and murder, became one of the most powerful Prohibition mobs when it began to control the smuggling of liquor products from Canada. In Cleveland, Chicago, New York, Boston, Philadelphia, and many other cities around the country, criminal groups that had been limited to various types of vice and violent crime (robbery, burglary, murder, gambling,* prostitution, etc.), or working as enforcers for the political machines, were transformed by Prohibition. It was not that they became less violent and murderous; rather, their devious skills for violence and corruption were energetically employed in organizing the manufacture and delivery of alcohol to a public that demanded it despite the fact that it had been declared illegal. It was through Prohibition that Alphonse Capone* gained recognition as the nation's best-known gangster; his income from bootlegging (selling illegal alcohol products) ran into the millions.

In New York, the criminal gangs that emerged in the slums and ethnic ghettos of the city's teeming immigrant populations struck it rich during Prohibition. The major gang bosses of the 1920s through the 1950s—Charles "Lucky" Luciano,* Frank Costello,* Meyer Lansky,* "Bugsy" Siegel*—got their start during Prohibition. Before Prohibition they were thugs in the street terrorizing shopkeepers, dealing drugs, and running illegal gambling* games (dice, cards) when not involved in theft and robbery. Booze changed them and the nature of the crime they committed. Crime became businesslike; gangs became "crime syndicates"* employing drivers, bookkeepers, guards, enforcers, and salesmen organized on a regional basis. It also meant wholesale corruption of police, politicians, and government officials at all levels. Where before Prohibition, politicians hired street goons to help them with elections and rewarded criminals with petty jobs and law enforcement policies that ignored mob operations, now the tables were turned, and gangsters bought politicians through massive corruption.

Public lawlessness was an outcome of Prohibition that its advocates and supporters failed to anticipate. Speakeasies sold liquor to anyone who paid. It was rumored that even a president of the United States, Warren G. Harding, ignored the law and served liquor in the White House.

The corruption of law enforcement became widespread in the United States. Gun fights in city streets were common, and hundreds of gangsters were slain in the "beer wars" and smuggling that went on for almost 15 years. Most Prohibition agents were easily corrupted and often cooperated with bootleggers and smugglers.

In 1932, the election of Franklin Delano Roosevelt doomed Prohibition, which by then everyone had recognized as unworkable. The Twenty-first Amendment to the Constitution repealed the Eighteenth Amendment in 1933, ending Prohibition. But the crime syndicates that were the offspring of the failed "Great Experiment" continued. The bootleg gangs and Mafia crime families that were formed during Prohibition stayed together and moved into new businesses—labor racketeering, drug trafficking, gambling, loansharking, and the penetration of legitimate businesses on a massive scale. *See also* COSTELLO, FRANK; LANSKY, MEYER; LUCIANO, CHARLES "LUCKY"

**SUGGESTED READINGS:** Joseph R. Gusfield, *Symbolic Crusade: Status Politics and The American Temperance Movement.* 1963; Martin Lender and J. Martin, *Drinking in America: A History.* 1982.


**PROVENZANO, ANTHONY.** ("Tony Pro") (b. May 7, 1917, New York City—d. Dec. 12, 1988, Lompac, CA, near the Federal Penitentiary). A major labor racketeer in the Teamsters Union, believed to be instrumental in the disappearance and murder of Jimmy Hoffa,* one of the most powerful labor union leaders in the United States.

Anthony Provenzano was one of six sons born to Sicilian immigrants living on the Lower East Side of New York City. He dropped out of school at the age of 15 and later became a truck driver in Hackensack, New Jersey. He had aspirations of becoming a professional prizefighter and bore the scars of an amateur career.

His reputation for violence brought him to the attention of Anthony Strollo, better known as "Tony Bender," a caporegime in the Genovese crime family* of La Cosa Nostra.* With Tony Bender's patronage, "Tony Pro"—as he was known to friends and foes alike—became a member of the Genovese crime family. Through his cunning and ruthlessness, he found his way into the leadership of the International Brotherhood of Teamsters,* Local 560, in northern New Jersey. By 1941, Provenzano was a shop steward, and in 1959, with the help of Jimmy Hoffa, he was elected president of the local. He was rewarded for his support of Hoffa's successful 1957 bid for the Teamster international presidency with an appointment to a International Brotherhood of Teamsters vice presidency; at the same time, he rose rapidly in the ranks of the Cosa Nostra, becoming a captain (caporegime) in the Genovese crime family.

Throughout these years, Tony Pro was involved in violent union election campaigns, federal and state investigations, and the disappearances and mysterious deaths of union opponents. His influence earned him the enmity of law enforcement officials and the homage and loyalty of Teamster rank and file.

Provenzano's leadership of Local 560 and his strategic connections with Hoffa and the international executive enabled him to embezzle funds and sign "sweetheart contracts" with trucking firms. Three of Provenzano's six brothers as well as his daughter had affiliations with Teamster Local 560.

In 1963, Tony Pro's salary of $113,000 made him the highest paid union official in the world. However, a conviction in that same year for extortion sent him to prison for seven years. During his imprisonment, his brothers Salvatore and Nunzio continued operations on his behalf. During the four and half years he served in prison and for the five years he was disqualified from holding union office, Provenzano's brothers ran the union affairs of the 13,000-member Teamster local headquartered in Union City, New Jersey.

Behind his rise and fall lay a shadowy world of criminal associates engaged in murder, mayhem, and corruption. Earlier in 1961, a rival challenged his leadership and was garroted with piano wire by mob executioners. In 1978, Provenzano was convicted of a murder and received a 25-year sentence. While serving his sentence, there were two additional convictions—one in 1978, for which he was sentenced to 4 years for arranging kickbacks on a $2.3 million pension fund loan; a year later, he received a 20-year prison sentence from a federal judge in New Jersey for labor racketeering.*

Perhaps Provenzano's most notorious activity in a career of racketeering and murder involved the disappearance of his onetime close associate Jimmy Hoffa. The Hoffa-Provenzano alliance was typical of the bargains Hoffa struck with gangsters around the country. In return for help in pushing him to the top, Hoffa arranged for several gangsters to obtain powerful union positions of authority, which enabled then to engage in moneymaking schemes including pension frauds, loansharking,* and employer extortion rackets.

Both Hoffa and Provenzano were serving prison terms in the federal correctional facility in Lewisburgh, Pennsylvania, when bad blood between the two former friends developed. Upon his release after serving a substantial part of his sentence and being pardoned by President Richard Nixon, Hoffa announced that he intended to seek the presidency of the Teamsters despite the opposition of his underworld partners and allies. On July 30, 1975, he vanished in Detroit and is believed to have been murdered by Cosa Nostra members fearful of his return. On the date he was reported missing, Hoffa was on his way to what he thought was a meeting with Provenzano, who was not in Detroit then but became a key suspect in Hoffa's disappearance. It was speculated that Provenzano's associates kidnapped Jimmy Hoffa, murdered him, and disposed of his body in a garbage shredder.

Provenzano's many jail terms did not interfere with his power in the Teamster locals. Through relatives, he exercised control, even from prison.

In 1984, a federal judge removed Local 560's executive board and placed it in a "trusteeship" until such time as the membership could freely nominate and elect new officers. After more than two years, Local 560 voted in the local's first contested election in over a quarter of a century. But even then, scandal invalidated the outcome when the FBI disclosed that a Genovese crime family boss was busy promoting a Provenzano associate. Local 560 may have been rescued from mob control, but the Provenzano grip on Local 84 in New Jersey and Local 522 in New York remains intact.

SUGGESTED READINGS: Steven Brill, *The Teamsters*. 1984; President's Commission on Organized Crime, *The Edge: Organized Crime, Business and Labor Unions*. 1986; President's Commission on Organized Crime, *Organized Crime and Labor-Management Racketeering in the United States*. 1985.

**PURPLE GANG.** Jewish bootlegging gang in Detroit.

Detroit's Jewish ghetto, "Little Jerusalem," spawned a collection of adolescent street gangsters before World War I. The origins of the gang name are not clear, but one of their early leaders was Samuel "Sammy Purple" Cohen.

When Prohibition (*see* PROHIBITION AND ORGANIZED CRIME\*) arrived, the Purples had the rudiments of an organization and a preestablished network. From their base in Detroit's downtown ghetto, they radiated out in a widening arc of control and domination. Under Benny and Joe Bernstein and Harry and Louis Fleisher, they maintained close ties to the Cleveland syndicate\* and its leaders "Moe" Dalitz\* and Chuck Polizzi. Detroit was an important locale during Prohibition because it served as a gateway for illegal liquor shipped across the Canadian border. As with most bootlegging organizations, the Purple Gang went into other illicit operations within their reach, including gambling,\* extortion, loansharking,\* and prostitution.

When the crime syndicate formed, Charles "Lucky" Luciano\* and Meyer Lansky\* insisted the Purple Gang join them, which they did. They disbanded their own organization and took a role in the crime cartel's gambling activities by providing the "muscle" to enforce the syndicate's decisions and activities.

SUGGESTED READING: Richard Cohen, *Tough Jews*. 1998.

**PURPLE GANG, MODERN.** At the height of the drug craze in the 1970s, a new gang formed in the bosom of the Cosa Nostra's stronghold, adopting the name the Purple Gang\* after the notorious Detroit outfit that emerged during Prohibition (*see* PROHIBITION AND ORGANIZED CRIME\*). In this case, however, the modern "Purples" were of Italian American background rather than Jewish. They were young and had graduated from small-time positions in the New York underworld, gravitating around Pleasant Avenue, between 110th and 117th Streets in New York City's Italian American enclave in Harlem.

The gang became dominant in large-scale drug distribution in the south Bronx and Harlem and operated as a sort of "sixth family" among the Cosa Nostra's established five families in New York City. Supplementing their drug activities, the Purples became involved in gun running and formed ties with Latino drug lords.

Mafia bosses worried about these young rebels because they did not respect the families and chose to forge partnerships in narcotics with non-Italians. The Purples were quite violent, and on top of every other protocol they ignored, they talked recklessly about controlling all narcotics activities on the East Coast.

In time, arrests and murders diminished their numbers. The gang dissolved in the 1980s.

**SUGGESTED READING:** David Durk and Ira Silverman, *The Pleasant Avenue Connection*. 1976.

# R

<br />

**RACKETEER INFLUENCED AND CORRUPT ORGANIZATIONS ACT.** *See* RICO

**RACKETEERING.** Racketeering is the criminal act of extortion through the threat of violence. The definition of the crime in the RICO* statute, which is the major legal instrument used by the federal government against organized criminal activity, includes any behavior or threats involving murder, kidnapping, arson, infiltration of legitimate business (including labor unions), bribery, embezzlement, loansharking* (usury), and mail and wire fraud.

Racketeers are not only those who belong to La Cosa Nostra* crime families but may be individuals who engage in extortion and conspiracies across a wide spectrum of criminal activities. Racketeers are indeed criminals who usually depend on their reputations for violence to intimidate victims into compliance. A labor racketeer, for example, is able to control a union local through fear and can extort money from builders because of his capacity to disrupt construction activities or ensure that operations proceed smoothly and uneventfully.

How may a whole industry be brought under the control of racketeers? Why is racketeer investment in legitimate enterprises considered a serious problem such that it warrants government attention? There are a number of possible responses to these questions. First, while it is preferable that criminals invest in real estate rather than in drug trafficking enterprises, it must be assumed, based on a long history of experience, that racketeers bring to their legal interests the same techniques of corruption, fraud, and intimidation that they employ in their illegal enterprises.* In effect, they pollute legal markets. Second, the intensity with which they pursue their illegal activities is only slightly diminished. Heroin importers who invest in wine imports do not, by doing so, pass up significant opportunities in the drug business. Third, investment in legal enterprises may actually facilitate or enhance illegal activities. For example, bar and restaurant ownership provides criminals with a legitimate front, with a public yet protected place to conduct business and a vehicle for laundering large amounts of small bills from vice rackets. Fourth, racketeers are likely to use their criminal assets (violence and corruption) to assist their legal enterprises and create disadvantages that frustrate their legitimate competitors.

**SUGGESTED READING:** Peter Reuter, "Racketeers as Cartel Organizers," in *The Politics and Economics of Organized Crime*, ed. H. Alexander and G. Caiden. 1985.

**RAGEN, JAMES M.** (b. 1881, Chicago, IL—d. Sept. 1946, Chicago, IL). Chicago gambling figure, 1930s.

James Ragen was the man picked to run the Chicago Continental wire service Moses Annenberg* built in the 1930s. The son of Irish immigrants, the product of a tough street gang, a veteran of Chicago's newspaper circulation war, Ragen shot and killed a man in 1906. Under Ragen the gambling wire, which contained up-to-date information on racetrack results in 223 cities in 30 states, did business with Abner Zwillman,* Meyer Lansky,* and other major gangsters.

Ragen came up in the Chicago underworld and learned the skills of a hoodlum under the tutelage of Charles Dion O'Banion.* His Continental Press Service met the needs of bookmakers so efficiently that the mob put pressure on Ragen to form a partnership. He resisted, so the mob set up Trans-American Publishing under "Bugsy" Siegel* and took over the California gambling* market. Ragen kept firm control over the rest of the country until June 1946, when he was shot in the street. Ragen blamed the mob, and several of its top leaders were questioned. In September 1946, Ragen died not from his wounds but from mercury poisoning. Apparently, as with "Kid Twist" Reles,* the mob could reach its enemies even when they were hiding behind police protection.

**RASTAFARIANS.** *See* AFRICAN AMERICAN ORGANIZED CRIME

**RASTELLI, PHILIP.** ("Rusty") (b. 1918, Brooklyn, NY—d. Dec. 27, 1991, NY). Boss (don)* of the Bonanno crime family.*

Women of Mafia men are usually kept away from the activities of their husbands, fathers, and brothers. But occasionally, a Mafia wife, or "princess," becomes involved and threatens to raise the veil on criminal activities. Rastelli's wife Connie was not a quiet wife who kept her mouth shut and turned a blind eye and a deaf ear to her husband's activities. She informed on her husband.

During the early 1970s, Rastelli was boss of the Bonanno crime family but stepped down when Carmine "The Cigar" Galante* was released from prison. In 1979, Galante was assassinated, and Rastelli returned to power, but the police suspected he had a role in Galante's death. His activities, like that of Galante, included drug trafficking, and it was these activities that led to the death of his wife in 1962. By informing on her husband, Connie Rastelli violated the code of omerta,* for which the penalty is death. It was unusual for a woman to be involved in crime, but Mrs. Rastelli had been a major asset to Rastelli by driving getaway cars during holdups, keeping track of illegal loans, maintaining the books for her husband's extensive gambling* operations, and running a new racket in the 1960s—abortion mills in poor neighborhoods.

True to the way of life of a mafioso, Phil Rastelli kept a mistress. Mrs. Rastelli would not tolerate the old Mafia tradition and attempted to kill her husband on a Brooklyn street when she learned about his romantic interlude in Canada with another woman. She emptied a gun on her husband, who managed to survive the wounds. When he did not return home, she threatened to talk to law enforcement officials about his activities. Under ordinary circumstances, Rastelli would have been killed by his Mafia associates for allowing his wife to participate in his activities, but the fighting within the Bonanno family at that time deflected attention away from the boss and his domestic problems. Connie Rastelli persuaded federal officials that she was a valuable informant when she gave them the correct address of a witness they were protecting in New Jersey that the mob planned to murder. Big John Ormento and others were convicted, but before a case could be mounted against Rastelli, his wife was shot to death by a mob assassin—presumably approved by her husband.

From the mid-1970s on, Rastelli had been in and out of prison on a variety of charges including extortion and labor racketeering. Because of his frequent imprisonment, it was expected that the Young Turks in the Bonanno crime family might topple him in that being in prison interfered with his position as family boss. With the murder of Paul Castellano* in 1985, Rastelli was placed under the protection of U.S. marshals in a secure location, which fueled speculation that he was cooperating. A 1986 RICO* conviction quelled the rebellion in the family, but that meant he could no longer function as boss. Within five years, he died of natural causes.

**SUGGESTED READING:** Joe Pistone, *Donnie Brasco: My Undercover Life in the Mafia.* 1989.


**REINA, GAETANO "TOMMY."** (b. 1889, Castellammarese, Sicily—d. Feb. 26, 1930, New York City). Boss of one of the original five crime families of Cosa Nostra.

"Tommy" Reina was a victim of the unscrupulous intrigues of gangsters who admired him. His murder in February 1930 marked the opening of the Castellammarese War* between Mafia factions in New York City. Actually, the battle lines in the struggle were murky, with individuals and groups switching sides and betraying each other. Reina was caught in the middle. As a capo* in the "Joe the Boss" Masseria Mafia clan, he played an important role in vice rackets and bootlegging in Manhattan and the Bronx; but he was also less than enthusiastic about a war against Masseria's rival, Salvatore Maranzano,* many of whose soldiers* and supporters such as Joseph Profaci* and Joseph Bonanno* were personal friends. A third force headed by Charles "Lucky" Luciano* emerged to lead a generational revolt against Masseria and Maranzano. Luciano represented the "Americanization" of the Mafia*; he, along with Frank Costello* and Gaetano Luchese,* had Jewish partners (Meyer Lansky* and "Bugsy" Siegel*) in their criminal enterprises and did not intend to abandon them for the sake of the ethnic purity the "Mustache Petes"*—Masseria and Maranzano—demanded. Because Luciano feared that Reina's influence could swing the struggle in Maranzano's favor, and thereby upset Lucky's plans to eliminate all the "Mustache Petes" who refused to change their traditional ways, Reina had to be eliminated. Vito Genovese* shot him to death in the driveway of his Bronx home, and that murderous act set in motion a 19-month period of gang war in which Maranzano, Masseria, and many others were murdered. A new, younger, more American generation of bosses, less tied to the customs of the old country, emerged to form La Cosa Nostra.*

**SUGGESTED READING:** Martin Gosch and Richard Hammer, *The Last Testament of Lucky Luciano*. 1974.

**RELES, "KID TWIST."** ("The Kid") (b. Abraham Reles, 1907, New York City— d. Nov. 12, 1941, Brooklyn, NY). Contract killer for Murder, Inc.* and mob informant.

During an interrogation where Kid Twist recanted the grisly murders he and his associates committed, the assistant district attorney Burton Turkus asked how he could kill with such ease and indifference to human life. "How did you feel when you tried your first case?" Reles replied. "I was rather nervous," said Turkus. "And how about your second case?" "It wasn't so bad, but I was still a little nervous." "And after that?" "Oh, after that I was all right. I was used to it." "You answered your own question," said Reles. "It's the same with murder. I got used to it."

When Reles decided to talk to the district attorney, he spoke compulsively, giving names, dates, details, where to look, whom to ask. Reles told the prosecutor not only what happened but how to make the case. And when word about Reles got out, a panic ran through the underworld with gangsters thinking back, trying to remember their dealings with Kid Twist. Never before had someone highly placed in the mob turned rat. Kid Twist knew many secrets: He talked about the murder of Dutch Schultz,* about beatings, assaults, shootings, stabbings, fires, robberies; his confessions filled 75 notebooks with details on more than 80 killings. When Reles started talking, there was a chain reaction, one confession leading to another until the air was full of voices. Several gangsters turned into informers: Dukey Maffeatore, Sholem Bernstein, Albert Tannenbaum, Pretty Levine, and Mickey Sycoff—some of the toughest assassins and gangsters in New York's Jewish underworld who had been members of the troop of murderers known as Murder, Inc., doing the killings and maimings for Louis Buchalter* and Albert Anastasia.*

Abe Reles grew up in the tough streets of Brownsville and East New York—

Jewish ghettos in the borough of Brooklyn in New York City. Reles left school by the end of the eighth grade and began a career as a thief and extortionist, preying upon small shopkeepers in Brownsville. By the start of the depression, he and "Pittsburgh Phil" Strauss,* "Buggsy" Goldstein, and others were killing members of the rival Strauss gang for control of territory. Thereafter, Reles and his "Boys from Brownsville" began doing murder for Buchalter and Anastasia.

Kid Twist (the nickname he adopted himself after an old-time thug from the Lower East Side of New York) was the leader of a troop of killers that carried out murders on order from the New York syndicate,* or "Combination," which consisted of loose partnerships among Italian and Jewish gangsters involved in the vice industries and labor racketeering.*

In 1940, Reles was picked up on a murder charge, and in order to save himself, he decided to talk. He described Murder, Inc. in grisly detail and implicated his associates in many murders. Most important, his grand jury testimony led to the conviction and execution in 1944 of Lepke Buchalter, a major syndicate boss.

While taking part in several trials, Reles was kept in protective custody in the Half Moon Hotel along the Coney Island seaside in Brooklyn. Kid Twist was preparing to give testimony on Albert Anastasia and "Bugsy" Siegel* concerning their ties to Murder, Inc. when during the early morning hours of November 12, 1941, he jumped, fell accidentally, or was thrown out of the sixth-floor window of his room. The case against mob kingpins went out the window with Reles. The murder has never been solved, but Charles "Lucky" Luciano* insisted shortly before his death that Frank Costello* paid the police $100,000 to murder Reles. Meyer Lansky,* years later, confirmed Luciano's account.

**SUGGESTED READING:** Rich Cohen, *Tough Jews: Fathers, Sons and Gangster Dreams.* 1998.

**RICCA, PAUL "THE WAITER."** (b. Paolo deLucia, 1897, Naples, Italy—d. Oct. 1972, Chicago, IL). Chicago Outfit boss, 1940s and 1950s.

Behind the elegant manners and neat appearance, Paul "The Waiter" Ricca was a cold-blooded killer. He became head of the Chicago Outfit* when Frank "The Enforcer" Nitti* committed suicide in 1944. Among all the individuals identified as the bosses (dons)* of the Chicago Outfit—Anthony Joseph Accardo* Sam Giancana,* Joseph John Aiuppa*—Ricca was always part of the decision-making apparatus that constituted the leadership.

He came to the United States in 1920, fleeing Italian authorities who wanted him in connection with several murders. Some historians believe that "Ricca" was a name he assumed of a man he had killed in a family feud. Eventually he managed to obtain work in Chicago restaurants, where he earned the name "Paul the Waiter." His involvement with Alphonse Capone* came about through his management of a theater Big Al owned; later, the theater background provided the invaluable knowledge he needed to set up the infiltration of the film industry through Willie Morris Bioff.* Eventually, Ricca was swept up in the indictments and prosecutions for extortion in the film industry based on Bioff's evidence, but he shortened his ten-year sentence through the intervention of the attorney general of the United States, Tom Clark. Although a man of violence, Ricca appreciated the value of corruption and the bribe, which he learned from his mentor Capone.

With his release Ricca and Accardo emerged as the leaders of the Chicago Outfit. In 1950 the Kefauver Committee* identified him as the "national head of the Crime Syndicate"; and the McClelland Committee* in 1958 referred to Ricca as the "most important" criminal in America.

In 1957 Ricca was subject to deportation, but the Italian government refused to permit his return. Indeed, over the next decade, appeals to 60 countries to allow his immigration also failed. The government was still seeking his deportation in 1972 when he died.

**SELECTED READING:** William F. Roemer, Jr., *Accardo: The Genuine Godfather.* 1995.

**RICO.** (The Racketeer Influenced and Corrupt Organizations Act).

RICO was enacted by Congress in 1970 as part of the Organized Crime Control Act. Its use by the Department of Justice has revolutionized the prosecution of organized crime. The purpose of RICO is to provide a tool to prosecute an entire multi-defendant organized crime group for all of its many criminal activities. The RICO statute authorizes the seizure of the proceeds and profits of illegal enterprises.* The most often used section of the RICO law (Sec. 18, 1962) makes it unlawful for any person to be employed by, or associated with, any enterprise engaged in racketeering* activity.

In effect, RICO created a new crime: belonging to an enterprise engaged in racketeering activities. The law does not require that a defendant actually commits the crime; only that he or she belongs to, or is associated with, an enterprise that does. In short, RICO makes it unlawful to acquire, operate, or receive income from racketeering.

In practice, RICO allows prosecutors to use numerous criminal acts that may have occurred over several years in one sweeping racketeering indictment. This method of prosecution has been widely used by the federal government against Mafia* families. Organized criminals fear RICO for other reasons. The penalties are substantial: Any individual or group that commits two or more indictable offenses within a ten-year period is subject to 20 years' imprisonment, fines up to $25,000, forfeiture of any interest in the enterprise, as well as civil damages and dissolution of the enterprise itself.

Today a steady parade of mobsters have gone to prison with life sentences resulting from RICO convictions. Indeed, the lengthy prison terms under RICO constitutes a threat that has been effectively used to gain the cooperation of defendants. In 1992, mainly on the testimony of "Sammy the Bull" Gravano,* the underboss (sottocapo)* of the Gambino crime family,* John Gotti,* its head, was convicted for the murder of Paul Castellano* (himself a capo* mafioso) and other charges. Gotti was sentenced to life in prison without the possibility of parole. Gravano did the arithmetic on the charges against him and the possible outcomes: If he cooperated with prosecutors, he would eventually be released; if not, a RICO conviction (which was likely) was a death sentence in that he would be incarcerated for the rest of his life.

Three major criticisms of RICO have been raised by defense attorneys. First, it involves the prosecution of persons who, though they may not have been implicated directly in criminal behavior, are connected to organized crime through indictments. Second, invoking RICO may result in assets being frozen even before a trial begins, which can effectively put a company out of business; or RICO charges may induce defendants to plead guilty when they believe themselves innocent. Third, a RICO action brings with it a stigma of being a "racketeer" affiliated with organized crime.

Prosecutors and law enforcement officials, on the other hand, see RICO as an effective crime control mechanism. Also, it is the only criminal statute, according to its author G. Robert Blakey, who proposed it as a recommendation in the 1967 Task Force Report on Organized Crime, that enables the government to present to a jury the whole picture of how an enterprise, such as an organized crime family,* operates and conducts its criminal activities through racketeering activities. Rather than pursuing the leader or boss of a group of individuals for a single crime or scheme, the government is able to indict the entire hierarchy of an organized crime family for the diverse criminal activities in which that "enterprise" engages. Instead of merely proving one criminal act in a defendant's career, RICO permits the exploration of a defendant's whole life in crime.

**SUGGESTED READINGS:** G. Robert Blakey, "RICO: The Federal Experience," in *Handbook of Organized Crime in the United States*, ed. Robert J. Kelly et. al. 1994; Rudolph W. Giuliani, "Legal Remedies for Attacking Organized Crime," in *Major Issues in Organized Crime Control*, ed. H. Edelhertz. 1987.


**RIESEL, VICTOR.** (b. 1917, New York City—d. Jan. 8, 1995, Los Angeles, CA). Newspaper columnist covering organized crime and labor affairs.

In the early morning hours of April 5, 1956, Victor Riesel made a radio broadcast in which he denounced the prevalence of racketeering* in Local 138 of the International Union of Operating Engineers on Long Island, New York. Riesel was a well-known journalist specializing in labor relations whose newspaper column was carried in almost 200 papers across the country and whose radio commentary was widely acclaimed.

After his broadcast, he stopped at Lindy's Restaurant in Manhattan, and when he left in the early morning hours, he was assaulted by a man who hurled sulfuric acid into his eyes, causing permanent damage that left the journalist blind.

The hoodlum who blinded Riesel had been hired by two hoodlums associated with Johnny Dio,* a labor union racketeer and a protégé of Louis Buchalter* and Jacob "Gurrah" Shapiro.* The attacker, Abraham Telvi, received $1,175 for his dreadful work; and when public furor following the attack increased, Telvi extorted Johnny Dio for more money. Then, shortly after, Telvi was found dead, in July 1956. In testimony before a federal grand jury, Johnny Dio and his associates were indicted. But charges against Dio were dropped when the other defendants refused to testify against him after threats were made against them and their families. Riesel never resumed his active career and was one of the few honest journalists who reported on the mob that was attacked by it.

**SUGGESTED READING:** Jonathan Kwitny, *Vicious Circles: The Mafia in the Marketplace.* 1979.

**RODRIGUEZ GACHA, JOSÉ GONZALO.** ("The Mexican") (b. 1946, Pacho, Colombia—d. Dec. 1989, Tolu, Colombia). Medellín cocaine cartel leader.

Gonzalo Rodriguez Gacha was fond of buying soccer teams with the millions he earned in the narcotics business. His role in the cartel involved assassinating informers and competitors (including public figures) and putting peasant farmers on the payroll to grow coca plants. He also negotiated an agreement with the Colombian terrorist guerrilla organization known as FARC (Revolutionary Armed Forces of Colombia) to provide security for the narcotics operation and laboratories of the Medellín cartel. "The Mexican" managed to turn proud political revolutionaries into little more than a band of gangsters who had sold out to the cocaine barons.

Rodriguez Gacha headed the Medellín's cartel's West Coast distribution and acquired Mexican airstrips to secretly accommodate aircraft loaded with cocaine destined for the United States.

He was the cocaine boss in Colombia's capital city Bogotá, and he got his start in the cocaine business by becoming a specialist in the transport of coca leaf from Peru and Bolivia to processing labs in Colombia. Gacha loved Mexico and things Mexican, and for this he was generally known as "El Mejicano" (The Mexican). A squat man of medium height, he was not considered a major player in the narcotics trade until 1983 when it was discovered that he had operated his transport routes from Peru and Bolivia, flying in paste to Colombian labs.

By 1988, with Pablo Emilio Gavoroa Escobar* occupied with gang war and Jorge Luis Vasquez Ochoa* out of the picture, Gacha stepped from the shadows to lead the Medellín cartel in an aggressive expansion into the southwest United States and Europe. He traveled to New York City in a bid to take over the Cali cocaine cartel's* distribution network in Queens County. This move may have triggered a version of the "War of the Cartels" back in the early 1980s as local cocaine and crack dealers contested turf. At the same time, Gacha may have mended fences between the two cartels and affected a truce—a process true to his character: He always viewed cocaine as just a business. In 1988 Gacha joined Escobar and Ochoa in *Forbes* magazine as one of the world's billionaires.

In the summer of 1989, the assassination of leading anticocaine cartel public figures reached a new level of intensity. A magistrate who ruled against the Medellín cartel bosses was killed by gunmen as he left his office; a leading candidate for president who favored extraditing drug barons was killed in the midst of a public address at a campaign rally. In a communiqué published in Colombian newspapers from "The Extraditables," as the drug bosses called themselves, they warned that the murders would continue against anyone who supported extradition. The government's response was a crackdown of the traffickers and the reactivation of the extradition treaty. Colombian police began to round up thousands of traffickers and their property.

Even with the war against the government in full swing and the struggle against the guerrillas who kidnapped cartel members and their relatives for ransom, the Medellín, Cali, Bogotá, and Baranquilla cartels still competed with each other vigorously for market share. In December, 1989 Gacha was discovered by police in Tolu near the Caribbean port of Covenos. It is believed that a Cali cartel informant helped law enforcement. After a brief gun battle, Gonzalo Gacha was killed.

**SUGGESTED READING:** Patrick Clawson and Rensselaer Lee III, *The Andean Cocaine Industry*. 1996.

**RODRIGUEZ-OREJUELA, GILBERTO.** ("The Chess Player") (b. 1939, Cali, Colombia—incarcerated). Founder and original member of the Cali cocaine cartel.*

For all Colombian cocaine traffickers, extradition was like a cross to a vampire. Gilberto Orejulea and his brother Miguel Angel* feared trial and imprisonment in the United States with its long prison sentences and intractable attitudes toward drug traffickers. With his brother Miguel, the Orjeuelas controlled the most powerful of the Cali organizations. The organization was involved in all aspects of the cocaine trade, including production, transportation, wholesale distribution, and money laundering.* The younger Gilberto was responsible for strategic long-term planning, whereas Miguel was the micromanager who was involved in the minuscule details of the organization's daily operations. Although the Rodriguez-Orejuela brothers did not take part in indiscriminate violence, they did engage in kidnapping and physical threats and occasionally in murder. More routinely they used bribes and threats to further their business.

The Rodriguez brothers usually contracted the services of independent Mexican drug transportation groups to smuggle cocaine from Mexico to the United States via land. Southern Florida was also used by their organization as a key point of entry for cocaine smuggled aboard ships. After the cocaine was smuggled into the United States, wholesale distribution operations were carried out in Houston, Los Angeles, Miami, New York, and other U.S. cities. The organization also ran drug money laundering operations in these U.S. cities.

Gilberto Orejuela had been sought since 1978 on drug trafficking warrants in Los Angeles and New York; in 1984, along with Jorge Luis Vasquez Ochoa,* Gilberto Orejuela was in Madrid, Spain, depositing large amounts of cash in local banks and buying real estate. The Spanish police discovered that Orejuela was traveling under a false Venezuelan passport and quickly identified him as a major drug trafficker. The DEA was alerted and issued an extradition request to the Spanish Foreign Ministry, requesting his arrest. Orejuela and Ochoa were arrested and their assets seized. Ultimately, the extradition failed because of the intervention of the Sandinista government of Nicaragua, which the DEA had accused of complicity in cocaine smuggling into the United States. Ochoa and Orejuela were cleverly portrayed by their lawyers as victims of American foreign policy. Orejuela would stand trial in Colombia for a false passport and avoid the U.S. courts. His ability to manipulate the Colombian judicial system clearly figured in his calculations. Not for nothing was this subtle man known as "The Chess Player."

On June 9, 1995, Gilberto Rodriguez-Orejuela was captured in an apartment in Cali, Colombia, by an elite unit of the Colombian National Police working with the DEA and the U.S. intelligence community. Gilberto Rodriguez-Orejuela was indicted in the United States numerous times, most recently in May 1995, in the Southern District of Florida.

A 1989 U.S. indictment for drug trafficking emanating in New Orleans and evidence shared with the government of Colombia provided the impetus for Rodriguez-Orejuela's arrest. He was indicted in Miami, along with other members of the Cali mafia,* for the illegal importation of over 200,000 kilograms of cocaine over the last ten years.

Colombian police staged several simultaneous raids on June 9, 1995. They were about to give up when Gilberto was found hidden in a secret closet of a luxury house. Gilberto, perhaps remembering the shootout that killed Pablo Emilio Gavoroa Escobar,* is reported to have said, "Don't shoot me. I will surrender," when faced with the police.

**SELECTED READING:** Francisco Thoumi, *Political Economy and Illegal Drugs in Colombia*. 1995.

## RODRIGUEZ-OREJUELA, MIGUEL ANGEL. ("Transportation Specialist") (b. 1943, Cali, Colombia—incarcerated). Cali cocaine cartel* leader.

Like his brother Gilberto* and José Santacruz Londono, Miguel Orejuela relied on an elaborate security system to protect himself against rivals in the Medellín cartel, the Colombian National Police, and the prying eyes of the American Drug Enforcement Administration (DEA) agents who were everywhere in the world, or so it seemed.

Miguel, who was born in 1943 in Cali, has been involved in drug trafficking since 1980. He was responsible for smuggling multiton quantities of cocaine from Colombia into the United States, Canada, and Europe using a wide variety of sophisticated transportation and smuggling techniques. Seventy percent of the cocaine destined for the U.S. market was smuggled through Mexico.

Miguel, also known as the "Transportation Specialist," was responsible for the day-to-day operations of the Rodriguez-Orejuela organization, the most powerful of the Cali groups. He micromanaged all aspects of their multifaceted trafficking ventures, which included production, transportation, wholesale distribution, and money laundering.* His older brother Gilberto had concentrated on "strategic planning" for the Cali group.

He was captured on August 6, 1995, when the Colombian National Police (CNP) broke down the door of his apartment and found him hiding in a secret closet in the bathroom. He had been the subject of an intense manhunt. According to Colombia's foreign minister, Miguel Rodriguez-Orejuela could receive a maximum sentence of 24 years in prison. Following the successful arrest of Miguel Rodriguez-Orejuela, General Miguel Serrano of the CNP proclaimed, "The Cali cartel died today."

**SELECTED READING:** Patrick L. Clawson and Rensselear W. Lee III, *The Andean Cocaine Industry.* 1996.

**ROSELLI, JOHN.** (b. Filippo Sacco, 1905, Esteria, Italy—d. Aug. 7, 1976, murdered, Miami, FL). Chicago Outfit* racketeer and Las Vegas, Nevada,* power broker.

Roselli was one of those gangsters who never got to the top of the criminal hierarchy but made an impact on events nonetheless. He came to the United States when he was 6 years old. His mother remained after his father's untimely death, and Roselli traces the beginnings of his criminal way of life to the influences of his stepfather. According to Roselli, it was his stepfather who talked him into an act of arson when he was 11 years old. After he quit school in the seventh grade, he abandoned his family and embraced the Alphonse Capone* gang. Filippo Sacco became Johnny Roselli and represented the Outfit's interests in Hollywood by threatening union leaders and extorting money from the big film studios. For extortion he did three years in prison.

Roselli loved the Hollywood lifestyle and returned after his prison term. And as Las Vegas developed into a lucrative target for criminals, Roselli saw to it that the Outfit got its cut of the gambling skim. Hollywood and Las Vegas were not the only projects that Roselli enjoyed: With his boss Sam Giancana* of Chicago, he became involved in Operation Mongoose*—the CIA/Mafia* plot to kill Fidel Castro, the Cuban dictator. Roselli quickly surmised that the mob-spy partnership was a hare-brained scheme but did nothing to persuade the CIA to abandon the operation.

In 1975, he testified before a Senate committee with oversight on intelligence-gathering operations, where he allegedly disclosed the details of Mongoose, claiming that his participation was based on purely patriotic sentiments. In August 1975, his body was discovered in a sealed 55-gallon drum floating in Bis-

Arnold Rothstein. Reproduced from the Collections of
the Library of Congress.

cayne Bay. Prior to his murder, Roselli was seen in the company of columnist
Jack Anderson, and it was feared that he may have talked too much about the
government/Mafia scheme.

**SUGGESTED READING:** Charles Rappleye and Ed Becker, *All American Mafioso: The
Johnny Rosselli Story*. 1991.

**ROTHSTEIN, ARNOLD "THE BRAIN."** (b. 1882, New York City—d. Nov. 4,
1928, New York City). Criminal mastermind, gambling* and syndicate* leader.
   The man who fixed the World Series of 1919 and transformed criminal activity from a haphazard endeavor into one marked by skill, expertise, and careful
administration was born into a law-abiding orthodox Jewish family. Arnold "The
Brain" Rothstein started his career as an expert billiards and pool player who
parlayed his winnings into usurious loans. As his gambling* enterprises expanded, he bought police and political protection. Indeed, during Prohibition
(*see* PROHIBITION AND ORGANIZED CRIME*), he significantly reorganized the way that bribery, graft, and corruption were operated. Until his time,
police would collect graft and payoffs with politicians off in the margins, un-
tainted by direct contact. This was the way—the tradition through the end of
World War I where politicians used gangs of criminals as they wished at election

time or to resolve conflicts between labor and management, for instance. Police were part of the political patronage machine and relegated to roles that ensured virtually no professional autonomy or independence of action.

With Prohibition and its enormous wealth, power shifted increasingly to the criminals. Rothstein could, and often did, buy the political leaders and insisted on direct payoffs to eliminate possible police defections or deceit, and, more to the point, bribery obliged politicians to deal directly with their criminal sponsors and partners. The police would receive separate payments and were assigned to roles that subordinated them to politicians and criminals.

Rothstein formed up syndicates that did not discriminate ethically or racially: His protégés were Irish, Jewish, Italian, German, even African American. His skills at corruption became legendary, and his organization of bootlegging became a model for most forms of racketeering* in the future. Important criminals—such as Meyer Lansky,* Louis Buchalter,* Frank Costello,* Charles "Lucky" Luciano*—learned from Rothstein how to create and sustain a criminal empire.

On November 4, 1928, he was shot dead at the Park Central Hotel in New York City. It seems that there was a dispute over a gambling debt in excess of $300,000. Rothstein allegedly maintained that the game was rigged. The prime suspects then were California gamblers but were never indicted. The case was never solved. No suspicion ever arose about his criminal associates Lepke Buchalter, Dutch Schultz,* or Lucky Luciano, who had close ties with him and benefited enormously when he was rubbed out.

Rothstein may have been the most influential innovator in organized crime before World War II.

**SUGGESTED READING:** Leo Katcher, *The Big Bankroll: The Life and Times of Arnold Rothstein.* 1959.

**ROYAL FAMILY.** In Chicago, where African Americans are at the bottom of the economic ladder, organized criminal groups have been active in the ghettos since the 1950s. One, known as the Royal Family, consisting of former inmates from the Statesville Penitentiary, modeled itself deliberately on the fictitious Corleone family in Mario Puzo's novel *The Godfather.* The Royal Family did not challenge the white Chicago Outfit* but allied with it, working as enforcers. *See also* GANGSTER DISCIPLES; EL RUKNS

**SUGGESTED READING:** William Kleinknecht, *The New Ethnic Mobs: The Changing Face of Organized Crime in America.* 1996.

**RUBY, JACK L.** (b. Jacob Rubinstein, 1911, Chicago, IL—d. Jan. 3, 1967, Dallas, TX). Dallas racketeer and assassin of Lee Harvey Oswald.

Ruby began a criminal career by running errands for Alphonse Capone* as a teenager, then working gambling* operations in California, returning to Chicago in 1937 for nightclub work and more union racketeering. From 1943 to 1946, Ruby served honorably in the U.S. Army Air Corps. With his discharge in 1947, the Chicago Outfit* sent him to Dallas to help secure control of rackets in Texas. These big plans, however, never materialized; The Chicago Outfit did not assume control of the vice industries in Dallas or other Texas cities because of the influence of the Bonanno crime family* in Tucson, Arizona and the New Orleans Mafia* family of Carlos Marcello,* which left Ruby with a string of tawdry strip joints rather than fancy restaurants and glittering gambling casinos.

During the fall of 1963, circumstances changed dramatically for Jack Ruby. He began meeting with top associates of Carlos Marcello of New Orleans and John Roselli* in Miami. And at various times in the autumn, Lee Harvey Oswald was seen with Ruby at his Carousel Club. Oswald was a familiar figure on the fringes of the underworld in Louisiana and Texas: He spent part of his childhood in New Orleans with his uncle Charles Murret, who worked in a gambling syndicate* under the control of the Marcello La Cosa Nostra* crime organization.

Two days after President Kennedy's assassination on November 22, 1963, Jack Ruby shot and killed Lee Harvey Oswald. He said he wanted revenge, and he said he killed Oswald for the sake of Jacqueline Kennedy and the grief-stricken family and nation. However, the real motives were doubtlessly more complex and sinister. Attending the midnight press conference in police headquarters (to which he had easy access because he knew many police officers), Ruby stood at the back of the room, and when the district attorney incorrectly identified Oswald as a member of the Anti-Castro Free Cuba Committee, Ruby pointedly, revealingly, corrected him: It was the pro-Castro, left-wing, Fair Play for Cuba Committee, he said. Then on Sunday, expecting leniency for his "patriotic" act, Ruby found his way to the police garage, where Oswald was being led for transfer to another jail, and murdered Oswald while television cameras carried the act across the country and the world.

In 1964, Ruby was tried and sentenced to death in Texas, but he died in prison presumably of natural causes while awaiting a second trial and insisting to the Warren Commission investigating President Kennedy's assassination that his life in any Texas prison was in jeopardy. *See also* MAFIA AND THE KENNEDY ASSASSINATION

**SUGGESTED READINGS:** Edward Jay Epstein, *Counterplot: The Assassination Chronicles.* 1992; Norman Mailer, "The Amateur Hit Man," *New York Review of Books,* May 11, 1995, 52–59.

**RUNYON, DAMON.** (b. Alfred Damon Runyon, 1884, Manhattan, KS–d. 1946, New York City). Writer and social historian of the underworld.

Like Walter Winchell,* Damon Runyon chose to write about the gangster world of nightclubs, prizefights, and racetracks. Based on his columns for the Hearst papers, he wrote his short stories about underworld life on Broadway, which were the basis for many films and a famous Broadway musical, *Guys and Dolls*.

Runyon did his research by associating with racketeers in New York's famous speakeasy-turned-nightclub, the Stork Club, by watching and listening.

His work is noteworthy because it described the gangsters/racketeers in their unusual ornamental idiom of the Broadway vernacular—everything in a conversation expressed in the present tense and acted in present time. Although they are fictional, Runyon's stories had an edge of historical truth and sociological clarity, as evident in some of his characters who were transparently based on real people: Armand Rosenthal was Arnold "The Brain" Rothstein* Waldo Winchester was Walter Winchell, and Black Mike was Alphonse Capone.*

The popularity of Runyon's romanticized soft, humorous image of mobsters as mischievous bad guys who exist because the public needs their services would survive permanently and perhaps explain in part why the press lacked the zeal to really go after the mob.

**SUGGESTED READING:** Jimmy Breslin, *Damon Runyon*. 1991.

**RUPOLO, ERNEST "THE HAWK."** (b. 1908, Brooklyn, NY—d. Aug. 27, 1964, Jamaica, NY). Genovese crime family* assassin and hit man.

Rupolo's career is of interest and importance because it illustrates the workings of the criminal code of "omerta"* and the criminal's psychology of murder.

In 1934, after years of petty theft, robberies, and jail terms from the time he was thirteen years old, Rupolo was recruited by top criminals in La Cosa Nostra* to do a "hit"* a contract murder. Rupolo was known as "The Hawk" because of his visual acuity. (Ironically, he lost an eye from a gunshot wound that occurred in an argument over dividing the money from a criminal enterprise. He survived, amazingly, and carried on in a criminal career that required good eyesight—that of an assassin.)

Vito Genovese* put a contract out on mobster Ferdinand "The Shadow" Boccia, who was a manager of one of Genovese's gambling places in Brooklyn in 1934. Boccia set up a swindle and fully expected to share the fleeced money with Genovese, but Genovese decided to kill Boccia and keep all the money for himself. Willie Gallo and "The Hawk" Rupolo were given the murder contract. Actually, Rupolo was given two contracts: He was told to kill Gallo, too, as soon as Boccia had been finished off.

Boccia was killed as planned; then Gallo was shot three times in the head but managed, remarkably, to live and name his assassins when he realized he had been double-crossed. Rupolo and Genovese were arrested. Rupolo went to prison, but Gallo reneged on implicating the deadly Genovese, and "Don Vitone" went free. Rupolo then revealed that there had been a witness to the Boccia shooting who could implicate Genovese. A gangster named Peter LaTempa was sought out, and on the strength of his testimony, Genovese was reindicted. Genovese's organization went into action: LaTempa was in protective custody in a Brooklyn jail, but somehow, someone got to the pills he took regularly for a stomach disorder. He was found dead of poison in his cell, and Genovese was freed once again in 1945.

Rupolo made Genovese's death list. The Hawk went free and left prison despite strong advice against leaving, but Rupolo knew that Genovese's power could reach into prison, as LaTempa's murder proved. For years nothing happened. In 1959, Genovese was arrested on drug trafficking, so Rupolo felt somewhat safe. The Hawk's life out of prison consisted of petty shakedowns and extortion in the neighborhoods he lived in, but he always remained vigilant, knowing that he violated the oath of omerta, of silence; he was a "rat" in the eyes of the mob—but a dangerous rat who had to be approached cautiously. Rupolo's torture may have been the anguish he experienced as he waited for Genovese to exact his revenge.

In 1964, Rupolo's mangled remains were found floating in Jamaica Bay, New York. He had been brutally murdered and then weighted down with cement blocks. This gruesome method of execution ensured that eventually his body would surface as a reminder to everyone about the consequences of cooperation with law enforcement authorities.

**SUGGESTED READING:** James Miller, *The Prosecutor*. 1969.

**RUSSIAN ORGANIZED CRIME.** Criminal life in the former Soviet Union equipped many Russian gangsters with skills perfectly suited to white-collar crime in the United States. In the wake of the collapse of the Soviet Union, in 1991 it seems fair to say that the state itself contributed to the creation of a criminal subculture where Soviet citizens were forced to negotiate and connive their way through the vast Communist bureaucracy. Papers were needed to work, to travel, to buy certain consumer goods, to get medical care, to buy a car, to get an apartment. In order to survive, ordinary citizens had to act like criminals; they had to master the intricacies of the corrupt state bureaucracy, learn how to bribe officials, and develop skills in forging and counterfeiting documents. In America, these skills have translated into fortunes for Russian gangsters whose sophisticated white-collar crimes routinely confound law enforcement authorities.

The Russian organized crime threat in the United States became increasingly serious about two decades ago where in several American cities a loose-knit assortment of thieves, extortionists, confidence men, and white-collar swindlers were labeled the "Russian mafia." These cunning and clever criminals, who call themselves the *Organizatsiya*, or "organization," are the newest cast of gangsters to gain a foothold in the United States. Most were veteran gangsters in the former Soviet Union where survival in the underworld meant evading the dreaded KGB (state security police) and conducting their illegal activities within the tight confines of a totalitarian system. Police in the Soviet system did not need search warrants, nor were they constrained from beating and torturing suspects. By comparison with police in Russia, American law enforcement is soft and easy to resist.

The emergence of Russian organized crime in the United States can be traced to the Cold War and its aftermath. In the early 1970s the Nixon administration put together a policy of detente, which attempted to reestablish and strengthen East-West relations. The United States pressured the Soviet Union to permit the emigration of Soviet Jews. Between 1975 and 1980, almost 100,000 Soviet Jews immigrated to the United States. Nearly a quarter of a million Russian emigres are now in the United States, the majority of whom have settled in the borough of Brooklyn in New York City in a community known as "Little Odessa." Other Russian immigrant neighborhoods have sprung up in Philadelphia, Los Angeles, Miami, and Chicago—urban areas with ethnically and racially diverse populations.

But among the law-abiding and industrious emigrants, an organized criminal element is present. The Russian mafia is distinct from other ethnic crime groups in that many of its participants did not come out of adolescent street gangs. The Russian criminal class is not a product of economic disadvantage, like earlier immigrants (and some recent groups as well); most of the Russians were already hardened career criminals when they arrived in America. Their reasons for coming to the United States, however, were no different from those of their honest compatriots—they sought economic opportunities.

The experiences that shaped the backgrounds of Russian criminals meant that they did not have to follow the pattern of other ethnic crime groups of confining their criminal enterprises to the ethnic enclave, forming street gangs, and over a generation, preying upon immigrants like themselves. Although their record shows that they had no qualms about victimizing other emigrants, Russian mobsters arrived here ready to operate in the community at large. Their early ventures included credit card swindles, fraudulent bank loans, and large-scale burglary and shoplifting rings.

The first Russian gangsters in Brighton Beach, Brooklyn, formed themselves into bands of confidence men swindling local neighborhood residents. Known as the "Potato Bag Gang," they took advantage of recent arrivals eager to acquire money through gold ruble exchanges only to discover that they had been cheated: instead of a bag of rubles for cash, a sack would be filled with potatoes. Russian hoods became involved in a multitude of rackets, the most ingenious of which was known as the "daisy chain" in fuel oils. The scam was designed to evade taxes by fleecing the government and by taking advantage of honest fuel suppliers. The racket was more evidence that Russian criminals, having negotiated the cruel and complicated Communist bureaucracy, were quite adept at handling American government agencies.

The typical scam set up a series of companies through which the gasoline or diesel fuel moved on paper. It began when a licensed firm purchased a barge or tanker load of fuel and passed it on paper to another company, which assumed ownership, and then to another and still another in the "daisy chain" of companies, involving as many as a dozen false business firms. One of the dummy companies in the chain would be designated as the "burn firm," the one supposedly responsible for the payment of applicable taxes. Documents showing transfer of the fuel from the burn company to another distributor, or to service stations, would show that the tax had been paid. The price of the fuel to the service station would include the amount of the tax. However, since the tax was never paid, the bogus company could sell the fuel to a service retailer several cents cheaper per gallon than a legitimate distributor who had paid the tax. In turn, the retailer was able to sell the fuel cheaper than his competitors and still make a substantial profit. When tax agents sought payment, they would discover that the distributing company was no more than an address and mailbox, a vacant lot or an empty store front that never existed or had conveniently disappeared.

Another version of the scheme involved the purchase of diesel fuel for home heating, which is not taxable, the full would be moved through the maze of paper companies, and somewhere along the line, a phony company would show an invoice or receipt for highway diesel fuel with taxes paid. The retailer would have bought the fuel at a reduced price and paid the tax to the bogus company, which then pocketed the tax money and disappeared. The Russians established networks of fuel buyers in many states, particularly among independent retail operators in New York, New Jersey, Pennsylvania, Texas, California, and Florida.

Among the first Mafia figures to see the potential in the fuel tax scams was a Colombo crime family* underboss (sottocapo)* who formed a partnership with several Russian mobsters. Estimates as to the money that had been made ranged from $60 to $100 million a month in stolen taxes alone, not considering legitimate profits from a market they could dominate by offering discounts of $.05 to $.10 a gallon.

Through the early 1990s, the Russian mafia in the United States had about 2,000 members who operated in small criminal bands (Figures 7 and 8). Because their structure and membership frequently changed, law enforcement authorities found it difficult to identify the membership and its leaders. But by 1991, when the Soviet empire collapsed, it set off a wave of crime in Russia that would have serious repercussions for America. Gangsters and former Communist officials strangled many private enterprises struggling to emerge in Russia's new market economy. Their power and influence in the capitalistic, entrepreneurial Russia may be compared to the criminal syndicates in the United States during the Prohibition era. Indeed, this comparison may be too modest: Russia's criminal syndicates may exceed in influence and power that of the Charles "Lucky" Luciano*/Meyer Lansky* or Alphonse Capone*/Johnny Torrio* criminal mobs.

Russian law enforcement after Perestroitka (the opening up of Russia to non-Communist economics and social organization) failed to erect the safeguards that the United States and now even Italy employs to prevent crime and control it. The banks, securities firms, and other financial institutions in the liberated economic sectors are unregulated, with the consequence that gangs openly extort

**Figure 7**
**Reported Russian Emigre Criminal Activities, 1991–1995**

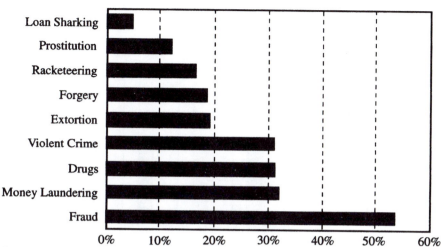

*Source:* An Analysis of Russian Emigre Crime in the Tri-State Region, June 1996. New York State Organized Crime Task Force and New Jersey State Commission of Investigation. Trenton, New Jersey.

money from new business firms and industries that have sprung up around the country.

Some of the gangs are led by professional criminals, *vory v zakone*, or "thieves-in-law," who made up the elite groups of criminals in the former Soviet Union. They were the obvious group to assume prominent positions in the new Russian underworld ready to prey on the developing economy. But they did not go unchallenged. Some of the toughest organized criminals in Russian are ethnic groups that have roots in other former Soviet republics such as Georgia, Chechnya, Ukraine, and Azerbaijan.

With relatively open borders, Russian crime groups have emigrated into western Europe, Israel, and the United States. But even earlier, during the late 1970s, the Soviet government released criminals from its prisons and commingled them with emigres leaving the USSR. Also, members of Soviet organized crime groups smuggled themselves out of the country, concealed themselves in Israel or various European cities, and later emigrated to the United States. International underground smuggling networks exist that were, and still are, accessible to these criminals.

The exact number and size of these groups is unknown. There are estimates that puts the membership between 400 to 500 in about a dozen groups in New York alone. They appear to be without the codes of secrecy and conduct or the hierarchical crime family structures of La Cosa Nostra.* Members range from street corner thugs to educated professionals. The criminal activities attributed

**Figure 8**
**Russian Emigre Crime Statistics, New York State**

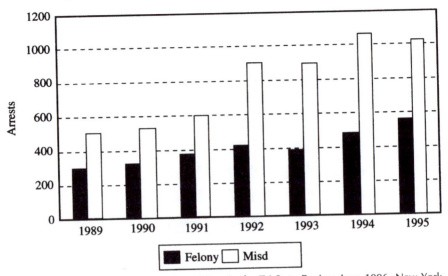

*Source:* An Analysis of Russian Emigre Crime in the Tri-State Region, June 1996. New York
State Organized Crime Task Force and New Jersey State Commission of Investigation.
Trenton, New Jersey.

to these groups include extortion, forgery, confidence schemes, racketeering,*
loansharking,* insurance and medical fraud, murder, arson, gun running, burglary, and drug trafficking.

Much still remains to be learned about Russian involvement in organized
crime in the United States. However, there is evidence that some of the conditions that favored Soviet Georgian criminal activity in Israel in the 1970s may
also be present in the United States. All of the emigrants from former Soviet
republics came from a society where corruption and hypocrisy were practically
normal activities in everyday life. Apart from that, not much is known about
the continuity of their various criminal networks nor about their internal structures. Are they hierarchical like Mafia crime families? How many members
belong to different crime networks? Is membership restricted to ethnic Russians?
There are many questions. *See also* AGRON, EVSEI; IVANKOV, VYACHES-
LAV

**SUGGESTED READINGS:** James Finckenauer and Dennis J. Kenny, *Organized Crime
in America.* 1995; Phil Williams, *Russian Organized Crime.* 1997.

# S

**SALERNO, ANTHONY.** ("Fat Tony") (b. 1911, East Harlem, NY—d. July 29, 1992, Springfield, MO, Federal Prison). Boss (don)* of the Genovese crime family.*

Anthony Salerno headed an underworld conglomerate with enterprises on both sides of what was for him a blurry line separating illegal from legal businesses. Known as "Fat Tony" ("Too fat to flee" was the chiding of his gangster cronies), his power did not stem solely from his position as head of the 300 or more members of the Genovese crime family. Even before he became boss in 1980, Salerno made more money than most Mafia* chieftains, mainly by skimming cash from casinos in Nevada and the Caribbean. "Skimming" is taking cash off the top of gambling proceeds before they are reported as taxable revenues. Law-abiding casinos take pains to prevent skimming; in mob-controlled casinos the practice is encouraged and widespread. The easiest way to skim is to simply walk into a casino counting room and take the money. In an indictment before his 1986 conviction of operating the Commission* of La Cosa Nostra,* Salerno and his cohorts were charged with managing a number of illegal gambling* joints for betting on numbers* and sports. In addition, Salerno and his criminal associates were charged with "extortionate extensions and collections of credit"—that is how the Department of Justice defines loansharking.* Salerno was accused of using threats and violence to force victims to pay illegal interest on their loans.

Salerno also had thriving business interests in the construction industry of New York City. In the Commission case in 1986 and in other racketeering indictments in 1981 and 1985, it was alleged that Salerno and his Mafia partners charged a 2 percent "Mafia tax" on New York City contractors pouring concrete for all superstructures costing more than $2 million. Salerno and the other New York godfathers ran a crime cartel that decided in advance which construction company would submit the winning bid on a project. To ensure that the favored firm would acquire the contract, the Mafia forced other firms to put in building bids that were unacceptably high. The 2 percent tax alone produced $3.5 million in profits for the Mafia on the 72 construction jobs that were investigated by the government, and that is a mere fraction of the buildings that have been erected in the real estate boom in the city for which the mob supplied the concrete.

Salerno, according to documents submitted to the President's Commission on Organized Crime, was a hidden partner in a covey of companies that bid on construction work worth more than $71 million. Any contractor who had the nerve to bid against the mob cartel faced a cutoff of supplies, union slowdown and strikes, and possibly death. Salerno had sway over Teamsters Local 28 whose members drive concrete delivery trucks and did create serious labor problems for uncooperative builders. He also helped to "select" Roy Williams to lead the International Brotherhood of Teamsters* in 1981. Along with Anthony Provenzano,* a capo* in the Genovese crime family and president of Teamster Local 560 in Union City, New Jersey, Salerno was believed to have been involved in the conspiracy to abduct and murder Jimmy Hoffa,* who wished to resume his presidency of the Teamsters but without mob influence.

Unlike younger Mafia leaders like John Gotti,* Fat Tony typified the old-fashioned gangster style—the cigar-chomping, gruff, tough guy who dressed in shabby clothes and frowned on flamboyance that might attract attention. Born in East Harlem, Salerno established his base there and never strayed far from the community, maintaining his headquarters at the Palma Boys Social Club on Pleasant Avenue.

In 1959 he was known as a gambler and policy operator and involved in professional boxing. Despite his gangster reputation, his first criminal conviction did not occur until 1978 when he pleaded guilty to federal tax evasion charges, for which he was sentenced to six months in prison.

During the 1980s, following the conviction of Frank Tieri,* Salerno became boss and broadened the crime family's involvement in a number of diverse rackets. In 1986, after a dramatic trial involving four of the five New York godfathers, Salerno was sentenced to 100 years for operating the Mafia's highest tribunal—the Commission. In yet a final trial in 1988, Salerno was convicted of participating in a criminal conspiracy that allocated construction contracts and obtained payoffs for construction jobs. On these charges, he was sentenced to 70 years.

Considered a major crime figure in the Cosa Nostra, not all officials and experts agree that Salerno was the sole boss of the Genovese crime family after Tieri. Some argue that "Fat Tony" was merely a figurehead and the real bosses were Philip ("Cockeyed Phil") Lombardo and Vincent "The Chin" Gigante.* Even if that were so, Salerno played a prominent role in Cosa Nostra rackets and in internal crime family affairs for nearly a decade.

**SUGGESTED READING:** Jules Bonavolanta and Brian Duffy, *The Good Guys: How We Turned the FBI Around and Finally Broke the Mob.* 1996.

**SANTACRUZ-LONDONO, JOSÉ.** ("Chepe") (b. 1942, Cali, Colombia—d. Mar. 5, 1996, Medellín, Colombia). Principal leader of the Cali cocaine cartel.*

José Santacruz-Londono was considered the number-three leader in the Cali drug mafia. He was characterized as a low-key, nonpresumptuous man who commanded respect from subordinates. However, he was also one of the more violent Cali kingpins. Although his talent rested in managing international cocaine transportation networks, his organization was also involved in drug production, wholesale distribution, and money laundering.* He also played a key role in the Cali cartel's intelligence collection efforts.

His major U.S. wholesale cocaine distribution and money laundering operations centered around the New York City metropolitan area. He is believed to have ordered the 1992 slaying of journalist Manuel de Dios, an investigative journalist whose articles on drug trafficking for a Spanish-language newspaper in New York angered the cartel. In addition, the Santacruz-Londono organization was linked to cocaine conversion production operations in the U.S. Northeast. In June 1992 the DEA seized two cocaine conversion laboratories in Brooklyn, New York, that were connected to Santacruz-Londono. DEA investigations also tied Londono to drug money laundering operations in various cities in Europe and the Americas.

Santacruz-Londono was arrested on July 4, 1995. Although he escaped on January 11, 1996, helped by corrupt prison officials, he was killed in a confrontation with the Colombian National Police (CNP) on March 5, 1996, in the outskirts of Medellín, which is 210 miles north of Cali. Medellín is the home of the rival cocaine cartel headed by Jorge Luis Vasquez Ochoa* and Pablo Emilio Gavoroa Escobar,* which fought a terrorist war against Cali and the state of Colombia for years. General José Serrano, the national police chief, said that the police were able to take advantage of the hostility in Medellín toward the Cali cartel to get good information on Santacruz's trial. He added that he believed Santacruz would never allow himself to be captured alive because he was bored in prison.

The Cali mafia is responsible for 80 percent of the world's cocaine supply and has an estimated annual income of $7 billion (eight times larger than the DEA budget). Financial records indicate Santacruz-Londono's net worth at several billion dollars.

Records also indicate two known arrests for Santacruz-Londono. The first occurred in 1976 when he traveled from New York to Costa Rica on a U.S. passport. The second took place in 1977 when he was arrested in Queens, New York, by the New York City Police on weapons charges. He served no jail time. Santacruz-Londono had been a DEA fugitive since April 1980 and was indicted four times in the United States, most recently in the Cali lawyer case (Operation Cornerstone) in Miami.

Santacruz-Londono was one of the premier drug traffickers in the world involved in large-scale cocaine trafficking for almost two decades.

**SUGGESTED READING:** Rensselaer W. Lee, *The White Labyrinth: Cocaine and Political Power.* 1990.

**SCARFO, NICKY.** ("Little Nicky") (b. Nicodemo Scarfo, Mar. 8, 1929, Atlantic City, NJ—incarcerated). Philadelphia/Atlantic City Cosa Nostra family boss.

"Bruno was a racketeer; I'm a gangster." (Pennsylvania Crime Commission Report 1990), Scarfo, like John Gotti* years later, saw himself in the image of Alphonse Capone*—a man of violent action patterned after the hoodlums of the 1920s and 1930s.

The murder of Angelo Bruno* in 1980 triggered a war of succession in the Philadelphia crime family that brought about a drastic change in its operating style. The family was frazzled by constant violence, murder, warfare, and reprisals in the wake of Bruno's death as the struggle for power and control raged in the streets of Philadelphia and Atlantic City, New Jersey.* Atlantic City was the home and territory of Little Nicky, a short (five-feet-five inches), hot-tempered hoodlum who was exiled there by Angelo Bruno before its revival with casino gambling. Back in 1963, Scarfo stabbed to death a longshoreman in a minor dispute in a restaurant over a seat. However, within ten years, Atlantic City was no longer a stagnant, depressed area, and Scarfo's power would expand accordingly.

With Bruno's murder, Scarfo became consigliere*—the third top slot in the family. A housecleaning within the family brought new members into the organization loyal to Philip ("Chicken Man") Testa, the new boss, and Nicky Scarfo; but Testa did not live long. A year later, in 1981, a bomb planted on the porch of his home blew Testa to bits. Scarfo succeeded him as boss and reorganized the crime family.

The idea was to redefine the relationship of the family to the wider underworld in the Philadelphia region. Like Paul Castellano,* the head of the Gambino crime family* who was assassinated in 1985 because he favored the legitimate business side La Cosa Nostra* over the vice activities of the street soldiers,* Angelo Bruno, too, was a benign leader less inclined to violence and criminal expansion. Further, the Philadelphia mob, in comparison to the powerhouse Mafia* families in New York City, was insular and weak in asserting its territorial rights over the Atlantic City money pot. The New York families were seeking influence in the casinos and did not concern themselves with Philadelphia.

In 1982, in the midst of an internal power struggle that cost more than 19 lives, Scarfo initiated shakedowns (extortion payments) of bookmakers, loansharks, drug dealers, thieves, and others for "protection" from the family. Those

Arthur "Dutch Schultz" Flegenheimer. Reproduced from the Collections of the Library of Congress.

who resisted, including made members of the family, who operated illicit businesses as independent criminal entrepreneurs, were targets for murder.

Scarfo also reached out to the New York families to develop mutually profitable criminal enterprises. Still, his flamboyant style and eagerness to freely use
violence against real or imagined enemies created turmoil in the family. By the
end of the 1980s, Scarfo himself was in prison—the first LCN boss to be convicted of first-degree murder. The fear he created among his own people induced
at least six former associates to turn state's evidence and enter into the Witness
Security Program.*

**SUGGESTED READING:** George Anastasia, *Blood and Honor: Inside the Scarfo Mob—
The Story of the Most Violent Mafia Family.* 1991.

**SCHULTZ, DUTCH.** (Charles Harman, "The Dutchman") (b. Arthur Flegenheimer, Aug. 1901, New York City—d. Oct. 24, 1935, Newark, NY). Organized
crime syndicate boss in New York City.

Part businessman, part brute, Schultz killed rivals, made millions, lived sen-
sationally, and died the same way in a hail of gunfire. Dutch Schultz was a
charismatic boss (don)* who could be quite charming but also capable of sheer
viciousness. It would be easy to consider him psychopathic.

Bored with school, he dropped out in the sixth grade. In Schultz's early teens, he joined a Bronx street gang and, at age 18, in November 1919 was arrested for burglary. The nickname "Dutch Schultz" was adopted to substitute for his real name, Arthur Flegenheimer, which would not fit into the headlines, as he vainly explained to news reporters.

In the 1920s, Schultz served, as had many other New York criminals who would become infamous, as a protégé of Arnold "The Brain" Rothstein.* During Prohibition (*see* PROHIBITION AND ORGANIZED CRIME*), the Dutchman (who was Jewish) became a bootlegger* and organized his own gang, which took over the illegal beer trade in the Bronx section of New York City. Schultz was soon known as the "Beer Baron" of the Bronx.

Despite his reputation for impulsive violence, Schultz was intelligent and a shrewd businessman who rivaled Charles "Lucky" Luciano* and even Meyer Lansky* with his keen sense for lucrative criminal opportunities. It was Schultz who first saw the enormous profits in the Harlem numbers* rackets. Though pennies, nickels, and dimes were bet on the outcome of the parimutuel results of specific racetracks, certain criminal entrepreneurs in Harlem's African American community were able to generate even more action by ensuring the honesty of the illegal game by using the last four digits of New York Stock Exchange results, which could not be fixed. As a result, thousands of dollars were bet daily on the numbers. Schultz sensed just how profitable the racket was and moved aggressively against Harlem's operators, using his influence with the corrupt political machine and the police to close down black-owned numbers banks. Thereafter, no one could operate without his protection.

Schultz's ego and self-absorption would not permit him to form cordial relationships with his underworld colleagues. Even his close associates were loyal only because of the money they could earn with him.

In 1931, Schultz and a former member of his gang, Vincent "Mad Dog" Coll,* went to war for control of liquor distribution. The ensuing street fighting left a five-year-old child dead in the streets. Coll was eventually trapped in a telephone booth and riddled with gunfire by Schultz's henchmen. These appalling events would lead to the Dutchman's fall from power.

The liquor rackets dried up with Repeal in 1933 with the passage of the twenty-first Amendment, but Schultz, ever the astute businessman, seems to have anticipated the end of Prohibition and formed in 1932 an association of restaurant owners. This extortion racket depended in large part on Schultz's reputation for violence and mayhem, so many restauranteurs sheepishly paid the $25,000 yearly to ensure labor peace and prevent acts of vandalism against their premises and patrons.

By 1933, New York rackets buster Thomas E. Dewey* promised to clean up New York and get the big-time gangsters, including Dutch Schultz. However, Schultz was indicted for tax evasion by the federal government on a reputed income from legal and illegal sources of $2 million per year. The Dutchman went on the lam, and while he awaited trial, Lucky Luciano, Meyer Lansky, and Abner Zwillman* considered taking over his beer, policy, and extortion rackets. Schultz attempted to negotiate a settlement for $100,000 with the government, but it turned down his offer. He went on trial in Syracuse, New York; the jury was deadlocked, and he was freed. The case was retried in Malone, New York, a small rural town in upstate New York. With great cunning and skill, Schultz confidently cultivated the victim image among local community residents. It worked; prospective jurors had been won over by Schultz's charm and charity. He delivered toys to sick children under the prosecutor's eyes and got away with it. This only proved that the Dutchman was a consummate salesman who sold beer and protection and also dreams to the hopeful.

In 1935 Schultz's celebrity and notoriety were challenged by opposing forces: Thomas E. Dewey, in his war on vice and racketeering,* turned his energies on Schultz and Luciano, an old rival, who wanted control of the Dutchman's protection and gambling interests. Predictably, Schultz wanted Dewey killed by the syndicate* because his operations, revenues, and freedom were threatened by the prosecutor. Indeed, he demanded that Dewey be assassinated before a stunned and shocked syndicate that realized it had no choice but to kill Schultz whose rage against Dewey seemed out of control. On October 23, 1935, Schultz and two of his top enforcers were meeting at the Palace Chop House and Tavern in Newark, New Jersey, when two gunmen entered, murdering Abbadabba Berman, Lulu Rosenkrantz, and Abe Landau—Schultz's associates—and shooting Schultz himself, who had been in the men's room when the shooting began. Fatally wounded, Schultz lingered more than 22 hours; in his delirium, he mumbled incoherently about his hidden money; he called for a priest, was baptized a Catholic, and died. During his last hours, Stephanie St. Clair,* a black numbers operator in Harlem whom Schultz had mercilessly intimidated, sent him a prophetic little note: "Ye shall reap what ye sow."

Schultz was just 34 years old when he was killed.

**SUGGESTED READING:** Paul Sann, *Kill the Dutchman!: The Story of Dutch Schultz.* 1971.

**SCOTTO, ANTHONY.** (b. 1934, Brooklyn, NY—   ). Gambino crime family* capo* and International Longshoremen's Association leader.

In 1963, with Carlo Gambino's* blessings, Anthony Scotto took over Local 1814 and was elected vice president of the ILA, a 16,000-member waterfront union in the Red Hook section of Brooklyn. Unlike his tough father-in-law Anthony Anastasio,* Scotto was a college graduate known for his charm and intelligence. He was also a caporegime in the Gambino crime family.

Scotto began to ingratiate himself with some of the nation's leading politicians; his high-level contacts extended to Vice President Lyndon Johnson and John V. Lindsay, mayor of New York City and a possible Republican candidate for the presidency. But in 1979 Scotto was arrested in connection with a federal probe of labor racketeering* along the Brooklyn waterfront.

Scotto managed to arrange a star-studded list of character witnesses including former governor of New York State, Hugh C. Carey, who referred to Scotto as energetic, trustworthy, and effective as a union leader. Two former mayors of New York City, Robert F. Wagner and John V. Lindsay, also testified on his behalf. Still, Scotto was convicted of manipulating ILA pension funds and welfare plans; of taking payoffs from maritime firms to guarantee "labor peace"; of accepting bribes from businessmen to secure union contracts; of awarding union business without competitive bidding to firms owned by his relatives; and of charges of featherbedding and loansharking* among ILA members.

He could have served twenty years but was let off lightly with a five-year prison term and a $75,000 fine.

**SUGGESTED READING:** President's Commission on Organized Crime, *The Edge: Organized Crime Business and Labor Unions.* 1986.

**SEABURY INVESTIGATIONS.** (1930–1932). Over a two-year period, Judge Samuel Seabury, a scion of a prominent New York City family and a crusading crime investigator, uncovered rampant municipal corruption intertwined with organized crime. Seabury's work led to the sensational resignation of Mayor Jimmy Walker. In 1933, Seabury put together the reform-minded Fusion Party, which selected Fiorello La Guardia* as its candidate for mayor. Aided by a split in Democratic ranks over Tammany Hall corruption, La Guardia swept into office and launched a vigorous effort against organized crime.

The Seabury investigations developed in 1931 in response to public concern over massive corruption. The state legislature in New York created an investigative committee to examine the relationships between politicians, police, and gangsters. During two years of hearings, solid evidence emerged of incompetence and crime in the magistrates courts. Evidence amassed by the investigation caused some magistrates to resign; inquiries into racketeering* activities in the Fulton Fish Market*—a huge seafood exchange and wholesale marketplace—revealed that criminals extracted regular protection payments from vendors, workers, fishermen, seafood processing firms, and shippers over a long period of time.

Seabury's meticulous work formed the basis for subsequent prosecutions of major underworld figures and their political cronies, including Charles "Lucky" Luciano* and Frank Costello* and their links to Judge Albert Marinelli; the relationships between Tammany Hall's political operative Jimmy Hines* and Dutch Schultz*; and Prohibition (*see* PROHIBITION AND ORGANIZED CRIME*) racketeers Owney Madden* and "Waxey" Gordon* partnerships with other gangsters.

Most important, Seabury set the stage for reform and the great era of New York City municipal government headed by the "Little Flower," Fiorello La Guardia.

**SELECTED READING:** Alan Block, *East Side–West Side: Organized Crime in New York City, 1930–1950.* 1983.

**SHAPIRO, JACOB "GURRAH."** (b. 1899, Odessa, Russia—d. 1947, Sing Sing Prison, NY). Labor racketeer, extortionist.

Among the most significant criminals to work in the garment industry were Louis Buchalter* and his partner Jacob "Gurrah" Shapiro. The two had virtual control of the Manhattan clothing industry from the late 1920s until 1940. As the enforcer for Lepke Buchalter, Shapiro was one of the most feared mobsters of his day. The nickname "Gurrah" derives from Shapiro's slurring of his pet phrase, "Get out of here." When he uttered this standard command of his in his gruff and growling voice, it sounded like "Gurra dahere"—hence the nickname.

Shapiro began his criminal career in the slums of New York's Lower East Side in 1914, stealing from pushcarts in the teeming streets where he eventually met Lepke and Meyer Lansky* and became a member of "Little Augie" Orgen's* gang, which provided muscle to employers as labor union strikebreakers. By 1927, after Little Augie was gunned down in the streets, Shapiro and Lepke organized truckers in the clothing industry. They later moved into the bakery unions, using their standard tactics of murder, bombings, arson, and hijacking.

Not all businesses and unions were easily intimidated by Gurrah's threats and his violent thugs: A determined and disciplined labor local of the Fur Dressers union in 1933 resisted with fists and union solidarity against the gangsters. It worked. Apparently, progressive labor unions with militant leaders and fearless rank and file could prevent penetration by organized crime.

Gurrah Shapiro achieved real power in the underworld in the 1930s when his partner Lepke joined the New York syndicate,* the "Combination," and directed, along with Albert Anastasia,* a band of murderers known as Murder, Inc.* Estimates vary, but the generally held view is that Lepke and Gurrah commanded about 250 men including experts in accounting, influence peddling, trade unions, and specialists in murder and mayhem.

Shapiro's violent streak was evident in 1935 when Dutch Schultz* wanted to kill Thomas E. Dewey,* who had targeted the Dutchman and his criminal enterprises for prosecution. Shapiro and Anastasia favored the idea of a murder contract on Dewey. Subsequently, after Schultz's murder, Dewey turned his sights on Charles "Lucky" Luciano,* Lepke, and Shapiro. It must have been cold comfort for Gurrah to remind his criminal partners that he was right about Dewey.

By 1936, Luciano became the focus of Dewey's attention and was convicted on prostitution charges; that same year the pursuit of Lepke and Shapiro began in earnest. Shapiro and Lepke went into hiding, but Gurrah, a sick man, could not hold out, and in April 1938, he surrendered unconditionally to authorities. "I got a bad reputation from the newspapers," he said as he was led off to jail.

In 1943, Gurrah was tried yet again on labor racketeering charges in the men's

Benjamin "Bugsy" Seigel. Reproduced from the
Collections of the Library of Congress.

clothing industry. The testimony against him laid out the whole mammoth system of protection, gangster locals, and sweetheart agreements that tainted entire segments of the New York economy. Shapiro died in prison in 1947.

**SUGGESTED READING:** Albert Fried, *The Rise and Fall of the Jewish Gangster in America.* 1980.

**SIEGEL, "BUGSY."** (b. Benjamin Hyman Siegel, Feb. 28, 1906, New York City—d. June 20, 1947, Los Angeles, CA). Associate of Meyer Lansky* and a key figure in the development of casinos in Las Vegas, Nevada.*

Best remembered, if inaccurately, for his role in developing Las Vegas, Nevada, as a major gambling* and casino resort area, Bugsy Siegel was a career criminal who emerged from the poverty and squalor of Jewish ghettos on the Lower East Side of New York City and Brooklyn. Early on, before he was 16 years old, Siegel was engaged in illegal gambling* and street vendor extortion, and it was in the teeming tenements of the city that he met Meyer Lansky.

Benjamin Siegel was a partner and friend of Meyer Lansky, the criminal wizard who managed to put crime on a business basis that remains with us today. Siegel and Lansky formed the Bug and Meyer Mob, a gang of young Jewish hoodlums who operated on New York's Lower East Side. Eventually, as the gang graduated from petty larcenies into more daring and violent crimes, Lansky, with Siegel as his elbow, joined forces with Charles "Lucky" Luciano* and Frank Costello.*

The Bug and Meyer Mob, as it was known, handled problems for bootleg gangs that Prohibition (*see* PROHIBITION AND ORGANIZED CRIME*) produced. It was Prohibition that gave them, as it gave many others, enormous opportunities. Arnold "The Brain" Rothstein,* the Henry Ford of the rackets, showed them the way. Lansky, Siegel, Costello, and Luciano worked closely together, supplying good whiskey to the speakeasies. Compared to the other three who were restrained and cautious, Siegel was explosive, capricious, and whimsical. He provided the protection services for the illegal liquor shipments and engaged in hijacking competitors' trucks.

Rothstein recruited Siegel and Lansky into bootlegging, but in spite of his violent inclinations, Siegel was compelled to become something of a businessman. The relationship Lansky and Siegel enjoyed was mutually rewarding and durable, and while Lansky was the brains of their operation and Siegel the muscle, Bugsy was no flunky; they were genuine partners.

As with other gangsters, Siegel lived a schizophrenic life: One world, the underworld, consisted of murder, mayhem, vice, and corruption; the other consisted of a wife, children, and a home in a decent neighborhood.

During the 1920s, Siegel was affiliated with Italian bootleggers, gamblers, and racketeers such as Luciano, Costello, Joseph Adonis,* Gaetano Luchese,* and Albert Anastasia*—all of whom would occupy major positions in La Cosa Nostra.* In the Castellammarese War*—an internal struggle among Italians for control of the Mafia* in the United States—Siegel participated in the assassination of "Joe the Boss" Masseria,* a key Sicilian leader opposed to another faction led by the mafioso Salvatore Maranzano.* Masseria's execution ended the war and propelled Siegel's friends and partners into the leadership of major national crime syndicates.

Bugsy Siegel was known among other criminals as a "cowboy," meaning that he was quick to resort to violence when problems arose. Siegel became a major player in Murder, Inc.*—a contract murder unit within the New York underworld.

In the 1930s Siegel left for Los Angeles to set up syndicate gambling enterprises. Sleek and pugnacious, Bugsy hobnobbed with Hollywood's elite. During the war years, he thought that Las Vegas, a dusty rail stop for troops on their way to the West Coast, might be turned into a gambler's paradise. In Nevada, gambling was legal, and Bugsy figured that Vegas could compete with, and surpass, Reno if it had mob help. His enthusiasm for a gambling equivalent of Disneyland, more lavish and more Hollywood than that cowtown Reno, attracted the mob's interest. Given Siegel's closeness with Lansky, underworld support and cash cows were found but ultimately double-crossed.

By 1935 Siegel was clearly aware that law enforcement officials in New York were determined to crush the syndicate by taking down its leaders—most notably, Charles "Lucky" Luciano. All the more reason to stay in California and out of harm's way in the person of Special Prosecutor Thomas E. Dewey* whose reputation as a rackets buster was attracting national attention. Siegel was sent to California to supervise syndicate gambling and union racketeering in the expanding film industry. With the backing of Lansky and Luciano, the local West Coast Mafia had little choice but to cooperate. Within a short period of time, Siegel took control of many narcotics and gambling enterprises by skillfully bribing police and local politicians.

Siegel proved to be not only an efficient hoodlum but also a social charmer. With George Raft (a New York actor), a suave Bugsy entertained and socialized with Hollywood stars including Clark Gable, Cary Grant, Jean Harlow, and Gary Cooper, who introduced him to the movie business and the unions representing studio workers.

The Hollywood experience, the romances with movie starlets, and various film industry people led to a bizarre episode where Siegel traveled to Italy with one of his mistresses to peddle a weapons component to Italian Fascist dictator Benito Mussolini. Staying with an Italian countess, Siegel met top Nazis such as Hermann Goering and Joseph Goebbels, whom he disliked because of their anti-Semitic politics. It was rumored that he planned their assassination but relented when his hostess pleaded with him that the plot would fail and they would be murdered.

In a film about Siegel, entitled *Bugsy*, the myth is perpetuated that Siegel "invented" Las Vegas, that he was the visionary. In fact, Las Vegas had gambling casinos and spas long before Siegel's Flamingo Hotel. By war's end in 1946, Miami and Havana were fairly well established mob territories with casinos in full swing. And on the West Coast, several Hollywood big shots were interested in casinos and hotels. The Flamingo itself was the brainchild of Billy Wilkerson, an entrepreneur with nightclubs and casinos in California and Nevada. Was the construction of the Flamingo a business project or a Taj Mahal for Virginia Hill*? Probably both. Virginia Hill became Siegel's mistress shortly after he arrived from New York. She was well known in the underworlds of Chicago, New York, and the Midwest as a high-class prostitute, money courier, and companion of several powerful gangsters. Bugsy was swept off his feet by Hill whose garish tastes he saw as high style. Bugsy gave her a free hand and unlimited bank roll to decorate and equip his "carpet joint," or, as it turned out, his heartbreak hotel. Hill was a thief as well as an accomplished prostitute, as she told the stunned Kefauver Committee* (behind closed doors, mercifully) in 1951. Siegel was smitten by Hill, who embezzled his and the mob's money. But Siegel may have been part of the ripoff. That doubt in the minds of his mob sponsors as to his complicity may have decided his fate.

The idea of Las Vegas as a gambling mecca was not something that struck Bugsy the moment he visited what was in the early 1940s a train stop for troops on their way to Pacific embarkation ports. In 1941, Siegel and associate Moe Sedway went to Las Vegas to escape from the bad publicity in Los Angeles.

At first it appeared that Siegel thought the idea of Las Vegas as a site for a gambling casino and hotel preposterous. However, along with Lansky's prodding and encouragement the challenge appealed to him, and he talked his syndicate associates into funding the project to the amount of $6 million. When the Flamingo finally opened, it was a financial disaster, and Lansky and Luciano demanded an accounting of their investment and profits. In early 1947, Siegel was in trouble. There were rumors that Siegel and Hill were stealing. It was possible that they conspired to skim money from construction funds and deposit them in secret Swiss bank accounts. Lansky's observation that Benny's "a dreamer" may have been an indirect attempt to save him; Siegel himself may have felt secure when by May 1947 the casino was showing a profit. But nobody—not even old and trusted friends—steals from the mob and gets away with it. Having failed to make good as a casino operator and impresario and, what is worse, having embarrassed and betrayed friends and associates, Bugsy's execution was ordered.

On June 20, 1947, Siegel returned to Los Angeles. While sitting in the living room of Hill's $500,000 Beverly Hills mansion, reading the newspapers, two shots were fired from a carbine rifle. The frustrated gangster and would-be movie star found himself in his most celebrated portrait, splayed across Miss Hill's couch, his handsome profile destroyed by gunfire. His murder was never solved. The killing done gangland style was almost certainly carried out on orders of Luciano and Lansky, who had financed and endorsed Siegel's operation. Both, naturally denied any responsibility.

Ironically, Bugsy's dream materialized but without Bugsy. For decades, Las Vegas was a mob money pot paying out millions in skimmed money to underworld gangs with hidden investments in the casinos or because of their control of some portion of the gambling through trade unions, primarily through Teamster pension funds borrowed illegally and then poured into Las Vegas.

**SUGGESTED READINGS:** Dean Jennings, *We Only Kill Each Other*. 1973; Robert Lacey, *Big Man*. 1993.

**SINDONA, MICHELE.** ("God's Banker") (b. May 8, 1920, Patti, Sicily—d. Mar. 22, 1986, Voghera, Italy). Major Mafia* bank swindler and money launderer.

In the days when the Sicilian Mafia was just beginning to make big drug money, especially in America, they could leave it in the hands of a single crooked banker. During the 1970s, Sicily's old guard bosses chose Don Michele Sindona, financial adviser to the Vatican and the most renowned international banker–crook of our time. Sindona's activities ruined thousands of depositors and investors before his life ended.

Sindona engineered the crash of the prominent Franklin National Bank in New York in October 1974, which was the biggest fraud on record in the United States, entailing a loss of $1.7 billion. But when Sindona tried to take the Mafia's money, they took his life.

By the late 1970s, Sicilian traffickers were clearing about $1 billion yearly in America, largely consigned to Sindona for laundering and investment. Unfortunately, he lost it on his way to jail in 1979, the year he went bankrupt. In March 1979, a U.S. Justice Department indictment cited him on 99 counts of fraud, perjury, and misappropriation of bank funds. He faced 25 years of imprisonment in the United States and as much again in Italy, if and when the courts there could lay hands on him.

While awaiting trial proceedings in August 1979, Sindona walked out of the Hotel Pierre in Manhattan in an odd chicken-skin disguise and vanished. He was smuggled to Palermo by Gambino crime family* members associated with Sicilian groups. Sindona was the Mafia's prisoner. After a month in captivity, he furnished his captors with compromising documents on the Vatican Bank and some 500 leading figures in Italy's political and financial world who were susceptible to Mafia blackmail. Sindona betrayed his former clients and was released. Shipped back to New York, he was sentenced to 25 years and then received a life sentence in Italy, where he died of strychnine poisoning in his cell the day after his trial.

**SUGGESTED READING:** Luigi DiFonzo, *St. Peter's Banker: Michele Sindona.* 1983.

**"SIT-DOWN."** A meeting between two or more La Cosa Nostra* members who attempt to settle a dispute over territory rights, proceeds from a criminal enterprise, or some personal matter.

Usually a dispute to be resolved is handled by individuals with some authority in a criminal organization—a capo,* for instance, who, if and when a conflict is peacefully and profitably resolved, may expect a lucrative piece of the action or a tribute from the aggrieved parties. When a boss (don) or authority figure makes a decision at a sit-down, it is final.

The appeal to higher authority for the "organization man" goes far beyond the settlement of arguments: It is used in advance to prevent problems from arising. The intelligent racketeer/gangster clears all proposed actions with higher authority, even when he knows there is little or no danger of conflict. Thus, the criminal checks with his boss and seeks his advice before launching a new project. Again, he might also think it wise to cut the boss in on a piece of the business. By doing this he not only curries favor, but he insures against future problems by offering his superiors economic incentives to prevent them.

In addition, the rule that authority figures are the final arbiters is actually a key to power that a boss has over his underlings. For his own safety and to avoid embarrassment among his peers, the boss must always know everything that is going on in his organization. The members are wise if they keep him informed.

**SUGGESTED READING:** Michael Franzese, *Quitting the Mob.* 1992.

**SOLDIERS.** The lowest-level positions in a La Cosa Nostra* crime family* are the "made men*"—inducted members of the Cosa Nostra who function in crews* that are parts of crime families. Sometimes they are called "wise guys," "buttons," or good fellows"; rarely are the terms "mafia" or "mafioso" used even among themselves. Soldiers live by the code of omerta*—their honor and rules of conduct are prescribed by a set of guidelines that go back to the genesis of mafia in Sicily and the south of Italy.

A soldier might operate an illicit enterprise for his boss (don)* on a share-cropping basis (the boss owns the operation that the soldier manages), or he might own the enterprise (gambling pad, drug business, loansharking* operation) and pay homage to the boss for "protection," the right to operate. All soldiers in good standing are guaranteed a livelihood and need not fear encroachment on their illicit operation by other soldiers. Further, they are guaranteed assistance in overcoming any threatened competition from nonmembers. They are also promised various security benefits such as near immunity from arrest, and when immunity cannot be maintained, they are sure of bail, legal assistance, and some unemployment compensation for their wives and kids in case they receive a prison sentence. To put this another way, bribery and violence are used to protect soldiers and all other Cosa Nostra members from anyone who might want to harm them physically or their businesses, whether the business is legal or illegal. Put still another way, the Cosa Nostra serves as a police force for the criminals and gangsters who can't go to the police when people threaten them or do them injury. In return for these protective services, the soldier serves at the pleasure of his capo* and boss.

Retiring from organized crime is not so simple. Part of the mythology, if not the reality, is that one is admitted by the gun and the knife, and one goes out by the gun or the knife. According to this point of view, there is no retirement plan: One leaves feet first. Nowadays, some members who are inactive and quite old are permitted to retire, as have some bosses such as Frank Costello* and Johnny Torrio.*

Soldiers can and do form business partnerships with other soldiers, capos, and even bosses. It usually occurs in a gambling operation, a dice or card game, a loansharking operation, or some ongoing illicit enterprise.

At one time, to be a soldier one had to have parents who were both Italian. This ethnic specification in recent times has been relaxed because of the difficulties in recruiting members; now at least one parent must be of Italian decent. Also, in the old country, a man could not be a soldier if his father was a member. That rule is not followed in the United States even though it works to the disadvantage of men without blood relatives in the family.

**SUGGESTED READING:** George Anastasia, *Blood and Honor: Inside the Scarfo Mob.* 1991.

**SOTTOCAPO.** *See* UNDERBOSS (SOTTOCAPO)

**SPILOTRO, TONY "THE ANT."** (b. Anthony Spilotro, 1936, Chicago, IL—d. Aug. 30, 1986, Enos, IN). Chicago Outfit* strong-arm and Las Vegas, Nevada,* gangster.

Spilotro, known as "The Ant" because of his small stature and ferocity, began his criminal career on Chicago's South Side as a mob enforcer and jewel thief. In stark comparison to his antisocial attitudes, his family was quite respectable, with an older brother serving honorably as an air force officer and dental surgeon. Like Louis Buchalter* and several others including "Sammy the Bull" Gravano,* "The Ant" chose the streets and a life of crime.

In 1964 he worked in Miami, Florida, gambling* operations with the Chicago Outfit's Frank ("Lefty") Rosenthal, who would later work with Spilotro in 1969 out of the mob-controlled Stardust casino hotel in Las Vegas.

Spilotro was in Las Vegas to protect the enormous racket of casino "skimming" of gambling dollars. Spilotro's ambitions, however, were not limited to baby-sitting casino ripoffs: He brought to Las Vegas a group of Chicago gangsters who proceeded to take over the street action in loansharking,* burglary, jewel theft, and drug trafficking. "The Ant's Hole-in-the-Wall-Gang" terrorized the town and forced the Nevada Gaming Commission to ban Spilotro from casino hotels.

In 1981, several members of his gang were arrested during a burglary. Thinking they had been betrayed, one of the gang agreed to become a witness against "The Ant," whose notoriety prompted the Gaming Commission to place his name in the "Black Book," which banned him from the casinos. With all the notoriety the gang generated, it jeopardized Spilotro's capacity to ensure that the "skim" share of gambling proceeds would reach the Chicago Outfit. The Ant violated another rule of mob etiquette by carrying on an affair with Rosenthal's wife. By 1983, the evidence of murder, drug trafficking, loansharking, and skimming gambling profits led to an indictment against Spilotro and members of the Outfit. In 1986, the Chicago bosses apparently had had enough: Spilotro was called back to Chicago with his brother Michael. They never made it. Both were beaten to death and buried in a shallow grave in Indiana farm country close to a farm owned by Joseph John Aiuppa*—Chicago Outfit boss who got into trouble because of the antics of "The Ant."

**SUGGESTED READINGS:** Nicholas Pileggi, *Casino.* 1995; William F. Roemer, Jr., *The Enforcer Spilotro: The Chicago Mob's Man over Las Vegas.* 1994.


**SQUILLANTE, VINCENT.** ("Jimmie") (    —disappeared Sept. 30, 1960). Racketeer in waste collection industry.

Vincent ("Jimmie") Squillante, a soldier* in the Luciano crime family,* who murdered Albert Anastasia's* underboss (sottocapo)* Frank ("Don Cheech") Scalise in June 1957, developed his criminal career not in the murder business per se as a professional "hit* man" for La Cosa Nostra* but in garbage.

Squillante was connected with the Teamsters local 813 that handled garbage collection among private industry business. Through guile, violence, and mob influence in the Teamsters, Squillante became head of the Greater New York Cartmen's Association.

Squillante also helped to discipline the industry's labor unions in Nassau and Suffolk counties on Long Island, which are suburban areas east of New York City. The garbage industry business banded together under Squillante and rigged bids on jobs, created customer allocation schemes, and settled territories for exclusive exploitation by Association members—all in violation of the law against restraint of trade. Firms that refused to join the garbage cartel were coerced by various means including equipment destruction, union strikes, and competition from Association "whip companies." A whip's mission was simple: Raid the customers of those firms that stepped out of line. In some cases, the whip company would offer to pick up a customer's garbage for practically no cost in order to force uncooperative garbage companies back into line. Squillante brought more than 46 known organized crime figures into the private waste hauling business, according to the investigations of the McClelland Committee.*

In late 1957, Squillante was arrested on charges of extortion. His case dragged on for nearly three years. Perhaps because of the notoriety, he became too great a liability for his criminal partners. On September 30, 1960 he disappeared, never to be seen again.

**SUGGESTED READING:** Peter Reuter, *Racketeering in Legitimate Industries: A Study in the Economics of Intimidation.* 1987.

**STACHER, JOSEPH.** ("Doc") (b. 1902, Poland—d. 1977, Israel). New York underworld figure and associate of Meyer Lansky.*

In 1931, Stacher functioned as the chief organizer of a meeting at the Franconia Hotel that included all the top Jewish gangsters in the New York area. It was decided that the Jewish gangs merge with the Italian Mafia and form a new national syndicate.* The meeting, sometimes referred to as the formation of the "Kosher Nostra" (in satirical contrast to La Cosa Nostra*), occurred around the time of the murder of Salvatore Maranzano* on September 10, 1931, which ended the Castellammarese War* fought among Italian mafiosi in the United States.

The merger included Meyer Lansky and Charles "Lucky" Luciano* and became a powerful model for organized crime in America throughout the twentieth century.

Stacher's specific criminal role was serving as the payoff man and as Lansky's representative in Las Vegas, Nevada.* He also handled corruption and bribes to the Batista regime in Cuba during the heyday of mob casino gambling operations in Havana.

Stacher came to the United States from his native Poland when he was ten years old and settled with his family in Newark, New Jersey, where he eventually became a member of the Meyer Lansky–"Bugsy" Siegel* bootleg mob. He was also affiliated with Abner Zwillman* and illegal gambling* activities in New Jersey.

In the 1960s Stacher faced income tax evasion charges. Rather than face a five-year sentence and/or deportation to his native Poland, he settled with the IRS and emigrated to Israel under the Israeli "Law of Return," which permits any Jew the right to become a citizen of Israel. To ensure against rejection of admittance on grounds of his criminal past—which his friend Meyer Lansky encountered when he sought Israeli citizenship—Stacher asked entertainer Frank Sinatra, a longtime friend, to intercede with Israeli officials. Stacher was allowed to immigrate, as were other Jewish underworld figures of lesser notoriety. He died peacefully in 1977 in Israel.

**SUGGESTED READING:** Howard Bloom, *Gangland: How the FBI Broke the Mob.* 1993.

**ST. CLAIR, STEPHANIE.** ("Madame Queen of Policy"). Harlem policy rackets operator.

Stephanie St. Clair, known as "Madame Queen of Policy," a black French woman from Marseilles, operated one of Harlem's big policy banks in the 1920s, from which she made a quarter of a million dollars a year. She was arrested on December 30, 1929, and served eight months. St. Clair claimed that her arrest and sentence were in retaliation for her whistle-blowing. Outraged by the unscrupulous behavior of the police to whom she paid protection, she placed several paid advertisements in local Harlem newspapers, making serious charges of graft and corruption against the police. Almost immediately, she was arrested on what she termed a "framed charge" and was sent to the workhouse on Welfare Island for eight months. *The New York Age* contained a report that, upon her release from prison in 1930, she appeared before Seabury investigations* (a government probe into corruption in the Manhattan and Bronx Magistrates Courts) and testified that she operated a policy bank from 1923 to 1928 and paid members of the police department $6,000 to protect her workers from arrests. She claimed that they double-crossed her and continued to arrest her workers. A police lieutenant and 13 men were suspended in December 1930 because of her testimony about paying "protection money."

In 1932, St. Clair complained that she was being pressured by the Dutch Schultz* gang to join their numbers* gambling* combination. She went to the mayor and the district attorney to protest that gangsters were trying to take over her policy business. Her outcries were unsuccessful. St. Clair attempted to interest other African American numbers bankers to join her in her fight with Dutch Schultz. They refused because they believed, correctly, that Schultz had the police and the politicians on his side. When Schultz lay dying of bullet wounds in a New Jersey hospital in October 1935, a telegram arrived saying, "As ye sow, so shall ye reap." It was signed "Madame Queen." Stephanie St. Clair is believed to have sent the telegram.

**SUGGESTED READING:** Rufus Schatzberg and Robert J. Kelly, *African-American Organized Crime: A Social History.* 1997.

**STRAUSS, "PITTSBURGH PHIL."** ("Pep," "Big Harry") (b. Harry Strauss, 1908, Brooklyn, NY—d. June 12, 1941, Sing Sing, NY). Contract killer for Murder, Inc.*

Pittsburgh Phil killed more than 30 men in over a dozen towns and cities across America. He traveled to his deadly assignments with a small leather case that held pants, underwear, a shirt, a gun, and a rope—the tools of his depraved trade. "Pep," as he was known to his associates in Brownsville's Murder, Inc., was the most prolific killer among men who earned their living as murderers. The Brooklyn District Attorney's Office, which presented evidence of his participation in 28 homicides, estimated, based on circumstantial evidence, that Strauss was involved in at least 100 murders around the country. Like "Kid Twist" Reles,* and others in the gang, Pittsburgh Phil killed on orders from the "Combination" the New York crime syndicate* headed by Louis Buchalter,* Charles "Lucky" Luciano,* and Albert Anastasia,* among others.

The troop of killers that made up Murder, Inc. were finally brought to justice in 1940 when Kid Twist Reles cooperated with authorities and provided evidence that put key members of the syndicate in prison or in the electric chair. Pittsburgh Phil paid with his life in 1941 when he was executed in Sing Sing Prison in New York State. To the end, he tried to project an image of an insane man hoping for a commuted sentence. During trial proceedings when indictments and overwhelming evidence of his ruthless acts were presented, he refused to shave, cut his hair, or wear presentable clothes. Finally, when he realized the ruse would not work, Strauss cleaned himself up but went to his death raging against Kid Twist Reles.

Pittsburgh Phil, a staff killer for the mob, was able to act out his sick compulsions and psychopathic tendencies in a cold-blooded manner because the criminal world in which he lived made murder a profitable business that rewarded men with his psychotic needs.

**SUGGESTED READING:** Burton Turkus and Sid Feder, *Murder, Inc.: The Story of the Syndicate.* 1974.

## ST. VALENTINE'S DAY MASSACRE. (February 14, 1929). Chicago gangland mass murder.

"Only Capone kills like that." These were the words of George "Bugs" Moran,* a Chicago gangster and arch enemy of Alphonse Capone,* when learning of the brutal murder of seven of his associates in a Chicago garage.

The garage execution of members of the North Side Irish mob was part of a raging war between Capone's forces and the survivors of Charles Dion O'Banion's* North Side gang. The struggle to control gambling,* alcohol, and vice appeared settled by Johnny Torrio,* who was known as "The Brain" much like his counterpart, Arnold "The Brain" Rothstein* in New York City.

Torrio brought Capone to Chicago to assist him in taking over the vice operations of his uncle Big Jim Colosimo. Torrio and Capone eliminated Colosimo because he would not or could not adjust to changing times and opportunities—especially the growing bootlegging industry. However, Torrio wanted cooperation rather than conflict among the numerous competing vice gangs in Chicago and the surrounding areas. So he arranged territories of control for each gang where they could operate without competition from others. Corruption would be streamlined by arranging things at the top—with the mayor's office. Anyone getting out of line would feel the wrath of Capone and his enforcers. More important, he persuaded tough Irish, Italian, and Polish gangsters that such an arrangement, where violence is minimized, would yield millions for all. But the syndicate* could not last because it could not work. War soon raged over bootlegging territories: O'Banion, the head of the North Side Irish gang, doublecrossed Torrio, who then in retaliation had O'Banion murdered in his florist shop.

The new boss of O'Banion's gang Earl "Hymie" Weiss,* ambushed Torrio, who suffered gunshot wounds in the chest, arm, and stomach. This was in 1925. Torrio survived after hovering near death for almost two weeks. He was 43 and a multimillionaire. He announced his retirement to Capone.

By 1929, a series of bosses had been murdered, and only George "Bugs" Moran was capable of leading the gang that Capone's best efforts could not destroy. Capone set up the North Side Moran gang by having a Detroit bootlegger* offer Moran a load of booze allegedly hijacked from Capone's trucks. Moran fell for it and arranged the delivery at the gang's headquarters—a garage on North Clark Street in Chicago.

What occurred on the morning of February 14, St. Valentine's Day, would not only shock Chicago but the entire nation. Several of Capone's mobsters dressed as policemen rushed into the garage. The truck loaded with stolen liquor never arrived. They lined up the seven occupants against the wall and let loose with powerful Thompson submachine guns, "Tommy Guns," as they were known to the public. All were killed, slaughtered mercilessly. The killers got into their car, still dressed as police, and left the scene. No one was ever arrested or indicted for the murder.

Moran and two of his associates were lucky enough to have been late for the meeting. As he rushed to the garage, he spotted three men dressed as police and two others in plain clothes entering the garage. Believing it to be a police shakedown, Moran decided to wait until they left. Minutes later machine gun fire rocked the streets. When he learned what happened, he was quoted as saying, "Only Capone kills like that." It was an observation that would haunt Capone, who was at the time vacationing in Florida on his estate, entertaining local officials and neighbors who would serve as solid alibis for Big Al.

After the massacre, Moran's stature as a gang boss diminished. Eventually he left Chicago and was arrested for various robberies, serving nearly 20 years in federal prisons. He died of cancer in 1957, forgotten.

Although Capone was believed by everyone to have been behind the murders, he was never indicted. About a year after the murders, the weapons were found in the home of a professional killer, Fred Burke, who was known to have done jobs for Capone. Burke was convicted of murdering a policeman in Michigan in 1930 and was sentenced to life imprisonment. With all the speculation ever since the murders, the executioners were never identified. Fred Burke was believed to have taken part and "Machine Gun" Jack McGurn (Vincent DeMora), a Capone enforcer, is alleged to have planned the murder. McGurn would be found murdered a year after the massacre, also on St. Valentine's Day. The underworld had its theories about the assassins.

Because of the outrage throughout the nation, Capone was criticized by his criminal colleagues at an Atlantic City, New Jersey,* conference of gangsters. They believed he brought too much attention to the underworld and that sooner or later they would become the targets of public anger. So a brief jail term on a gun charge was arranged in Philadelphia in order to appease an aroused public that found the gangland murders too shocking and intolerable. *See also* CAPONE, ALPHONSE; PROHIBITION AND ORGANIZED CRIME; TORRIO, JOHNNY

**SUGGESTED READINGS:** John Kobler, *Capone: The Life and World of Al Capone* 1971; Frank Spiering, *The Man Who Got Capone.* 1976.

**SULLIVAN, "BIG TIM."** ("Dry Dollar," "Big Feller") (b. Timothy Sullivan, 1863, New York City—d. 1913, New York City.) New York political leader and Irish crime boss (don).*

At 250 pounds, standing more than six feet tall, "Big Tim" Sullivan was an imposing figure who was also very shrewd and smart. A powerful political leader in Tammany Hall, Big Tim was also affiliated with the Whyos, a vicious gang of thieves and murderers, who came into existence in the slums of New York City after the Civil War. As a criminal organization, it reached its zenith of power in the 1880s. The Whyos helped Sullivan win election to the state legislature, where he represented the Bowery district in lower Manhattan. It was an area of cheap amusement resorts, lodging houses for transients and vagrants, and tenements housing Jewish and Italian immigrants. Big Tim mobilized the criminal elements of his district into an army that could be relied on to win elections through the use of repeat voters and through terrorist tactics against legitimate voters at the election polls.

Among the underworld leaders helpful to Sullivan in his climb to power was Monk Eastman,* whose organizing skills enabled Big Tim to put together several street gangs of criminals into a large, efficient criminal federation. The vice and prostitution interests in the Bowery were important segments of Sullivan's organization. Big Tim headed a gambling* syndicate* that enabled him to exercise a dominant influence over the flourishing vice industries throughout New York City. Through a series of alliances with other political leaders and underworld bosses, Big Tim had by the turn of the century established a vice and crime empire unequaled then or since in the city's history.

Sullivan's political formula, which depended on agreements and alliances with the underworld, was the real reason for his success. It made him a state senator; it helped him win a congressional election and serve a term in the U.S. House of Representatives. His claim to distinction as a congressman was winning the pinochle championships of Congress.

A serious challenge to Sullivan's political/criminal empire did not come as might have been expected from the reform-minded Theodore Roosevelt, who objected to Sullivan's control over boxing through his National Athletic Club, which staged many of the top prizefights in the country. Rather, the challenge to Sullivan as district leader came from a local political contest in lower Manhattan. Big Tim played his trump card. Through arrangements with gang leader Paul Kelly* (Paolo Vaccarelli), a steady stream of Italian gunmen poured into the Second District and intimidated supporters of candidates opposed to Sullivan and his machine.

For many years Sullivan had been the dominant figure in New York City's gambling rackets and political corruption schemes. In 1912 Big Tim went insane. He was kept in a sanitarium, but in 1913, he eluded his caretakers and guards and was later found dead near a railroad freight yard in Westchester County. At his funeral, a testament to his influence and power and also an indication of the networks Sullivan created between gangsters and politicians, over 25,000 persons attended the funeral services, including three U.S. senators, a delegation of 20 members of the House of Representatives, and justices of the New York Supreme Court; and marching in somber homage were also less-upstanding citizens such as Paul Kelly, "Joe the Boss" Masseria,* and Arnold "The Brain" Rothstein.*

**SUGGESTED READING:** Donald Cressey, *Theft of a Nation.* 1969.

**SYNDICATE.** A syndicate is an association, either formal or informal, legal or illegal, of individuals who come together to carry out the activities of an enterprise.

Two basic types of criminal syndicates can be identified. One is the "enterprise syndicate," which operates in the arena of illicit enterprises such as gambling,* narcotics, pornography, smuggling, and so on. The second type is the "power syndicate" (a term coined by Alan Block), which refers to an organization that deals in extortionate violence (see Table 1). The power syndicate operates in two worlds: in the arena of vice activities and in the legitimate world of labor-management disputes and conflicts. Labor racketeering* is the most visible form of power syndicate activities in this area.

Some syndicates display characteristics of both power and enterprise. Syndicates are not the same as La Cosa Nostra,* the Mafia,* or the "underworld." Syndicates may include Mafia members or be run by them, but they, syndicates, existed before Cosa Nostra crime families* and continued after the consolidation of the crime family structure of Cosa Nostra. Louis Buchalter* operated a power syndicate as a labor racketeer, as did Carlo Gambino*; Dutch Schultz* did both: He offered protection to Harlem numbers* rackets and restaurants in Manhattan (power) and also ran gambling and bootlegging syndicates (enterprise) in the

**Table 1**
**Characteristics of Power and Enterprise Syndicates**

| SYNDICATE TYPE | SERVICE PRODUCT | SIZE | LONGEVITY | SPECIALIZATION | CLIENTELE |
|---|---|---|---|---|---|
| **I. Enterprise Syndicates** | | | | | |
| a. Freelance or integrated criminal entrepreneur activities | Gambling, theft, robbery, loansharking, prostitution, extortion | Small | Short-lived | Variable | Small; variable |
| b. Specialized, diversified monopolies & mergers | Gambling, drug importation and distribution, loansharking | Large | Durable | Variable | Large; variable |
| **II. Power Syndicates** | | | | | |
| a. Corrupters, Brokers, Bribers | Arrange and guarantee illicit transactions; protection | Small | Durable | None | Small |
| b. Extortionists | Violence | Small | Short-lived | None | Small |
| c. Financiers & Fences | Capital; money laundering; illicit and licit investment opportunities | Variable | Variable | None | Small |
| d. Mediators & Conflict Resolving Racketeers | Violence | Large | Durable | Some | Variable |

*Source:* Adapted from Alan Block (1983) *East Side—West Side: Organizing Crime in New York, 1930–1950* New Brunswick, NJ: Transaction Books.

Bronx and Westchester counties. Within criminal syndicates there was a great deal of ethnic cooperation in bootlegging, gambling, and labor racketeering.

**SUGGESTED READINGS:** Alan Block, *East Side–West Side: Organizing Crime in New York, 1930–1950.* 1983; Joseph Coffey and Jerry Schmetterer, *The Coffey Files: One Cop's War Against the Mob.* 1991.

**TABLE.** *See* SIT-DOWN

**TEAMSTERS UNION.** *See* INTERNATIONAL BROTHERHOOD OF TEAM-STERS

**TERESA, VINCENT CHARLES.** ("Fat Vinnie") (b. Nov. 28, 1928, Revere, MA—Federal Witness Protection Program). Mob informer.

A sudden flash of moral righteousness did not inspire Vincent Teresa to change his criminal ways and go straight. As with other mob informers like Joseph Valachi* and "Sammy the Bull" Gravano,* he betrayed his former associates and friends in order to survive and avoid life behind bars. Revenge was part of Teresa's motives: By his own account, he was the number-three man in the New England Mafia family headed by Raymond L. S. Patriarca* and knew where the bodies were buried. He decided to talk, he said, because his criminal associates stole his money and did not help his wife and children when he was doing a prison term.

Teresa was an "earner"—a mafioso with many interests and involvements that generated a great deal of cash. Thus, his knowledge of mob activities and personalities beyond Boston, Massachusetts, and New England was extensive. The evidence he provided led to the indictment of some 50 underworld figures. His style was such that he attracted the attention of journalist Thomas C. Renner, who did a book with Teresa, *My Life in the Mafia* (1973); the book dramatically described Fat Vinnie's 28-year criminal career of illegal gambling,* securities and stock fraud and theft, fencing,* fixed horse races, and mob rubouts.

When Teresa finished as an expert government witness in 1970, he was placed in the Witness Security Program* with a new identity. In 1984, he surfaced as Charles Cantino of Maple Valley, Washington, when a federal grand jury indicted him and five members of his family on charges of smuggling hundreds of exotic birds and reptiles on the endangered species list.

**SUGGESTED READING:** Vincent Teresa and Thomas C. Renner, *My Life in the Mafia.* 1973.

**THIEVES WORLD.** For decades, the prisons of the Soviet Union had been home to the world's most extraordinary criminal society. For almost a century, it had been known as *vorovskoi mir*, the Thieves World. From their cells, crime bosses planned and organized their operations across the country. Lieutenants, often called *brodyagi* (vagabonds), conducted formal dealings with the outside. The so-called vagabond brotherhood provided the network for transmitting orders and collecting profits. In the Soviet era, the gangs operating from their prison bases were no threat to ordinary civilians. Their enemy and rival was the Communist Party, for which they bore an old and long-standing grudge.

Once the Soviet Union had collapsed, however, criminal organizations emerged from their lofty isolation. It was no longer necessary to guard against Communist infection. A modern gang leader could manage his empire from outside prison walls without shame; in fact, the new opportunities available for profit made this nearly a requirement. And even for those who remained inside, there was no risk of embarrassment or censure in bargaining with straight society. Like caged lions who suddenly realized their strength, the leaders of the Thieves World were ready to take what they considered their rightful place in the pecking order of the New Russia and elsewhere, especially the United States and western Europe.

**SUGGESTED READING:** Stephen Handelman, *Comrade Criminal: Russia's New Mafiya.* 1995.

**TIERI, FRANK.** ("Funzi") (b. 1904, Castel Gondolfo, Italy—d. Mar. 15, 1981, New York City). Boss (don)* of the Genovese crime family.*

In 1980, Tieri had the distinction of being the first boss ever of a La Cosa Nostra* crime family* to be convicted for that very reason. According to the government, as a boss of a Cosa Nostra crime family, Tieri was connected to a pattern of racketeering,* which violates provisions of the RICO* statute. Though sentenced to ten years, he never served a day. He died two months after his conviction from a long and complicated illness.

Tieri was born in Italy and emigrated to the United States in 1911, and apart from an armed robbery conviction in 1922 at the age of 18, Tieri would not be prosecuted again until the end of his life, despite numerous allegations and indictments.

Tieri's leadership was much less violent than other crime bosses. He oversaw gambling* and loansharking* operations in New York City, Westchester County, Long Island, New Jersey, Florida, and Las Vegas, Nevada*—wherever the Genovese crime family exerted its influence. His approach to crime appealed to many Cosa Nostra soldiers*; and many desired to join his family. While hardly a peace-loving pacifist, Tieri did not resort to violence unless it was absolutely necessary. He played a key role in Mafia* Commission* decisions to eliminate Carmine "The Cigar" Galante,* who attempted to depose the crime family bosses and declare himself "boss of bosses"; Tieri also played a role in persuading Joseph Bonanno* to retire to Arizona rather than try a comeback in the tumultuous underworld of New York.

"Funzi," a nickname close associates would use, lived a relatively quiet, un-assuming life much like Carlo Gambino.* He owned a modest two-family home in an Italian American working-class section of Brooklyn known as Bath Beach. With so many layers of insulation between himself and street criminals doing his bidding, his life appeared normal, and he could be easily mistaken for an aging, successful businessman.

His great passion was opera. Tieri's longtime mistress was a former opera singer from Italy whom he helped in her career and then supported after her retirement. His mistress's home was his base of operations, where he carefully examined gambling and loansharking rackets managed by a group of very ac-complished criminals including two men who would succeed him as boss of the family: Anthony Salerno* and Vincent "The Chin" Gigante.*

Tieri was also notable for his business sense: He invested heavily into legit-imate businesses and controlled one of the most successful Italian food product retail outlets in the New York metropolitan area.

**SUGGESTED READING:** Virgil W. Peterson, *The Mob: 200 Years of Organized Crime in New York*. 1983.

**TOA YUAI JIGYO KUMIANI.** Japanese-Korean crime group.

The Toa Yuai Jigyo Kumiani (TYJK) is still something of a mystery to ex-perts. Also known as the East Asia Friendship and Enterprise Union, it was founded by a billionaire president and founder of a Tokyo-based business. It has a membership of 850 with six subgroups. Koreans comprise approximately 1.5 percent of the TYJK, and most of the upper echelon is of Korean ancestry. This organization is involved in criminal activity in Japan and the United States. Despite TYJK's smaller membership, they have extensive involvement in drug trafficking and money laundering* in the United States, which rivals that of the other three large Yakuza* (a.k.a. Boryokudan) groups. Officials estimate that this group could quickly become a significant player in drug trafficking since it has a worldwide network of legitimate businesses already established.

**SUGGESTED READING:** Hiroaki Iwai, "Japanese Organized Crime," in *Organized Crime: A Global Perspective*, ed. Robert J. Kelly. 1986.

**TONGS.** Roughly translated as "meeting hall," Tongs were established in big-city Chinatowns as mutual aid societies for new immigrants. Serving legitimate business, fraternal, and political purposes, Tongs continue to serve a socially useful function within Chinese communities. However, these organizations inevitably attract a criminal element seeking to take advantage of its established power base and stature in the community. While the degree of criminal infiltration varies greatly, it is reported that some of the largest and most respected Tongs serve as fronts for Asian organized crime.*

The criminally influenced Tongs' primary operation is illegal gambling,* where violence is used to protect the illegal enterprise. They are also involved in extortion, murder, drug trafficking, bribery, and prostitution. Tongs have working relationships with various Chinese and Vietnamese street gangs that operate at the direction of older Chinese businessmen and community leaders to protect gambling operations using violence or threats of violence. Their targets are Chinese immigrants and Asian Americans, and they are becoming increasingly violent in exerting their control over Chinese communities.

Tongs were first established in San Francisco in the 1850s by the first wave of Chinese immigrants. Prior to the emergence of Tongs, Chinese communities in the United States were controlled by the dominant family or district associations. Immigrants whose last name was shared by few others or who came from a small district were not readily accepted by the established associations and were left unprotected. In order to fend for themselves, they banded together and established the Tongs. Because recruitment by the Tongs was without restrictions, they expanded rapidly. Rival Tongs were soon drawn into street battles known as the "Tong wars." The secretive nature of the Tongs and the strong alliances among themselves when they fought with family and district associations enabled them to become the more powerful associations in the Chinese communities, prompting members of family and district associations to join a Tong for additional protection.

Like the family and district associations, the Tongs provided many needed services to immigrants who could not otherwise obtain them. The Tongs also acted as power brokers mediating individual and group conflicts within the community. More than 30 groups were formed in the United States including the Chih Kung, Bing Kung, and Hop Sing, which are some of the most active Tongs in America.

The On Leong Merchant Association (a Tong) was formed in 1894 in Boston. Ten years later, the On Leong headquarters was moved to New York City. In the mid-1970s, Eddie T. C. Chan,* a former sergeant with the Hong Kong Police Department, arrived in New York City. Chan was alleged to have been involved in extensive corruption while he was in Hong Kong. Soon after his arrival, Chan became a businessman and was elected president of the On Leong. During his tenure, he also became the vice president of a Chinatown bank and the president of the Chinese American Welfare Association (a nationwide advocate group located in Washington, D.C.). Through his connections with leading New York City politicians, Chan came into contact with many local and federal political leaders.

Law enforcement authorities charged that the On Leong leader had links with

Chinese gang members. Chan was alleged to be the man behind the shootings of the disgruntled Ghost Shadows street gang in Chicago by gang members from New York City. He was also accused of ordering the killing of a gang leader who was extorting money from him. Chan was implicated in the fraudulent activities carried out by the Continental King Lung Group, an investment company he established. A Chinese Triad* member in Hong Kong had identified Chan as the "dragon head" (crime boss) of New York Chinatown's underworld. When subpoenaed by the President's Commission on Organized Crime in 1984 to testify at the commission's hearings, Chan fled the United States.

In 1990, leaders of the On Leong in New York, Chicago, and Houston were indicted in Chicago for racketeering* activities. Twenty-nine core members of the On Leong were arrested, close to half a million dollars of gambling cash was confiscated, and the building owned by the Chicago On Leong was forfeited. The case, however, ended in a hung jury, and the On Leong remains a powerful organization in the Chinese community.

Another powerful Tong is the Hip Sing Association, which was formed in 1855 (Figure 9). The headquarters of Hip Sing is located in New York City's Chinatown. Benny Eng is the permanent chief adviser of the Hip Sing. He also is the leader of the Chih Kung Tong. Little is known about Eng, except that he was imprisoned for murder in 1936 and was paroled 18 years later. He had been arrested for assault, robbery, gambling, and drug offenses before his 1936 conviction for murder. In 1976, he was sentenced to prison for bribery.

Other associations in New York City resemble the Tongs in terms of their affiliation with Chinese gangs and extensive involvement in gambling operations. They are the Tung On Association, the Tsung Tsi Association, and the Fukien American District Association. Immigrants from two areas of Canton province, Tung Kwong and Po On, formed the Tung On Association. Federal agents believe that the association is active in running gambling operations in Chinatown and that it is well connected with the Sun Yee On Triad Society in Hong Kong.

The Tsung Tsin was established in 1918. Members of the association are predominantly Hakka (meaning "guest"), an ethnic group that migrated to the southern part of China from midwest China during a period of war and famine. The Tsung Tsin's headquarters is only a few buildings away from the Tung On, and like the Tung On, it is heavily involved in gambling activities. The physical proximity between the two associations had enabled the Tung On gang to provide protection for gambling operations of both associations.

The Fukien American District Association is probably the fastest growing community association in New York City's Chinatown. With the dramatic influx of both legal and illegal Fukienese migrants in the past decade, the association, which was established in 1942, is now in control of the newly expanded areas east and north of Chinatown. Members of the association are alleged to be active in illegal smuggling, promoting gambling and prostitution, and heroin trafficking.

**Figure 9**
**The Hip Sing Tong**

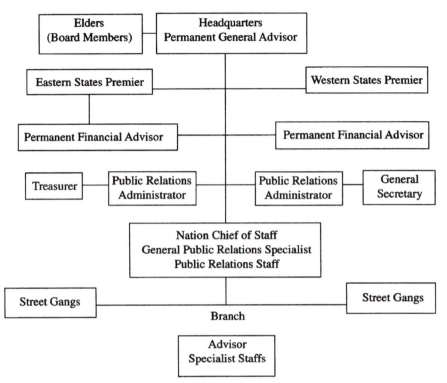

*Source:* Adapted from Ko-lin Chin, *Chinese Subculture and Criminality.* Westport, CT: Greenwood Press, 1990; p. 58.

**SUGGESTED READING:** Ko-lin Chin, *Chinese Subculture and Criminality.* 1991.

**TORRIO, JOHNNY.** (b. 1882, Naples, Italy—d. 1957, Brooklyn, NY). Chicago
racketeer and syndicate* boss (don).*

Like Louis Buchalter* in New York City, Johnny Torrio was a bureaucrat of
organized crime. They both believed strongly in organization, and both believed
that murder decisions be made collectively and go through channels. A member
of the crime syndicate wanting to do murder in order to solve a problem would
lay his case before his associates and partners. In New York City, Murder, Inc.*
was put together by the crime syndicate as a small, tightly knit team of specialists and experts in murder. Torrio invented the idea during Prohibition (*see*
PROHIBITION AND ORGANIZED CRIME*) of syndicate organization on a
mass scale where all of the warring gangs could be brought together. In Chicago,
he created territories for bootlegging and vice and used Alphonse Capone* to
provide the protection and muscle that would keep the peace. Torrio

gave Capone his start in the mob and carefully groomed him from a bouncer in a brothel to one of the most influential mob bosses in the United States.

The neat territorial arrangements Torrio created among the tension-ridden Italian, Irish, Polish, and Jewish gangsters broke down. Gangsters were killed in the streets and retaliations followed. When Charles Dion O'Banion,* the leader of the powerful North Side gang in Chicago, was murdered, Torrio was attacked and seriously wounded. After he recovered from his wounds, he retired and turned over the reins of power to Al Capone. He returned to Brooklyn, New York, and served as an adviser to the La Cosa Nostra* Commission* and to important gang leaders until his death in 1957.

**SUGGESTED READING:** Jack MacPhaul, *Johnny Torrio: First of the Gang Lords*. 1970.

**TOUHY, ROGER.** ("The Terrible") (b. 1898, Chicago—d. 1959, Chicago). Prohibition gangster, Chicago and Midwest.

His memoirs suggest that Roger Touhy never considered any rackets until Prohibition (*see* PROHIBITION AND ORGANIZED CRIME*). His father was a Chicago policeman, and the family was typically a large, Irish Catholic working-class home bustling with seven children. He got into bootlegging because his work as a car dealer made trucks available for renting. A beer distributor offered him a partnership, and Touhy began operating in the suburbs north and West of Chicago. At their peak, Touhy and his brothers had ten fermenting plants, a half-dozen tank trucks, and a weekly volume of a thousand barrels of bootleg beer. A barrel costs $5 to produce and sold for $55 to saloons and nightclubs. As Touhy observed in his very discreet book *The Stolen Years*: "[T]here was no stigma to selling beer." But the price could be awfully high when your competitor was Alphonse Capone.*

With his five brothers armed to the teeth with machine guns, Touhy masterfully projected the tough image of a vicious gangster but in fact only used violence when it was absolutely necessary. His skill was in bribery and "the fix."

In 1933 Touhy was arrested for the alleged kidnapping of an international con man with ties to the Capone organization. It was a frame-up, but Touhy was convicted. In 1950 he won a rehearing and was finally released in 1959 but was murdered after doing 25 years.

**SUGGESTED READING:** Roger Touhy, with Roy Brennan, *The Stolen Years*. 1959.

**TRAFFICANTE, SANTOS, JR.** (b. 1915, Tampa, FL—d. Mar. 17, 1987, Tampa, FL). Reputed Mafia boss of Tampa, Florida, and one of the key figures in the plot to assassinate Fidel Castro.

Santos Trafficante, Jr. assumed the leadership of numerous Florida La Cosa Nostra* enterprises in 1954 upon the death of his father, Santos Trafficante, Sr. A Sicilian-born immigrant, Trafficante, Sr. ruled Tampa with an iron fist. When he died, his son Santos, Jr. assumed the position of boss (don)* and, in collusion with powerful gangland figures in Chicago, New York, and Cleveland, began organizing casino gambling operations in Havana, Cuba, with the cooperation of its dictator Fulgencio Batista.

Cuba under Batista was a simple and brutal state. Crime syndicate* gamblers from the United States paid cash to the dictator for casino concessions; Havana was a wide-open city for any and all kinds of recreation that was illegal at home. Meyer Lansky,* Charles "Lucky" Luciano,* and top mafiosi in the Chicago Costa Nostra invested with Trafficante and exerted influence throughout Florida and Cuba. However, when Castro took over, he exhibited the usual puritanical attitudes of young revolutionaries and closed the casinos. Trafficante found himself jailed temporarily along with other "enemies" of the revolution in Cuba. Eventually he was freed, but all his casino holdings were seized by the Castro regime.

In 1963, Trafficante's power and stature in the underworld was publicly revealed during Senate hearings investigating labor racketeering.* It was before the McClelland Committee* where Tampa police department officials presented evidence that there was a criminal syndicate organization in Tampa led by Trafficante. Trafficante had also been a delegate to the 1957 Apalachin meeting* in upstate New York, where some major criminal leaders had gathered to discuss the assassination of Albert Anastasia,* a New York Cosa Nostra boss, and drug trafficking operations in the United States.

Trafficante played a role in several major criminal intrigues in the course of a career that was remarkably free of jail time. In 1966, he was one of 13 people arrested in Queens, New York, when the police broke up what they believed to be a meeting of mafia leaders from all over the country. At the time, the press dubbed it "Little Apalachin." Not only did he avoid arrest and prosecution over his long career as a mob boss, but throughout the dangerous gangland wars in which he participated, Trafficante suffered only an arm wound from a shotgun blast in 1953.

In an appearance before the House committee looking into the assassinations of Martin Luther King, John F. Kennedy, and Robert F. Kennedy,* Trafficante admitted that he participated in a plot arranged by the CIA to assassinate Fidel Castro in 1960. Granted immunity to testify, Trafficante described the details that involved unnamed members of the Chicago Mafia. He claimed that his role in the plot was modest—limited to translating Spanish-language documents and messages. The conspiracy never materialized, as one Mafia participant after another met death. Trafficante claimed, somewhat disingenuously, that his motives were purely patriotic; he saw himself, he claimed, as helping the U.S. government—his government. His real motives, however, may have been revenge: In 1959 when Castro seized power and outlawed casino gambling, Trafficante lost his businesses and was held in prison for two months in Cuba before friends obtained his release by buying his way out of prison.

Trafficante denied that he was part of a Mafia plot to kill President John F. Kennedy despite rumors and speculations that he, Carlos Marcello,* Cosa Nostra boss of the Louisiana crime family, and Jimmy Hoffa,* head of the Teamsters Union, arranged the murder. The House Committee Hearings revealed that Trafficante, in wiretapped conversations with Marcello and Hoffa, spoke angrily about Attorney General Bobby Kennedy's crackdown on mob operations across the country after the Cosa Nostra had supported Kennedy in the 1960 presidential election. Suspicions intensified when it was shown that Trafficante's henchman, Hoffa, had been hounded by Bobby Kennedy's Justice Department, and Carlos Marcello had been illegally deported to Guatemala in 1961.

In 1994, Frank Ragano, who spent three decades as a lawyer representing organized crime figures that included Jimmy Hoffa, Carlos Marcello, and Santos Trafficante, Jr., published a book where he describes a conversation he had with a gravely ill Trafficante shortly before his death. According to Ragano, without implicating himself specifically, Trafficante indicated that Marcello and Hoffa were instrumental in arranging the assassination of the president because Kennedy had betrayed them. Their motives were to neutralize Bobby Kennedy by killing his brother. The conspirators believed that with the president gone, the attorney general would not long remain in his job, and the harassment by the Justice Department would end. This terrible disclosure seemed credible to Ragano, given the events and circumstances of 1960.

**SUGGESTED READING:** Frank Ragano and Selwyn Raab, *Mob Lawyer.* 1994.

**UNDERBOSS (SOTTOCAPO).** Higher than the level of the consigliere* counselor in the structural skeleton of a La Cosa Nostra* crime family* is the staff position of "underboss" (sottocapo). Beneath the boss, and enjoying his confidence, is that of an executive vice president—to use the analogy of the legitimate business corporation—the "sottocapo," whose job is to function as a deputy director of the enterprise in the larger La Cosa Nostra crime families in the United States. The person in the position is picked by the boss and collects information, relays messages to him, and passes on the boss's orders and decisions down to the men below him in the hierarchy. In the absence of the boss for relatively short periods of time, the underboss acts on his behalf.

Not every underboss moves up to the position of boss when the latter is incarcerated, murdered, or indisposed because of illness or aggressive law enforcement surveillance. Indeed, when a boss dies or loses power, his entourage of underboss, consigliere, and capos* are usually replaced.

**SUGGESTED READING:** Gerard O'Neill and Dick Lehr, *The Underboss: The Rise and Fall of a Mafia Family.* 1989.

**U.S. DEPARTMENT OF JUSTICE ORGANIZED CRIME STRIKE FORCES.** (1967–1990). Between January 1967 and April 1971, the Organized Crime and Racketeering Section (OCRS) of the Department of Justice established 18 "strike forces" around the country in order to meet the goals and aims of crime control policy outlined by Attorney General Robert F. Kennedy* and the President's Task Force on Organized Crime.

The tasks of the strike forces were to: (1) coordinate law enforcement activities against organized crime; (2) to initiate and supervise investigations; (3) to accumulate and correlate intelligence data; (4) to formulate general prosecutive policies; and (5) to assist federal prosecuting attorneys throughout the nation.

The OCRS established federal strike forces across cities in the United States where organized crime was present. The first strike force became operative in Buffalo, New York, and directed its resources against the Cosa Nostra crime family of Stefano Magaddino.* The strike forces were staffed with Department of Justice attorneys and representatives of other federal investigative and law enforcement agencies. As of December 1976, strike forces were active in Boston, Brooklyn, Buffalo, Chicago, Cleveland, Detroit, Kansas City, Los Angeles, Miami, Newark, Philadelphia, San Francisco, and Washington, D.C. Participating agencies included: Bureau of Alcohol, Tobacco and Firearms (BATF); U.S. Customs Service; Department of Labor; Drug Enforcement Administration (DEA); Federal Bureau of Investigation (FBI); Immigration and Naturalization Service (INS); Internal Revenue Service (IRS); Securities and Exchange Commission (SEC); U.S. Postal Service; U.S. Marshalls Service; and the U.S. Secret Service.

Early on, the strike force concept was highly praised. The Buffalo Strike Force initiated a program of "going for the serpent's head"—meaning that it aimed to bring down the boss and the power structure of the local criminal enterprise. Targeting those individuals in a criminal group whose removal would most severely damage criminal operations became the operational practice throughout the strike forces across the country. The targets were usually mob bosses. Cases were initially investigated by a participating agency in the local strike force as a whole for investigation, followed by indictment and prosecution. By 1983, strike forces obtained about 80 percent of their case initiations from investigations conducted by BATF, DEA, FBI, and the IRS. The FBI supplied about 55 percent of the cases for prosecution.

One of the most attractive attributes of the task force structure of the strike forces was its ability to place prosecutional resources across jurisdictional boundaries, which until now often frustrated law enforcement efforts that were paralyzed by turf battles among agencies that led to inaction.

However, even with these distinct advantages of combining strength, streamlining bureaucratic procedures, by the late 1980s plans were developed by the attorney general of the United States to do away with strike forces because their investigations were autonomous and competed with the activities of local U.S. attorneys in the 94 federal judicial districts across the country. In 1990, the strike forces were integrated into the offices of the U.S. attorneys and not heard from again.

The primary effect of the merger appears to have been to limit the interagency scope and interjurisdictional effort of organized crime investigations.

**SUGGESTED READING:** Patrick J. Ryan, "A History of Organized Crime Control: Federal Strike Forces," in *Handbook of Organized Crime in the United States*, Robert J. Kelly, Ko-lin Chin, and Rufus Schatzberg, ed. 1994.

# V

**VALACHI, JOSEPH.** (b. Sept. 22, 1904, East Harlem, New York City—d. 1971, La Tuna Penitentiary, El Paso, TX). La Cosa Nostra* defector and informer.

Valachi had a remarkable impact on organized crime. Fearing for his life and angry at Vito Genovese* for attempting to murder him in the federal prison in Atlanta, Joseph Valachi, a soldier* in the Genovese crime family,* decided to break his oath of silence and talk. Before the McClelland Committee* of the U.S. Senate investigating labor racketeering* Valachi described in riveting detail the Mafia* underworld. During his testimony he coined the name "Cosa Nostra" (Our Thing), using it to denote the Italian American criminal organization he had been a sworn member of for more than 30 years and whose oaths he had betrayed. Other Cosa Nostra defectors in the years following Valachi's disclosures have been helpful in putting major organized crime figures behind bars for life. The great majority of books, articles, and films that depict the structure of organized crime in America rely heavily on his testimony. And over the years new information has generally confirmed Valachi's views. His contributions had more to do than simply informing the public and putting hoodlums behind bars: His information led to the creation of new laws and new strategies to control organized crime in the United States.

Valachi's career in the Cosa Nostra began in 1930 during the Castellammarese War.* He served on Salvatore Maranzano's* side until its climax in 1931 and then worked for Vito Genovese, a capo* in the Luciano crime family.* As a soldier, or "button man," in the mob, his duties included murder, extortion, and drug pushing.

Confined to Atlanta federal prison on drug charges, he was serving a 20-year sentence when Genovese, also imprisoned, suspected Valachi of informing. Genovese ordered his death. The attempt was foiled by Valachi who mistakenly killed an innocent inmate he thought was assigned to murder him. He decided to turn informer and get federal protection.

By the time Valachi appeared before the televised hearings of the Senate Committee, he was protected by 200 U.S. marshals when the Mafia put out a $100,000 "contract" on his life. The committee and the nation were mesmerized by this gangster's tale of organized crime—how members were selected; how the organization worked; its code of secrecy; its businesses; means of coercion; corruption of police and public officials; and above all, how Cosa Nostra managed its affairs across the entire country. The public was stunned. Although his testimony did not lead to the arrest of any criminal, its effects on the Mafia have been devastating.

**SUGGESTED READING:** Peter Maas, *The Valachi Papers.* 1968.

**VIETNAMESE ORGANIZED CRIME.** The first of two distinct waves of Vietnamese immigrants occurred just prior to the fall of Saigon in 1975. It was composed of immigrants who were generally older, well educated, and somewhat familiar with American culture. With the fall of Saigon, another wave poured in, many of whom were younger and less educated than their predecessors. Among them were criminals who formed groups to prey on the wealthier and more established immigrants from the first wave. In Vietnam, these criminals were involved in extortion, drug trafficking, prostitution, and gambling. After emigrating to the United States, they continued these activities, preying on Asian immigrants and Asian American businesses. New immigrants were particularly vulnerable to crime because they were reluctant to go to the police. In their homeland, the police were frequently agents of oppressive political regimes and not to be trusted.

Vietnamese organized crime groups range from street gangs engaged in drug trafficking and armed home invasions to highly sophisticated groups specializing in extortion, gambling,* drug trafficking, and smuggling. They are known to be very violent, having been trained in the use of weapons and explosives. Members of some of the more sophisticated groups were associated with the South Vietnamese Army, which was known for its brutality. The gangs are also active in the expanding enterprise of high-tech crime, such as theft or robbery of computer parts, which are later sold on the black market or to underdeveloped nations.

Historically, these groups were less formally structured than other Asian organized crime* (AOC) groups, and this remains true, particularly with the street gangs. However, as individuals grow older, they take on planning and advisory roles for the group, whereas younger members execute the crimes. Over time, as the organization has become more sturdy and the hierarchy more clearly defined, they are more skillful in executing their operations. Vietnamese groups have not yet reached the level of other organized crime groups. *See also* ASIAN ORGANIZED CRIME; CHINESE STREET GANGS

**SUGGESTED READING:** U.S. Senate, *Asian Organized Crime.* 1991.

# W

## WATERFRONT RACKETEERING AND THE INTERNATIONAL LONG-SHOREMEN'S ASSOCIATION.

The port of New York is the best natural harbor in North America. This fact made New York one of the greatest of American cities and provided the setting for organized criminal activity along its waterfront. New Orleans, also another great port, generated its own crime not unlike that which occurred on the New York/New Jersey docks.

The New York waterfront was enormous: It covered over several hundred miles of shoreline with wharves and deep-water piers. When a ship entered port, unloading and reloading had to be done quickly: A ship sleeping in port made no money. The stevedores, longshoremen, worked night and day, often under nasty conditions. The workforce consisted of low-skilled manual laborers, many of whom were ex-convicts. In such conditions of unskilled labor, hiring bosses could demand "kickbacks" (part of a longshoreman's earnings) from those workers in a "shape-up" (a gang of day-to-day workers).

Beyond the docks, the conditions for moving freight to and from ships also invited criminal activity. The streets were narrow and congested with trucks; this led to abuses where for a fee, truckers could get their vehicles loaded or unloaded; truckers also paid other "fees" to advance their place in line to the piers.

These two aspects of the waterfront, the shape-up and loading activities, caused most of the crime along the docks. Because these rackets were so lucrative, they attracted the attention of criminal gangs. The gangs insinuated themselves into the longshore unions or helped to form them. Throughout the nineteenth century, the docks belonged to Irish gangsters, but in the twentieth century, wars raged between the Irish and Italians with the massive influx of Italian immigrants into the port cities of New York, Boston, Philadelphia, and Chicago.

The ILA (International Longshoremen's Association) was organized on the

Great Lakes in 1892 but controlled by the rapidly expanding New York locals by 1910. In Manhattan and Brooklyn, the stevedores were mostly Irish, but during and after World War I, new piers were built near Italian neighborhoods in south Brooklyn, Hoboken, New Jersey, and Staten Island, New York City. Slowly the Italians under Paul Kelly* and later Albert Anastasia,* Anthony Anastasio,* Joseph Adonis,* and Vincent Mangano* gained dominance over the Irish. By 1925, the last important leader of the White Hand Society* was murdered, and the Italian gangsters won the docks on the East River piers. Meanwhile, Irish gangs hung on to the West Side docks in Manhattan in the midtown area including the terminals servicing transatlantic passenger liners.

The president of the ILA had political connections that enabled him to regularize the union's extortion activities against shippers and waterfront trucking companies. On the Brooklyn waterfront, the Mangano crime family consolidated its control on hiring and shakedowns of shipping and trucking firms. On both waterfronts, shippers had to pay to guarantee timely loading and unloading of cargo; dockworkers were coerced into paying kickbacks to hiring bosses; and loansharking* became widespread as regular work became less certain.

Just prior to World War II, Anastasia and his brother "Tough Tony" directly controlled six ILA locals in Brooklyn. Those union members who dared to challenge mob control would wind up in the river, face down. Waterfront conditions were described in newspaper exposes, in investigations, and in government hearings. But none of this much affected the situation of criminal control. Not until the 1950s, after successive waves of reformers and lawmen, was mob control on the waterfront effectively challenged. Finally the murder of Anastasia in 1957 and his brother Tony's death in 1963 led to significant changes on the waterfront. The Waterfront Commission formed in 1953 was now energized to act: Longshoremen were required to register with the commission; the "shape-up" method of hiring was eliminated; pier superintendents, hiring agents, and port watchmen had to be licensed. The Waterfront Commission was a giant step in the right direction. To further weaken the grip of the gangsters on the piers, the AFL (American Federation of Labor) expelled the ILA in 1953 when it failed to comply with demands that the union purge its ranks of criminals.

The final blow came in 1979 when Anthony Scotto,* president of the ILA and a capo* in the Gambino crime family,* was convicted of labor racketeering charges.


**WEISS, EARL "HYMIE."** (b. Earl Wajciechowski, 1898, Poland—d. Oct. 11, 1926, Chicago, IL). Chicago North Side gang boss.

With Charles Dion O'Banion's* assassination in 1924, Hymie Weiss swore vengeance against Alphonse Capone* and Johnny Torrio.* Unlike many racketeers, who let their wives pray for their sins, Weiss was a devout Catholic (it was generally assumed he was a Jew, which is how he acquired the nickname "Hymie"); he regularly carried rosary beads wherever he went, frequently attended Mass, and apparently had no difficulty reconciling his spiritual inclinations with his everyday criminal activities.

Weiss was born in Poland, and in his teens in Chicago, he became friendly with Dion O'Banion. In the Polish and Irish Catholic slums of Chicago, Weiss and O'Banion began their careers in crime: They stole, robbed, and worked as goons in the newspaper circulation wars and in labor union battles. With Prohibition (*see* PROHIBITION AND ORGANIZED CRIME*), new opportunities loomed, and Weiss, along with O'Banion, ruthlessly exploited the criminal opportunities illegal alcohol offered. At the height of the gang wars in Chicago's bootleg empires, Weiss originated the term "one-way ride," where a victim is taken on an automobile ride but never returns.

O'Banion's murder by the Torrio-Capone syndicate* set Weiss off on a killing spree. In January 1925, months after O'Banion's murder, Weiss, along with George "Bugs" Moran,* a top gun in the O'Banion gang, attacked Capone as he drove to a restaurant. Two bodyguards were wounded, but Capone narrowly escaped injury. Hymie next turned his wrath against Torrio, who also escaped with his life, though his chauffeur and dog were killed in the attack. Two weeks later, on January 24, 1925, Torrio and his wife were ambushed in front of their apartment building as they returned from shopping. Weiss and Moran wounded Torrio severely, forcing his retirement, but Capone proved elusive. All the while Capone's gunmen hunted Hymie Weiss and Bugs Moran. The war continued.

The Chicago public was stunned when on September 20, 1926, a fleet of cars filed past the Hawthorne Inn restaurant in Cicero, a suburb of Chicago, and fired more than a thousand bullets from submachine guns into the restaurant where Capone was dining. Again, Capone was not hit, but a bodyguard and an innocent bystander were wounded. The motorcade attack occurred in broad daylight in the downtown area in full view of hundreds of people. Three weeks later, on October 11, 1926, Weiss became the target. Capone's hit* men stalked him for days and finally brought him down, along with a bodyguard, in a hail of gunfire as he made his way to his headquarters above O'Banion's flower shop. Weiss was 28 years old and thought to be worth about $1.5 million. As with other well-known mobsters, his floral entourage numbered more than a dozen automobiles. But Weiss's execution did not consolidate Capone's grip on organized crime in Chicago. Other gangsters had to be confronted before the public decided it had had enough of the shootings and murders.

**SUGGESTED READING:** Howard Abadinsky, *Organized Crime.* 5th edition. 1997.

**WHITE HAND GANG.** Irish waterfront racketeers, 1900–1925.

Between 1900 and 1925 a war between Irish and Italian waterfront gangsters raged over control of profitable rackets. The White Hand Gang of Irish criminals formed to confront the challengers, The Black Hand (La Mano Nera)* of mafiosi recently arrived from Italy and Sicily. When William Lovett* was murdered in 1923, his successor "Peg Leg" Lonergan continued the struggle until he was killed in 1925 by none other than Alphonse Capone* in a south Brooklyn saloon owned by friends of Joseph Adonis,* Vincent Mangano,* and Albert Anastasia.* These mobsters challenged the Irish for control of the Brooklyn piers in the predominantly Italian immigrant section of Red Hook, Brooklyn.

**SUGGESTED READING:** Thomas Pitkin and Francesco Cordasco, *The Black Hand.* 1977.

**WHITE HAND SOCIETY.** Anti–Black Hand vigilante group (1910).

In New York City produced infamous Black Hand extortionist Ignazio "Lupo the Wolf" Saietta and his law enforcement nemesis, Sergeant Joseph Petrosino,* but Chicago, in the first decade of the twentieth century when Italian immigration was at its peak, had a more severe problem with immigrant extortion. It was so bad that by 1907 an exasperated community of Italian business and professional men, the Italian Chamber of Commerce and several ethnic organizations, put together the White Hand Society, an organization to fight criminals who preyed like parasites on Italian families, businesses, and communities. This was an unusual step; the common tendency for ethnic minorities was to feel embattled by the larger society and to cope defensively with criticisms about criminal activity labeling them as slurs against the entire ethnic group. However, the situation in Chicago was particularly bad—much worse, in fact, than in other large cities with Italian ethnic groups. The Black Hand (La Mano Nera)* extortionists were rampant in the community and had the temerity to victimize racketeers such as Big Jim Colosimo and Johnny Torrio.* People and their families were threatened with maiming or death. Many, but not all, of the extortion rings were mafiosi or camorristi (gangsters from Naples and the province of Campania in Italy).

At first, the White Hand consisted of upstanding persons who were threatened by The Black Hand; in the spirit of lawfulness, which they respected and on which they depended, attorneys were hired and private detectives engaged to gather and share information with the police so that The Black Hand could be properly exterminated legally with convictions against its participants. The enthusiasm of the group quickly faded, however. Police inactivity against The Black Hand—which was a reason behind the citizen's formation of the White Hand—did not increase with new information, nor was the department energized by community interest in the problem. Several Black Hand extortionists were driven from the city or convicted, but too many were quickly released on parole when their associates corrupted public officials. There was fear that the White Hand Society members, out of frustration with the corruption and lax administration of justice, might take matters into their own hands, as happened tragically in other communities where frenzied posses administered summary justice, often with tragic results. Another problem the White Hand faced was a public relations and image issue: The success of their efforts to expose crime in the Italian community was leading to a backlash against all Italians by other Chicago citizens. By 1913, the White Hand disbanded, but The Black Hand continued for at least another decade.

**SUGGESTED READINGS:** Humbert S. Nelli, *The Business of Crime.* 1976; Joseph Albini, *The American Mafia, Genesis of a Legend.* 1971.

**WILD COWBOYS.** (Dominican drug gang).
This was the first drug gang headed by American-born Dominicans. The Wild Cowboys were quite violent; law enforcement officials believe that since the mid-1980s the gang had been responsible for 30 murders in the New York City boroughs of Brooklyn, the Bronx, and Manhattan. Their crack cocaine business grossed more than $20 million a year.

Lenin and Nelson Sepulveda, two brothers who led the gang, organized it with a corporate like structure where street dealers known as "pitchers" and a group of enforcers who were well armed reported to managers and supervisors. The gang was headquartered in the Washington Heights section of New York, where other Dominican drug traffickers congregated, but its main distribution points were in the Bronx where thousands of vials of crack under brand names like "Red Top" and "Orange Top" were sold.

Street warfare for sales territory was a common occurrence on the streets of Latino enclaves in New York during the 1980s and 1990s. In December 1991, five members of the Wild Cowboys killed rival gang members in the Bronx, and in the melee, three innocent bystanders went down in the hail of gunfire. The massacre outraged authorities, who put together a large task force to target the gang. After an intensive two-year investigation, the Sepulveda brothers and nearly three dozen of the Wild Cowboys were arrested and indicted on many charges. Nelson Sepulveda fled the country but was arrested in Santiago, Dominican Republic, in 1994 and returned to the United States to face trial.

The growth of Dominican criminal organizations is a sad outcome of the ravenous demand for drugs, especially crack cocaine. The influence of the Colombian connection, which used Dominicans as retailers for cocaine, cannot be underestimated: It has enabled these criminal groups to branch out beyond their home base in Washington Heights and to set up distribution networks in many northeastern cities. Dominican crack gangs have been identified in Pennsylvania, Maine, Rhode Island, Connecticut, and Massachusetts.

**SUGGESTED READING:** Diego Vigil, *Barrio Gangs.* 1988.

**WILLEBRANDT, MABEL WALKER.** (b. May 23, 1889, Woodsdale, KS—d. Apr. 6, 1963, Riverside, CA). Assistant attorney general for Prohibition (*see* PROHIBITION AND ORGANIZED CRIME\*) enforcement.
Mabel Walker Willebrandt, hailed by her contemporaries as the "First Lady in Law," was assistant attorney general of the United States from 1921 to 1929 at the height of the Prohibition era. In the early phases of her legal career, she was appointed an assistant public defender with responsibility for criminal cases

involving women. She worked on the defense of over 2,000 women, and her sympathetic handling of prostitution cases resulted in a changed practice in court procedures as judges began to mandate the appearance of both men and women before the bench.

During World War I, she was appointed head of the Legal Advisory Board for draft cases in Los Angeles. Senator Hiram Johnson and every member of the bench in southern California recommended her for the post of assistant attorney general in the Harding administration.

Only the second woman to receive an appointment as an assistant attorney general and the first to serve an extended term, Willebrandt was responsible for the division in the Justice Department that dealt with tax, prison, and Prohibition matters. Before her appointment, Willebrandt was not a Prohibitionist; in office, however, she was determined to uphold the law. The major obstacles she noted in her book *The Inside of Prohibition* were political interference, official incompetence, and public indifference.

Willebrandt insisted that government agents chase the bootleggers* with enthusiasm. Her major focus was on the Prohibition Bureau and the law enforcement establishment with the responsibility of enforcing the Volstead Act. Because of her age (32) and her sex, she was at first overlooked by older, skeptical men in the Justice and Treasury Departments who ran the government's enforcement apparatus. There existed in the government a kind of indifference toward enforcement bred by the overriding fact that people still wanted to drink. The twist in the law was that Prohibition had been forced on working-class drinkers by middle-class moralists. And now with alcohol consumption illegal, one had to be middle class, at least, to get a good drink and powerful enough not to worry about raids on speakeasies by Prohibition agents.

Further complicating the problems was the fact that the Prohibition Bureau's agents were underpaid and easily bribed. Many were dismissed for corruption, and many others quit to become bootleggers. But Willebrandt did not give up. She focused on the U.S. attorneys' performance in Prohibition cases because her authority did not extend to local law enforcement. Many of the U.S. attorneys around the country displeased her. Their performance in bringing cases to trial ranged from inefficient to obstructionist. Under Attorney General Harlan Stone, she was able to secure the dismissal of several attorneys hostile to the prosecution of Prohibition violations.

Despite the obstacles, major cases were broken under Willebrandt's direction. In 1923, the Big Four of Savannah (Georgia), allegedly the largest bootleg ring in the country, was cracked, as were the Cincinnati operations of bootlegger George Remus. The attorney general's annual report for 1925 noted that of 48,734 cases brought by Willebrandt's division between June 1924 and June 1925, 39,072 ended in convictions. Willebrandt submitted 278 cases on certiorari (judicial review of lower court proceedings) to the Supreme Court dealing with the defense, clarification, and enforcement of the Prohibition Amendment and the Volstead Act. She also argued over 40 Supreme Court cases, a total that has been rarely exceeded. Particularly noteworthy were her victories in cases controlling liquor sales on American and foreign vessels.

Earning the title of "Prohibition Portia," Willebrandt wrote and spoke extensively urging public support of the law. She consistently argued that the government should aim at the major offenders, complaining that going after the hip pocket and speakeasy cases was like trying to dry up the Atlantic Coast with a blotter.

In her efforts to enforce the law, Willebrandt proposed the reallocation of federal judges to respond more flexibly to Prohibition case loads, the transfer of enforcement from the Treasury to the Justice Department, better articulation of law enforcement activities, and stiffer, more consistent sentences for convicted offenders. She also recommended J. Edgar Hoover* to head the Federal Bureau of Investigation.

In 1929, Willebrandt resigned and observed that federal enforcement does not need more men, more money, and more ammunition, just more commitment. Ironically, shortly after her resignation, she became a counsel of California Fruit Industries, which made a grape concentrate that was easily and widely transformed into serviceable table wine. *See also* PROHIBITION AND ORGANIZED CRIME

**SUGGESTED READING:** Mabel Walker Willebrandt, *The Inside of Prohibition.* 1929.

**WILSON, FRANK J.** (b. 1887—d. 1970). IRS agent in Chicago; Investigator of Al Capone.

How to get Alphonse Capone?* He seemed invulnerable; government agencies at all levels were frustrated by their failure to put him behind bars.

In 1927 the Supreme Court ruled that even illegal income was subject to taxation. Elmer Irey's Intelligence Unit of the IRS came up with the idea of prosecuting Capone on tax evasion; but it was an idea not easily implemented because evidence of Capone's financial dealings proved elusive: bootlegging,* vice, and gambling*—indeed, the entire spectrum of Capone's rackets—were all cash businesses.

The IRS devised a scheme to determine how much money Capone was spending as a way to estimate how much taxable income he was earning. What made the idea plausible was the fact that Capone had not been paying his taxes.

Frank J. Wilson led the investigation. Previously, he had success in uncovering illegal financial chicanery of lesser gangsters. Wilson fit the stereotype of the accountant/civil servant: When he began his work, he was about 40 years old, balding, with wire-rimmed eyeglasses—a man who proved to be an obsessive investigator. Despite the inherent danger of the assignment, Wilson and his wife moved to the Sheridan Plaza Hotel in Chicago where he passed himself off as a tourist. He did not tell his wife the precise nature of his work in Chicago; all she knew was that her husband was looking into the affairs of someone called "Curly Brown." Wilson would spend three years (1928–1931) digging for the elusive information to send Capone to prison. Given Capone's vast income and lavish spending habits, this may have sounded easy enough to do; in fact, it proved nearly impossible. As Wilson discovered, Capone was completely anonymous when it came to income. He did all his business through front men or third parties.

When he got wind of the efforts to get him, Capone put a murder contract on Wilson. But the threat didn't intimidate Wilson: The IRS and other federal agents approached Johnny Torrio,* Capone's former mentor and partner, and warned Torrio that if Capone did not cancel the hit,* there would be warfare in the streets. The murder contract was null and void within 24 hours.

Wilson managed to track mob accountants and bookkeepers who were able under intense questioning to establish Capone's spending patterns and his net worth—a crude but nonetheless effective measure that Capone's lawyers managed to challenge on grounds of admissible evidence. Capone was sentenced to 11 years for tax evasion.

With Capone's fall, Wilson's career did not sunset in 1931. In 1936 he became head of the Secret Service and tackled the problem of counterfeiting. In this work, too, his dedication and concentration worked well, so well that the amount of counterfeit money in circulation fell drastically.

**SUGGESTED READING:** Frank Spiering, *The Man Who Got Capone.* 1976.

**WINCHELL, WALTER.** ("The King of Broadway") (b. Apr. 7, 1897, New York City—d. Feb. 20, 1972, New York City). New York gossip columnist and mob reporter.

"Good evening Mr. and Mrs. North America and all the ships at sea." This famous refrain was the opening statement of Walter Winchell's nationally popular radio news and comment show. Winchell pioneered what we refer to today as "talk radio" with the exception that he did not conduct on-air conversations with his listeners. Because of his influence—1,000 newspapers carried his column at the height of his popularity, and his radio broadcast was among the top ten—Winchell used organized crime and the police as material for his show and column.

His mentor Damon Runyon,* who wrote *Guys and Dolls*, a successful Broadway musical about gangsters and their girlfriends, introduced Winchell to many underworld figures at New York's famous Stork Club. In 1939, Winchell played a role as a go-between for the FBI and its long manhunt of Louis Buchalter,* a boss (don)* in the New York syndicate.*

During his career, Winchell reported on Frank Costello,* Charles "Lucky" Luciano,* and the trials of the Murder, Inc.* gang to a fascinated public. His celebrity (60 million people read his column or listened to his radio show in 1937) ended ignominiously when the public tired of his brash style. He died in 1972 with only his daughter at his graveside.

SUGGESTED READING: Neal Gabler, *Winchell: Gossip, Power, and the Culture of Celebrity*. 1994.

## "WISE GUY." *See* SOLDIERS

WITNESS SECURITY PROGRAM. The U.S. Marshals Service provides for the security, health, and safety of government witnesses and their immediate dependents whose lives are in danger as a result of their testimony against organized crime and major criminals.

Since 1971, more than 5,600 witnesses (not including family members) have entered the Witness Security Program (WITSEC) and have been protected, relocated, and provided with new identities by the Marshals Service.

The successful operation of this program by the Marshals Service has provided a unique and valuable tool in the government's war against major criminal conspiracies and organized crime. Since the inception of the program, an overall conviction rate of 86 percent has been obtained as a result of protected witnesses' testimony.

Final determination that a witness qualifies for WITSEC protection is made by the attorney general or his designee. The decision is based on recommendations by U.S. attorneys assigned to major federal cases throughout the nation. In a state court case, the determination is based on a request from a state attorney general through the appropriate U.S. attorney's office.

After the witness receives a preadmittance briefing by Marshals Service personnel and agrees to enter the program, the procedure usually involves the immediate removal of the witness and his/her immediate family members from the danger area and their relocation to a secure area selected by the Marshals Service. In addition, it typically involves obtaining a court-ordered name change and providing new identities with authentic documentation for the witness and family. Among the types of assistance provided to the witness are: housing, medical care, job training, and employment. Subsistence funding to cover basic living expenses also is provided to the witness until the program participants become self-sufficient in the relocation area.

The Marshals Service provides 24-hour protection to all witnesses while they are in a "threat" environment and upon their return to a danger area for pretrial conferences, testimony at trials, or other court appearances.

Organizationally, the program is operated from three levels: Marshals Service Headquarters; 12 regional offices; and Metro units, which have a highly trained Witness Security Inspector to provide assistance to witnesses and to serve as an adviser to the local marshal on witness security matters.

The recidivism rate (witnesses with prior criminal histories who entered into the program and were later arrested and charged with crimes) is less than 23 percent. (This rate of recidivism among program participants is less than half the rate of those released from the nation's prisons.) In both criminal and civil matters involving protected witnesses, the Marshals Service cooperates fully with local law enforcement and court authorities in bringing witnesses to justice or in having them fulfill their legal responsibilities.

The Witness Security Program was authorized in 1970 by the Organized Crime Control Act of 1970 (Public Law 91–452) and was amended by the Comprehensive Crime Control Act of 1984 (18 U.S.C. sections 3521–3528).

**SUGGESTED READING:** Robert J. Kelly, Ko-lin Chin, and Rufus Schatzberg, "Without Fear of Retribution: The Witness Security Program," in *Handbook of Organized Crime in the United States*, ed. Robert J. Kelly, Ko-lin Chin, and Rufus Schatzberg. 1994.

# Y

**YAKUZA.** (a.k.a. Boryokudan). Japanese organized crime group.

Although this group is not known to be operating extensively in the United States, their physical presence is not required for the impact of the Japanese Boryokudan to be felt. They are known to be extremely innovative in finding ways to make money. Through associations with other criminal groups, including La Cosa Nostra,* Chinese Triads,* and Colombian drug cartels,* and through investments in legitimate and illegitimate businesses in the United States, the Boryokudan has transcended boundaries and is becoming deeply entrenched in the economic infrastructure of the United States.

Headquartered in Japan, the Boryokudan is perhaps the largest and oldest criminal organization in the world, with roots dating back some 300 years. Over 2,500 different criminal groups are affiliated with the Boryokudan, and their membership is estimated at over 85,000 worldwide. The word "Boryokudan" means "violent gang." Members of this group prefer to be called "Yakuza." The term "Yakuza" originally referred to the worst possible numbers combination in a gambling game but has evolved to mean "outlaw."

The Yakuza are famous for their tattooed bodies and their practice of self-inflicted body maiming. Members of various groups adorn their bodies with intricate tattoos, and when they fail in an assignment or job, they apologize to their bosses by cutting off their fingers.

While still involved in drug trafficking, extortion, prostitution, violent crimes, and gun smuggling, the current objective of the Boryokudan is to find investment opportunities, particularly real estate, in which to launder ill-gotten profits and establish havens abroad where they can seek refuge if necessary. With all of the legitimate Japanese investment activity occurring in the United States, there is little doubt that the Boryokudan will gain a substantial foothold in the American real estate market. At the same time, it is feared that expansion of legitimate business investment will result in increasing corporate extortion. The

Boryokudan is currently targeting companies that are Japanese-owned or U.S. companies that employ Japanese executives. Adept at assimilating into the criminal infrastructure in the United States, law enforcement experts believe it is only a matter of time before the Boryokudan targets U.S. corporations for extortion.

In Japan, this group has amassed tremendous economic and political power. For many years, it was tolerated and allowed to operate openly. Like most organized crime groups, the Boryokudan relies heavily on bribing corrupt public officials. The National Police of Japan estimated Boryokudan gambling and drug trafficking alone accounted for almost $10 billion in revenue in 1988. *See also* ASIAN ORGANIZED CRIME; TOA YUAI JIGYO KUMIANI; YAMAGUCHI-GUMI

**SUGGESTED READING:** Alec Dubrow and David Kaplan, *Yakuza*. 1986.

**YALE, FRANKIE.** (b. Francesco Ioele, 1893, Calabria, Italy—d. July 1, 1928, Brooklyn, NY). Brooklyn racketeer and feared assassin.

Alternately killer and benefactor, he elicited wild and contradictory passions in Brooklyn, but on one point, at least, there was a general agreement: Nobody defied Frankie Yale. Before he was 20, he was famous (or infamous), compact, muscular, and very dangerous looking. The stories about him say that he murdered a dozen men, or more, before he was 21 years old.

Yale was not his real name; that was contrived deliberately. Nor did he belong to the Mafia* he was born in Calabria, one of the poorest rural provinces in Italy, in 1893 and came to the United States as a child. Yale spent his adolescence in a youth gang affiliated with the Five Points in lower Manhattan and got himself into many scrapes until he married in the 1920s and became partners with Johnny Torrio* in the Harvard Inn. During Prohibition (*see* PROHIBITION AND ORGANIZED CRIME*) he also developed many sidelines in labor union racketeering* and extortion.

Yale got into the ice business—a necessity before refrigeration—and organized local monopolies that controlled supply and competition in Brooklyn's Italian neighborhoods. Then there was the laundry business that Yale controlled in parts of Brooklyn by threatening and scaring off union organizers. Tobacco, especially small cigars featuring his name "Frankie Yale," became yet another racket. Shop owners who did not stock them risked broken shop windows and possibly broken necks, too.

After he opened his Coney Island bar and dance hall, the Harvard Inn, Yale needed a bouncer and bartender capable of combining a winning manner and sheer brutality when necessary. Torrio sent him Alphonse Capone.* When Torrio assembled his empire of vice based on illegal alcohol, he needed to get rid of his boss Big Jim Colosimo. Yale was doing a booming business in Brooklyn and wanted more; he saw opportunities in Chicago and assassinated Colosimo in 1920; but Yale's attempt to destabilize Torrio's control of the Chicago racket backfired. The removal of Big Jim actually consolidated the power of the Torrio organization, which in turn froze Yale out. But Yale appeared undeterred and still worked for Torrio/Capone. In 1924, Yale, John Scalise, and Albert Anselmi, Capone's favorite gunman, shot Charles Dion O'Banion,* the leader of the North Side gang, in his floral shop. This event was the major step in the spread of Capone's power throughout Chicago.

By 1928, the relationship between Capone and Yale deteriorated because Capone suspected Yale of a double cross: Frankie was hijacking Capone's truckloads of imported liquor intended for the Midwest along the Long Island coastline and New England beaches.

Despite the obvious betrayal, Capone did not react immediately: Alcohol smuggling and manufacture were huge industries generating illicit wealth that supported thousands of people in the business. Few, including Capone, would dare to act recklessly or in ways that might threaten the business. So the "Big Fella" waited until an opportune moment arrived.

Sunday, July 1, 1928, Brooklyn, New York: Yale was out riding alone in his new car, which featured a bulletproof chassis. A black sedan pulled alongside, filled with Capone assassins from Chicago who unleashed a storm of bullets. "Machine Gun" Jack McGurn, Scalise, and Fred "Killer" Burke, a St. Louis gunman who later participated in the grisly St. Valentine's Day Massacre,* shot Yale dead. The Thompson submachine gun and .45 revolvers burst through the windows of Yale's car—the part that was not bulletproof. This was the first time a "Tommy gun" had been used in a mob murder.

The funeral took place on July 5, and 100,000 people turned out to pay respects to Yale and to gape at the spectacular floral arrangements, which were more outlandish than even those at Dion O'Banion's funeral, which had been considered, up until 1924, Chicago's grandest display of the underworld in mourning.

Although Frankie Yale died on a Brooklyn street and not in Chicago, his murder was among the most significant gangland hits of the decade, for next to Al Capone, Yale had been one of the best-known, most-feared racketeers of the Prohibition Era. Yet at the time of his murder, few knew why he was killed or who had him murdered.

**SUGGESTED READING:** Ralph Salerno and John S. Tompkins, *The Crime Confederation.* 1969.


**YAMAGUCHI-GUMI.** Japanese crime group.

Yamaguchi-Gumi is one of the largest and most powerful Yakuza* (Boryokudan) subgroups, with over 20,000 members in more than 750 subgroups. It has influence in over 80 percent of Japan's prefectures and is known to be operating in the United States through legitimate companies. It hides behind legitimate company names to camouflage its operation, while it expands by recruiting new members and laundering money. The Yakuza group's operations are very lucrative, and much of the profit is invested in companies in the United States. They launder a great deal of money through the purchase of real estate in Hawaii. When asked why the Yamaguchi-Gumi is so interested in acquiring property in Hawaii, one Yakuza member responded, "First we buy the property, then we buy the people." *See also* YAKUZA

**SUGGESTED READING:** Minour Yokoyama, "Trends of Organized Crime by Bar-yokudan in Japan," in S. Einstein and M. Arnis, eds., *Organized Crime: Uncertainties and Dilemmas.* 1999.

**YOUNG BOYS, INC.** One of the first African American drug gangs of the 1980s that pioneered many techniques that would become standard operating procedures for drug gangs around the country: the use of young adolescents in drug transportation (they usually do not get prison time if prosecuted and convicted); the use of brand names on packets of drugs; the use of violence to attain control of street-level distribution in neighborhood until a "territory" is under the gang's control.

Milton (Butch) Jones put together the Young Boys in the squalid streets of Detroit's west side ghetto when he was a young man. Not fitting the image of the sleek, glamorous drug dealer, Jones was short, plain-looking, stockily built, who often brooded and scowled. He did not drink, use drugs, or circulate through nightclubs and after-hours clubs. But he was smart and tough and had served a prison sentence on an assault charge.

With Sylvester (Seal) Murray, a major heroin wholesaler, Jones put together an army of some 300 people to sell drugs on the streets and in the hallways of public housing projects.

The Young Boys functioned like a competent, legitimate retail business: Jones would obtain bulk heroin from Murray, process it in a "cutting mill," and package it with colorful names like "Rolls-Royce" and "Renegade" for street sale. The timetable was a model of efficiency, with "hook-up crews" dressed in blue jogging suits delivering heroin to street dealers. During the day, money runners dressed in red jogging suits would pick up the cash from sales. Each drug-selling location was supervised by a "top dog" who supervised the runners and dealers in his area.

Although the Young Boys were suspected of several murders, they were not particularly violent, as were some other gangs. Problems requiring violent resolutions were typically handled by the "Wrecking Crew," a group of enforcers that were part of the Young Boys organization.

In 1983, Butch Jones and some 40 other members of the drug gang were convicted and sentenced to long prison terms. *See also* AFRICAN AMERICAN ORGANIZED CRIME; CHAMBERS BROTHERS; CRIPS AND BLOODS; EL RUKNS; FORT, JEFF

**SUGGESTED READING:** Rufus Schatzberg and Robert J. Kelly, *African-American Organized Crime: A Social History.* 1997.

# Z

ZERILLI, JOE. (b. Joseph Zerilli, 1898, Terrasini, Sicily—d. Oct. 30, 1977, Grosse Pointe, MI). Detroit La Cosa Nostra* boss (don).*

Until Joe Zerilli assumed prominence in the Detroit crime scene, the Purple Gang,* which was composed mainly of tough Jewish bootleggers* with close ties to Cleveland racketeers such as "Moe" Dalitz,* ruled the underworld of the motor city. Zerilli and another mafioso joined the Purple Gang and rose quickly to the top as it began to transform itself into a more sophisticated criminal enterprise.

Zerilli was born in Sicily and arrived in the United States as a teenager, then worked as a laborer in construction. After joining the Purple Gang, he built a criminal enterprise that included loansharking,* narcotics, labor racketeering,* and extortion. Even prostitution—which many mafiosi disdained as beneath them—was part of the Zerilli empire.

In Detroit for the purposes of appearances, Zerilli posed as a good citizen who was devoted to his family and bakery business. He lived well and carefully managed the affairs of his crime family.* Among the mafiosi in the country he was one of only two non–New Yorkers to sit on the Commission*; but his service there was very low-keyed: Not believing in external interference in the affairs of Cosa Nostra families, Zerilli practiced restraint in reaching decisions that would overrule local bosses. He himself always paid close attention to activities in his territory and always respected the territorial prerogatives of other groups.

In the early 1970s Zerilli retired after installing his son Joseph, Jr. as his successor. But in 1975 he was forced to return after his son received a four-year prison sentence and when Jimmy Hoffa* was released from prison expecting to resume the leadership of the powerful Teamsters Union. Hoffa was angry and wanted the mob's man, Frank Fitzsimmons, to resign. At this point, it is believed that Zerilli intervened. The conventional wisdom has it that Hoffa disappeared and was murdered on July 30, 1975, by Anthony Provenzano,* head of Teamster Local 560 in New Jersey who also served as a capo* in the Genovese crime family,* and Russell Buffalino, a Pennsylvania mafioso who headed a Cosa Nostra family in Pittstown, Pennsylvania. Hoffa was scheduled to meet a Zerilli associate, Tony Giacalone; that plus the fact that Zerilli allowed nothing to occur in his territory without his knowledge and approval strongly suggest that he had a hand in Hoffa's disappearance and murder.

**SUGGESTED READING:** Dennis J. Kenney and James O. Finckenauer, *Organized Crime in America*. 1995.

**"ZIPS."** A slang, derogatory term describing Italian and Sicilian mafiosi. Its origins are probably linked to the reaction of Americans describing Sicilian-speaking immigrant criminals uttering the Sicilian dialect so fast that it was incomprehensible.

Large numbers of mafiosi and Camorristi (gangsters from Naples) entered the United States during the Mafia wars that raged across Sicily and southern Italy from 1980 through 1983. The struggle developed to gain control of the lucrative drug markets that the La Cosa Nostra* families organized and maintained. Italian law enforcement estimates are that the war cost the lives of more than 500 members of the Mafia families and camorrista gangs. Scores of members were arrested and held for trial, and a pattern of flight and illegal immigration occurred reminiscent of decades earlier when Fascist dictator Benito Mussolini decided to destroy the Mafia.

The escalating violence and mass trials of Mafia suspects, combined with a need for their services in the drug markets in the United States, have served to foster illegal immigration of these criminals into the United States. *See also* LA COSA NOSTRA; MAFIA

**SUGGESTED READING:** Claire Sterling, *Octopus: The Long Reach of the International Sicilian Mafia*. 1990.

**ZWILLMAN, ABNER.** ("Longy") (b. 1899—d. Feb. 26, 1959, NJ). Leader in the East Coast Prohibition syndicate and crime boss of New Jersey.

"Longy" Zwillman grew up in a tough Jewish neighborhood in Newark, New Jersey, at the turn of the century. As a teenager, he worked briefly as a huckster selling fruits and vegetables from a wagon, but with his boyhood friends, who would later emerge as important figures in the Prohibition (*see* PROHIBITION AND ORGANIZED CRIME*) alcohol rackets—namely, Joseph Stacher* and "Niggy" Rutkin—Zwillman ran with a street gang called the Ramblers. Over time, bootlegging and hijacking made Zwillman rich enough to regard himself as a philanthropist. Zwillman's speciality as a bootlegger* was enforcement, the threat and use of violence. He also played a very prominent role in a Newark political club that was influential in the democratic machine that controlled politics in northern New Jersey. The club provided Zwillman with a headquarters for his various enterprises and a respectable front that disguised his criminal activities.

Zwillman's expertise as a violent hoodlum enabled him to become a partner of "Waxey" Gordon,* a daring and imaginative criminal entrepreneur who acquired large holdings in breweries and distilleries during Prohibition. In 1930, probably for much the same reasons, Zwillman acquired a 50 percent interest in the Reinfeld syndicate,* a huge bootlegging operation that sprawled all over New Jersey. As bootlegging spread and became a major business enterprise across the entire country, Zwillman joined the "Big Six" combination, another major illegal alcohol syndicate that included such underworld celebrities as Meyer Lansky,* Frank Costello,* Charles "Lucky" Luciano,* Joseph Adonis,* Anthony Joseph Accardo,* and Al Capone's chief financial adviser Jake Guzik.*

Zwillman worked closely with the New York bosses of the syndicate and formed a partnership with Frank Costello's associate in New Jersey, Willie Moretti.* Moretti served as additional muscle and provided a link with the Luciano crime family,* of which Frank Costello was a boss, and with Albert Anastasia* of the Vincent Mangano.* Cosa Nostra family, who was a fearsome killer heading Murder, Inc.*

Zwillman's wealth conferred power, and as his influence rose, his political power increased as well. In 1946, the governor of New Jersey, Harold G. Hoffman, personally sought Zwillman's support. In 1949, the mobster brashly suggested to the Democratic candidate for the governship that he would support him if he allowed Zwillman to name the state's attorney general, the chief law enforcement officer. The Democratic candidate, to his credit, refused and then lost the election.

With Moretti at his side and the power of the regional Cosa Nostra behind him, Zwillman worked his rackets in extortion, hijacking, and gambling. A plush gambling casino in the Riviera nightclub on the Hudson River Palisades (just above the George Washington bridge connecting New York and New Jersey) was opened by Zwillman and his associates, featuring star entertainers.

Zwillman sought to sustain a respectable image throughout his criminal career. As early as 1932, for example, when the search for the kidnapped Lindbergh baby caused a national furor, he posted a large reward for information leading to the kidnapper; in the 1950s his civic-minded image was enhanced when he donated $250,000 for a Newark slum clearance project. But when the McClelland Committee* on labor racketeering* turned its spotlight on his activities, the facade of the good, upstanding citizen dissolved. Subpoenaed by the McClelland Committee and subjected to a tax investigation, Zwillman's public image was shattered.

Problems with the government were compounded by internal conflicts in the underworld. Unfortunately for Zwillman, he backed the wrong competitors in a struggle for power in the Cosa Nostra. Vito Genovese* returned from Italy, where he stayed during World War II in order to avoid arrest on a murder charge. He was interested in revitalizing Cosa Nostra and wanted to assume control of the crime family that Costello held in stewartship for the deported crime boss, Lucky Luciano. Genovese also wanted to develop lucrative drug trafficking operations with the Sicilian Mafia. Zwillman backed Costello and Anastasia against Genovese. After Anastasia was murdered in 1957, and an attempt that same year was made on Costello's life by a Genovese henchman, Vincent "The Chin" Gigante* (who many years later would become boss of the Genovese crime family*), Zwillman's power eroded rapidly.

Shortly before he was scheduled to appear before the McClelland Committee in 1959, Abner "Longy" Zwillman appeared to have committed suicide. Doubts were raised as to whether Zwillman did indeed take his own life or had been murdered on orders of Genovese and his associates—mainly Carlo Gambino,* the new boss of the Anastasia crime family and close associate of Genovese. Evidence suggests that Zwillman was murdered, and the reasons for it are not hard to ascertain. Associates of Zwillman may have feared that he might turn informer (as had Joseph Valachi* in his appearance before the McClelland Committee) in order to avoid prison. The underworld version of Zwillman's death is that he was murdered in order to silence him, and his former partner, Meyer Lansky, had to approve it.

**SUGGESTED READING:** Hank Messick, *The Silent Syndicate*. 1967.

# GENERAL BIBLIOGRAPHY

From the wealth of books devoted to organized crime, a number are recommended to supplement the information provided in this volume. The following bibliography is organized into categories for the convenience of the reader. The recommended reference works cover subjects involving organized crime in the United States during the twentieth century. They contain a mass of information on individuals and events in various historical periods. Some general works examine the role of organized criminal activity in society and the legal and economic environments in which criminal enterprises operate; others examine specific groups or organized criminals. Memoirs, personal accounts, and biographies include those by and about individuals who led a life of crime and those who fought organized crime as law enforcement officers and officials. Important government reports can be consulted for information compiled by government agencies. Finally, fictional and cinematic portrayals of organized crime are presented as examples of popular cultural responses to organized crime.

## REFERENCE WORKS

Inciardi, James, ed. *Handbook of Drug Control in the United States*. Westport, CT: Greenwood Press, 1990.

Kelly, Robert J., Ko-lin Chin, and Rufus Schatzberg, eds. *Handbook of Organized Crime in the United States*. Westport, CT: Greenwood Press, 1994.

Sifakis, Carl. *The Mafia Encyclopedia*. New York: Dell, 1987.

## GENERAL WORKS

Abadinsky, Howard. *Organized Crime*. 5th ed. Chicago: Nelson Hall, 1997.

Albanese, Jay S. *Organized Crime in America*. Cincinnati, OH: Anderson, 1996.

Albini, Joseph. *The American Mafia: Genesis of a Legend*. New York: Appleton-Century-Crofts, 1971.

Anastasia, George. *Blood and Honor: Inside the Scarfo Mob—The Story of the Most Violent Mafia Family*. New York: Morrow, 1991.

Block, Alan. *East Side–West Side: Organizing Crime in New York, 1930–1950.* New Brunswick, NJ: Transaction Books, 1998.

Block, Alan A., and Frank R. Scarpitti. *Poisoning for Profit: The Mafia and Toxic Waste in America.* New York: William Morrow, 1985.

Blum, Howard. *Gangland: How the FBI Broke the Mob.* New York: Pocket Books, 1993.

Blumenthal, Ralph. *The Gotti Tapes.* New York: Random House, 1992.

Chin, Ko-lin. *Chinatown Gangs: Extortion, Enterprise, and Ethnicity.* New York: Oxford University Press, 1996.

Cressey, Donald R. *Theft of the Nation: The Structure and Operations of Organized Crime in America.* New York: Harper Colophon Books, 1969.

Davis, John H. *Mafia Dynasty: The Rise and Fall of the Gambino Crime Family.* New York: HarperCollins, 1993.

Fox, Stephen. *Blood and Power: Organized Crime in Twentieth Century America.* New York: William Morrow, 1989.

Fried, Albert. *The Rise and Fall of the Jewish Gangster in America.* New York: Holt, Rinehart and Winston, 1980.

Haller, Mark H. *Life Under Bruno: The Economics of an Organized Crime Family.* Conshohocken: Pennsylvania Crime Commission, 1991.

Handelman, Stephen. *Comrade Criminal: Russia's New Mafiya.* New Haven, CT: Yale University Press, 1995.

Hess, Henner. *Mafia and Mafiosi: Origin, Power, and Myth.* New York: New York University Press, 1998.

Ianni, Francis, A. J. *A Family Business: Kinship and Social Control in Organized Crime.* New York: Russell Sage Foundation, 1972.

Jacobs, James B., with Christopher Paranella and Jay Worthington. *Busting the Mob: United States vs. Cosa Nostra.* New York: New York University Press, 1994.

Kaplan, David E., and Alec Dubro. *Yakuza: The Explosive Account of Japan's Criminal Underworld.* Reading, MA: Addison-Wesley, 1986.

Kelly, Robert J. *The Upperworld and the Underworld: Case Studies of Racketeering and Business Infiltrations in the United States.* New York: Kluwer Academic/Plenum Publishing, 1999.

Kelly, Robert J., and Rufus Schatzberg. *African-American Organized Crime: A Social History.* Newark, NJ: Rutgers University Press, 1997.

Kenney, Dennis J., and James O. Finckenauer. *Organized Crime in America.* New York: Wadsworth, 1995.

Lee, Renssalaer W. III. *The White Labyrinth.* New Brunswick, NJ: Transaction Books, 1990.

Maas, Peter. *The Valachi Papers.* New York: Bantam Books, 1968.

Mills, James. *The Underground Empire: Where Crime and Governments Meet.* New York: Dell, 1986.

Nelli, Humbert. *The Business of Crime.* New York: Oxford University Press, 1976.

O'Neill, Gerard, and Dick Lehr. *The Underboss: The Rise and Fall of a Mafia Family.* New York: St. Martin's Press, 1989.

Peterson, Virgil W. *The Mob: 200 Years of Organized Crime in New York.* Octavia, IL: Green Hill Publishers, 1983.

Reuter, Peter. *Disorganized Crime.* Cambridge, MA: MIT Press, 1983.

Smith, Dwight, Jr. *The Mafia Mystique.* New York: University Press of America, 1990.

Sterling, Claire. *Octopus: The Long Reach of the International Sicilian Mafia*. New York: W. W. Norton, 1990.

Turkus, Burton, and Sid Feder. *Murder, Inc: The Story of the Syndicate*. New York: Farrar, Straus, & Young, 1951.

Vaksberg, Arkady. *The Soviet Mafia*. New York: St. Martin's Press, 1991.

Volkman, Ernest, and John Cummings. *Goombata: The Improbable Rise and Fall of John Gotti and His Gang*. Boston: Little, Brown, 1990.

## BIOGRAPHIES AND MEMOIRS

Bergreen, Laurence. *Capone: The Man and the Era*. New York: Simon & Schuster, 1994.

Blakey, Robert, and Richard Billings, eds. *The Plot to Kill the President*. New York: Times Books, 1981.

Blakey, Robert, Ronald Goldstock, and Charles H. Rogovin, eds. *Rackets Bureau*. Washington, D.C.: U.S. GPO, 1978.

Bonanno, Joseph, with S. Lalli. *A Man of Honor: The Autobiography of Joseph Bonanno* New York: Simon & Schuster, 1983.

Bonavolanta, Jules, and Brian Duffy. *The Good Guys: How We Turned the FBI 'Round— and Finally Broke the Mob*. New York: Simon & Schuster, 1996.

Breuer, William. *Vendetta: Castro and the Kennedy Brothers*. New York: John Wiley, 1997.

Cohen, Richard. *Tough Jews*. New York: Simon & Schuster, 1998.

English, Thomas J. *Born to Kill*. New York: Morrow, 1995.

Epstein, Edward Jay. *The Assassination Chronicles*. New York: Carroll & Graf, 1992.

Franzese, Michael. *Quitting the Mob*. New York: Harper Paperbacks, 1992.

Garrison, Jim. *On the Trail of the Assassins*. New York: Sheridan Square, 1988.

Giancana, Antoinette, and Thomas Renner. *Mafia Princess: Growing Up in Sam Giancana's Family*. New York: Avon, 1985.

Gies, Joseph. *The Colonel of Chicago: A Biography of Robert McCormick*. New York: Dutton, 1979.

Goddard, Donald. *Joey: The Life of "Crazy Joe" Gallo*. New York: Harper & Row, 1974.

Hersh, Seymour. *The Dark Side of Camelot*. New York: Little, Brown and Company, 1997.

Jacobs, James B., Coleen Friel, and Robert Roddick. *Gotham Unbound*. New York: New York University Press, 1999.

Kleinknecht, William. *The New Ethnic Mobs: The Changing Face of Organized Crime in America*. New York: Free Press, 1996.

Lupska, Peter A. "Transnational Narco-Corruption and Narco Investment: A Focus on Mexico," *Transnational Organized Crime* 1 (Spring 1995): 84–101.

Maas, Peter. *Underboss: Sammy the Bull Gravano's Story of Life in the Mafia*. New York: Harper Paperbacks, 1997.

Massing, Michael. "In the Cocaine War, the Jungle Is Winning," *New York Times Magazine* (March 4, 1990): 26, 88, 90, 92.

Meskil, Paul S. *Don Carlo: Boss of Bosses*. New York: Popular Library, 1973.

Mustain, Gene, and Jerry Capeci. *Mob Star: The Story of John Gotti, the Most Powerful Criminal in America*. New York: Franklin Watts, 1988.

Neff, James. *Mobbed Up: Jackie Presser's High-Wire Life in the Teamsters, the Mafia, and the FBI*. New York: Atlantic Monthly Press, 1988.

O'Brien, Joseph, and Andriss Kurins. *Boss of Bosses: The FBI and Paul Castellano*. New York: Dell, 1991.

Pileggi, Nicholas. *Casino*. New York: Pocket Books, 1995.

———. *Wiseguy: Life in a Mafia Family*. New York: Pocket Books, 1987.

Pistone, Joseph D. *The Ceremony: The Mafia Initiation Tapes*. New York: Dell, 1992.

———, with Richard Woodley. *Donnie Brasco: My Undercover Life in the Mafia*. New York: New American Library, 1987.

Potter, Gary. *Criminal Organizations: Vice, Racketeering, and Politics in an American City*. Prospect Heights, IL: Waveland, 1994.

Reppetto, Thomas. *The Blue Parade*. New York: Free Press, 1978.

Reynolds, Marylee. *From Gangs to Gangsters: How American Sociology Studied Organized Crime, 1918–1994*. Albany, NY: Harrow & Heston, 1995.

Rockaway, Robert A. *But—He Was Nice to His Mother: The Lives and Crimes of Jewish Gangsters*. Jerusalem, Israel: Gefen Publishing House, 1993.

Roemer, William F., Jr. *Accardo: The Genuine Godfather*. New York: D. Fine, 1995.

———. *The Enforcer Spilotro: The Chicago Mob's Man over Las Vegas*. New York: Ivy Books, 1994.

Roppleye, Charles, and Ed Becker, eds. *All-American Mafioso: The Johnny Rosselli Story*. New York: Doubleday, 1991.

Rudolph, Robert. *The Boys from New Jersey*. New York: Morrow, 1992.

Russo, Gus. *Live by the Sword: The Secret War Against Castro and the Death of J.F.K.* Baltimore, MD: Bancroft Press, 1998.

Talese, Gay. *Honor Thy Father*. New York: World Publishing, 1971.

Teresa, Vincent, and Thomas C. Renner. *My Life in the Mafia*. Greenwich, CT: Fawcett, 1973.

Webster, Barbara, and McCampbell, Michael S. *International Money Laundering: Research and Investigation Join Forces*. Washington, D.C.: NIJ, 1992.

## GOVERNMENT REPORTS

The most recent major government report on organized crime in the United States is *The Impact: Organized Crime Today*, Report to the President and the Attorney General, President's Commission on Organized Crime (Washington, DC: GPO, April 1986). Over the past 35 years two presidential commissions have focused on organized crime: before *The Impact*, the *Task Force Report of 1967* (Washington, DC: GPO, 1967) took up the task of defining organized crime, describing the principal activities of organized crime groups and their structures. Both reports also looked at the role of organized crime in private and public corruption and at law enforcement crime control strategies.

At state and local levels, crime commissions carry on investigations and hearings. The structure of investigation and enforcement resources brought to bear against organized criminal activities varies from state to state and from locale to locale. Analysts and practitioners in the United States have developed varied responses ranging from rackets bureaus and strike forces to coordinated teams of specialists housed in organized crime control units within police departments. Since 1967 and the passage of RICO legislation in 1970, the scope and power of investigative agencies and units within law enforcement have increased dramatically. See, for example, U.S. Comptroller General, *Drug Investigation: Organized Crime Drug Enforcement Task Force Program's Accomplishments* (Washington, D.C.: GPO, 1987); and Herbert Edelhertz, ed. *Major Issues in Organized Crime Control* (Washington, D.C.: U.S. Department of Justice, 1987).

## Other Useful Government Reports

New York State Organized Crime Task Force. *Corruption and Racketeering in the New York City Construction Industry*. New York: New York University Press, 1990.
President's Commission on Organized Crime. *America's Habit: Drug Abuse, Drug Trafficking, and Organized Crime*: 1986.
————. *The Cash Connection: Organized Crime, Financial Institutions, and Money Laundering*. Washington, D.C.: GPO, 1984.
————. *Organized Crime of Asian Origin*: 1984.

## FICTION

Daley, Robert. *The Year of the Dragon*. Boston: Houghton Mifflin, 1982.
Puzo, Mario. *The Godfather*. New York: G. P. Putnam and Sons, 1969.
Watson, Peter. *Capo*. New York: Ivy Books, 1998.

## FEATURE-LENGTH FILMS

*Bonnano: A Godfather's Story* (1999)
*Bugsy* (1991)
*Carlito's Way* (1993)
*Donnie Brasco* (1997)
*The Freshman* (1990)
*The Godfather* (1972)
*The Godfather, Part II* (1974)
*The Godfather, Part III* (1991)
*Goodfellas* (1990)
*Hoffa* (1992)
*King of New York* (1990)
*Lansky* (1999)
*Mafia Princess* (1990)
*Miller's Crossing* (1990)
*My Blue Heaven* (1990)
*Once Upon a Time in America* (1984)
*Prizzi's Honor* (1985)
*Scarface* (1991)
*The Untouchables* (1993)
*Year of the Dragon* (1985)

In all these films, with the exception of *Year of the Dragon* and *Scarface*, Italian American mobsters either are the central characters or play important supporting roles. Of the films listed here, only *Hoffa* and *Godfather, Part III* deal explicitly with the political/criminal nexus. All contain ethnic and racial stereotypes of Asians, Latinos, African Americans, and white ethnics, and with one or two exceptions—*Year of the Dragon* and *Scarface*—the Mafia image is the most dominant and enduring. Only in *Goodfellas*, based on Nicholas Pileggi's popular book *Wiseguy*, which is the true story of Henry Hill, a Mafia associate turned informer, is there any effort to divest mobsters of a romantic or glorified aura. *Wiseguy* reveals them to be the vicious, petty hoods that they really are.

# INDEX

(**bold** indicates main entries in text; 'i' indicates an illustration; 't' indicates a table)

**About the Author**

ROBERT J. KELLY is Broeklundian Professor of Social Sciences at Brooklyn College and Professor of Criminal Justice and Sociology at the Graduate School, City University of New York. He has served as a consultant to numerous government agencies concerning terrorism, organized crime, prison administration, and extremist politics. Kelly is author of *Hate Crimes: The Politics of Global Polarization* (1998), *African-American Organized Crime: A Social History* (1997), *Handbook of Organized Crime in the United States* (Greenwood, 1994), and *The Upperworld and the Underworld* (1999).